EUROPEAN
REVIEW
OF SOCIAL
PSYCHOLOGY

EUROPEAN REVIEW OF SOCIAL PSYCHOLOGY

Editorial Board

Editors

Wolfgang Stroebe	Utrecht University, The Netherlands
Miles Hewstone	University of Wales, Cardiff, UK

About the editors

Wolfgang Stroebe has published widely on the topics of attitudes, group processes and health psychology. A former President of the European Association of Experimental Social Psychology and a fellow of the Society of Personality and Social Psychology, he is currently Professor of Social, Organizational and Health Psychology at the University of Utrecht (The Netherlands) and Director of the Inter-university Research Institute 'Psychology and Health', and Editor of *Psychologische Rundschau*.

Miles Hewstone has published widely on the topics of attribution theory and intergroup relations. He was awarded the British Psychology Society's Spearman Medal in 1987 and was a Fellow at the Center for Advanced Study in the Behavioral Sciences, Stanford, California. He is Professor of Psychology at the University of Wales, Cardiff, UK.

EUROPEAN REVIEW OF SOCIAL PSYCHOLOGY

VOLUME 8

WOLFGANG STROEBE
Utrecht University, The Netherlands
and
MILES HEWSTONE
University of Wales, Cardiff, UK

JOHN WILEY & SONS

Chichester · New York · Weinheim · Brisbane · Singapore · Toronto

National   01243 779777
International   (+44) 1243 779777
e-mail (for orders and customer service enquiries): cs-book @wiley.co.uk
Visit our Home Page on http://www.wiley.co.uk
or http://www.wiley.com

European Review of Social Psychology
ISSN 1046–3283
Published annually by John Wiley & Sons

For information on other volumes
in this series please complete the subscription notice
at the back of this volume

British Library Cataloguing in Publication Data

European review of social psychology. Vol 8. 1998.
 – (European review of social psychology)
  I. Stroebe, Wolfgang   II. Hewstone, Miles
  III. Series
  302.094

ISBN 0-471-97949-X

Typeset in 10/12pt Times by Dorwyn Ltd, Rowlands Castle, Hants
Printed and bound in Great Britain by Bookcraft (Bath) Ltd
This book is printed on acid-free paper responsibly manufactured from sustainable forestry, in
which at least two trees are planted for each one used for paper production.

Contents

About the Editors   ii

Contributors   vii

Preface   ix

Acknowledgements   xi

Introduction to Volume 8   xiii

Chapter 1 Cognitive Dissonance Theory: A Radical View
               Robert-Vincent Joule and Jean-Léon Beauvois   1

Chapter 2 Affect, Attitudes and Decisions: Let's Be More Specific
               Joop van der Pligt, Marcel Zeelenberg, Wilco W. van Dijk,
               Nanne K. de Vries and René Richard   33

Chapter 3 Affective Priming
               Karl Christoph Klauer   67

Chapter 4 Hindsight Bias: Impaired Memory or Biased
               Reconstruction?
               Dagmar Stahlberg and Anne Maass   105

Chapter 5 Cognitive and Social Consequences of the Need for
               Cognitive Closure
               Donna M. Webster and Arie W. Kruglanski   133

Chapter 6 The Context/Comparison Model of Social Influence:
Mechanisms, Structure and Linkages that Underlie Indirect
Attitude Change
William D. Crano and Eusebio M. Alvaro   175

Chapter 7 The Group as a Basis for Emergent Stereotype Consensus
*S. Alexander Haslam, John C. Turner, Penelope J. Oakes,
Craig McGarty and Katherine J. Reynolds*   203

Chapter 8 Outgroup Prejudice in Western Europe
*Thomas F. Pettigrew, James S. Jackson, Jeanne Ben Brika,
Gerard Lemaine, Roel W. Meertens, Ulrich Wagner and
Andreas Zick*   241

Author Index   275
Subject Index   283
Contents of Previous Volumes   293

Contributors

EUSEBIO M. ALVARO, *Department of Communication, University of Arizona, Tucson, AZ 85721, USA*

JEAN-LÉON BEAUVOIS, *Laboratoire de Psychologie Sociale de la Cognition, Université de Nice—Sophia Antipolis, France*

JEANNE BEN BRIKA, *L'École des Hautes Études en Sciences Sociales, Paris, France*

WILLIAM D. CRANO, *Department of Communication, University of Arizona, Tucson, AZ 85721, USA*

NANNE K. DE VRIES, *University of Amsterdam, Vakgroep Sociale Psychologie, Roetersstraat 15, NL-1018 WB Amsterdam, The Netherlands*

S. ALEXANDER HASLAM, *Department of Psychology, The Australian National University, Canberra, ACT 0200 Australia*

JAMES S. JACKSON, *University of Michigan, USA*

ROBERT-VINCENT JOULE, *Laboratoire de Psychologie Sociale, Université de Provence, 2 Av. Robert Schuman, 13621 Aix-en-Provence Cedex 1, France*

KARL CHRISTOPH KLAUER, *Psychologisches Institut, University of Bonn, Römerstr. 164, D-53117 Bonn, Germany*

ARIE W. KRUGLANSKI, *Department of Psychology, University of Maryland, College Park, MD 20742, USA*

GERARD LEMAINE, *L'École des Hautes Études en Sciences Sociales, Paris, France*

ANNE MAASS, *Department of General Psychology, University of Padua, Padua, Italy*

CRAIG McGARTY, *Department of Psychology, The Australian National University, Canberra, ACT 0200, Australia*

ROEL W. MEERTENS, *University of Amsterdam, Vakgroep Sociale Psychologie, Roetersstraat 15, NL-1018 WB Amsterdam, The Netherlands*

PENELOPE J. OAKES, *Department of Psychology, The Australian National University, Canberra, ACT 0200, Australia*

THOMAS F. PETTIGREW, *Stevenson College, University of California, Santa Cruz, CA 95064, USA*

KATHERINE J. REYNOLDS, *Department of Psychology, The Australian National University, Canberra, ACT 0200, Australia*

RENÉ RICHARD, *University of Amsterdam, Vakgroep Sociale Psychologie, Roetersstraat 15, NL-1018 WB Amsterdam, The Netherlands*

DAGMAR STAHLBERG, *Lehrstuhl Sozialpsychologie, Universität Mannheim, D-68131 Mannheim, Germany*

JOHN C. TURNER, *Department of Psychology, The Australian National University, Canberra, ACT 0200, Australia*

JOOP VAN DER PLIGT, *University of Amsterdam, Vakgroep Sociale Psychologie, Roetersstraat 15, NL-1018 WB Amsterdam, The Netherlands*

WILCO W. VAN DIJK, *University of Amsterdam, Vakgroep Sociale Psychologie, Roetersstraat 15, NL-1018 WB Amsterdam, The Netherlands*

ULRICH WAGNER, *Philipps-Universität Marburg, Marburg, Germany*

DONNA M. WEBSTER, *Department of Psychology, Winthrop University, USA*

MARCEL ZEELENBERG, *University of Amsterdam, Vakgroep Sociale Psychologie, Roetersstraat 15, NL-1018 WB Amsterdam, The Netherlands*

ANDREAS ZICK, *Bergische Universität, Wuppertal, Germany*

Preface

Social psychology is an international endeavour. This fact, which underlies our decision to make the *European Review of Social Psychology* an international review that publishes outstanding work of authors from *all* nations rather than restricting it to Europeans, is again reflected by the scholars who contributed to this volume. However, even though the *European Review of Social Psychology* is worldwide in terms of the nationality of the authors, it is European in terms of the nationality of the editors who select the contributions and shape the editorial policies. Our goal in publishing the *European Review* is to further the international exchange of ideas by providing an English-language source for important theoretical and empirical work that has not been previously published in English. With the help of an editorial board consisting of senior scholars drawn from across the globe, we invite outstanding researchers to contribute to the series. The emphasis of these contributions is on critical assessment of major areas of research and of substantial individual programmes of research, as well as on topics and initiatives of contemporary interest and originality. Volumes contain three types of contribution:

(1) Reviews of the field in some specific area of social psychology, typically one in which European researchers have made some special contribution.
(2) Reports of extended research programmes which contribute to knowledge of a particular phenomenon or process.
(3) Contributions to a contemporary theoretical issue or debate.

This is the eighth volume. The *European Review of Social Psychology* is widely accepted as one of the major international series in social psychology. Not only have reviews been very complimentary, but many of the chapters published in previous volumes have been widely cited in the international literature.

Acknowledgements

We would like to thank the following reviewers, who helped us and the authors to shape these chapters into their final versions:

Dominic Abrams, Monica Biernat, Herbert Bless, Gerd Bohner, Michael Diehl, Carsten de Dreu, Alice Eagly, Klaus Fiedler, Dieter Frey, Ralph Hertwig, Mike Hogg, Klaus Jonas, Charles M. Judd, Diane Mackie, Tony Manstead, Robin Martin, David Messick, Penelope J. Oakes, John Rijsman, Bernard Rimé, Norbert Schwarz, Gün Semin, Charles Stangor, Fritz Strack, Stephen Sutton, Theresa Vescio, Thomas Wills.

Introduction to Volume 8

The eight chapters of this volume of the *European Review of Social Psychology*, which includes authors from Europe, North America and Australia, can, although we eschew formal grouping of chapters into parts, be structured into three sections, each of which is central to social psychology: attitudes, social cognition, and group processes.

The first two chapters concern attitudes, the first dealing with attitude change, and the second looking more at attitudes and the prediction of behaviour. Chapter 1 by *Joule and Beauvois* presents a radical view of dissonance theory. Their view is radical in the sense that they reject all reformulations of the theory as unnecessary and misleading. They argue for a return to the original version of dissonance theory as presented in 1957, except that they want it supplemented by an axiom stating the necessity of commitment or, more specifically, the free choice of compliance. Thus, even according to the radical view, dissonance is unlikely to be aroused unless participants felt free to refuse to comply with the experimenter's request. However, the authors' concept of commitment is somewhat different from that accepted in the literature. With commitment to compliance, for example with regard to the classic task of counter-attitudinal advocacy, the authors mean that subjects have to know, when agreeing to the task, that they would have to write a counter-attitudinal essay. They do not have to know the topic of the essay. The chapter reviews the results of the authors' extensive research programme aimed at testing predictions from reformulated versions of dissonance theory against the radical (or nearly original) version.

Chapter 2 by *van der Pligt, Zeelenberg, van Dijk, de Vries and Richard* focuses on the role of affect in attitudes and decision-making, or more specifically, the role of anticipated post-behavioural affective consequences, such as anticipated regret in motivating behaviour. The main thesis of this chapter is that people anticipate affective consequences of their actions in deciding between behavioural alternatives. In support of this proposition the authors present evidence from their own research programme to demonstrate: (1) that inclusion of measures of anticipated post-behavioural affective outcomes can improve the predictive validity of expectancy-value models, such as Ajzen's model of planned behaviour; and (2) that inducing individuals to anticipate the regret they would feel after engaging in certain risky behavioural alternatives can increase risk aversiveness. With regard to the first point, evidence is pre-sented that inclusion of a measure of individuals' expectations of the extent to which they would regret having had sex without using a condom substantially improved predictions of the model of planned behaviour. With regard to the second point, evidence is presented to demonstrate the impact of induced anticipatory regret on behavioural intentions and actual behaviour. Implica-tions of these findings for the study of affect in expectancy-value models of behaviour, as well as for designing attitude change interventions, are discussed.

The next three chapters are concerned with social cognition, ranging from basic processes to the interface between cognition and motivation. Chapter 3 by *Klauer* deals with evaluative processes in social cognition, argued by some to be automatic, spontaneous and possibly prior to cognitive analysis of stimuli. Klauer focuses on the use of an affective priming paradigm. In affective priming—which he refers to as "an effect" rather than "a mechanism"—evaluation of a prior stimulus affects processing of subsequent stimuli, perhaps by increasing the accessibility of similarly affectively-toned information in memory. Klauer reviews the results of previous research in this area, including his own, and casts doubts on the generality of the affective-priming effect, but also provides a detailed and useful analysis of when and why significant effects have been found, or not. Based on explanations derived from semantic priming, he reviews accounts of affective priming in terms of spreading activation, expec-tancy and post-lexical mechanisms. His preferred and new explanation, however, is in terms of the Stroop paradigm, which addresses interference effects among competing stimuli.

Chapter 4 by *Stahlberg and Maass* addresses "hindsight bias", originally identified by Fischhoff and sometimes called the "knew-it-all-along-effect". This bias refers to people's tendency to believe, falsely, that they would have predicted the outcome of an event, once the outcome is actually known. Stahlberg and Maass focus on the contrast between "memory impairment" (Fischhoff's explanation) and "biased reconstruction" explanations of hindsight bias. According to the memory-impairment view, memory for the original pre-diction is altered by subsequent outcome information. According to the biased reconstruction view, for those people who have forgotten the original informa-tion, post-event information—if remembered—can be used as a basis for guess-ing how they originally responded (thus this account emphasizes anchoring, response bias and metacognitive processes). Disentangling these two theoreti-cal accounts is far from simple, but is the focus of Stahlberg and Maass's own research. Their results argue strongly in favour of the biased-reconstruction view, although they do not rule out memory processes under certain circumstances.

Chapter 5 by *Webster and Kruglanski* reviews the research programme of Kruglanski and colleagues on the antecedent conditions and the cognitive and social consequences of the need for closure. This need is conceptualized as involving a desire for definite knowledge on some issue as opposed to confusion or uncertainty, and as deriving from situational or personality factors that influence the subjective costs or benefits of possessing definite closure. It is assumed to influence the knowledge-construction process through two general tendencies, namely an urgency tendency to attain closure quickly, and a permanence tendency to maintain closure once achieved. Empirical evidence regarding a broad range of effects exerted by closure motivation is reviewed. These include direct social cognitive effects, such as less extensive information processing and hypothesis generation, elevated judgemental confidence, greater preference for prototypical rather than diagnostic evidence, as well as the more indirect effects on interpersonal and group level phenomena, such as lowered perspective taking and empathic concerns for dissimilar others, greater linguistic abstraction in interpersonal communication, and increased desire for consensus in a group. These studies constitute impressive empirical support for the theory.

The last three chapters span the extent of group processes, ranging from studies of social influence, through stereotyping and on to wider patterns of racism in society. Chapter 6 by *Crano and Alvaro* is one of a series of important chapters on minority influence that have appeared in the *European Review*. It outlines the Context/Comparison Model of social influence, and applies it to indirect influence by a minority source. As other researchers have acknowledged, Crano and Alvaro assume that minorities do not typically effect change in established or vested beliefs. But in-group minorities can bring about change by making the targets of their message enter a "leniency contract". This is associated with resistance of overt change in the direction of the minority, but the source is not derogated and its message is actively elaborated with little counter-argumentation. Resulting imbalance in attitude structure can be relieved by changing beliefs close to the focal attitude in the target's belief configuration (i.e., indirect influence). A major theoretical contribution of this chapter is its detailed and constructive analysis of indirect influence. In particular, the authors' set of four criteria for indirect attitudes should guide and clarify future research.

Chapter 7 by *Haslam, Turner, Oakes, McGarty and Reynolds* deals with an under-researched and under-explained aspect of stereotyping—stereotype consensus, or the extent of agreement about the content of stereotypes, whether referring to ingroups or outgroups. As these authors argue, this neglect can be traced to the general trend towards individual, rather than social, measures of stereotypes. Haslam *et al.* use self-categorization theory to develop prior work by Tajfel, who mentioned the links between group membership and the psycho-logical activity underpinning stereotype consensus, into a theoretical analysis of how stereotype consensus develops. In their view, consensus is produced by social identification, or social identity salience, and collective coordination of perception and behaviour. They critically review previous work and summarize some of their own studies showing how stereotype consensus varies as a func-tion of social context, particularly frame of reference in terms of other groups rated, and the specific nature of the rating task. This research programme underlines the authors' claim that, far from being expendable, the concept of consensus is crucial to our understanding of stereotypes as social phenomena.

The final contribution, Chapter 8 by *Pettigrew, Jackson, Ben Brika, Lemaine, Meertens, Wagner and Zick* reviews an ambitious research programme using public opinion data from Europe to test whether psychological principles of prejudice—largely identified using African-Americans as target group—generalize across societies and target groups. Using seven national samples from Europe, rating a range of ethnic minorities, Pettigrew and colleagues provide support for the notion that social-psychological factors operate in simi-lar ways across different nations and target groups. For example, prejudice levels and immigration policies differ widely across samples, but the relation-ships between measures of prejudice and immigration attitudes are similar. These authors also reveal, with the help of sophisticated analyses, that social-psychological variables (acting as proximal causes) mediate the effects of social factors (operating as distal causes) on prejudice. For example, the effect of education on prejudice was consistently mediated by such variables as political conservatism, group relative deprivation, intergroup contact and national pride.

Chapter 1

Cognitive Dissonance Theory: A Radical View

Robert-Vincent Joule
Université de Provence
Jean-Léon Beauvois
Université de Nice-Sophia Antipolis

ABSTRACT

A radical view of dissonance theory is presented. The view is radical in the sense that it rejects all reformulations of dissonance theory as unnecessary and misleading. The chapter argues for a return to the original version of dissonance theory as presented in 1957, but supplemented by an axiom stating the necessity of commitment, or more specifically the free choice of compliance. The chapter reviews the results of an extensive research program aimed at testing predictions from reformulated versions of dissonance theory against the radical version. Although individual studies may sometimes allow for interpretations alternative to the one offered, the total body of evidence presented is supportive of the radical view presented by the authors.

Social psychology is now re-embracing one of its greatest theories: the theory of cognitive dissonance (Aronson, 1992). This is quite gratifying for those researchers who never ceased working with it. The return to this theory has not been cost-free, however. In fact, the new theory is based on a number of theoretical options that have taken it quite far away from the proposals set forth in the original theory (Festinger, 1957a, 1957b).

One such option is the often blind acceptance of a number of amendments (or rather "revisions") made to the theory over the years. These modifications

European Review of Social Psychology, Volume 8. Edited by Wolfgang Stroebe and Miles Hewstone.
© 1998 John Wiley & Sons Ltd.

have gradually transformed the original theory into a cognitive-defense theory describing the mechanisms used by the "moral self" to preserve an image of worth and responsibility (Aronson, 1968, 1969; Wicklund & Brehm, 1976; Cooper & Fazio, 1984). Yet, although they are based on an undeniable fact, namely, the importance of what Kiesler (1971) called "external commitment" (free choice, salience of an act's consequences, irrevocability of an act, etc.), the need for these amendments has not really been demonstrated (Greenwald & Ronis, 1978; Beauvois & Joule, 1996). In any case, they have not generated any truly new hypotheses (or genuinely new experimental paradigms) as robust or as challenging as the ones derived from the initial theory back in the late 1950s and early 1960s. Moreover, the revisions do not seem to stem from any predictive insufficiencies discovered in the original theory. As early as 1962, for instance, Brehm and Cohen proposed the first revised version, apparently "for purposes of explicitation", not to enhance the predictive power of the initial theory. Their "explicitation" did not produce new hypotheses, however, since the foundations for all of the studies presented in their book can be found in the 1957 theory.

Even more intriguing, certain hypotheses derived from theories traditionally considered to be dissonance-theory rivals have been explicitly or implicitly accepted in the regeneration of dissonance theory. A number of theorists thus casually proceed to integrate certain competing principles into dissonance theory itself. Leippe and Eisenstadt (1994), for instance, go so far as to propose an appalling "integrated view of dissonance" which captures "traditional dissonance" (actually, the later versions of dissonance theory) as well as competing theories like self-presentation theory (Baumeister, 1982), impression-management theory (Tedeschi, 1981), and self-affirmation theory (Steele, 1988).

It is our claim that such compromises are useless, whether within dissonance theory (unquestioning adoption of the amendments) or beyond its bounds (acceptance of competing theoretical principles), and that dissonance theorists, even if they feel obligated to incorporate the notion of commitment into their new versions, must also acknowledge the specificity of the 1957 theory. In support of this claim, the first section of this paper will present a number of studies conducted in France. These studies test several hypotheses that can be directly deduced from the 1957 theory provided they are supplemented by one axiom, which is the necessity of commitment, and more specifically, the free choice of compliance or non-compliance. In the process of validating these hypotheses we shall see that dissonance theory is clearly different from both its revised versions and its rivals. The second section will attempt to show why we need what we call a "radical" interpretation of the theory (Beauvois, 1994; Beauvois & Joule, 1981, 1996; Joule, 1986a, 1986b). We believe the merits of such a radical interpretation are threefold: (a) the radical view focuses on that which is specific to the process of dissonance reduction; (b) this specificity can be demonstrated without having to rely on ego-based concepts (cognitive self-defense, self-enhancement) as in the various new versions; and (c) the radical theory has given rise to new experimental paradigms (double forced compliance and act rationalization).

As we shall see, the radical conception is original with respect to current theories of dissonance, for at least three reasons. It is original because it reflects the desire to return to the strictly theoretical propositions of the initial 1957 version (what we call the "basic core" of 1957), and in particular, to the ratio used by Festinger to measure dissonance. More importantly, it is original because it formulates some implications of the basic core that have never been formulated before, be it by Festinger himself or his successors. Finally, it is original because it makes commitment (and more specifically, free choice) a prerequisite to the very operation of the theory, in such a way that the dissonance reduction process can still be described using the terms employed initially in 1957. It will become clear that these three features make dissonance theory into a theory of the rationalization of behaviors to which the subject is committed, particularly ones manifested in situations of compliance.

THE 1957 DISSONANCE THEORY AND THE VARIOUS REFORMULATIONS

Two Principles Underlying the Reformulations of the Theory

It is not very difficult to pinpoint two of the basic principles or assumptions used as a foundation for both the revised versions of dissonance theory and the other competing reformulations.

The first is based on common sense. It is the principle of consistency between cognitions, or between cognitions and behavior. This principle works in two ways. First, and essentially for Bem (1972), it acts by allowing individuals to make self-perception inferences of the type "behaviors → internal states": if nothing in the situation can account for my behavior, given that I am free to act as I please, then I cannot be anything but consistent; my attitude follows from my behavior. For other researchers, the consistency principle also acts by providing information about people's worth, through the implicit but general axiom that consistency between attitudes and behaviors is a social norm (see Cialdini, 1984). "Personal worth" is established either in the individual's own eyes or in the eyes of others. In the former, self-image case (Aronson: "What kind of an individual would I be if I were inconsistent to the point of having done something that goes against my own values?"), an attitude change serves to maintain the subject's image of his/her own consistency (Wicklund & Brehm, 1976; Cooper & Fazio, 1984: "I cannot admit to being responsible for a behavior that produced consequences which are inconsistent with a value I believe in"). A necessary assumption here is that the re-establishment of some degree of consistency between an attitude and a behavior (or its consequences) serves to uphold the subject's image of his/her own worth. In the latter, social-image case ("People are going to think I'm an unworthy person if it looks like I do things that don't conform to my own attitudes"), the expression of a new attitude which is consistent with the behavior is a means of avoiding looking "bad" (self-presentation, impression management). Thus, without the principle of consistency, along with the hypothesis that consistency is a valued norm, neither the revised versions nor the rivals of Festinger's theory (1957a) can persist for long. It would only be necessary to prove that the purpose of the dissonance reduction process is not to re-establish this type of consistency, for an indispensable foundation to crumble. As the radical conception is not founded on such a premise, we shall demonstrate the need for a radical view by reporting some experiments which show that the ultimate and necessary purpose of the dissonance reduction process is not to achieve consistency but to rationalize behavior. We shall then discover that the effects obtained, fully predicted by the 1957 basic core theory, are incompatible with the various reformulations.

The second principle underlying the revisions of dissonance theory is a representation of the individual as the bearer of a moral ideal (an individual in the service of ideals). To be operational, this representation needs the principle of consistency, but it adds something else: inconsistency is all the more important since it means "I'm going against some fundamental ideal or value" (this is Aronson's morally good self"). This representation is what pulls dissonance theory closer to a theory of self-defense and of the cognitive management of personal responsibility. Cooper and Fazio push this to an extreme in claiming that it is the predictability of morally "aversive" consequences that creates dissonance. One of the results of this change is that it led dissonance theorists to neglect the decision-making paradigm, and, in the case of forced compliance, to fail to analyze rather commonplace situations in which people, acting under mildly constraining conditions, execute behaviors which oppose the ones they would spontaneously produce, but which have no obvious moral implications. Some examples are getting up when you would rather stay in bed, refraining from drinking before driving, doing a boring job, etc.[1]

As the radical conception is not founded on this type of premise, we shall demonstrate the need for a radical view by reporting some experiments which show that the aim of the dissonance reduction process is not moral worth. And we shall discover once again that the effects obtained, entirely predicted by the 1957 theory, are incompatible with the various reformulations.

---

[1] This is why, to our knowledge, dissonance theory has never been called upon to account for the cognitive effects of disciplinary events that are part of liberal child-raising which apparently represent 60% of all parent–child interactions between the ages of 3 and 8.

And What If Dissonance Theory Were Not a Theory of Consistency?

This section will be devoted to presenting experiments which demonstrate that dissonance theory cannot be likened to a theory of consistency, precisely because one can derive hypotheses from it that go against the consistency principle. Five experiments were selected from among the many that support this point of view (Experiment 1: Joule & Leveque, 1993; Experiment 2: Beauvois & Rainis, 1993; Experiments 3 and 4: Beauvois, Joule, & Brunetti, 1993; Experiment 5: Joule, 1996). In discussing the results, only those differences with a statistical significance level of $p < 0.05$ will be considered.

Experiment 1: Argumentation and Attitude Change

Festinger and Carlsmith (1959) realized that the condition that produced the greatest attitude change also produced less argumentation about the position being defended. Rabbie, Brehm, and Cohen (1959) observed incidentally that in a counter-attitudinal role-playing situation, participants who had found the greatest number of arguments in favor of the position being defended were also the ones whose attitudes changed the least. These observations suggested an inverse relationship between the elaborateness of the argumentation and the attitude change. In fact, these findings were never formalized by dissonance theorists who, on the contrary, mentioned them as mere curiosities. Yet they clearly fit quite well into the strict (let us say "radical") view of the 1957 theory: the counter-attitudinal arguments that subjects produce furnish cognitions which are consistent with the counter-attitudinal behavior precisely because this kind of behavior consists of defending the argued viewpoint. There is nothing shocking about this statement to a dissonance theorist, who "naturally" recognizes that cognitions which are consistent with the initial private attitude may involve the opposing behavior: writing an attitudinal essay. As such, every argument that psychologically implies the viewpoint being defended must be regarded as a consonant cognition, and as such, is a dissonance-reducing cognition. It is thus easy to see why, in a counter-attitudinal role-playing situation, the more arguments subjects find against their initial attitude, the less dissonance they experience, and consequently, the less they change their minds. Beauvois, Ghiglione, and Joule (1976) obtained results supporting this hypothesis, that there is an inverse relation between argumentation and attitude change. They found that for subjects declared free to choose, unlike those with no choice, the more time allotted to supporting the counter-attitudinal position, the less the subjects' attitudes changed. Joule and Lévèque tested this hypothesis more recently using a 2×3 factorial design with subjects in a classical counter-attitudinal role-playing situation (individual training). In this experiment, 120 subjects who were literature students at the University of Provence had to write a persuasive essay favoring the counter-attitudinal position that "leisure activities are a waste of time for students". All subjects had volunteered to participate in what was said to be a study on persuasion. Half were also told they were free to accept or refuse to write the essay ("free-choice" instructions), while the other half heard no such statement. A third of the subjects were given 20 minutes to write the advocacy before assessing their attitude on a 21-point scale. Another one-third were given 5 minutes before making the attitude assessment, and the final one-third expressed their attitudes right away, before beginning to write. The arguments produced by the subjects in the 20-minute condition substantially and significantly outnumbered those generated in the 5-minute condition. The attitude ratings are given in Table 1.1. The expected interaction between the two independent variables was significant and did indeed exhibit the predictable pattern: in the free-choice condition, the more time the subjects had to find arguments, the farther away their post-experimental attitudes were from the position being defended. The opposite pattern was obtained in the no-choice condition.

The results observed in the free-choice condition, like the ones obtained by Beauvois, Ghiglione and Joule (1976), support the hypothesis that finding arguments reduces the dissonance generated by the behavior executed during the counter-attitudinal role-playing.[2] Note that they are incompatible with self-perception theory: no self-perception view could possibly be used to derive the idea that subjects are less likely to adhere to the position they are defending as the number of arguments they find increases. Among the alternative explanations of these results is the frequently proposed idea that subjects find unconvincing and even stupid arguments, and so all the more as the allotted time increases, in such a way that they change their minds less and less as the amount of time available for realizing that the arguments are stupid increases. This explanation is inconsistent with the data. First of all, blind

Table 1.1 Effects of counter-attitudinal advocacy on attitude

	Free-choice condition			No-choice condition		
	0 min	5 min	20 min	0 min	5 min	20 min
No. of arguments	0	2.85	5.05	0	2.8	5.4
Attitude	6.2	3.4	2.5	1.3	2.9	8.0

The higher the figure, the more closely the measured attitude conforms to the counter-attitudinal act. In a control group ($n = 20$), the mean attitude was 2.6. Blind judges were asked to assess the arguments furnished by the subjects. The arguments given in the 5-minute conditions were also found in the 20-minute conditions, along with new arguments deemed acceptable by the judges. From Joule and Lévêque, 1993.

---

[2] Those subjects in the no-choice condition who did not experience dissonance no doubt underwent a self-persuasion process.

judges asked to analyze the arguments (see footnote to Table 1.1) found the same arguments in the 20-minute condition as in the 5-minute condition, along with others also deemed acceptable. Second, if this alternative hypothesis is correct, it should apply to all subjects whether or not they are given the choice. But this is not what happened: subjects who were not free to choose, unlike those who were free, changed attitudes more when there was more time. So having more time did not bring them to regard their arguments as stupid. We have seen that our results fit fully with the 1957 theory. If our hypothesis has not yet been added to the "corpus" of dissonance theory, it is probably because it goes against the widely accepted idea (see the classical presentations of dissonance theory: Feldman, 1966; and especially Zajonc, 1968) that dissonance theory is a theory of consistency. It is indeed difficult to see how there could be a consistency effect in the fact that subjects change their attitudes even less when they come up with numerous arguments against them. Brehm and Cohen (1962), somewhat embarrassed, even judged dissonance theory to be ambiguous in this respect, claiming that another hypothesis opposing the one we have just set forth was just as compatible with the theory and, needless to say, more compatible with the consistency axiom ("the higher the quality of the subject's arguments, the more dissonance there should be, assuming an initial disagreement with the advocated position", p. 34). Faced with this predicament, they suggested "holding constant the quantity of persuasive material written" (p. 35). But as we have already seen, the inverse relationship between argument quantity and attitude change is not ambiguous from the standpoint of dissonance theory. And as we shall soon see, other results show that this is not the sole case that goes against the idea that dissonance theory is a theory of consistency.

Experiment 2: Negative Feedback and Attitude Change

The preceding experiment shows that the dissonance reduction process is not aimed at re-establishing harmonious or consistent cognitions. If this were the case, the subjects who found more arguments would have displayed the attitude that conformed the most to those arguments. But consistency can be more than just an optimal state of equilibrium towards which the cognitive universe is drawn. It can also act as an internal-state/behavior correspondence principle, upon which the subject can count to infer his/her own attitude. This is the essential assumption of any self-attribution view of the effects of dissonance and, in particular, of self-perception theory (Bem, 1965, 1967, 1972). Festinger probably had this kind of assumption in mind when he confessed that he saw no difference between his theory and Bem's (Jones, 1990). We shall now discover that the dissonance reduction process is not based on such a principle.

Our demonstration of this will use the change in attitude subjects undergo when given negative feedback about their performance on a tedious task just

willingly performed for an experimenter. By virtue of psychological implication, the knowledge that one has freely agreed to carry out a tedious task is
inconsistent with the knowledge that the task is tedious, and therefore gener-
ates dissonance. However, the knowledge that by accomplishing it one is
doing a favor for an experimenter is consistent with the accomplishment of
the task, and will therefore reduce the dissonance. In this "tedious-task"
paradigm, the most direct way to reduce dissonance is to find the task more
interesting or worthwhile.

Imagine that after carrying out a tedious task as a favor for an experimenter,
the subjects are informed that their work was too poor to be used. Two hypotheses can be proposed to predict the effect of this negative feedback. The first is
based on a principle of consistency between one's internal state and one's
behavior, whereby subjects can be expected to infer from their poor performance that the task did not interest them much. From this, we can predict that
negative feedback will reduce the attractiveness of the task. This was in effect
the kind of reasoning—quite similar to Bem's—exhibited by the observers of an
interpersonal simulation devised by Beauvois and Joule (1982), who predicted
that the task would be less attractive after negative feedback was received. The
1957 version of dissonance theory calls for an opposing hypothesis. Learning
from the experimenter that one's work is unusable eliminates the consistent
cognition "I am doing a favor for the experimenter". The subject should therefore experience more dissonance, and as a result, undergo a greater change in
attitude about the task by finding it more interesting. Reasoning of this kind, as
well as the counter-intuitive hypothesis that follows from it, requires juggling
solely with psychological implications that are strictly in line with the 1957
theory. This idea was validated by two studies (Beauvois & Joule, 1982; Beauvois & Rainis, 1993), the more recent of which will be reviewed here. These two
studies are in line with Freedman's research, and they test the same hypotheses.
They differ, however, on one essential point: the feedback here does not pertain
to the usefulness of the task (important vs. unimportant), but to the subject's
work on the task (good vs. poor). This difference is important in that the results
obtained by Freedman can easily be reinterpreted in self-perception terms,[3]
unlike the ones presented below.

The boring task in the Beauvois and Rainis experiment consisted of spending 20 minutes gluing tiny paper squares over certain letters in a long text. The
86 subjects were sociology students. The 20 subjects in the control group had
to describe the task as carefully as possible but were not required to perform
it. The subjects in the three experimental groups (22 per condition), all volunteers, were told they were free to choose whether or not to do the task. In two

---

[3] The fact of having agreed to carry out a task knowing that it is not very useful should facilitate
an inference that leads to the belief that the reason for accepting the task was that it is inherently
interesting.

of the conditions, after the task was completed and the experimenter had pretended to correct the papers, she informed the subjects either of the excellent quality and scientific usefulness of their work (positive-feedback condition) or of how poor it was, making it scientifically useless (negative-feedback condition)[4]. In the third condition (no feedback) no comments were made about the work. All subjects then rated their attitude towards the task on an 11-point scale. The results are given in Table 1.2.

All of the experimental conditions differed significantly from the control group. The negative-feedback group differed from the other two experimental groups, which did not differ from each other. The expected paradigmatic effect was thus observed, since the no-feedback subjects found the task more interesting than the control group. The negative-feedback effect more specifically supports our viewpoint: subjects having learned that their work was poor and useless found the task more interesting than the others, as expected. This negative-feedback effect is comparable to one already observed in a similar situation where the testing was collective and the feedback was given to the group as a whole (Beauvois & Joule, 1982). The same was true for the positive feedback. As in 1982, the positive feedback *per se* had no effect, as the subjects in the positive-feedback condition did not differ from those in the no-feedback condition. This is easy to understand, since the positive feedback merely emphasized a cognition which was consistent, granted, but which already existed in the subject's cognitive universe. It is indeed obvious for everyone, especially for students, that the work requested by an experimenter (here, doing a boring task) is scientifically useful.

As in the preceding experiment, by adhering as closely as possible to the original theory, we were able to derive—and validate—a hypothesis which sets the dissonance reduction process apart from processes governed by a principle of consistency. In fact, the negative-feedback hypothesis turns out to be based solely on psychological implication. This forces us to take the

Table 1.2   Effects of feedback on attitudes about a boring task

Positive feedback	Negative feedback	No feedback	Control
4.3	7.8	4.6	2.4

The higher the figure, the more positive the attitudes towards the task. From Beauvois and Rainis, 1993 (11-point scale), with permission.

---

[4] As we can see, our instructions emphasized the scientific uselessness of the subject's behavior in the negative feedback condition. On this basis, two interpretations are possible, both compatible with the data. Either one insists, as we do, on the elimination of a consistent cognition in this group ("My work will serve the cause of science") or one insists on the introduction of a new, inconsistent cognition ("My work will serve no purpose"). These two interpretations end up at the same experimental hypothesis and both are totally compatible with the radical conception since they are based on the dissonance ratio and posit the behavior as the generating cognition.

relationships between cognitions two at a time. Note also that, as in Experiment 1, such a radical view suffices to generate hypotheses which are incompatible with a self-perception view of the dissonance reduction process.

Experiments 3, 4 and 5: Act Rationalization

One of the essential points in the 1957 theory, now thoroughly validated (see Elliot & Devine, 1994), is that the state of dissonance is a state of unpleasant motivational tension which the dissonance reduction process is designed to alleviate. Now, while certain theorists have acknowledged this aspect of the matter, one of the nevertheless direct implications of this idea has been largely ignored: the selection of one means of reducing dissonance effectively renders all other means useless. In other words, if a subject resorts to a given means of reduction, none of the others need be used. Granted, the handful of researchers who have studied the various dissonance reduction modes have accepted this implication (see the hydraulic view: Gotz-Marchand, Gotz, & Irle, 1974; Sherman & Gorkin, 1980) by assuming, for example, that the trivialization of the behavior reduces the magnitude of the attitude change (see Simon, Greenberg, & Brehm, 1995). Yet, to our knowledge, few researchers have emphasized the point that this implication removes dissonance theory from the field of consistency theories because there are situations where inconsistency must be predicted. This occurs in particular in cases where one way to reduce dissonance is to agree to engage in another behavior, as in studies on act rationalization (Joule, 1996; Beauvois, Joule, & Brunetti, 1993; Fointiat, 1996; Joule, 1996; for a review, see Beauvois & Joule, 1996).

  Imagine a subject who has just agreed to perform a discomforting act (counter-attitudinal or counter-motivational). While attitude change has traditionally been studied as a means of reducing the dissonance generated by a discomforting behavior, other modes of reduction are still conceivable. There is one such mode which has not attracted enough attention: agreeing to execute a new behavior which is equally if not more discomforting than the first. Accordingly, Joule (1986b) found that smokers who agreed to refrain from smoking for a short period (18 hours) were only prone to agree to a longer abstinence period (3 days) when they were unable to use the classical cognitive means (attitude change regarding how hard it is not to smoke) to reduce the dissonance generated by the acceptance of the first abstinence. When the experimenter gave them the opportunity to reduce the initial dissonance, they tended on the contrary to refuse the new abstinence period. Apparently, agreeing to a new, highly discomforting act is a means of reducing dissonance that is functionally equivalent to an attitude change. From this initial observation, several experiments were conducted to test three new hypotheses, namely: (a) recourse to the cognitive mode of dissonance reduction lowers the probability of the behavioral mode; (b) inversely, preventing recourse to the cognitive mode increases the probability of the behavioral mode; and (c) when the behavioral mode is used, the cognitive mode need not be used. Although each of these hypotheses has been validated several times, only three experiments will be presented here.

In Experiment 3 (Beauvois, Joule, & Brunetti, 1993, Experiment 1), volunteer subjects were recruited in the morning for an experiment to be held in the late afternoon of the same day (115 male and female science students at the University of Provence, smokers). Half were informed during the recruitment that the experiment would involve 18 hours of abstinence from smoking (informed condition). The other half were given this information upon arriving at the laboratory that afternoon (uninformed condition) (independent variable 1). All subjects had been submitted to a highly effective compliance procedure without pressure (caught-in-the-gears procedure; see, e.g., Joule, 1987) designed to reduce the number of refusals. Once in the laboratory, 50% of the subjects were asked to write down the reasons why they had agreed to refrain from smoking for 18 hours. The other subjects were not asked to provide any such reasons (independent variable 2). Then, as they were leaving the laboratory to begin the 18 hours of abstinence, all subjects were asked whether they would like to participate in a future experiment requiring 6 days of abstinence. The dependent variable was the acceptance of the second abstinence period (2 × 2 design). The subjects in the control condition were asked right away to participate in the 6-day abstinence experiment. The data are given in Table 1.3.

The first of the three hypotheses presented above was clearly validated here. Reliance upon a cognitive means of dissonance reduction does seem to lessen the probability of a behavioral means. Let us look at the uninformed subjects first: more subjects who had to supply the reasons for their acceptance of a short abstinence refused the longer abstinence than did those who had not been asked to come up with any reasons. One might think that the reasons they produced would help lower the dissonance induced by the acceptance of the 18-hour abstinence. In fact, an analysis of the reasons actually given showed that they were all acceptable, and were usually internal explanations (I like to be helpful, to assist researchers; I thought it would be a good opportunity to see how I would hold up under withdrawal . . .). The processes

Table 1.3 Acceptance of 6 days of abstinence from smoking

	Informed subjects	Uninformed subjects
Reasons	62.5% (15/23)	26.1% (6/23)
No reasons	47.8% (11/23)	82.6% (19/23)

In the control group, 21.7% (5/23) of the subjects agreed to 6 days of abstinence. From Beauvois, Joule, and Brunetti, 1993, with permission.

were quite different for the informed subjects. Once in the laboratory, all of the informed subjects probably found good reasons for having accepted. It is thus likely that they had already reduced the dissonance. Their acceptance of the new period of abstinence cannot have served to reduce dissonance that had already been reduced. For these subjects, then, we must find some other process than dissonance reduction. Having to write down reasons they had probably already found may have instigated a self-perception process that led them to be more willing to accept a new abstinence period than if they had not had to state the reasons.

This experiment thus shows that when subjects are given the time they need for cognitive rationalization, or when rationalization is facilitated, the likelihood that a behavioral means will be chosen decreases. The next experiment will show, in line with the second hypothesis, that the use of a behavioral means can be promoted by hindering the use of a cognitive means.

In Experiment 4 (Beauvois, Joule, & Brunetti, 1993, Experiment 2), dissonance was induced by leading subjects (438 male and female customers of a large supermarket) to accept an initial discomforting behavior which they would gladly have done without: filling out a long questionnaire about cancer in the supermarket parking lot right when they were loading their groceries into their cars. Before beginning the questionnaire, the experimenter prointo their cars. Before beginning the questionnaire, the experimenter proposed a second discomforting behavior: a long, home interview on the same issue. This two-behavior sequence may remind the reader of a foot-in-the-door type of manipulation. However, contrary to what happens in a classic foot-in-the-door situation, the first behavior (questionnaire) was already very costly and was thereby dissonance-generating.[5] Just before requesting the home interview, the experimenter informed some of the subjects of the uselessness of the questionnaire (negative-information condition); others were told on the contrary that it would be highly useful (positive-information condition), and still others received no information (no-information condition). The subjects in the control group were asked directly whether they would agree to a home interview. The dependent variable was the acceptance of the interview. The data are given in Table 1.4.

Table 1.4 Agreeing to a home interview

Negative information	Positive information	No information	Control
39.4% (48/122)	13% (14/107)	25.7% (28/109)	10% (10/100)

From Beauvois, Joule, & Brunetti, 1993, with permission.

---

[5] Whatever the cause may be, our hypotheses do not pertain to a potential foot-in-the-door effect, but to variations of that effect related to the occurrence of a process of rationalization (cognitive vs. act).

The second of the three hypotheses presented above found solid validation in these results. As expected, subjects who had just agreed to execute a discomforting behavior (lasting approximately 20 minutes in a parking lot after shopping) and who had clearly been told that it would serve no purpose, outnumbered all others in agreeing to an even more discomforting behavior. Apparently, preventing the dissonance reduction process from occurring via the most direct cognitive means ("What I do serves some purpose") increases the probability that the subject will adopt the behavioral mode: agreeing to an even more discomforting act (the home interview). Note here that, contrary to what happened in Experiment 2, the positive information had an effect and, as could be expected compared with no-information, this effect was symmetrical, causing the probability of accepting the interview to decrease. We can account for the discrepancy between the two experiments (effect in the present experiment, no effect in Experiment 2) in terms of the differences between the two experimental situations. Here, the experimental manipulation immediately followed the subject's acceptance of the first behavior, which itself came right before the dependent variable was measured. These subjects did not have time to think about the utility of their discomforting act, whereas the subjects in Experiment 2 had over 20 minutes to do so. Furthermore and above all, the positive information supplied here went beyond merely announcing the scientific utility of the act, since it was accompanied by the provision of new information (subjects were told that the study was methodologically well-designed, that the results were needed soon by the Department of Health, that money was already available for initiating the measures suggested by the outcome of the survey, etc.).

With the results of these two studies behind us, we now know that the two modes of dissonance reduction are alternatives. The following experiment will show that agreeing to execute a second discomforting behavior is indeed a reflection of a smaller change in attitude towards the first behavior, i.e. less frequent use of the cognitive mode to reduce dissonance.

In Experiment 5 (Joule, 1996), subjects (90 male science students at the University of Provence, all smokers) were submitted to a low-ball—accomplished-act—procedure (Joule, 1987) so they would participate in a study requiring refraining from smoking for 24 hours. The procedure consisted of having subjects come to the laboratory without having been informed that they would have to stop smoking on the spot. Thus, it was only after the fact, once they were in the laboratory, that they were told and then forced to decide, at the last minute, to refrain from smoking for 24 hours. They came back to the laboratory 24 hours later, at the end of the abstinence period. The dependent variable was the subject's attitude about how difficult the tobacco deprivation was (rated on an 11-point scale), knowing that in experiments involving abstinence (from drinking, eating, etc.) the most direct means of reducing dissonance is to minimize the apparent difficulty of the abstinence.

The subject's attitude was measured either before or after the experimenter had proposed a new experiment involving 5 days without smoking. The acceptance vs. refusal of this new abstinence period was taken as an invoked independent variable, making a 2 × 2 design for presenting the data in Table 1.5.

The important thing here is what happens after the subjects have accepted or refused the second abstinence period. We discover that those who agreed to the second deprivation (act rationalization) had a lesser need to cognitively reduce the dissonance induced by the first, and therefore found it difficult. In contrast, those who refused and who did not engage in act rationalization, rationalized cognitively and lowered the dissonance induced by the first deprivation, thereby finding it quite easy. It is indeed the refused or accepted act that created this difference by bringing in a new cognition that was consistent or inconsistent with the first deprivation. Indeed, before the second abstinence period was proposed, the subjects did not differ in attitude. Apparently, the acceptance of a highly counter-motivational behavior cancels the need to reduce the dissonance generated by a previous behavior, and on the contrary, refusal of the highly counter-motivational act increases that need. From a more theoretical standpoint, the cognition behind the second behavior is consistent in this case with the cognition behind the first behavior (the cognition, "I am capable of not smoking for 5 days" psychologically implies the cognition, "I agreed not to smoke for 24 hours").

The above results—and many others (for a more comprehensive review, see Beauvois & Joule, 1996)—indicate that there is a behavioral means of reducing dissonance. Indeed, we discovered here that the subject's acceptance of a second act which is even more counter-motivational than the first has all the properties of a dissonance reduction mode: it acts as an alternative to the more traditional cognitive modes and renders those modes functionally useless. Insofar as the dissonance reduction process can be defined as a rationalization process, this is a case of act rationalization.

It is important to realize here that the behavioral mode of dissonance reduction can be a conveyor of inconsistency. In the three experiments just presented, the hypotheses set forth and validated predict inconsistency between the cognitive realm and the behavioral realm. In the first experiment,

Table 1.5 Attitude about 24-hour abstinence from smoking

	Agreed	Refused
Attitude before	−0.4 (n = 20)	−0.2 (n = 25)
Attitude after	−2.7 (n = 26)	1.2 (n = 19)

The lower the figure, the higher the perceived difficulty of the abstinence (11-point scale). From Joule, 1996, with permission.

subjects who found good reasons for having accepted a counter-attitudinal act refused a new act of a comparable nature. In the second, subjects who knew about the uselessness of an initial discomforting act agreed to a second act of a comparable nature. In the third, subjects who agreed to a highly counter-motivational act found a previous counter-motivational act of a comparable nature more difficult.

The inconsistency of the subjects who had reduced their dissonance here is quite similar to the inconsistency manifested by the subjects in Experiments 1 and 2. With this data in hand, we are now in a position to contend that the dissonance reduction process is not governed by a principle of consistency, whether it is a matter of cognitive consistency or cognition–behavior consistency. This conclusion runs counter to at least two sorts of conceptions of the dissonance reduction process: (a) it invalidates views which, like self-attribution, consider the reduction of dissonance to be a series of inferences subjects make on the basis of a postulate of consistency between their own behaviors and attitudes; (b) it invalidates views which account for dissonance reduction in terms of an orientation towards consistency, either by postulating that cognitive dynamism itself is orientated towards a state of consistency (cognitive consistency theories), or by postulating the existence of self-valuing strategies based on the worth of those states (self-enhancement theories).

Now that we have shown that dissonance theory can do without the first principle included in a number of the revised versions and rival theories (principle of consistency), we shall attempt to demonstrate that it has no need for the second either (the morally good self).

And What If Dissonance Theory Had Nothing To Do With Morals?

It seems to us that, starting in 1962 when Brehm and Cohen published the first book summarizing dissonance theory, the principal reformulations (Aronson, 1968, 1969; Cooper & Fazio, 1984; Wicklund & Brehm, 1976) have gradually turned the theory into a cognitive-defense theory describing the mechanisms used by responsible subjects concerned about their own morality. The reformulations date back to the discovery in the 1960s that certain situational factors are required in order to obtain the classical forced compliance effect (free choice, consequences of an act, etc.), factors which Kiesler (1971) considered to be the conditions for external commitment.

We would now like to demonstrate that even if one agrees that the commitment conditions are necessary, they do not have to be interpreted in terms of personal responsibility and the morally good self. Let us begin by showing that we can derive hypotheses from dissonance theory that are incompatible with this interpretation. After that, we shall present our view of the role of what, following Kiesler, we call the "commitment cognitions" (see Beauvois & Joule, 1996).

Experiment 6.   When Telling the Truth Increases Dissonance: Festinger and Carlsmith Revisited

The famous experiments by Festinger and Carlsmith (1959) should pose a serious problem for the advocates of the "moral self" view. After all, the subjects who were "bought" at the highest price were the ones to experience the least amount of dissonance. But this is not all. Contrary to what the versions based on the morally good self and centered around the idea of "lying" ($20 for a lie!) would lead us to expect, we shall see that in the same situation, dissonance can be increased by a perfectly moral act: telling the truth.

But first, let us analyze this situation. Subjects are induced to accomplish two consecutive behaviors likely to generate dissonance. The first consists of accomplishing a particularly boring and mindless task (tedious task paradigm). The second consists of telling a peer that the task is interesting (counter-attitudinal role-playing paradigm). Joule and Girandola (1995) demonstrated that this situation has to be regarded as a situation of double compliance (Joule, 1991), making it necessary to consider the relationship between the two behavioral cognitions. This relationship is obviously consonant if we confine ourselves to dual relationships involving two cognitions only, as required by the 1957 definition of psychological implication. Psychological implication indeed only looks at relationships between two cognitions. Dissonance theory treats relationships two at a time, and in this respect, it differs from Heider's theory where the balance between more than two cognitions can be considered. Saying that a task is interesting goes quite well with having carried out that task when the occasion arose, and this is true regardless of one's attitude towards the task, which constitutes a third cognition. In short, the actual accomplishment of the task provides the Festinger and Carlsmith subjects, who say the task is interesting, with a consonant cognition. They should thus experience less dissonance than subjects who said the same thing but who have not had the occasion to carry out the task.

What happens when subjects are led to tell the truth, namely, to say that the task is uninteresting? This time, the two acts are inconsistent with each other. The requested statement, which involves telling the truth, should thus increase the dissonance induced by task execution. In short, once they have executed the tedious task, subjects having "lied" should experience less dissonance than subjects having "told the truth". These conjectures were confirmed by the experiment conducted by Joule and Girandola (1995) (one of several experiments in a research project designed to study attitudinal role-playing and counter-attitudinal role-playing separately). The subjects, all volunteers, were 80 female literature students at the University of Provence assigned to the four cells of a 2×2 design. Half had to accomplish a tedious task (turning knobs on a board for 13 minutes). The other half simply had the task described to them and were clearly told they would not have to perform it. Then all subjects presented the task to a peer, either positively (counter-attitudinal role-playing) or negatively (attitudinal role-playing), using arguments supplied by the experimenter (e.g. "It was very enjoyable", "I had a lot of fun", vs. "It was tedious", "I got bored", etc.). Finally, the subjects rated their attitude towards the task on an 11-point scale (−5 to +5). This scale was strictly identical to the first one used by Festinger and Carlsmith (1959) (the scale that produced the most significant findings). The results are given in Table 1.6.

Festinger and Carlsmith's main finding was replicated: subjects who had to accomplish and positively present the task had a better attitude towards it than control group 2 subjects, who only had to assess it. But what these results show above all is that subjects having performed the tedious task found it more interesting after telling a peer it was boring than after claiming it was interesting. We can see in addition that subjects having carried out and negatively presented the task found it more interesting than control condition 1 subjects, who only had to carry it out. Thus, it is not the immorality of the "lie" that is behind the dissonance experienced by the Festinger and Carlsmith subjects, or the fact that they tricked the peer. They would have felt even more dissonance had the researchers asked them to tell the truth, as Joule and Girandola did. This conclusion urges us to think about the role played by the consequences of the act. Indeed, it is probably because they shared this somewhat "moral" interpretation of dissonance that certain researchers (in particular, Cooper & Fazio, 1984) insisted so strongly on the importance of what they called the act's "aversive" consequences (here, tricking a peer), to the point of making it the core of their "new look". Granted, we are not questioning the necessity of the commitment or, even less, the importance of the act's consequences as a commitment factor. Nevertheless, having shown in this situation that telling the truth to a peer (and in doing so, suggesting that he/she not agree to perform the tedious task) leads to an

Table 1.6 Attitude towards a tedious task

	Positive presentation ("counter-attitudinal" interesting)	Negative presentation ("attitudinal" boring)
With task	−0.5	1.5
Without task	1.4	−1.3

The higher the number, the more interesting or enjoyable the subjects found the task (11-point scale = −5/+5). In control situation 1 of simple compliance (task execution only), the subjects' attitude about the task was −0.2. In control situation 2 of simple task assessment, the attitude of the subjects who neither executed nor presented the task was −2.1. From Joule and Girandola, 1995, with permission.

increase in dissonance, compels us to reconsider the theoretical role some-times ascribed to these consequences. As we have just seen (see also Harmon-Jones *et al.*, 1996), they need not be morally "aversive" at all for dissonance to be generated. Note once again that we have adhered strictly to the stipula-tions of the 1957 theory.

Experiments 7 and 8.   Commitment to Compliance

Several times now we have said that it was the discovery in the 1960s of the conditions for commitment—in particular, being free to choose and the con-sequences of the act—that very quickly (as early as Aronson, 1968) drew dissonance theory towards today's widely accepted view that the dissonance reduction process is aimed at helping the individual cope with being held responsible (even morally responsible) for his/her acts. We do not challenge this discovery, or the importance attributed to it. We willingly agree that subjects who are not committed to an act do not experience dissonance. However, we have reasons to believe that the theoretical role of the commit-ment factors has not been properly clarified. The discovery of these factors has modified the essence of the original 1957 theory, even though they could very well have been incorporated into it. We shall return to this possibility later. This experimental section will be limited to clarifying the meaning of the most important factor of commitment: free choice.

Indeed, the traditional way to manipulate free choice ("You are entirely free to do or not to do what I ask you. It's up to you . . .") authorizes two interpretations with very different theoretical implications. Free choice can mean that the subject agrees (or in a few cases, refuses) to execute the particu-lar act requested of him/her, such as write an essay in favor of police interven-tion, refrain from eating or drinking, stop smoking temporarily, say that a task is interesting, etc. No one would deny that this is the traditional interpreta-tion. Yet manipulating free choice can be interpreted to mean something else, namely, that the subject agrees (or in a few cases, refuses) to comply with the obedience relationship proposed by an experimenter in a research frame-work. Replying, "No, I don't want to do that particular thing, but you can ask me to do some other thing", is not the same as replying, "I have no reason to comply with your demands". In the first case, accepting means agreeing to perform a specific act (and thus, to be held responsible for that act), as several post-Festinger theorists assume. In the second case, which is closer to our idea of what a "forced compliance contract" is (Beauvois & Joule, 1996), accepting means being willing to comply with the experimenter, in which case the ex-perimenter can be held responsible for whatever happens. Experiments 7 (Beauvois *et al.*, 1993, Experiment 1) and 8 (Beauvois, Bungert, & Mariette, 1995, Experiment 2) show that the second interpretation is in fact the right one. The subjects in Experiments 7 and 8, all seniors in a high school (tested individually), had to write a counter-attitudinal essay. Three possible choices were offered for the topic of the essay (vacations should be shortened, teenage driving should be eliminated, schools should be more selective about who gets scholarships). The clearly counter-attitudinal nature of all three topics had been pre-tested on other high school students in the city. Either the experimenter or the subjects themselves made the choice (independent variable 1). Before the topic was chosen, however, the free-choice variable was manipulated (commitment to compliance: independent variable 2).

In experiment 7 (2 × 2 design), subjects (100 high school students) were asked individually to come to the experimentation room. Once there, the experimenter who claimed to be conducting a national survey on the opinions of high school students, privately said right away to each subject that he/she would have to write an essay on one of the various issues. As an example, the experimenter mentioned the three experimental issues, while making it very clear that the students were expected to produce controversial advocacies. At that point, half of the subjects were told they were free to participate or not to participate in the survey (commitment to compliance) while nothing was said to the other half (non-commitment to compliance). Once this manipulation was achieved, the experimenter went on to manipulate the second independent variable (chosen vs. non-chosen issue): either he asked the subjects to choose one of the three issues, or he informed them that they would write about the "issue of the day". For this condition, the issues were paired with the ones chosen in the other condition. After the essays were written, the subjects were given an 11-point scale to assess their attitude about the issue in question. The results (2 × 2 design) are given in Table 1.7.

We can see in Table 1.7 that the subjects who changed attitudes the most, and thereby reduced dissonance the most, were the ones who had been given the free choice (committed to compliance) but were required to write about the issue of the day. This result has important theoretical implications. If the traditional "free choice" were indeed the choice to execute or not to execute the specific behavior requested, then the choice of one particular act among three in Experiment 7 would indeed be the best approximation of this type of

Table 1.7 Attitude towards a chosen vs. non-chosen issue

	Commitment to compliance	Non-commitment to compliance
Chosen issue	3.44 (8.4)	3.32 (6.5)
Non-chosen issue	5.28 (1.2)	3.76 (0.9)

The higher the figure, the closer the measured attitude to the counter-attitudinal act (11-point scale). In parentheses, data from an interpersonal simulation. From Beauvois *et al.*, 1993, with permission.

free choice.[6] Yet being able to choose one of three acts did not generate dissonance in this case. On the contrary, it seems to have reduced it when the subject was committed to compliance, and this is what we expected.[7] Imagine a subject who has just agreed to comply with the experimenter, knowing that he/she will have to execute a counter-attitudinal behavior but without knowing which. Once this commitment to compliance is obtained, the subject is given the choice between various obviously counter-attitudinal behaviors. In such a decision-making situation, being able to choose must reduce the dissonance ratio, compared to a classical forced compliance situation in which the subject is proposed one and only one act. Indeed, insofar as the chosen alternative is the least discomforting for the subject (the lesser of two evils), it must reduce the total amount of dissonance by creating consistent cognitions (the higher cost of the non-selected alternatives psychologically implies choosing the selected one). The fact that having chosen one out of three acts in Experiment 7 reduced the dissonance is thus perfectly compatible with Festinger's theory.

But the most important point in this experiment is that commitment to compliance must be taken as the factor that aroused the dissonance in the commitment-to-compliance/non-chosen-issue situation. These results were confirmed in Experiment 8.

In Experiment 8, subjects ($n = 176$) were assigned to one of two conditions. The first (paradigm condition) was an exact replication of Experiment 7. The second (out-of-paradigm condition) was used to manipulate commitment to compliance in another way. In the previous experiment, the commitment manipulation involved providing the subjects with information about the actual act they would execute, since the three experimental issues were announced to the subjects at the outset as examples of counter-attitudinal acts. This was no longer the case in the out-of-paradigm condition of Experiment 8. Here, before manipulating the commitment to compliance (statement of subject's free choice to participate in the experiment), the experimenter gave examples of counter-attitudinal acts that were very different from the ones the subjects would actually have to accomplish (examples given: glue a piece of confetti on every occurrence of the letter "a" in a long text, copy three pages of the telephone book, take a lengthy test involving crossing out symbols, etc.). Then, once the commitment to compliance was manipulated, the experimenter claimed she had made a mistake and told the subject that the task would be something completely different from what had just been said.

---

[6] Moreover, an interpersonal simulation (described in Beauvois et al., 1993, Experiment 3) demonstrates the validity of this interpretation: only those observers who had put themselves in the shoes of subjects who had to choose one of three acts, attributed the subjects an attitude that conformed to the act, as if our "choice of act" was in fact the only one that permitted self-attributional inferences.

[7] The interaction between these two independent variables was statistically significant.

Without repeating the statement that subjects were free to participate, she went on to the counter-attitudinal essays and manipulated the chosen/ non-chosen topic variable. Finally, after the completion of the essays, a post-experimental questionnaire was used to assess three attitudes (vacations, driving, scholarships). Insofar as the results of the paradigm condition replicated those obtained in Experiment 7 (including the interaction effect discussed above), Table 1.8 only gives the outcome of the out-of-paradigm condition. There were two dependent variables, the attitude towards the topic supported, and the mean attitude towards the other two topics.

As expected, we discovered that subjects who committed to compliance by agreeing to perform boring tasks modified their attitude in favor of the essay topic when it was imposed. Here again, the choice of one of three counter-attitudinal acts did not induce dissonance *per se*. However, in the commitment-to-compliance condition, being able to choose a topic does not seem to have reduced the dissonance (as in Experiment 7 and in the paradigm condition of this new experiment). This is probably due to the fact that in the out-of-paradigm condition, the subjects had been told nothing about the two non-chosen topics when they had to pick one of three, so they had not already implicitly agreed to write about them (during the commitment-to-compliance manipulation). In effect, avoiding two topics one has never heard about and therefore never agreed to write about, does not provide any consonant cognitions, unlike the case where subjects could say something like, "Out of the three I had agreed to write about, I chose the least problematic".

In opposition to the traditional understanding of free choice, it is indeed commitment to compliance and not commitment to a particular counter-attitudinal act—that turns out to be the condition needed to induce a state of dissonance. The results of Experiments 7 and 8 point out the limitations of a view of the dissonance reduction process which reduces it to the management of responsibility, and that is why they fall fully within the realm of a "radical" conception. In our minds, revisions based on responsibility, the moral self, the anticipation of aversive consequences, and other similar concepts, stem from

Table 1.8 Attitude towards the topic supported and mean attitude towards the other two topics in the experiment

	Out-of-paradigm	
	Commitment to compliance	Non-commitment to compliance
Chosen topic	4.72 (2.17)	2.77 (1.36)
Non-chosen topic	4.82 (2.26)	2.05 (2.03)

The mean attitude towards the other two topics is shown in parentheses. From Beauvois, Bungert & Mariette, 1995, with permission.

a poor interpretation of what free choice really is in classic forced-compliance experiments. It is quite understandable that subjects who experience the feelings involved in having chosen to perform the particular counter-attitudinal act just performed, having some problems about their own values and have trouble accepting that the act has morally "aversive" consequences. Note first of all, against this view, that dissonance is induced in a number of situations void of moral implications. Such is the case in situations of abstinence from smoking, for example, or in situations involving eating an unappetizing dish. Note also, and still opposing this view, the traditional "free-choice" effects are not incompatible with very slight though real differences in the feeling of freedom between subjects said to have a free choice and those given no choice—either they all globally experience a strong feeling of constraint (Steiner, 1980) or, on the contrary, they all experience a strong feeling of freedom (Beauvois *et al.*, 1996). In the studies mentioned by Steiner, as well as in those described by Beauvois *et al.*, dissonance effects are only observed in subjects said to have a free choice. The results of Experiments 7 and 8 described here and those of Experiment 1 by Beauvois, Bungert, & Mariette (1995) more clearly pinpoint the limits of personal responsibility in a "morally good self", and the ideological confusion this view implies: are subjects "morally" responsible when they accept a condition of obedience and perform an imposed, unexpected act—which they do (no refusals observed) simply because they accept their state of compliance with the experimenter? Even if we obviously have to answer "No" to this question, the results show that subjects nevertheless experience cognitive dissonance right from the very moment they are told they are free to comply or not to comply.

WHY IS A RADICAL VIEW NECESSARY?

As is often the case, the above experiments taken one by one fit with a number of alternative hypotheses (for example, reactance for Experiment 4, the selection phenomenon for Experiment 7). Even so, there is still no single alternative hypothesis that can account for all of our results, something which only the "radical" theory appears capable of doing. One might criticize us for having submitted subjects to only one scale that was directly related to the hypothesis being tested. In doing so, we neglected supplementary measures that were either associated with intermediating mechanisms, or that assessed the effectiveness of the experimental manipulations (manipulation checks). This stems from a deliberate choice concerning what we are theorizing about. We believe that as soon as subjects are presented with more than one or two scales, they build a theory about the experiment, and this theory shows up in their responses. We are not interested in subjects' implicit theories but in a process to which they have no access: rationalization. An illustration of this is the so-called "free-choice" manipulation, where we saw that the important thing was not the strength of the feeling of freedom subjects could express on a post-experimental scale, but the fact of having been declared free by the person with whom they were complying via an unconscious process. The radical conception we are defending makes no statements about the way subjects "construct" the experimental situation.

The "radical" interpretation of dissonance theory can account for the results just presented. To differentiate it more clearly from the other versions of the theory, it is useful to distinguish two types of positions: epistemological positions, which are in some sense the prerequisites of our theoretical argumentation and provide an epistemological base for the radical theory; and theoretical positions proper, whose function is to account for the experimental results as economically and concisely as possible.

Three Epistemological Positions

One epistemological position is the consideration that it is not scientifically acceptable to throw away theoretical proposals that have been fruitful, unless they have been proved false. From this standpoint, it seems quite bizarre that as time went by, researchers began totally ignoring the calculation of the total amount of dissonance—which constitutes one of the most original contributions of the 1957 theory—and began deriving hypotheses from simple intuitions about inconsistency between cognitions. Yet the specificity and the non-triviality of the initial theory lie precisely in the calculation of total dissonance (Brehm & Cohen, 1962). We know of no study showing that a revision is justified on the grounds that the dissonance ratio has been experimentally invalidated.

Another epistemological position amounts to considering that the discovery of a factor necessary to the operation of a theory does not necessarily have to give rise to a modification in the theory. The discovery of such a factor can simply lead to a more accurate specification of the conditions necessary to the operation of the theory, or of the framework in which the process under study takes effect. As such, the discovery during the 1960s of what, following Kiesler (1971), we call the factors of commitment (free choice, consequences of an act, etc.), did not call for the major revisions the initial theory underwent. A more parsimonious position would be to say that these factors provide a clearer picture of the situational conditions under which the unchanged theory can function.

A final epistemological position consists of admitting that several processes can be at work in a given paradigmatic situation and that it might be useless to search for a unique theory to account for them all. The important thing is to have a series of theories, each of which describes one process and can predict when that process will take effect. It is indeed probable that in a situation as rich as forced compliance, other processes may precede or succeed the dissonance reduction process (behavioral self-control, self-enhancement, self-consistency, etc.). Insofar as we have a theory to account for the dissonance reduction process within its own paradigms, it is not scientifically relevant to criticize the theory because it does not also account for other processes, or because its hypotheses are incompatible with some theory about those other processes.

These three positions could be taken to reflect a lack of theoretical ambition. It nevertheless seems to us that in bypassing them, Festinger's heirs have gradually modified the scope of the dissonance reduction process, even though the findings did not make that step necessary. In the 1957 theory, this process is a very specific one, but it is also one encountered on an everyday basis. The various amendments have made it into an overly complex process which only takes place on the rare occasions when an individual's image of worth and moral integrity is severely threatened. As such, dissonance theory has lost much of its ecological value. The most striking example is what happens to the now-neglected tedious task. It is true that accomplishing a tedious task does not threaten the subject's self-image of integrity. But it is also true that every day, people carry out tasks which hardly interest them, and that the simple psychological implication, "I don't like this task → I don't do this task", suffices to understand that dissonance is in fact being experienced. Just as the equally simple psychological implication, "I believe in X → I say X", suffices to understand that people experience dissonance if they agree to speak against their own beliefs (which is perhaps even rarer). It is puzzling that today's dissonance theorists more readily consider the second case as a dissonance situation than the first. Perhaps this is because the second is not as common as the first, and perhaps also because it is difficult to admit that every day, each of us experiences a virtual state of dissonance (and thus, is potentially in a position to rationalize).

Theoretical Positions

No theory other than the radical theory of dissonance can make sense out of all of the effects presented in this paper, or of many others which are variations of them (see Beauvois & Joule, 1996). This holds true, as stated above, for the theories devised by Festinger's critics, and even of the revised versions proposed by his followers. Yet if dissonance theory indeed remains the only theory that can make sense out of these effects, then it is not just any theory of dissonance. Does the "radical" theory diverge that far from the 1957 theory? We shall see that the answer to this question is "No". The radical theory requires two main conditions.

1. Strictly Calculating the Dissonance Ratio and Accepting Its Implications

The use of this ratio has several repercussions. Here are the major ones:

(a) Insofar as the state of dissonance is calculated from relationships (both dissonant and consonant) between cognitions, the calculation requires making the important theoretical distinction between the state of dissonance and the presence (vs. absence) of dissonant relationships between cognitions. The fact that Festinger used the word "dissonance" to refer to both of these instances may have led to the assumption that a state of dissonance exists whenever dissonant relationships between cognitions exist. Although a state of dissonance cannot exist without dissonant relationships, the converse is not necessarily true, i.e. there can be dissonant relationships without a state of dissonance. This is indeed what was shown by the long-standing line of research in which free choice was manipulated. Subjects not declared free indeed have dissonant relationships in their minds, but they are not in a state of dissonance because of it. This distinction prepares us for a later position concerning the role of commitment cognitions. In another publication (Beauvois & Joule, 1996), we pointed out the merits of using two different words to refer to these two concepts, and suggested employing the term "inconsistent" rather than dissonant to talk about the relationships between two cognitions, one of which implies the obverse of the other.

(b) Taking the calculation of the total amount of dissonance seriously also means recognizing that all cognitions do not have the same status. To make the calculation, one of the cognitions must be designated as the "generating" cognition, as we call it. It is this cognition that allows us to say that the other cognitions (the ones we put in the numerator or denominator of the dissonance ratio) are consistent (whenever there is psychological implication) or inconsistent (whenever there is implication of the obverse of the generating cognition). The other cognitions only enter into play as a result of potential psychological implications which link them to that cognition or the opposing one. Note that this goes against the former practices of the "balance" theorists, who calculated the state of imbalance by ascribing the same status to all cognitions. It is therefore not surprising that certain theorists, hoping to make it easier to grasp (Zajonc, 1968) or seeking to perfect it (Rajecki, 1990), implicitly or explicitly proposed a way of calculating the total amount of dissonance which combines all consistent and inconsistent relationships (hence ignoring the generating cognition), and which resembles the calculation of the degree of imbalance in any structure. Of course, other theorists of dissonance were aware of the need for setting one particular cognition apart from the others (our generating cognition). Almost systematically, they considered this cognition to be the one that was the most resistant to change. Given that experimentally, this "most change-resistant" cognition always pertains to one of the subject's behaviors, dissonance theory appears to be more of a theory of the rationalization of behavior (Beauvois & Joule, 1981) than a theory of cognitive consistency. And it is precisely as such that the radical version we advocate makes the theory operate. We have seen (Experiment 1) that Wicklund and Brehm (1976) were in an uneasy situation when it came to finding a hypothesis about the effect of the number of arguments produced during counter-attitudinal role-playing. Their uneasiness was rooted in the fact that they proposed two opposing hypotheses, one that took the behavior as the generating cognition (the one we ourselves set forth), and another that took the private attitude as the generating cognition. This dilemma no longer exists for us: every time the problem arose, the experiment proved that the behavior was in fact the generating cognition.

(c) Taking the dissonance ratio seriously also means only considering those relationships involving the generating cognition. Indeed, relationships are only included in this calculation to the extent that they link the generating cognition (or its obverse) to other cognitions. This implies that certain relationships, and in particular those between the cognitions in the numerator or denominator of the dissonance ratio, are not part of the calculation of the total amount of dissonance. For instance, anyone would agree that Festinger and Carlsmith were correct in ignoring the potential relationship between the personal attitude and the reward, i.e. between two cognitions included in the dissonance ratio because of the relationships (inconsistency for the former, consistency for the latter) they had with the generating cognition (the counter-attitudinal behavior). Note in passing that in the present case, the relationship between these two cognitions is irrelevant. But there may exist cases where there is a relevant relationship between two cognitions in the dissonance ratio. If so, should it also be ignored in the calculation of total dissonance? The answer is "Yes". We have even seen that total dissonance could be decreased by the generation of new inconsistencies between the cognitions in the dissonance ratio. In Experiment 1, for instance, the counter-attitudinal advocacy that led to the production of cognitions that were inconsistent with the subject's personal attitude was accompanied by less overall dissonance, since the total amount of dissonance was reduced by those cognitions. Along these same lines, studies on double compliance (Joule, 1991) have shown (see below) that less total dissonance is generated when subjects execute two behaviors which are inconsistent with their own personal attitude than when they execute two behaviors, of which only one is inconsistent with the personal attitude. Take the case of smokers having agreed to temporarily stop smoking (generating cognition) who feel less dissonance after writing an essay against smoking (hence counter-attitudinal) than after writing an essay in favor of smoking (hence attitudinal). It is this consequence of the Festinger definition of the dissonance ratio that takes his theory out of the paradigm of consistency theories.

(d) Finally, taking the total dissonance calculation seriously implies considering only those relationships which link two cognitions (two-term relationships). Coming back to the role of the reward in "$20 for a lie", we can agree once again—because the findings support their reasoning—that Festinger and Carlsmith were quite right to call "consistent" the relationship between the reward and the counter-attitudinal behavior. Yet it would suffice to bring a third cognition into the picture, the personal attitude, for the relationship between the reward and the behavior to change in nature, since the subjects might think that they are being bribed by the experimenter. In this case, the reward would become outright immoral, even "aversive", and should generate dissonance. We know that this type of reasoning is invalid, since the findings clearly show that rewards reduce dissonance. So why, then, would this reasoning become valid when we look at other possible cases of relationships between three cognitions, and in particular, when the consequences of the act are at stake? Indeed, the very idea of "aversive consequences" (Cooper & Fazio, 1984), presumably responsible for dissonance, relies on the consideration of three-term relationships (the relationship between my act and its consequences being modified by my personal attitude). It is hard to imagine an epistemological principle which could lead one to apply in one situation a kind of reasoning that is known to be poor in another. Either the consequences are "aversive", and then so is the reward, or the reward is not aversive and the consequences have no reason—as far as dissonance theory is concerned—to be so.[8] Moreover, as in Experiment 6, remember that informing a peer of the "truth" (in which case the consequences are anything but aversive!) can increase the dissonance experienced by a subject who has just accomplished a tedious task.

2. *Granting a Particular Status to Commitment Cognitions*

We have stressed that the discovery of commitment factors had a strong impact on the evolution of dissonance theory. Was it really necessary to change it? First of all, one must admit that if we limit ourselves to two-term relationships, which are the only ones defined in the theory, then what we call commitment cognitions ("I was told I was free to accept or refuse", "What I

---

[8] The consequences, just like the rewards, can obviously be so from another point of view than that of dissonance theory. See our third epistemological position.

do will have such and such a consequence", etc.) do not really fall within the scope of the 1957 theory. Such cognitions are obviously relevant, since they condition the dissonance reduction process. They are definitely not inconsistent with the act. Indeed, it makes no sense to contend that knowing one is free to do something (psychologically) implies that one does not do it. It sometimes happens, although rarely, that these cognitions are consonant with the act. This is the case of a successful counter-attitudinal act of persuasion when the forced compliance contract involves the subject's success in convincing a peer. Accordingly, Beauvois, Ghiglione, and Joule (1976) found that high school students who had explicitly agreed to try to convince a peer of the existence of extra-terrestrial beings underwent less change in attitude when they had managed to convince the peer, than when they had failed to so do. Commitment cognitions thus pose a real theoretical problem: while relevant, they are not inconsistent with the act, even though their presence is necessary to induce a state of dissonance. This is the reason why theorists quickly veered away from the theoretical constraints of the 1957 version, especially those involving the calculation of the famous dissonance ratio. They began to reason in a very flexible and anthropomorphic fashion by intuitively ascertaining a state of dissonance that subjects experience as they engage in a sort of reasoning in their heads based on three cognitions ("I say X but I am against X and yet I was free not to say X"; or "I say X but I am against X and it is even worse since my act is going to have such and such a consequence"), if not four ("Now I am still sure that I am a worthy person"). We think there is an alternative to this anthropomorphism, one which is in keeping with the experimental practices and data. This alternative fits into one proposition: commitment to an act is a necessary condition (but insufficient, because the act must also be discomforting, i.e. counter-attitudinal or counter-motivational) for the induction of a state of dissonance. This proposition has two implications. The first goes without saying: the 1957 theory can remain unchanged. The second is that it forces us to carefully examine this mandatory dissonance-inducing commitment. Reflection about this problem should give rise to a second branch of a more complete theory. Experiments 7 and 8 dealt with this question.

In our minds, looking more closely at this commitment has another advantage. It accounts for why there is a "strong" effect that should have been observed in the literature on dissonance but was not. In our opinion, the subject must be committed in order to experience dissonance, but the magnitude of that dissonance is not dependent upon the commitment (commitment cognitions are not included in the calculation of the dissonance ratio). This is not the case for the last few versions of Festinger's theory. In these versions, commitment cognitions do not act as conditions necessary to the induction of a state of dissonance but as actual constituents of that state. It therefore seemed natural to show that what we call commitment is proportional to the magnitude of the dissonance, by demonstrating, for instance, that the more aversive the consequences, the greater the attitude change on the part of the subjects, or yet again, the freer they feel, the more they change their minds. To say the least, this experimental effect is poorly documented in the literature.

CONCLUSION

The radical theory of dissonance paves the way for more fruitful research on attitude changes following the execution of a discomforting behavior at both the experimental and theoretical levels.

At the experimental level, the radical theory (i.e., our strict interpretation of the 1957 theory) has made it possible to test new effects in the classical forced compliance situation (effect of argumentation time, type of feedback, number of discomforting acts proposed, etc.). Furthermore, by focusing on the generating cognition as a behavior-related cognition and on the rationalization of behavior, the radical theory has made it possible to explore two new paradigms (for a review, see Beauvois & Joule, 1996): double forced compliance (see Experiment 6 above) and act rationalization (see Experiment 4 above). In the former, we are interested in the dissonance reduction process following the execution of two behaviors, at least one of which is discomforting. In the latter, we are interested in the conditions that are likely to lead a subject who has just carried out a discomforting act to rationalize that act by carrying out another discomforting act.

At the theoretical level, the radical theory (and more specifically, the way commitment is treated here) has led to a new understanding of the subject–experimenter rapport, and more generally, of the role of rationalization in power relations. In particular, the idea of commitment to compliance (see Experiments 7 and 8) led us to consider situations of forced compliance in relation to disciplinary encounters, whose role in the internalization process (Hoffman, 1983) is well known. Examination of the link between rationalization and internalization in power relations has barely begun. The radical theory still needs an in-depth analysis of the concept of commitment, so that this theory can be extended to social realities other than merely how subjects manage their cognitive universe.

In summary, the radical theory reclaims the basic core of 1957 in its entirety, and incorporates what proved to be true at the onset of the revisions of the initial theory, namely, the need for the subject to be committed by an act. Together, these two points have a dual consequence. They narrow the field of application of dissonance theory back down to what it was before the theory started being used as an ordinary theory of cognitive consistency or self-defense. On the other hand, they open the theory up to other paradigmatic registers, particularly the analysis of the cognitive consequences of power relations like the privileged relations of liberal power systems (see Beauvois, 1994; Dubois, 1994).

REFERENCES

Aronson, E. (1968). Dissonance theory: Progress and problems. In R. P. Abelson *et al.* (Eds), *Theories of Cognitive Consistency: A Sourcebook.* Chicago: Rand-McNally.

Aronson, E. (1969). The theory of cognitive dissonance: A current perspective. In L. Berkowitz (Ed.), *Advances in Experimental Social Psychology* (Vol. 4). New York, Academic Press.

Aronson, E. (1992). *The Social Animal.* San Francisco, CA: Freeman.

Baumeister, R. F. (1982). A self-presentational view of social phenomena. *Psychological Bulletin, 91*, 3–26.

Beauvois, J. L. (1994). *Traité de la Servitude Libérale. Une Analyse de la Soumission.* Paris: Dunod.

Beauvois, J. L., Bungert, M., Rainis, N., & Tornior, L. (1993). Statut d'agent, rationalisation et explications causales dans la soumission forcée. In J. L. Beauvois, R. V. Joule & J. M. Monteil (Eds), *Perspectives Cognitives et Conduites Sociales* (Vol. 4), *Jugements Sociaux et Changement des Attitudes.* Neuchâtel: Delachaux et Niestlé.

Beauvois, J. L., Bungert, M. & Mariette, P. (1995). Forced compliance: Commitment to compliance and commitment to activity. *European Journal of Social Psychology, 25*, 17–26.

Beauvois, J. L., Ghiglione, R., & Joule, R. V. (1976). Quelques limites des réinterprétations commodes des effets de dissonance. *Bulletin de Psychologie, 29*, 758–65.

Beauvois, J. L., & Joule, R. V. (1996). *A Radical Dissonance Theory.* London: Taylor and Francis.

Beauvois, J. L., & Joule, R. V. (1981). *Soumissions et Idéologies.* Paris: Presses Universitaires de France.

Beauvois, J. L., & Joule, R. V. (1982). Dissonance versus self-perception theories: A radical conception of Festinger's theory. *Journal of Social Psychology, 117*, 99–113.

Beauvois, J. L., Joule, R. V., and Brunetti, F. (1993). Cognitive rationalization and act rationalization in an escalation of commitment. *Basic and Applied Social Psychology, 14*, 1–17.

Beauvois, J. L., Michel, S., Py, J., Rainis, N., & Somat, A. (1996). Activation d'explications internes et externes du comportement problématique dans une situation de soumission forcée. In J. L. Beauvois, R. V. Joule & J. M. Monteil (Eds), *Perspectives Cognitives et Conduites Sociales* (Vol. 5), *Contextes et Contextes Sociaux.* Neuchâtel: Delachaux et Niestlé.

Beauvois, J. L., & Rainis, N. (1993). Dissonance reduction and causal explanation in a forced compliance situation. *European Journal of Social Psychology, 23*, 103–7.

Bem, D. J. (1965). An experimental analysis of self-persuasion. *Journal of Experimental Social Psychology, 1*, 199–218.

Bem, D. J. (1967). Self-perception: An alternative interpretation of cognitive dissonance phenomena. *Psychological Review, 74*, 183–200.

Bem, D. J. (1972). Self-perception theory. In L. Berkowitz (Ed.), *Advances in Experimental Social Psychology* (Vol. 6). New York: Academic Press.

Brehm, J. W. & Cohen, A. R. (1962). *Explorations in Cognitive Dissonance*. New York: Wiley.

Cialdini, R. B. (1984). *Influence*. New York: William Morrow.

Cooper, J., & Fazio, R. H. (1984). A new look at dissonance theory. In L. Berkowitz (Ed.), *Advances in Experimental Social Psychology*, (Vol. 17), pp. 229–66. New York: Academic Press.

Dubois, N. (1994). *La Norme d'Internalité et le Libéralisme*. Grenoble: Presses Universitaires de Grenoble.

Elliot, A. J., & Devine, P. G. (1994). On the motivational nature of cognitive dissonance: Dissonance as psychological discomfort. *Journal of Personality and Social Psychology, 67*, 382–94.

Feldman, S. (1966). Motivation aspects of attitudinal elements and their place in cognitive interaction. In S. Feldman (Ed.), *Cognitive Consistency*. New York: Academic Press.

Festinger, L. (1957a). *A Theory of Cognitive Dissonance*. Stanford, CT: Stanford University Press.

Festinger, L. (1957b). The relation between behavior and cognition. In J. S. Bruner (Ed.), *Contemporary Approaches to Cognition*. Cambridge, MA: Harvard University Press.

Festinger, L., & Carlsmith, J. M. (1959). Cognitive consequences of forced compliance. *Journal of Abnormal and Social Psychology, 58*, 203–10.

Fointiat, V. (1996). Rationalisation cognitive versus rationalisation en acte dans le paradigme de la fausse attribution. *Cahiers Internationaux de Psychologie Sociale, 30*, 10–21.

Gotz-Marchand, B., Gotz, J., & Irle, M. (1974). Preference of dissonance reduction mode as a function of their order, familiarity, and reversibility. *European Journal of Social Psychology, 4*, 201–28.

Greenwald,, A. G., & Ronis, D. L. (1978). Twenty years of cognitive dissonance: Case study of the evolution of a theory. *Psychological Review, 85*, 53–7.

Harman-Jones, E., Brehm, J. W., Greenberg, J., Simon, L., & Nelson, D. E. (1996). Evidence that the production of aversive consequences is not necessary to create cognitive dissonance. *Journal of Personality and Social Psychology, 70*, 5–16.

Hoffman, M. L. (1983). Affective and cognitive processes in moral internalization. In E. T. Higgins, D. Ruble, & W. W. Hartup (Eds), *Social Cognition and Social Development. A Socio-cultural perspective*. Cambridge: Cambridge University Press.

Jones, E. E. (1990). *Interpersonal Perception*. New York: Freeman.

Joule, R. V. (1986a). Twenty-five years on: Yet another version of cognitive dissonance theory? *European Journal of Social Psychology, 16*, 65–78.

Joule, R. V. (1986b). Rationalisation et engagement dans la soumission librement consentie. Doctoral Dissertation, Pierre Mendès France University, Grenoble.

Joule, R. V. (1987). Tobacco-deprivation: The foot-in-the-door technique versus the low ball technique. *European Journal of Social Psychology, 17*, 361–5.

Joule, R. V. (1991). Practicing and arguing for abstinence from smoking: A test of the double forced compliance paradigm. *European Journal of Social Psychology, 21*, 119–29.

Joule, R. V. (1996). Une nouvelle voie de réduction de la dissonance: La rationalisation en acte. In J. L. Beauvois, R. V. Joule, & J. M. Monteil (Eds), *Perspectives Cognitives et Conduites Sociales* (Vol. 5), *Contextes et Contextes Sociaux*. Neuchâtel: Delachaux et Niestlé.

Joule, R. V., & Girandola, F. (1995). Tâche fastidieuse et jeu de rôle dans le paradigme de la double soumission. *Revue Internationale de Psychologie Sociale*, **8**, 101–16.

Joule, R. V., & Lévèque, L. (1993). Le changement d'attitude comme fonction du temps d'argumentation. Laboratory of Social Psychology, Provence University (unpublished manuscript).

Kiesler, C. A. (1971). *The Psychology of Commitment. Experiments Linking Behavior to Belief*. New York: Academic Press.

Leippe, M. R., & Eisenstadt, D. (1994). Generalization of dissonance reduction: Decreasing prejudice through induced compliance. *Journal of Personality and Social Psychology*, **67**, 395–413.

Rabbie, J. M., Brehm, J. W., & Cohen, A. R. (1959). Verbalization and relations to cognitive dissonance. *Journal of Personality*, **27**, 407–17.

Rajecki, D. J. (1990). *Attitudes*. Sunderland: Sinauer.

Sherman, S. J., & Gorkin, L. (1980). Attitude bolstering when behavior is inconsistent with central attitude. *Journal of Experimental Social Psychology*, **16**, 388–403.

Simon, L., Greenberg, J., & Brehm, J. (1995). Trivialization: The forgotten mode of dissonance reduction. *Journal of Personality and Social Psychology*, **68**, 247–60.

Steele, C. M. (1988). The psychology of self-affirmation: Sustaining the integrity of the self. In L. Berkowitz (Ed.), *Advances in Experimental Social Psychology*, (Vol. 21). New York: Academic Press.

Steiner, I. D. (1980). Attribution of choice. In M. Fishbein (Ed.), *Progress in Social Psychology*,, Hillsdale, NJ: Erlbaum.

Tedeschi, J. T. (1981). *Impression Management Theory and Social Psychological Research*. New York: Academic Press.

Wicklund, R. A., & Brehm, J. W. (1976). *Perspectives on Cognitive Dissonance*. New York: Wiley.

Zajonc, R. K. (1968). Cognitive theories in social psychology. In G. Lindsay and E. Aronson (Eds), *Handbook of Social Psychology* (Vol. 1). Reading, MA: Addison-Wesley.

Chapter 2

Affect, Attitudes and Decisions: Let's Be More Specific

Joop van der Pligt, Marcel Zeelenberg, Wilco W. van Dijk, Nanne K. de Vries and René Richard
University of Amsterdam

ABSTRACT

This chapter focuses on the role of affect in attitudes and decision-making. First we will briefly discuss the role of affect in attitude-formation and -change processes. Two issues have played an important role in this research area: first, the distinction between affect-based and cognition-based attitudes; second, the effects of mood on persuasion. Generally these traditions rely on a crude dichotomy between positive and negative affect and rather general, holistic measures of affect. Moreover, these traditions tend to emphasize automatic information processing. We focus on controlled information processing and continue with a discussion of the role of affect in expectancy-value models of behaviour such as Ajzen's theory of planned behaviour. Affect received only limited attention in these models. It will be argued that people anticipate *post-behavioural* affective consequences of their actions, and take these into account when deciding about their behavioural preferences. We will argue that the inclusion of anticipated postbehavioural affective outcomes could improve the predictive validity of expectancy-value models. Next, we will contrast research on affect and attitudes with research on behavioural decision-making. The latter area tends to focus on more specific affective determinants of behaviour. One of these is anticipated regret. Antecedents of anticipated regret will be discussed and the predictive validity of anticipated regret will be tested in the context of Ajzen's theory of planned behaviour. Finally we will show that it is relatively easy to increase the salience of postbehavioural affective reactions such as regret and worry and

European Review of Social Psychology, Volume 8. Edited by Wolfgang Stroebe and Miles Hewstone.
© 1998 John Wiley & Sons Ltd.

that this increased salience has an impact on both behavioural intentions and self-reported behaviour. Implications for the study of affect in expectancy-value models of behaviour will be briefly discussed.

Preferences are a central issue in social psychology and are examined in research on attitudes, impression formation, interpersonal relationships, decision-making, and many other fields. For the past few decades the prevailing paradigms in these fields of research treated preferences as the outcome of a cognitive process focusing on utilities and values. Moreover, decomposing these utilities and values into more elementary components was a general solution to improve our understanding of these processes. The one factor often missing in these approaches was affect. This emphasis on cognition was corrected in the 1980s, resulting in a marked increase in research on the role of affect in social judgment, attitude-formation and -change processes, and decision-making.

In this chapter we will discuss research on the role of affect in attitudinal processes. First, we will briefly summarize research on affective information processing and the effects of mood on attitudes. Next we turn to the main issue of this chapter, the role of affect in expectancy-value models of attitudes. We will focus on the conscious processing of affect and contrast research on the role of affect in expectancy-value models of attitudes with research on behavioural decision-making. We will show that affect can play an independent role in attitudes and behavioral decisions. It will be argued that incorporating affective factors in expectancy-value models such as Ajzen's theory of planned behaviour requires less holistic measures of affect, should focus on specific emotional reactions, and should also take account of anticipated, postbehavioural affective reactions.

The renewed interest in the role of affect can be traced to Zajonc's (1980) influential paper on affective vs. cognitive information processing. Zajonc, on the basis of his mere exposure studies, argued for separate systems and suggested that affective and cognitive processes may proceed independently from one another and that affective reactions could even precede and influence cognition. Basically, he argued that the affective quality of a stimulus can be processed outside of conscious awareness. Researchers of the affect–cognition interface often used subliminal presentation of affective primes to demonstrate evaluative reactions to stimuli that cannot be traced to some conscious computation of liking. For instance, Edwards (1990) and Murphy and Zajonc (1993) used subliminal presentation of faces showing a positive or negative emotion to prime affective reactions to a subsequent (ambiguous) stimulus. Generally, this research relies on a "crude" dichotomy of affect by valence (good or bad), and it can be placed in the context of a larger tradition in social psychology concerning the role of awareness and control on a person's judgements, and research on automatic phenomena in social judgement (see Bargh, 1994). More recent findings (Bargh *et al.*, 1996) in this line of research confirm the so-called automatic evaluation effect, and show that attitudes can be activated without conscious processing and facilitate or interfere with the conscious and intended evaluation of a target stimulus.

Based on Zajonc's (1980) distinction between feeling and thinking, Abelson *et al*. (1982) explored comparisons between conventional semantic judgements focusing on a cognitive appraisal of attitude objects, and affective responses to these objects. In two large-scale surveys, respondents were asked to ascribe personality traits to prominent national politicians as well as to report the feelings that these politicians elicited. Affect elicited by the politicians was highly predictive of political preference, and this effect was independent of, and more powerful than, the effect of trait judgements. On the basis of these findings, Abelson *et al*. (1982) concluded that affective responses add to the predictive validity of attitude measures beyond that available from standard semantic judgements. Moreover, both Zajonc (1980) and Abelson *et al*. (1982) proposed that individual preferences can be based on affect *per se*.

Other researchers did not deal directly with this question but obtained results suggesting that affect does influence attitudes. A variety of research findings including behaviours such as energy conservation (Seligman *et al*., 1979), health behaviour (Ajzen & Timko, 1986), responses to victimization (Tyler & Rasinsky, 1984), and contraceptive behaviour (Fisher, 1984) suggests that affect can have a strong and independent impact on attitudes. Zanna and Rempel (1988) also propose to distinguish affective and cognitive aspects of attitudes. They regard an attitude as the categorization of a stimulus object along an evaluative dimension, and argue that this evaluation can be based upon three different sources of information: (a) cognitive information, (b) affective/emotional information, and (c) information concerning behaviour in the past. Their view goes back to Rosenberg and Hovland's (1960) "three-component" view of attitudes. Zanna and Rempel build upon this early work, and argue that it is possible for an attitudinal judgement to be dependent strictly on cognitive beliefs, but also on affect or on past behaviour *vis-à-vis* the attitude object. These beliefs, feelings and behaviours are not mutually exclusive and constitute different ways in which the attitude is formed and experienced. Moreover, the three components need not be consistent and can have different valences. It needs to be added that Zanna and Rempel's approach seems to have the same shortcoming as Rosenberg and Hovland's view; i.e., it is not specified when and under what conditions attitudes will be based on one source of information rather than another. Most important for our discussion is that Zanna and Rempel's conceptualization implies that evaluation and affect are different components of attitudes. Further support for this view is provided by Breckler (1984) and Breckler and Wiggins (1989).

Breckler and Wiggins (1989) proposed to use the term *"evaluation"* (as opposed to "cognition") to refer to attitudes based on judgements *about* the attitude object because cognition can include the appraisal of emotions and emotion-related functioning (see also Lazarus, 1981, 1982, 1984). They reserved the term "affect" for emotional responses and feelings engendered by an attitude object. In their study they collected multiple measures of evaluation and affect in six attitude domains (blood donation, legalized abortion, computers, nuclear weapons, standardized admission tests, and college comprehensive examinations). Although they relied on self-report measures, correlations between affective and evaluative responses showed considerable variation. Results of a second study on attitudes towards blood donation indicated a modest correlation between affect and evaluation and a stronger relationship between affect and (self-reported) behaviour than between evaluation and behaviour.

Other research focused on affect in the context of attitude change processes and persuasion. For instance, Edwards (1990) distinguished between affect- and cognition-based attitudes, and investigated the effectiveness of affective and cognitive means of persuasion. Her findings showed that affect-based attitudes (created by a subliminal or supraliminal affective prime) exhibit more change under affective means of persuasion than under cognitive means of persuasion. Cognition-based attitudes (created by the provision of information about the attitude object) exhibited equal change under both forms of persuasion. It needs to be added, however, that research on this topic has yielded conflicting findings. Millar & Millar (1990) found that cognition-based attitudes were more easily changed by affective means than cognitive means, and vice versa. Contrary to Edwards (1990) who used Chinese ideographs as attitude objects, they relied on attitude object with which people were already familiarized.

Mood (as a general affective state without a specific focus) has also been related to attitudinal change processes, especially in the context of Petty and Cacioppo's Elaboration Likelihood Model (e.g. Bless *et al.*, 1990; Petty *et al.*, 1994). Generally, individuals in an elated mood are less likely to engage in systematic message elaboration than individuals in a neutral or depressed mood. According to the Elaboration Likelihood Model (Petty & Cacioppo, 1986), affective (peripheral) cues are particularly potent determinants of attitude change when the ability or motivation to process issue-relevant information is low.

Both the literature on mood and persuasion and the literature on affect vs. cognition-based attitudes focus on the role of a universal and ubiquitous characteristic of affect—valence. This seems partly a consequence of the tendency to contrast affect with cognition (especially in research on the primacy of affect and research on cognition vs. affect-based attitudes). One unfortunate consequence of this contrast is that much attention has been paid to this (sometimes rather artificial) dichotomy at the expense of adequate and differentiated measures of cognitive and affective determinants of attitudes and behaviour.[1]

Some of the studies described earlier (e.g. Breckler & Wiggins, 1989) relied on scales that present generally applicable evaluative word pairs and instruct respondents to indicate how (e.g. good or bad) the attitude object makes them *feel* (to assess affect) or how good or bad the attitude object *is* (to assess evaluation). Using the same scales to assess the affective and cognitive component of attitudes has some advantages. For instance, Eagly, Mladinic, and Otto (1994) argue that the use of different sets of items to assess affective and cognitive components of attitudes might result in one set being more saturated with evaluative meaning than the other set. The disadvantage of using the same set of items is, however, that one has to rely heavily on general evaluative terms that can be used meaningfully when accompanied by questions referring to feelings triggered by the attitude object as well as when accompanied by questions referring to characteristics of the attitude object. As argued before, one inevitable consequence of such an approach is that the measurement of affect is limited to a crude positive–negative classification. Another disadvantage is that, because of the rather general and widely applicable items, one could miss (cognitive or affective) attributes that are extremely relevant for judging a specific attitude object. Moreover, if the under-representation of relevant attributes is not evenly distributed over the affective and cognitive components of attitudes, this could have serious consequences for the assessment of their relative impact on attitudes.

Crites, Fabrigar, and Petty (1994) argued that the assessment of affective and cognitive properties of attitudes is plagued by a number of problems. They mention a lack of consistency in procedures across studies, the possible impact of structural characteristics of the measures of affect and cognition on responses, and the limited attention paid to the reliability and validity of scales to assess these properties of attitudes. Crites, Fabrigar, and Petty (1994) developed scales for assessing the affective and cognitive properties of attitudes and examined their reliability and validity. Their aim was to develop more general scales that could be applied to a variety of attitude objects. Their affective scale was based on eight affective word pairs; their cognitive scale focused on more utilitarian dimensions and consisted of seven "cognitive" pairs. Their analyses showed that the measures were applicable to multiple attitude objects and had good and stable psychometric properties. Contrary to most of the literature discussed earlier in this chapter, Crites,

---

[1] There is one notable exception: research on the effects of fear-arousing messages on (preventive) behaviour. This older tradition (Janis, 1967; Leventhal, 1970; Rogers, 1975) differs from the research described in the previous paragraphs because it focuses on one specific emotion (fear) as opposed to general affect, and it also tends to pay more attention to behavioural consequences.

Fabrigar, and Petty (1994) stress that affect is *not* an undifferentiated component of attitudes but consists of discrete, qualitatively different emotions. Although Crites, Fabrigar, and Petty propose a more differentiated approach, they still focus on a more general index score, combining the various items into an overall score that primarily reflects the valence of the affective determinants of attitudes.

Most of the research described in this section focused on attitudes without explicitly addressing behaviour. For instance, Abelson *et al.* (1982) studied attitudes towards political candidates, and Edwards (1990) used Chinese ideographs as attitude objects. In the remainder of this chapter we will focus on attitudes towards behavioural options. This brings us to research on attitude–behaviour models.

AFFECT IN ATTITUDE–BEHAVIOUR MODELS

Fishbein and Ajzen's (1975) *theory of reasoned action* and Ajzen's (1985, 1991) *theory of planned behaviour* assume that attitudes are an important determinant of intentions. In their approaches attitudes are based on the summed products of the likelihood of consequences associated with behavioural actions and the evaluation of these consequences. Thus, the more positive consequences are associated with a specific behaviour and the more likely their occurrence, the more attractive the behaviour is. Fishbein and Ajzen (1975) also incorporated perceived social norms in their model, and Ajzen added perceived behavioural control as a third determinant of behavioural intentions. Both theories have been applied to a wide variety of behaviours, such as shopping (Madden, Ellen, & Ajzen, 1992), food intake (Sparks, Hedderly, & Shepherd, 1992), violations of traffic regulations (Parker *et al.*, 1992) weight reduction (Schifter & Ajzen, 1985), dental hygiene (McCaul *et al.*, 1993) and contraceptive use (Middlestadt & Fishbein, 1995; Chan & Fishbein, 1993).

Both the theory of reasoned action and the theory of planned behaviour thus assume an informational foundation of human conduct, focusing on the expected outcomes of behavioural action. Individuals are expected to respond to the analytic features of stimuli. This approach is also central to normative theories of decision-making to which we will turn later. Initially, Fishbein and Ajzen were rather unspecific about the role of affect, as illustrated by the following quote:

> The term "affect" and "evaluation" are used synonymously throughout this book. Although it might be argued that there is a difference between a person's judgement that an object makes him feel good and his evaluation that the object is good, there is little evidence to suggest that a reliable empirical distinction between the two variables can be made (Fishbein & Ajzen, 1975, p. 11).

This view is different from Zanna and Rempel's (1988) proposal discussed earlier. In the theory of reasoned action affect is represented through evaluations of each of the possible outcomes (outcome evaluations) and through an overall evaluation of the attitude object (attitude). Fishbein and Ajzen (1975) argue that learning (both classical conditioning and other forms of learning) may determine affective reactions towards particular behaviours, objects or specific outcomes. Fishbein and Ajzen thus also rely on a simple positive–negative dichotomy of affect and, more importantly, "evaluation" and "affect" are used synonymously and both are assumed to be determined by outcome related beliefs and their evaluations.

Ajzen's (1989) theory of planned behaviour also pays limited attention to the role of affective processes. Ajzen admits that the role of affect is not spelled out very clearly in the Ajzen–Fishbein framework. In his view, affective reactions may depend at least in part on cognitions and, like cognitions, they may feed into the overall evaluative response to an attitude object. Moreover, "Affect may also be associated with the perceived attributes of the attitude object and thus also determine the evaluative direction and intensity of a person's beliefs" (Ajzen, 1989, p. 248).

Manstead and Parker (1995) argue that the evidence showing that evaluative responses based on affective reactions (i.e., specific emotions) are empirically distinguishable from measures of evaluative responses based on beliefs about the attitude object is sufficiently strong to also incorporate this distinction in attitude–behaviour models. Their view is supported by the findings of Breckler and Wiggins (1989) and Edwards (1990), discussed earlier in this chapter. More recently, Eagly, Mladinic, and Otto (1994) and Pfister and Bohm (1992) provided further support for this distinction. Indirect evidence for this view is provided by research focusing on the relative contribution of direct, holistic measures of attitudes and indirect (belief-based) measures of attitudes. Quite often the two measures do not correspond as well as they should (see, e.g., Terry, Gallois, & McCamish (1993)). This could be related to the fact that some relevant beliefs are not included in the set of beliefs presented to the respondents. Another reason for this modest correspondence could be that the direct measure of attitudes is more likely to also tap affective reactions that generally are not included in the indirect belief-based measure. The latter tends to be dominated by (instrumental) outcome beliefs, in which affective or emotional outcomes play only a minor role.

Manstead and Parker (1995) define *affective* evaluations of behaviour as referring to an individual's positive or negative *feelings* about performing the behaviour in question. This is in contrast to the behavioural beliefs typically tapped in the context of attitude–behaviour models such as the theory of planned behaviour. As indicated in the previous paragraphs, these beliefs usually focus on the utilitarian aspects of the outcomes of the behaviour (i.e., costs and benefits). This is in accordance with subjective expected utility

(SEU) approaches on which Fishbein and Ajzen's theory is based. Later in this chapter we will discuss SEU theory in more detail.

Ajzen and Driver (1991) were probably the first to investigate directly the usefulness of the distinction between affective evaluations and behavioural beliefs in relation to the theory of planned behaviour. Their study focused on leisure activities. Results provided some support for the discriminatory validity of the measures of these two variables, but treating the two variables as separate factors did not result in a significant improvement in the predictive ability of the model. Manstead and Parker (1995) also report some preliminary findings showing that measures based on affective evaluations (feelings associated with the behaviour) correlate only moderately with measures based on behavioural beliefs (beliefs about the outcomes of a behavioural action). In their research on driving behaviour they report correlations as low as 0.14 and 0.29. These modest correlations between affect-based and cognition-based measures were obtained in one specific domain (driving violations). Manstead and Parker rightly argue that it would be interesting to see whether similar findings are found in other domains. Richard, van der Pligt, and de Vries (1996a) attempted to do this; and it is to that research we turn next.

Research on the impact of affect on attitudes usually relies on a general measure of positive/negative affect associated with the behaviour. Attitude–behaviour models, however, deal with *future* behaviour, and belief-based measures of attitudes focus on the possible *consequences* of behavioural actions. Generally, research in this tradition presents respondents with a set of possible consequences of a behavioural action and asks them to assess their likelihood and their evaluation. Richard van der Pligt and de Vries (1996a) argued that it would be appropriate to also incorporate *anticipated postbehavioural affective reactions* as possible consequences of behavioural actions.

In their study, Richard, van der Pligt, and de Vries (1996a) assessed the *evaluative* response (attitude) towards a number of behaviours, *affective* reactions towards these behaviours, and *anticipated* postbehavioural affective reactions. These three concepts differ in terms of time perspective and the affect–evaluation distinction. The aim of their study was to investigate the discriminant validity of the three measures. The inclusion of both general affective reactions and anticipated affective reactions allowed them to investigate the predictive utility of *anticipated* affective reactions and general affect over and above attitudes and other components of the theory of planned behaviour. Richard, van der Pligt, and de Vries selected four behaviours: eating "junk food", using soft drugs (marijuana, hashish), drinking alcohol, and studying hard. They relied on a direct attitude measure; respondents were asked to evaluate each of the four target behaviours on three semantic differential scales: *pleasant–unpleasant, nice–awful,* and *good–bad.* Next, respondents were asked to indicate their general feelings and their anticipated postbehavioural feelings towards each of the target behaviours on the same set of scales. Thus the same scales were used to assess the three evaluative scores (attitudes, general feelings and anticipated postbehavioural feelings). Richard, van der Pligt, and de Vries (1996a) did this to prevent one set of items being more saturated with evaluative meaning than the other set (see our earlier discussion of the arguments presented by Eagly, Mladinic, & Otto, 1994).

As expected, eating junk food, using soft drugs, and drinking alcohol were associated with negative anticipated affective reactions, and these were more negative than both the evaluations of, and general affective reactions towards, the target behaviours. Similarly, anticipated affective reactions after "having studied hard" were more positive than both attitudes and general affective reactions towards this behaviour. Overall, evaluations (attitudes) towards each target behaviour did *not* differ significantly from the general affective reactions associated with the behaviour. *Anticipated* affective reactions, however, differed substantially from both evaluations and general affective reactions.

Richard, van der Pligt, and de Vries (1996a) compared two models, one with two separate factors (evaluations and anticipated affect) and one which combined these two factors into one overall factor. The two-factor models fitted the data well, whereas all one-factor models were statistically rejected. More importantly, further testing revealed that for all four behaviours the two-factor model (separating anticipated affect and evaluation) fitted the data significantly better than the one-factor model. Overall, these findings supported the discriminant validity of their measure of *anticipated* affect; anticipated affect proved different from both more cognitive evaluations and general affect associated with the behaviour.

For three of the four investigated behaviours, anticipated postbehavioural affective reactions predicted a significant proportion of variance in behavioural expectations, over and above the components of the theory of planned behaviour. The only exception concerned the behaviour with relatively positive anticipated postbehavioural affective reactions ("studying hard"). Thus, the results of this study show that the predictive power of the theory of planned behaviour may improve if anticipated postbehavioural affective reactions are incorporated in the model. Figure 2.1 illustrates the findings for "using soft drugs". The regression parameters in this Figure should be interpreted as β-weights; zero-order correlation coefficients are given in brackets. Although the estimated correlation between "anticipated affect" and "attitudes" was 0.76, the two-factor model fitted the data better than the one-factor model combining anticipated affect with attitudes.

Two shortcomings of the research by Richard, van der Pligt, and de Vries (1996a) need to be noted. First, they opted for the solution to use the same

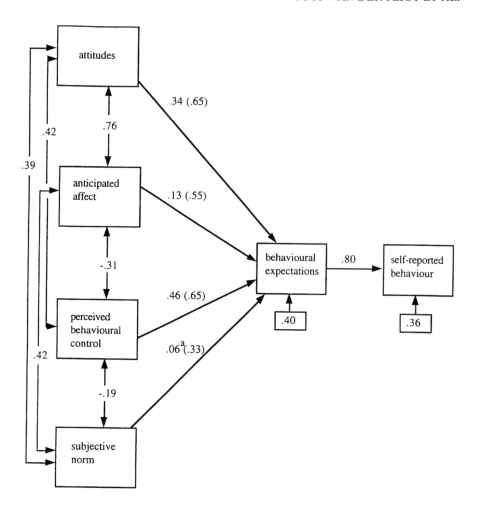

Figure 2.1   The role of anticipated affect as a determinant of "using soft drugs". Note: parameter estimates are standardized; all parameters are significant at $p < 0.01$ except [a]$p < 0.10$. Adapted from Richard, van der Pligt, and de Vries (1996a, p. 122)

scales to assess evaluations (attitudes), general affect and anticipated affective reactions. They did not include a belief-based indirect measure of attitudes, but relied on a general, direct measure of attitudes. Obviously, anticipated postbehavioural affective reactions can also be included in the set of possible outcomes that constitutes the indirect attitude measure. Opting for such a solution would have allowed another test of the independent contribution of anticipated affect. Moreover, it would have allowed for the assessment of the subjective probability of the anticipated affective outcomes. People are likely to have different views on the subjective probability of particular affective outcomes just as they tend to vary with regard to the subjective probabilities they attach to other kinds of outcomes.

A second potential shortcoming of the study is that Richard, van der Pligt, and de Vries (1996a) as many other studies in this field of research, relied on a simple dichotomy, positive vs. negative affect, and assessed (anticipated) affective reactions at a rather general level (e.g., "expecting to feel good vs. expecting to feel bad") without paying attention to more specific affective reactions that could determine attitudes and/or behaviours. Overall, the main contribution of Richard, van der Pligt, and de Vries's (1996a) paper is that it points at the possible role of anticipated postbehavioural affective reactions in attitude–behavioural models. However, more research is needed to assess the independent role of anticipated affect in expectancy-value approaches to attitudes. This research should not only rely on general measures of affect but also include specific anticipated affective reactions in the set of outcome beliefs that constitutes the indirect measure of attitude.

Interestingly, research in the related area of behavioural decision-making emphasizes the role of specific affective reactions and does not rely on the crude positive–negative dichotomy of affect we tend to see in research on attitudes. Several researchers in the area of behavioural decision-making stressed the need to look at more specific emotions and studied the impact of a variety of anticipated emotions on human decision-making. These include guilt, sadness and anger (Baron, 1992), regret and disappointment (e.g., Bell, 1982, 1985; Loomes & Sugden, 1987b), and envy and gloating (Loewenstein, Thompson, & Bazerman, 1989).

Research on emotions has also spent considerable effort to distinguish between the various emotions. There is some dispute as to whether there are such things as "basic emotions" (see, e.g., Ortony & Turner, 1990), but present-day emotion theorists agree that there are important differences between emotions. Research findings show that emotions can be differentiated by their accompanying thoughts and feelings, by their appraisal, physiological activity, expression, action tendencies, and behavioural actions (Frijda, Kuipers, & ter Schure, 1989; Roseman, Wiest & Swartz, 1994). This research also indicates that different emotions with the same valence have different implications for behaviour. For example, fear evokes a tendency to flight, whereas anger evokes a tendency to fight. Similarly, the experience of regret tends to make people active and problem-oriented, while disappointment, albeit its strong relation to regret, tends to be related to a more passive reaction focusing our attention away from the problem (Zeelenberg *et al.*, 1997b).

Distinguishing between various affective or emotional states could help our understanding of anticipated, postbehavioural affective reactions and their role in attitudinal and decision processes. As mentioned earlier, researchers in the area of behavioural decision-making have focused on more specific emotions. In the next section we turn to this field of research.

AFFECT AND DECISION-MAKING

The increased attention for affect since the early 1980s was not restricted to research on emotions and social cognition but is also apparent in research on behavioural decision-making. While the renewed interest in affect in social psychology can be traced to Zajonc's 1980 article on preferences and inferences, the renewed interest in the area of decision-making was mainly caused by the inability of normative models of decision-making to explain and describe preferences. Interestingly, research on decision-making did not rely on the rather holistic approach to affect that dominated social psychological research on attitudes, but focused on more specific emotions. This could well be caused by methodological differences between the two areas. One important difference between the two fields is that behavioural decision-making research almost always uses choice of some sort as a dependent variable, whereas attitude research focuses on evaluative judgements and behavioural intentions. The fact that behavioural choice is a prime dependent variable in research on decision-making probably resulted in a preference to study concrete emotions with clear consequences for (choice) behaviour. To illustrate how this came about we will first briefly describe the normative model of decision-making that is central to this field of research.

Edwards' (1954) *Subjective Expected Utility* (SEU) Theory is a normative theory of decision-making and has had a profound impact on research on behavioural decision-making. His expectancy-value approach also inspired Fishbein and Ajzen's (1975) theory of reasoned action and Ajzen's (1991) theory of planned behaviour. Edwards assumed that people generally aim to maximize utility and prefer behavioural options that are associated with the highest expected utility. The overall utility or desirability of a behavioural alternative is assumed to be based on the summed products of the probability and utility of specific outcomes or consequences. Thus:

$$SEU_j = \sum_i P_{ij} \cdot U_{ij}$$

where SEU_j is the *SEU* of action or behavioural alternative j; P_{ij} is the perceived probability of outcome i of action j; U_{ij} is the subjective utility or desirability of outcome i of action j. Each action or behavioural alternative may have a different subjective expected utility because of the outcomes associated with that action and/or the probabilities of these outcomes. Quite often, however, people do not behave in accordance with SEU-theory, and this behaviour is frequently called "irrational". There is considerable disagreement about the use of the term "irrational" in this context (see, e.g., Cohen, 1981), and it has been argued that discrepancies between normative models such as SEU-theory and actual decision-making does not warrant the use of this term. Some researchers attempted to improve the descriptive validity of SEU-theory and suggested further refinements (e.g., Kahneman & Tversky, 1979). Others proposed to incorporate additional aspects that should be taken into account when investigating decision-making processes.

Kahneman and Snell (1992) argued that most research and theorizing in decision-making rely on a severely impoverished conception of utility. In their view, rigid operationalism has led to a situation in which little is left of the original broader sense of utility in the writings of Bentham and Bernoulli, who related utility to the hedonic quality of experience. Kahneman and Snell (1990) propose to distinguish two concepts of utility: first, the *decision utility* of an outcome which is defined as the sign and weight of that outcome in the context of choice; second, the *experienced utility*, which is defined by the quality and intensity of the hedonic experience with that outcome. Decision utility focuses on the decision rather than on experience and is linked to the basic assumption of rationality: i.e., rational individuals can be trusted to know what will be good for them and are entitled to their sovereignty (cf. Kahneman & Snell, 1990, p. 296). This basic assumption is also central to expectancy-value models such as those of Fishbein and Ajzen. Kahneman and Snell (1992) investigated people's ability to predict experienced utility over time for stimuli such as ice creams, yoghurt and short musical pieces. This ability turned out to be limited. The major contribution of their approach is that they tried to broaden the concept of utility, partly in order to improve the descriptive validity of decision theory. Other researchers opted for more specific solutions, and to these we turn next.

Regret and Decision-making

Bell (1982) and Loomes and Sugden (1982) argued that incorporating one specific emotion (*anticipated regret*) in SEU theory could help to improve its descriptive validity. Regret theory differs from classical theories of decision-making, such as SEU theory, which are based on the same premises as attitude–behaviour models such as those of Ajzen and Fishbein. In regret theory the utility of a choice option additionally depends on the *feelings* evoked by the outcomes of rejected options. Regret theory rests on two basic assumptions (Loomes & Sugden, 1982). The first holds that people compare the actual outcome with what the outcome would have been, had a different choice been made, *and* that they experience emotions as a consequence. People experience regret when the foregone outcome would have been better, and rejoicing when the foregone outcome would have been worse. The second assumption of regret theory is that the emotional consequences of decisions are *anticipated* and taken into account when making decisions. Thus, the tendency to avoid negative postdecisional emotions such as regret, disappointment and self-recrimination, and to strive for positive feelings and emotions such as rejoicing, elation and pride, are assumed to be important determinants of individual decision-making.

According to Bell (1982) and Loomes and Sugden (1982), the expected utility of a specific behavioural option *x* should be modified by incorporating the amount of regret for not choosing *y*. More formally:

Modified $SEU_x = SEU_x \pm \text{Regret}_{not-y}$

Regret is thus defined as the difference between the value of the obtained outcome and that of the alternative(s) not chosen.

Summarizing, research on regret attempts to explain violations of the principles of rationality assumed by SEU-theory by postulating that people sometimes sacrifice utility in order to prevent the experience of regret. This approach thus assumes that the anticipation of future regret affects current choices (Bell, 1981, 1982; Loomes & Sugden, 1982, 1987a), and this assumption has received considerable empirical support (Loomes, 1987; Loomes and Sugden, 1987a; Ritov, 1996; Simonson, 1992; Zeelenberg et al., 1996), although there are some exceptions (Harless, 1992; Starmer & Sugden, 1993).

The first work in social psychology paying attention to post-decisional regret is Festinger's dissonance theory (e.g. Festinger & Walster, 1964). In their work, regret is almost always conceptualized as the reversal of the initial decision. Janis and Mann (1977) also pay attention to the role of anticipatory regret in decision-making. They conceive of anticipatory regret as a "hot" cognition and argue that:

> Before undertaking any enterprise "of great pith and moment", we usually delay action and think about what might happen that could cause regret . . . *Anticipatory regret* is a convenient generic term to refer to the main psychological effects of the various worries that beset a decision-maker before any losses actually materialize . . . Such worries, which include anticipatory guilt and shame, provoke hesitation and doubt, making salient the realization that even the most attractive of the available choices might turn out badly (Janis & Mann, 1977, p. 222).

Regret is generally regarded as a cognitive-laden or cognitively-determined emotion. Hampshire (1960) argued that the question of whether one regrets a decision induces people to think about the decision and not merely to inspect their feelings. Landman (1993) argues that:

> Regret is a more or less painful cognitive and emotional state of feeling sorry for misfortunes, limitations, losses, transgressions, shortcomings, or mistakes. It is an experience of felt-reason or reasoned-emotion (p. 36).

Thus, cognitive evaluations of the outcomes received and the outcomes foregone underlie the comparison of different states of the world that can lead to the experience of regret.

Why focus on this specific emotion? Research findings show that regret is a powerful predictor of behaviour and it thus seems a prime candidate to be incorporated in attitude–behaviour models. For instance, Josephs *et al.* (1992) found that the threat of regret reduced the tendency to take risky decisions. Larrick and Boles (1995) found that the tendency to avoid regret affects negotiation decisions; Beattie *et al.* (1994) found that anticipated regret can make people reluctant to make decisions. Bar-Hillel and Neter (1996) argued that people's reluctance to exchange lottery tickets could well be a function of the perceived possibility of postbehavioural regret. Regret can also be related to Kahneman and Snell's distinction between decision utility and experienced utility. Regret is unpleasant and thus affects the experienced utility of the decision. Next, we address the possible antecedents of anticipated, post-behavioural regret.

Antecedents of regret

Knowledge about the outcomes of both the chosen and the unchosen option(s) is central to regret theory: if you cannot compare "what is" with "what would have been", there should be no reason for regret. In economic approaches to regret it is assumed that regret *only* arises if the outcomes of the rejected alternatives are revealed. In other words regret will only occur if people receive feedback about chosen and unchosen alternatives. Zeelenberg *et al.* (1996) studied the role of feedback more closely. In accordance with regret theory they assumed that people are *regret-averse* and are therefore motivated to make *regret-minimizing* choices. In three experiments respondents were given a choice between a risky and a safe gamble. Possible feedback on one of the options was manipulated orthogonally to the riskiness of the gambles. Respondents always expected to learn the outcome of the chosen option; sometimes they could also receive feedback on the foregone outcome. Those who expected to receive feedback on the safe option, regardless of their choice, had a preference for this option, thereby protecting themselves from threatening feedback for the foregone outcome. Likewise, respondents who expected to receive feedback on the risky option tended to choose the risky option. When asked to *explain* their preferences, respondents quite often referred to the anticipation of regret. Thus, findings of Zeelenberg *et al.* (1996) confirm the role of feedback as one of the determinants of regret.

There is evidence showing that the extent to which people feel regret when confronted with the outcome of a decision does not depend solely upon the comparison of that decision with the possible outcomes of other courses of action, but also on *how* the outcome is achieved. Outcomes achieved through action tend to lead to more extreme regret than the same outcomes achieved through inaction (Kahneman & Tversky, 1982a; Gleicher *et al.*, 1990; Landman, 1987). This can be illustrated by Kahneman and Tversky's (1982a) study in which they presented the following scenario:

> Mr. Paul owns shares in company A. During the past year he considered switching to stock in company B, but he decided against it. He now finds out that he would have been better off by $1200 if he had switched to the stock of company B. Mr George owned shares in company B. During the past year he switched to stock in company A. He now finds out that he would have been better off by $1200 if he had kept his stock in company B. Who feels greater regret? (Kahneman & Tversky, 1982a).

In Kahneman and Tversky's study more than 90% of the respondents thought that Mr. George, whose misfortune stems from an action taken, would experience more regret. Kahneman and Tversky argue that Mr. George seems more likely to be plagued by thoughts of what "might have" or "should have" been, partly because it tends to be easier to imagine oneself abstaining from actions that one has carried out, than carrying out actions that were not performed. Landman (1987b) termed this *"the actor effect"*. Thus, if feedback is not actually present people are assumed to simulate mentally what could have been different. This process has been termed "counterfactual thinking". Unfortunately none of the studies dealing with this explanation (e.g. Landman, 1987b; Kahneman & Tversky, 1982a; Gleicher *et al.*, 1990) provide *direct* evidence for these processes. The only direct test of the effects of counterfactual thoughts resulted in mixed findings (N'gbala & Branscombe, 1997).

The explanation focusing on the role of counterfactuals differs from the economic approach to the study of regret. As argued before, economic theorists generally assume that regret does not arise if the outcomes of the rejected alternatives are not revealed (Bell, 1982, 1983; Kelsey & Schepanski, 1991; Sage & White, 1983). Thus, as argued by Gilovich and Medvec (1995), no allowance is made for the fact that individuals might consider (and even be tormented by) what they *imagine* to be the outcomes of alternatives not chosen. Psychological research on counterfactual thinking (Kahneman & Tversky, 1982b; Kahneman & Miller, 1986) stresses that events are not evaluated in isolation, but are compared to alternative events that "could have" happened. Research on counterfactual thinking thus has focused on two issues: (a) the rules by which counterfactual alternatives are generated (i.e., some alternatives are more easily imagined than others); and (b) the consequences of comparing actual events with imagined events that might have happened.

Another possible explanation for the actor-effect focuses on differences in the *perceived responsibility* for the outcome, and assumes that outcomes for which a person is responsible give rise to more extreme affective reactions.

According to this explanation actions imply greater personal responsibility than inaction. This can be related to research on attributions indicating that affective reactions following success and failure are to a large extent determined by attributions (McFarland & Ross, 1982). Weiner (1986) argues that affective reactions to outcomes are different and more extreme when the outcome is attributed to the actor as opposed to situational factors. According to this reasoning, actions will lead to more extreme affective reactions because outcomes following action tend to be attributed to the actor. Outcomes following inaction, however, can be attributed to any external event that preceded the outcome. This line of reasoning is also supported by the fact that actions, compared to inactions, are more salient, more often used to infer one's own attitude, and are perceived to be more informative (see for instance Fazio, Sherman, & Herr, 1982). Further support is provided by research showing that people who cause harm by acting are judged to be more immoral and more personally responsible than people who cause the same harm not by acting (Spranca, Minsk, & Baron, 1991; Ritov & Baron, 1990). Zeelenberg, van der Pligt, and de Vries (1997a) investigated the role of attributions and counterfactuals as determinants of the experience of regret. Their results showed that attributions and affective reactions to outcomes are highly correlated; outcomes after action were associated with both more internal attributions and more extreme affective reactions. Zeelenberg *et al.* (1997c) argued that attributions are likely to mediate the counterfactual–emotion relation.

Research discussed in this section points at a limited number of factors that can influence the experience of regret. Both counterfactual thinking and attributions seem important determinants of the amount of regret experienced after misfortune. In the next section we will focus on the *consequences* of anticipated regret.

ANTICIPATED REGRET AND THE THEORY OF PLANNED BEHAVIOUR

As discussed earlier in this chapter, general *anticipated* affect assessed with the same scales as evaluations and general affective reactions can improve the predictive power of the theory of planned behaviour. In this section we will focus on the role of *anticipated regret* in the context of other behavioural determinants incorporated in Ajzen's theory of planned behaviour. We investigated this for behaviour characterized by the possibility of a clear discrepancy between evaluative reactions towards the behavioural act itself and postbehavioural feelings; i.e. unsafe vs. safe sex.

Richard, van der Pligt, and de Vries (1995) tested the effects of anticipated regret on intentions to engage in (un)safe sex. In a first study a total of 822 adolescents participated. Anticipated regret was assessed in accordance with

Janis and Mann's (1977) definition of regret. They use the concept "anticipatory regret" as a generic term for the various worries that beset a decision-
maker before any negative outcomes materialize. Their definition is more
general than the one proposed in regret theory. Attitudes towards condom
use with new and/or casual partners were assessed with a coherent 12-item
scale. Perceived behavioural control was assessed with eight items, and subjective norms were also assessed in accordance with the theory of planned
behaviour. Anticipated regret was assessed with three semantic-differential
scales (*regret–no regret; worried–not worried;* and *tense–relaxed*).

Richard, van der Pligt, and de Vries (1995) tested their model for two behavioural actions: "refraining from sexual intercourse" and "condom use". For
each behaviour respondents were asked to indicate their expectations for three
different situations (e.g. "Suppose you meet a boy/girl you like and both of you
want to make love"; "Suppose you have a date with a person from your
school—after a great evening both of you want to make love") and these scores
formed a reliable index score. Figure 2.2 summarizes the results of their
LISREL analysis for the behaviour "condom use". The regression parameters
should be interpreted as β-weights; zero-order correlation coefficients are given
in brackets. Anticipated regret was assessed with the three scales mentioned
earlier and we calculated the difference score between anticipated affect associated with not having used a condom and anticipated affect associated with
having used a condom. A higher score indicated that higher levels of anticipated regret were associated with unsafe sex (not using a condom). Results
show that anticipated regret has an independent and significant impact on
behavioural expectations. For "condom use" the correlation between anticipated regret and behavioural expectation was 0.37 and slightly higher than the
correlation between attitudes and behavioural expectations (0.33). While for
"refraining from sexual intercourse" these correlations were 0.48 and 0.51 respectively. The four independent factors explained nearly 40% of the variance in
expectations to refrain from casual sexual intercourse, and nearly 30% of the
variance in expectations to use a condom when having sex with a casual partner.

Richard, van der Pligt, and de Vries (1995) also compared the fit of the
models in which anticipatory regret and attitudes were reflected by a single
latent construct (with five indicators) with the model shown in Figure 2.2. If
anticipated regret and attitudes are essentially equivalent, the overall fit of the
proposed alternative model should not differ significantly from the overall fit
of the two-factor model. This was not so; the possibility that anticipated regret
was similar to attitudes was statistically rejected for both refraining from
sexual intercourse and condom use.

The same model was also tested in a slightly older group of respondents
(Richard, de Vries, & van der Pligt, 1998 in press). A total of 451 students
from the University of Amsterdam participated in this study, in which the
model combining attitudes, subjective norms, perceived behavioural control

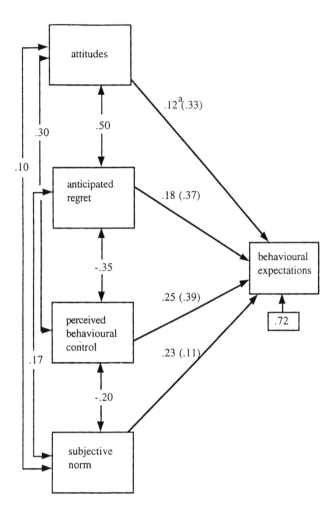

Figure 2.2   The role of anticipated regret as a determinant of safe sex (condom use).
Note: parameter estimates are standardized; all parameters are significant at $p < 0.01$
except [a]$p < 0.10$. Adapted from Richard, de Vries and van der Pligt (1998, in press)

and anticipated regret explained 65% of the variance in behavioural expectations (in this case condom use when having sex with a new and/or casual
partner). The correlation between expectation and self-reported behaviour
was 0.58, thus expectations explained 35% of the variance in contraceptive
behaviour of the respondents who had (casual) sex in the 4 weeks following
the first session of the study. The number of respondents who had engaged in
casual sex in this period was considerably lower than the total number of
respondents, hence self-reported behaviour could not be included in the
LISREL analysis summarized in Figure 2.3.

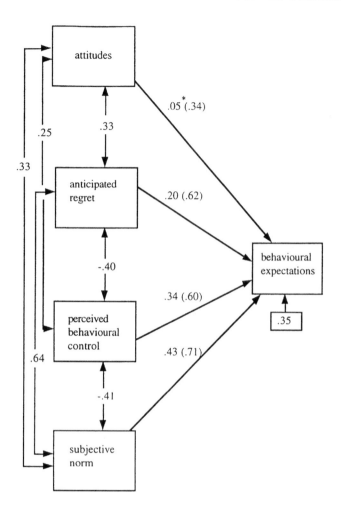

Figure 2.3 The role of anticipated regret as a determinant of safe sex. Note: parameter estimates are standardized; *n.s, all other parameters are significant at $p < 0.01$. Adapted from van der Pligt, de Vries and Richard (1997)

Thus, results of this study show that anticipated regret (in Janis and Mann's broader sense) can add to the prediction of behavioural expectations and (self-reported) behaviour, at least in the context of sexual risk-taking behaviour. Parker, Manstead, and Stradling (1995) also tested the role of anticipated regret in the context of the theory of planned behaviour. Their study focused on intentions to commit each of three driving violations (cutting across traffic to leave a motorway; weaving in and out of two lanes of slow moving traffic; and overtaking on the inside). Results of their study showed substantially improved predictive ability of the model when anticipated regret was included. In their approach anticipated regret was conceptualized as part of a moral norm which was measured by items such as, "It would be quite wrong for me to . . ." (followed by the violation in question) and, "Having committed a violation would make me feel really sorry for doing it". On average their model explained approximately 50% of the variance in intentions to commit driving violations.

To provide further evidence for the causal role of anticipated affective reactions such as regret and worry, Richard, van der Pligt, and de Vries (1996b) carried out two studies in which they attempted to induce anticipatory, postbehavioural negative affect and test its impact on behavioural expectations and actual behaviour. To this we turn next.

INCREASING THE SALIENCE OF ANTICIPATORY POSTBEHAVIOURAL AFFECT

Wilson and Hodges (1992) argued that people often have contradictory beliefs about a topic, and that their attitude towards a topic (which could be an object, a person or a specific action) depends on the subset of beliefs to which they attend. This also applies to affective reactions associated with certain behaviours. Quite often people have mixed emotions about behaviours. For example, one could have positive feelings about drinking alcohol and smoking cigarettes, but also negative feelings. The latter most likely stem from the possible more long-term effects of these behavioural practices. Often, as in this case, there is a temporal pattern to these different feelings. The feelings associated with performing the behaviour are positive, but the feelings towards the possible consequences are negative. This can be related to research on intertemporal choice showing that people tend to discount more remote future outcomes, and that their decisions are mostly based on more proximate outcomes (see, e.g., Loewenstein, 1992; Roelofsma, 1996). Consequently, we expect that feelings about performing a behaviour will generally receive more weight than the anticipated postbehavioural feelings when deciding whether to perform the behaviour or not. As argued by Wilson and Hodges, the beliefs (and feelings) people attend to are likely to be influenced by both contextual factors and thought processes, and they present evidence that attitudes and behaviour are easily changed if people are led to attend to a particular subset of beliefs. Thus, when people think about their feelings *about* a specific behavioural action, different beliefs may be salient than what they think about the feelings they would experience *after* carrying out the action. The earlier presented evidence that anticipated regret adds to the predictive power of attitude–behaviour models indicates that people differ in the extent to which they consider postbehavioural affective outcomes. The distinction between people's feelings *about* an action and their anticipated feelings *after* an action seems most relevant for domains in which there is a clear evaluative and/or affective discrepancy between the behavioural action itself and the (possible) postbehavioural outcomes.

Richard, van der Pligt, and de Vries (1996b) investigated whether students' unsafe sexual practices (i.e., not using condoms with casual partners) would be reduced by stimulating them to extend their time perspective and think about their postbehavioural feelings. Condom use is often associated with reduced sexual pleasure, and for this reason people's feelings about not using a condom may be relatively positive. However, an important negative postbehavioural consequence of not using a condom is a possible infection with a sexually transmitted disease (STD). Thus, if a person failed to use a condom in a casual sexual interaction, he/she is likely to worry about a possible STD (including HIV infection) and experience regret and other negative feelings. Since worry and regret are negative feelings that are more likely to be experienced *after* risky sexual behaviour, these feelings are likely to become more salient when people think about how they would feel afterwards. Thus, by stimulating respondents to focus on their feelings *after* unsafe sex, we expected them to become increasingly aware of the negative affective consequences of unsafe sexual behaviour. In line with van der Pligt and Richard (1994), Richard, van der Pligt, and de Vries (1996b) predicted that this increased awareness would make people more risk-averse and would reduce the likelihood of engaging in risky sexual practices.

In the first study, respondents were asked to imagine the following hypothetical situation: "Suppose you are on a holiday and you meet a very attractive boy (girl) and after spending some time with him (her) the two of you have sex". Respondents were randomly allocated to two groups. Respondents in the "feelings about" condition were asked to describe the feelings they would have about having sex (in the above situation) when *not* using a condom. On the next page they were asked to describe the feelings they would have about sexual intercourse (in the same situation) when using a condom. Respondents in the "feelings after" condition were also asked about the feelings they would have, but now the questions referred to *anticipated* feelings *after* having had safe or unsafe sex.

Feelings were assessed with a list of 40 affect-terms, of which 18 were positive and 22 negative. Examples of these are "elated", "active" and "excited" for positive affect terms, and "regretful", "fearful", "guilty" and "worried" for negative affect terms. In each case, respondents described their feelings by selecting 10 affect terms. Overall, affective reactions to unsafe sex were much more negative than were affective reactions to safe sex (use of condoms). More importantly, results also showed a significant main effect of time perspective on the number of negative feelings mentioned with respect to the risky behaviour (unsafe sex), with significantly more negative affect terms being selected in the "feelings after" condition.

Further analyses showed that the increased tendency to endorse negative affect terms in the "feelings after" condition was largely due to a greater endorsement of the terms "regret" and "guilt". For unsafe sex, the "feelings after" condition resulted in nearly 60% of the respondents selecting the term "regret", which was nearly twice as many as in the "feelings about" condition. The observed greater endorsement of negative terms in the "feelings after" condition was largely at the expense of positive affect terms (such as "excited", "pleasurable" and "energetic") associated with the act itself. The increased salience of negative (postbehavioural) feelings with respect to unsafe sex was related to increased expectations to engage in safe, preventive behaviour; in the "feelings after" condition respondents indicated stronger expectations to use condoms in future casual sexual interactions than in the "feelings about" condition.

Richard, van der Pligt, and de Vries (1996b) also tested the effects of the time-perspective manipulation on actual behaviour in a second study which included two follow-up measures of condom use in casual encounters over a period of 5 months. In this study respondents were asked to report their actual condom use in new or casual sexual encounters after 1 and 5 months. Respondents indicated their feelings on 10 nine-point scales referring to the following affective states: *regretful, enjoyable, contented, worried, tense, pleasant, anxious, satisfied, good*, and *ill-at-ease*. For each of these terms respondents were asked to indicate whether the affect term was more strongly associated with safe sex (condom use) or with unsafe sex (not using a condom). As expected, respondents in the "feelings after" condition associated unsafe sex more strongly with negative feelings, and the use of condoms more strongly with positive feelings. This difference was obtained for all positive and negative affect terms. Thus, people associated negative feelings (e.g., regret, anxiety, worry) more with unsafe sex than with safe sex, but *only* when they were asked to describe their postbehavioural feelings. This difference was not obtained when respondents indicated their feelings about the behaviour itself. Again, respondents in the "feelings after" condition had stronger expectations that they would use condoms because they associated the use of other contraceptives more with negative affect and the use of condoms more with positive affect. Moreover, relative to respondents who focused on the feelings they have about the behavioural act itself, those who focused on their anticipated feelings after the behavioural alternatives also reported a more frequent use of condoms in sexual encounters in the 5 months following the experimental manipulation. Thus, a simple manipulation intended to focus respondents on postbehavioural affective consequences of risky behaviour had a clear impact on behavioural intentions and also an actual behaviour as measured 5 months after the manipulation. These findings suggest that interventions stressing postbehavioural affect could be useful in applied settings such as health education.

Although additional research seems to be required to illuminate the precise mechanisms underlying our findings, they suggest that increasing the *awareness* that an action can have negative postbehavioural affective consequences is an important factor in producing behavioural change. Simonson (1992) used an experimental manipulation similar to ours in an attempt to influence consumer behaviour (e.g., a cheap consumer good of an unknown brand and quality vs. a more expensive alternative from a respectable producer). In his study respondents were asked to anticipate how they would feel if, after choosing between two alternatives, the wrong decision were made. The remaining respondents were not asked how they would feel. Results showed that respondents in the experimental condition were more risk-averse (i.e., made more conventional choices) than were those in the control condition. Simonson also asked respondents to think aloud as they made their decisions. Protocol analysis revealed that the main difference between the conditions was that in the experimental condition respondents tended to base their decisions more on anticipated regret. Thus, Simonson's findings also show that asking people to indicate postbehavioural feelings makes them aware of the affective consequences which are subsequently taken into account when they make their decision. Our own findings revealed modest but significant and stable effects due to a simple rating task requiring little effort. It would be interesting to study ways to enhance the effectiveness of the time perspective manipulation and test whether more demanding tasks (e.g., writing a short essay about postbehavioural feelings) increase the size of the effect.

SUMMARY AND CONCLUSIONS

Since the early 1980s there has been a dramatic increase in research on the impact of affect on attitudinal judgement, attitude-change processes and decision-making. Unfortunately, the term "affect" is used to denote many different things. For instance, Zajonc (1980) refers to affect as the outcome of valenced holistic processes that may proceed automatically without awareness, and are independent from cognitive processes. Others (e.g., Petty *et al.*, 1993) studied affect by focusing on the impact of mood on information processing and attitude change. In the context of expectancy-value approaches to attitudes and behaviour, the term "affect" is used to refer to rather holistic, undifferentiated affective reactions to the attitude object. Still others study affect by looking at specific emotions. In this chapter the emphasis was on affect as the outcome of a cognitive appraisal. We discussed recent theoretical and empirical developments concerning the role of affect in attitudinal judgement and decision-making. Several studies indicate that it is possible to distinguish between affective and more cognitive, analytical determinants of attitudes and behavioural decisions. We argued that this distinction should be extended to attitude–behaviour models such as the theory of planned behaviour. Most research on the role of affect in attitudes relies on holistic measures of affect and a rather crude dichotomy of positive vs. negative affect. Early attempts to incorporate affective determinants of behavioural intentions in the theory of planned behaviour resulted in only marginal improvements of its predictive validity (see, e.g., Ajzen & Driver, 1991). Later research (see, e.g., Manstead & Parker, 1995) supported the view that more specific measures of affect-based beliefs can make an independent contribution to the prediction of behavioural intentions. Their research focused on driving behaviour. The findings of Richard, van der Pligt, and de Vries (1996a), discussed earlier, point to the independent role of anticipated affect as a determinant of intention in other behavioural domains.

This evidence thus provides further support for the usefulness of the affect–cognition distinction in the context of attitude–behaviour models. Generally, research based on these models emphasizes utilitarian beliefs about the outcomes of behavioural alternatives. Research using the models of Fishbein and Ajzen tends to rely on elicitation techniques to assess the modal set of beliefs that require respondents to list advantages and disadvantages of the target behaviour. This wording may induce respondents to focus more on the utilitarian consequences and pay less attention to the possible affective or emotional consequences of the behaviour. Paying explicit attention to both components could provide more information about the structure of attitudes and the relative importance of affect- and belief-based considerations.

Most research on the role of affect in attitudinal judgement, attitude formation and attitude change relies on a simple dichotomy between positive and negative affect. We argued that it is essential to be more specific about affective determinants of attitudes, behavioural intentions and behaviour, especially when we are dealing with controlled as opposed to automatic aspects of information processing. Even if we rely on a simply dichotomy between positive and negative affect, it seems essential to assess whether we are dealing with general affective reactions towards the behavioural act itself or with *anticipated*, postbehavioural affective reactions. Especially in the context of attitude–behaviour models, it is not only crucial to distinguish between the evaluation of the behaviour and affect associated with the behaviour, but also between the latter and anticipated postbehavioural affective consequences.

Interestingly, most belief-based measures of attitudes focus on specific possible consequences of the behaviour in question, while studies incorporating affect tend to rely on rather general affective associations with the behavioural activity itself. We would like to argue that an approach paying attention to both utilitarian and affective consequences of behavioural actions is to be preferred. Thus, it seems essential to distinguish between the various possible affective reactions towards behavioural actions, and go beyond the rather crude distinction between positive and negative affect. Crites, Fabrigar, and Petty (1994) also argue in favour of a differentiated measure of affect and recommend that affect should be conceptualized in terms of discrete emotional reactions. In this chapter we have paid attention to one specific emotion, i.e., anticipatory regret. Research in the area of decision-making has shown that this emotion can have profound effects on behavioural choice. The discriminant validity of measures of anticipatory regret seems adequate, and the anticipation of this emotion is especially relevant in domains that are characterized by a discrepancy between the affective responses to the behavioural act itself and postbehavioural affective reactions.

Some issues remain unresolved, however. The studies presented in this chapter do not provide an answer to the question whether affective and cognitive determinants of attitudes can be really separated and related to different information-processing systems. The view of separate systems was advanced by Zajonc (1980, 1984), but his claims for the primacy of affect and the independence of cognitive appraisal and affective judgement have proved controversial (see, e.g., Birnbaum, 1981; Lazarus, 1982, 1984). This controversy partly revolves around definitional issues concerning the nature of cognition. Moreover, Zajonc's view of affect makes it difficult to distinguish it from cognitive mechanisms that can proceed automatically, without awareness. Buck (1985) suggested that Zajonc's definition of affect resembles what Tucker (1981) called "*syncretic* cognition" (holistic and vague), while his definition of cognition resembles what Tucker called "*analytic* cognition". Although Zajonc acknowledges that affect and cognition influence each other, he tends to emphasize their autonomy. The main contribution of Zajonc's work is that it showed that automatic processes can also influence attitudes. His proposal to distinguish two separate systems has also influenced attitude research but has generated a sometimes mysterious discussion and has often relied on rather contrived assessment techniques (e.g., presenting the same rating-scales preceded by questions about one's thoughts (cognition) or feelings (affect)).

Assessment techniques requiring respondents to think about their affective responses tap cognitions about these responses and seem far removed from the automatic processes Zajonc referred to. We argue that if we focus on cognitions about affect it seems unwise to treat affect as an undifferentiated, valenced response and recommended decomposing affect into concrete emotions. In the context of attitude–behaviour models this emphasis should also include anticipated postbehavioural emotions. One of these is regret, which seems a powerful predictor of behaviour. This is especially the case when there is the possibility of alternative actions with different outcomes and when some of these outcomes are irrevocable. This suggests that it could be useful for expectancy-value models to also consider alternative courses of action. This might capture the decision process better (see also Ronis, 1992).

Interestingly, the counterpart of regret (rejoicing) seems to have less predictive power. Much theorizing and research has focused on (anticipated) regret and related negative emotions, while positive emotions such as rejoicing and elation have received far less attention. One reason for this could be that the impact of (anticipated) positive emotions is far less pronounced than that of negative emotions. It seems that Tversky and Kahneman's view that "losses loom larger than gains" not only applies to utilitarian beliefs but also to anticipated emotions. In the one study where we attempted to test for the effects of anticipated elation (Richard, van der Pligt, & de Vries, 1996a) we found very modest effects; moreover, more recent attempts (van der Pligt & de Vries, in preparation) show similar (non-)effects of the positive counterpart of regret. This seems in accordance with emotion research. Attempts to develop a taxonomy of emotions tend to differentiate between many more negative emotions (each with their own characteristics and action tendencies) than positive emotions (see for instance Ortony & Turner, 1990).

Are there other negative emotions that should receive attention in the context of attitude–behaviour models apart from regret? One obvious candidate is disappointment. Disappointment is studied in research on behavioural decision-making (e.g. Bell, 1985; Kelsey & Schepanski, 1991; Loomes, 1987; van Dijk & van der Pligt, 1997) and the anticipation of disappointment can affect expectations (Sheppard, Oulette, & Fernandez, 1996) and attitudes towards different goals and/or tasks. Empirical evidence for the impact of *anticipated* disappointment on attitudes and behaviour is limited, and this also applies to other anticipated emotions that could have an impact on attitudes such as fear, guilt, embarrassment and shame. On the positive side one could think of (anticipated) emotions such as pride, relief and joy. As mentioned before, empirical evidence concerning the possible impact of these anticipated emotions is extremely limited. Our main argument is that the various possible anticipated emotions should receive more attention in belief-based measures of attitudes. If we want to learn more about the role of affective vs. more cognitive determinants of attitudes and behaviour, both should be assessed adequately and be based on a similar time perspective. Moreover, both should be assessed at the same level of specificity. Too often, utilitarian beliefs are assessed in great detail, while affect is assessed at a more general level, often with only one or two items.

An added benefit of focusing on specific emotions may be that it helps us to get rid of the sometimes artificial contrast between affect and cognition. Clore (1994) argued that all emotions require cognitions. The anticipation of postbehavioural affective consequences such as regret requires considerable cognitive processing. It requires thinking through various courses of action and estimating the likelihood of regret by comparing a chosen action with non-chosen actions. The anticipation and experience of regret thus obviously requires cognition and can hardly be seen as affect in terms of the crude dichotomy discussed earlier. The same applies to related emotions such as disappointment, which is a function of the difference between expectations and the obtained outcomes of one's behaviour.

The findings of the last two studies presented in this chapter show that it is relatively easy to increase the salience of anticipated regret and related (negative) affective reactions. A simple procedure requiring respondents to take a slightly longer time perspective made these emotions more salient, and this also influenced behavioural intentions and self-reported behaviour as shown by the results of Richard, van der Pligt, and de Vries (1998, in press). Their findings were limited to sexual risk-behaviour but there is other evidence suggesting that the *awareness* that an action can have negative postbehavioural affective consequences is an important factor in producing behavioural change. For instance, Simonson (1992) used a similar experimental manipulation to influence consumer behaviour.

The applied value of this research is that these outcomes point to the potential usefulness of focusing on more immediate affective consequences of risky behaviour, such as regret and worry, to foster behavioural change. This seems especially relevant in the context of health behaviours, because many negative consequences can be seen as a long way off and are more likely to be discounted (van der Pligt & de Vries, 1998, in press). Health education campaigns that stress rather immediate postbehavioural affective consequences could help to increase the willingness to engage in preventive behaviour. Moreover, stressing postbehavioural affective consequences seems a less extreme manipulation than fear appeals. Research has shown that the amount of fear aroused by a communication is predictive of intentions to adopt the recommended action independently of cognitive, more utilitarian considerations. However, it has also been shown that excessive levels of fear can trigger maladaptive coping-styles and reduce the effectiveness of recommendations to change one's behaviour (e.g. Liberman & Chaiken, 1992; Joseph *et al.*, 1987). It could be that stressing postbehavioural affective consequences results in lower anxiety levels and still stimulates preventive behaviour.

Summarizing, affect seems to have regained its place in research on attitudes and decision-making. Expectancy-value models of attitudes and behaviour can benefit from this renewed interest in affect. This would be enhanced if research in this tradition also focuses on specific affective reactions or emotions and also takes account of their time-perspective. Holistic assessments of affective associations with behavioural acts are less likely to help improve our understanding of the role of affect in controlled information processing underlying attitudes and decisions. More correspondence of measurement between outcome-related beliefs and expected affects, as well as a differentiated approach to the measurement of affect, should help to increase the expected utility of expectancy-value approaches to attitudes and behaviour.

ACKNOWLEDGEMENTS

We would like to thank Tony Manstead, Dave Messick, Miles Hewstone, Wolfgang Stroebe, Herbert Bless and Stephen Sutton for their comments on an earlier draft of this paper. Marcel Zeelenberg is currently at Tilburg University.

REFERENCES

Abelson, R. P., Kinder, D. R., Peters, M. D., & Fiske, S. T. (1982). Affective and semantic components in political person perception. *Journal of Personality and Social Psychology, 42,* 619–30.

Ajzen, I. (1985). From intentions to actions: A theory of planned behavior. In J. Kuhl & J. Beckmann (Eds), *Action-control: From Cognition to Behavior* (pp. 11–39). Heidelberg: Springer.

Ajzen, I. (1989). Attitude structure and behavior. In A. R. Pratkanis, S. J. Breckler & A. G. Greenwald (Eds), *Attitude Structure and Function.* Hillsdale, NJ: Erlbaum.

Ajzen, I. (1991). The theory of planned behavior. *Organizational Behavior and Human Decision Processes, 50,* 179–211.

Ajzen, I., & Driver, B. E. (1991). Prediction of leisure participation of leisure participation from behavioral, normative, and control beliefs: An implication of theory of planned behavior. *Leisure Sciences, 13,* 185–204.

Ajzen, I., & Timko, C. (1986). Correspondence between health attitudes and behavior. *Journal of Basic and Applied Social Psychology, 7,* 259–76.

Bargh, J. A. (1994). The four horsemen of atomaticity: Awareness, intention, efficiency, and control in social cognition. In R. S. Wyer, Jr & T. K. Srull (Eds), *Handbook of Social Cognition* (Vol. 1): *Basic Processes* (pp. 3–40). Hillsdale, NJ: Erlbaum.

Bargh, J. A., Chaiken, S., Raymond, P., & Hymes, C. (1996). The automatic evaluation effect: Unconditional automatic attitude activation with a pronunciation task. *Journal of Experimental Social Psychology, 32,* 104–28.

Bar-Hillel, M., & Neter, E. (1996). Why are people reluctant to exchange lottery tickets? *Journal of Personality and Social Psychology, 70,* 17–27.

Baron, J. (1992). The effect of normative beliefs on anticipated emotions. *Journal of Personality and Social Psychology, 63,* 320–30.

Beattie, J., Baron, J., Hershey, J. C., & Spranca, M. D. (1994). Psychological determinants of decision attitude. *Journal of Behavioral Decision Making, 7,* 129–44.

Bell, D. E. (1981). Explaining utility theory paradoxes by decision regret. In J. Morse (Ed.), *Proceedings of the Fourth International Conference on Multiple Criteria Decision Making* (pp. 28–39). New York: Springer.

Bell, D. E. (1982). Regret in decision making under uncertainty. *Operations Research, 21,* 961–81.

Bell, D. E. (1983). Risk premiums for decision regret. *Management Science, 29,* 1156–66.

Bell, D. E. (1985). Disappointment in decision making under uncertainty. *Operations Research, 33,* 1–27.

Birnbaum, M. H. (1981). Thinking and feeling: A skeptical review. *American Psychologist, 36,* 99-101.

Bless, H., Bohner, G., Schwarz, N., & Strack, F. (1990). Mood and persuasion: A cognitive response analysis. *Personality and Social Psychology Bulletin,* **16**, 331–45.

Breckler, S. J. (1984). Empirical validation of affect, behavior and cognition as distinct components of attitude. *Journal of Personality and Social Psychology,* **47**, 1191–1205.

Breckler, S. J., & Wiggins, E. C. (1989). Affect versus evaluation in the structure of attitudes. *Journal of Experimental Social Psychology,* **25**, 253–71.

Buck, R. (1985). Prime theory: an integrated view of motivation and emotion. *Psychological Review,* **92**, 389–413.

Chan, D. K-S., & Fishbein, M. (1993). Determinants of college women's intentions to tell their partners to use condoms. *Journal of Applied Social Psychology*, **23**, 1455–70.

Clore, G. L. (1994). Why emotions require cognition. In P. Ekman & R. J. Davidson (Eds), *The Nature of Emotions: Fundamental Questions* (pp. 181–91). New York: Oxford University Press.

Cohen, L. J. (1981). Can human irrationality be experimentally demonstrated? *Behavioral and Brain Sciences,* **4**, 317–31.

Crites, S. L. Jr, Fabrigar, L. R., & Petty, R. E. (1994). Measuring the affective and cognitive properties of attitudes: Conceptual and methodological issues. *Personality and Social Psychology Bulletin,* **20**, 619–34.

Eagly, A. H., Mladinic, A., & Otto, S. (1994). Cognitive and affective bases of attitudes towards social groups and social policies. *Journal of Experimental Social Psychology,* **30**, 113–37.

Edwards, W. (1954). The theory of decision making. *Psychological Bulletin,* **51**, 380–417.

Edwards, K. (1990). The interplay of affect and cognition in attitude formation and change. *Journal of Personality and Social Psychology,* **59**, 202–16.

Fazio, R. H., Sherman, S. J., & Herr, P. M. (1982). The feature-positive effect in the self-perception process: does not doing matter as much as doing? *Journal of Personality and Social Psychology,* **42**, 404–11.

Festinger, L., & Walster, E. (1964). Postdecision regret and decision reversal. In L. Festinger (Ed.), *Conflict, Decision, and Dissonance* (pp. 100–112). Stanford, CA: Stanford University Press.

Fishbein, M., & Ajzen, I. (1975). *Beliefs, Attitudes, Intention, and Behavior: An Introduction to Theory and Research*. Reading, MA: Addison-Wesley.

Fisher, W. A. (1984). Predicting contraceptive behaviour among university men: The role of emotions and behavioral intentions. *Journal of Applied Social Psychology,* **14**, 104–23.

Frijda, N. H., Kuipers, P., & ter Schure, E. (1989). Relations among emotion, appraisal and emotional action readiness. *Journal of Personality and Social Psychology,* **57**, 212–28.

Gilovich, T., & Medvec, V. (1995). The experience of regret: What, when and why. *Psychological Review,* **2**, 379–95.

Gleicher, F., Kost, K. A., Baker, S. M., Strathman, A. J., Richman, S. A., & Sherman, S. J. (1990). The role of counterfactual thinking in judgments of affect. *Personality and Social Psychology Bulletin,* **16**, 284–95.

Hampshire, S. (1960). *Thought and Action*. London: Chatto and Windus.

Harless, D. W. (1992). Actions versus prospects: The effect of problem presentation on regret. *American Economic Review,* **82**, 634–49.

Janis, I. L. (1967). Effects of fear arousal on attitude change: Recent developments in theory and experimental research. In L. Berkowitz (Ed.), *Advances in Experimental Social Psychology* (Vol. 3, pp. 166–224). San Diego, CA: Academic Press.

Janis, I. L., & Mann, L. (1977). *Decision Making: A Psychological Analysis of Conflict, Choice, and Commitment.* New York: Free Press.

Joseph, J. G., Montgomery, S. B., Emmons, C. A., Kirscht, J. P., & Kessler, R. C., *et al.* (1987). Perceived risk of AIDS: Assessing the behavioral and psychological consequences in a cohort of gay men. *Journal of Applied Social Psychology, 17,* 231–50.

Josephs, R. A., Larrick, R. P., Steele, C. M, & Nisbett, R. E. (1992). Protecting the self from the negative consequences of risky decisions. *Journal of Personality and Social Psychology, 62,* 26–37.

Kahneman, D., & Miller, D. T. (1986). Norm theory: Comparing reality to its alternatives. *Psychological Review, 93,* 136–53.

Kahneman, D., & Snell, J. (1990). Predicting utility. In Hogarth, R. M. (Ed.), *Insights in Decision Making* (pp. 295–310). Chicago: The University of Chicago Press.

Kahneman, D., & Snell, J. (1992). Predicting a changing taste: Do people know what they will like? *Journal of Behavioral Decision Making, 5,* 187–200.

Kahneman, D., & Tversky, A. (1979). Prospect theory: Analysis of decision under risk. *Econometrica, 47,* 263–91.

Kahneman, D., & Tversky, A. (1982a). The psychology of preferences. *Scientific American, 246*(1), 160–73.

Kahneman, D., & Tversky, A. (1982b). The simulation heuristic. In D. Kahneman, P. Slovic & A. Tversky (Eds), *Judgement Under Uncertainty: Heuristics and Biases* (pp. 201–8). Cambridge: Cambridge University Press.

Kelsey, D., & Schepanski, A. (1991). Regret and disappointment in taxpayer reporting decisions: an experimental study. *Journal of Behavioral Decision Making, 4,* 33–53.

Landman, J. (1987). Regret and elation following action and inaction: Affective responses to positive versus negative outcomes. *Personality and Social Psychology Bulletin, 13,* 524–36.

Landman, J. (1993). *Regret: The Persistence of the Possible.* New York: Oxford University Press.

Larrick, R. P., & Boles, T. L. (1995). Avoiding regret in decisions with feedback: a negotiation example. *Organizational Behavior and Human Decision Processes, 63,* 87–97.

Lazarus, R. S. (1981). A cognitive reply to Zajonc on emotion and cognition. *American Psychologist, 36,* 222–3.

Lazarus, R. S. (1982). Thoughts on the relations between emotion and cognition. *American Psychologist, 37,* 1019–24.

Lazarus, R. S. (1984). On the primacy of cognition. *American Psychologist, 39,* 124–9.

Leventhal, H. (1970). Findings and theory in the study of fear communications. In L. Berkowitz (Ed.), *Advances in Experimental Social Psychology* (Vol. 5, pp. 119–86). San Diego, CA: Academic Press.

Liberman, A., & Chaiken, S. (1992). Defensive processing of personally relevant health messages. *Personality and Social Psychology Bulletin, 18,* 669–79.

Loewenstein, G. (1992). The fall and rise of psychological explanations in the economics of intertemporal choice. In G. Loewenstein & J. Elster (Eds), *Choice Over Time* (pp. 3–34). New York: Russel Sage Foundation.

Loewenstein, G. F., Thompson, L, & Bazerman, M. H. (1989). Social utility and decision making in interpersonal contexts. *Journal of Personality and Social Psychology, 57,* 426–41.

Loomes, G. (1987).   Further evidence of the impact of regret and disappointment in choice and uncertainty. *Economica,* **55**, 47–62.

Loomes, G., & Sugden, R. (1982).   Regret theory: an alternative theory of rational choice under uncertainty. *Economic Journal,* **92**, 805–25.

Loomes, G., & Sugden, R. (1986).   Disappointment and dynamic consistency in choice under certainty. *Review of Economic Studies,* **53**, 271–82.

Loomes, G., & Sugden, R. (1987a).   Some implications of a more general form of regret theory. *Journal of Economic Theory,* **41**, 270–87.

Loomes, G., & Sugden, R. (1987b).   Testing for regret and disappointment in choice under uncertainty. *Economic Journal,* **97**, 118–29.

Madden, T. J., Ellen, P. S., & Ajzen, I. (1992).   A comparison of the theory of planned behavior and the theory of reasoned action. *Personality and Social Psychology Bulletin,* **18**, 3–9.

Manstead, A. S. R., & Parker, D. (1995).   Evaluating and extending the theory of planned behaviour. In W. Stroebe & M. Hewstone (Eds), *European Review of Social Psychology* (Vol. 6, pp. 69–95). Chichester: Wiley.

McCaul, K. D., Sandgren, A. K., O'Neill, H. K., & Hinsz, V. B. (1993).   The value of the theory of planned behavior, perceived control, and self-efficacy expectations for predicting health-protective behaviors. *Basic and Applied Social Psychology,* **14**, 231–52.

McFarland, C., & Ross, M. (1982).   Impact of causal attribution on affective reactions to success and failure. *Journal of Personality and Social Psychology,* **43**, 937–46.

Middlestadt, S. E., & Fishbein, M. (1995).   Evaluating the impact of a national AIDS prevention radio campaign in St. Vincent and the Grenadines. *Journal of Applied Social Psychology,* **25**, 21–34.

Millar, M. G., & Millar, K. U. (1990).   Attitude change as a function of attitude type and argument type. *Journal of Personality and Social Psychology,* **59**, 217–28.

Murphy, S. T., & Zajonc, R. B. (1993).   Affect, cognition, and awareness: Affective priming with optimal and suboptimal stimulus exposures. *Journal of Personality and Social Psychology,* **64**, 723–39.

N'gbala, A., & Branscombe, N. B. (1997).   When does action elicit more regret than inaction and is counterfactual mutation the mediator of this effect? *Journal of Experimental Social Psychology,* **33**, 324–43.

Ortony, A., & Turner, T. J. (1990).   What's basic about basic emotions. *Psychological Review,* **97**, 313–31.

Parker, D., Manstead, A. S. R., & Stradling, S. G. (1995).   Extending the theory of planned behaviour: The role of personal norm. *British Journal of Social Psychology,* **34**, 127–37.

Parker, D., Manstead, A. S. R., Stradling, S. G., Reason, J. T., & Baxter, J. S. (1992).   Intention to commit driving violations: An application of the theory of planned behavior. *Journal of Applied Psychology,* **77**, 94–101.

Petty, R. E., & Cacioppo, J. T. (1986).   The elaboration likelihood model of persuasion. In L. Berkowitz (Ed.), *Advances in Experimental Social Psychology* (Vol. 19), Orlando, FL: Academic Press.

Petty, R. E., Schumann, D. W., Richman, S. A., & Strathman, A. J. (1993).   Positive mood and persuasion: Different roles for affect under high- and low-elaboration conditions. *Journal of Personality and Social Psychology,* **63**, 5–20.

Pfister, H., & Bohm, G. (1992).   The function of concrete emotions in rational decision making. *Acta Psychologica,* **80**, 105–16.

Richard, R., van der Pligt, J., & de Vries, N. K. (1995).   The impact of anticipated affect on (risky) sexual behavior. *British Journal of Social Psychology,* **34**, 9–21.

Richard, R., van der Pligt, J., & de Vries, N. K. (1996a). Anticipated affect and behavioral choice. *Basic and Applied Social Psychology*, **18**, 111–29.

Richard, R., van der Pligt, J., & de Vries, N. K. (1996b). Anticipated regret and time perspective: Changing sexual risk-taking behavior. *Journal of Behavioral Decision Making*, **9**, 185–99.

Richard, R., de Vries, N.K., & van der Pligt, J. (1998). Anticipated regret and precautionary sexual behaviour. *Journal of Applied Social Psychology*, in press.

Ritov, I. (1996). Probability of regret: anticipation of uncertainty resolution in choice. *Organizational Behavior and Human Decision Making Processes*, **66**, 228–36.

Ritov, I., & Baron, J. (1990). Reluctance to vaccinate: Omission bias and ambiguity. *Journal of Behavioral Decision Making*, **3**, 263–77.

Roelofsma, P. H. M. P. (1996). Modelling intertemporal choice: An anomaly approach. *Acta Psychbologica* (in press).

Rogers, R. W. (1975). A protection motivation theory of fear appeals and attitude change. *Journal of Psychology*, **91**, 93–114.

Ronis, D. L. (1992). Conditional health threats: Health beliefs, decisions, and behaviors among adults. *Health Psychology*, **11**, 127–34.

Roseman, I. J., Wiest, C., & Swartz, T. S. (1994). Phenomenology, behaviors, and goals differentiate discrete emotions. *Journal of Personality and Social Psychology*, **67**, 206–11.

Rosenberg, M. J., & Hovland, C. I. (1960). Cognitive, affective and behavioral components of attitude. In M. J. Rosenberg, C. I. Hovland, W. J. McGuire, R. P. Abelson, & J. W. Brehm (Eds), *Attitude Organization and Change*. New Haven, CT: Yale University Press.

Sage, A. P., & White, F. B. (1983). Decision and information structures in regret: Models of judgment and choice. *IEEE: Transitions on Systems, Man, and Cybernetics*, **13**, 136–43.

Schifter, D. B., & Ajzen, I. (1985). Intention, perceived control, and weight loss: An application of the theory of planned behavior. *Journal of Personality and Social Psychology*, **49**, 843–51.

Seligman, C., Kriss, M., Darley, J. M., Fazio, R. H., Becker, L. J., & Pryor, J. B. (1979). Predicting summer energy consumption from homeowners' attitudes. *Journal of Applied Social Psychology*, **9**, 70–90.

Sheppard, J. A., Ouelette, J. A., & Fernandez, J. K. (1996). Abandoning unrealistic optimism: Performance estimates and temporal proximity of self-relevant feedback. *Journal of Personality and Social Psychology*, **70**, 844–55.

Simonson, I. (1992). The influence of anticipating regret and responsibility on purchase decisions. *Journal of Consumer Research*, **19**, 105–18.

Sparks, P., Hedderley, D., & Shepherd, R. (1992). An investigation into the relationship between perceived control, attitude variability and the consumption of two common foods. *European Journal of Social Psychology*, **22**, 55–71.

Spranca, M., Minsk, E., & Baron, J. (1991). Omission and commission in judgment and choice. *Journal of Experimental Social Psychology*, **27**, 76–105.

Starmer, C., & Sugden, R. (1993). Testing for juxtaposition and event splitting effects. *Journal of Risk and Uncertainty*, **6**, 235–54.

Terry, D. J., Gallois, C., & McCamish, M. (Eds), (1993). *The Theory of Reasoned Action: Its Application to AIDS-preventive Behaviour*. Oxford: Pergamon.

Tucker, D. M. (1981). Lateral train function, emotion, and conceptualizaiton. *Psychological Bulletin*, **89**, 19–46.

Tyler, T. R., & Rasinsky, K. (1984). Comparing psychological images of the social perceiver: Role of perceived informativeness, memorability, and affect in mediating the impact of crime victimization. *Journal of Personality and Social Psychology*, **46**, 308–29.

van der Pligt, J., & de Vries, N. K. (1998).   Expectancy-value models of health behaviour: The role of salience and effect. *Psychology and Health*, in press.

van der Pligt, J. & de Vries, N. K (1997).   Anticipated regret and elation as determinants of behavioural intentions (manuscript in preparation).

van der Pligt, J., & Richard, R. (1994).   Changing adolescents' sexual behaviour:
Perceived risk, self-efficacy, and anticipated regret. *Patient Education and Counsel-
ing*, **23**, 187–96.

van Dijk, W. W., & van der Pligt, J. (1997).   The impact of probability and magnitude
of outcome on disappointment and elation. *Organizational Behaviour and Human
Decision Processes*, **69**, 277–84.

Weiner, B. (1986).   Attribution, emotion and action. In R. M. Sorrentino & E. T.
Higgins (Eds), *Handbook of Motivation and Cognition* (pp. 281–312). Chichester:
Wiley.

Wilson, T. D., & Hodges, S. D. (1992).   Attitudes as temporary constructions. In L. L.
Martin & A. Tesser (Eds), *The Construction of Social Judgments* (pp. 37–65). Hillsdale, NJ: Erlbaum.

Zajonc, R. B. (1980).   Feeling and thinking: preferences need no inferences. *American Psychologist*, **35**, 151–75.

Zajonc, R. B. (1984).   On the primacy of affect. *American Psychologist*, **39**, 117–23.

Zanna, M., & Rempel, J. K. (1988).   Attitudes: A new look at an old concept. In
D. Bar-Tal & A. Kruglanski (Eds), *The Social Psychology of Knowledge* (pp. 315–
34). Cambridge: Cambridge University Press.

Zeelenberg, M., Beattie, J., van der Pligt, J., & de Vries, N. K. (1996).   Consequences
of regret aversion: Effects of expected feedback on risky decision making. *Organizational Behavior and Human Decision Processes* (in press).

Zeelenberg, M., van der Pligt, J., & de Vries, N. K. (1997a).   The role of attributions
in post-decisional affect (manuscript under review).

Zeelenberg, M., van Dijk, W. W., Manstead, A. S. R., & van der Pligt, J. (1997b).   The
experience of regret and disappointment. *Cognition and Emotion* (in press).

Zeelenberg, M., van Dijk, W. W., van der Pligt, J., Manstead, A. S. R., van Empelen,
P., & Reinderman, D. (1997c).   The role of behavior-focused and situation-focused
counterfactuals in the experience of regret and disappointment (manuscript under
review).

Chapter 3

Affective Priming

Karl Christoph Klauer
University of Bonn

ABSTRACT

It is frequently assumed that people spontaneously evaluate any incoming stimulus as pleasant or unpleasant, liked or disliked, good or bad. This evaluative reaction is sometimes held to be automatic and unconditional, and it is claimed to precede cognitive analysis of the stimulus. Evaluative processes of this kind play a central role in current theories of emotion and attitude. One avenue to studying the evaluative response has been the affective priming paradigm. Affective priming investigates whether the evaluation of a first stimulus, the prime, that is to be ignored, affects the processing of subsequent stimuli. The pattern of results and explanations of affective priming effects are reviewed. Explanations of affective priming have traditionally been adapted from explanations of semantic priming. The evidence for automaticity of affective priming is critically assessed. Furthermore, it is argued that the Stroop paradigm may be a more appropriate point of reference than the semantic priming paradigm in accounting for affective priming. The conceptual implications for the role of evaluative processes, the role of consciousness, the nature of judgement and evolutionary theorizing are discussed.

The evaluative dimension is defined by a number of classic dimensions of "good–bad", "safe-dangerous", "like–dislike", and so forth (Osgood & Suci, 1955). An assumption of long standing (e.g. Arnold, 1960; Lazarus, 1966; Martin & Levey, 1978) is that a characteristic reaction to any stimulus is to evaluate it on this evaluative dimension at a level which is typically well removed from intense automatic arousal and well before actual approach–avoidance behaviour as well as cognitive analysis of the stimulus. Martin and

European Review of Social Psychology, Volume 8. Edited by Wolfgang Stroebe and Miles Hewstone.
© 1998 John Wiley & Sons Ltd.

Levey (1978) have termed this covert reaction the "subjective evaluative response".

From a social-cognition point-of-view, human information-processing is not geared simply to the acquisition of knowledge, but must enable the organism to act in an environment full of opportunities and risks, hospitable and hostile stimuli. In this vein, it is frequently argued that a mechanism for recognizing hostility or hospitality in the environment is necessary for the survival of the organism, and that the immediate evaluation of incoming stimuli, i.e., the evaluative response, serves this adaptive function.

Given the unconditional and ubiquitous role that is often assigned to the evaluative response, it is not surprising that many lines of research in social and clinical psychology have explored, in one way or another, the nature and antecedent and consequent conditions of this evaluative process. For instance, evaluation is a central concept in current theories of *emotion* (Hermans, 1996). According to Ortony and Turner (1990), for example, emotions are, above all, positive or negative evaluations. Similarly, cognitive appraisal models of emotion (Lazarus, 1991; Scherer, 1988) assume that stimuli are evaluated as positive or negative at an early stage in the elicitation of emotions.

Another research tradition of more immediate relevance to the present chapter sought to exploit the assumed reflex-like nature of the evaluative response to explain the acquisition of evaluations and attitudes by means of *classical conditioning*. The rationale is as follows: if the evaluation of a positive or negative stimulus (e.g., a positive or negative word) is accessed spontaneously and reliably, then it should be possible to condition this evaluative response on a previously neutral stimulus (e.g., a nonsense syllable) presented contingently with the positive or negative stimulus. In so-called attitude conditioning (Staats & Staats, 1957, 1958) as well as evaluative conditioning (Martin & Levey, 1978), classical conditioning of evaluations has in fact been found effective for a variety of materials and classical conditioning techniques.

More recent work has demonstrated that the effects can be obtained even when the positive or negative stimulus is presented under conditions that prevent awareness of its presence (De Houwer, Baeyens, & Eelen, 1994; Krosnick et al., 1992; Murphy & Zajonc, 1993; Murphy, Monahan, & Zajonc, 1995; Niedenthal, 1990). Krosnick et al. (1992), for example, presented slides of a person going about normal daily activities. Each slide was preceded by a briefly presented affect-arousing slide, which in the first group depicted a positive scene (e.g., a pair of kittens) and in the second group a negative scene (e.g., a bucket of snakes). During the subsequent attitude-testing phase, the subjects in the first group reported more positive attitudes toward the person shown in the conditioning phase than subjects in the second group, even though none of the subjects had detected the affect-arousing pictures. While awareness of the affect-arousing stimulus thus appears not to be necessary for evaluative conditioning, the effects are even disrupted under conditions that encourage a more conscious and reflective processing of the relevant stimuli (Martin & Levey, 1978; Murphy & Zajonc, 1993). It should be noted that although these studies are often discussed under the label of classical conditioning, some of them employed procedures more reminiscent of the affective priming paradigm, and these latter studies will be considered again below.

A third major line of relevant research is attitude research. Attitudes are favourable or unfavourable dispositions toward social attitudes. The evaluative or affective component of attitudes is one of their defining attributes (e.g., Krech, Crutchfield, & Ballachey, 1962, p. 139; Osgood, Suci, & Tannenbaum, 1957, p. 189) that is often stressed to the exclusion of other (cognitive and conative) components. The influence of the affective component of social attitudes on social judgements is well established.

For example, early studies by Zillig (1928), whose work influenced Heider (1944, 1958), demonstrated that pupils' attitudes toward each other biased their judgements of success and failure in simple tasks. Liked pupils were judged to perform better than disliked pupils, irrespective of actual performance. More recently, Lord, Ross, and Lepper (1979) observed subjects' attitudes toward capital punishment to affect their evaluations of empirical evidence concerning the deterrent efficacy of capital punishment.

The studies just mentioned, as well as many others, make it evident that the perceiver's attitude plays an important role in how a stimulus is judged (Greenwald & Banaji, 1995). There is a clear tendency for evaluation-congruent judgements, sometimes termed the halo bias, even when this is objectively inappropriate and when subjects seem motivated to avoid biased processing (Klauer, 1991; Nisbett & Wilson, 1977; Wetzel, Wilson, & Kort, 1981).

From a social-cognition point of view, social judgements are complex processes involving perception, attention, memory and reasoning processes. Much recent research has addressed the question at which stage or at which stages the affective component of attitudes exerts its influence. In the course of this endeavour, researchers have turned to more elementary tasks than social judgements to isolate possible components and mechanisms, by which affect influences cognitive processes.

In informationally rich environments, only a small subset of the available information can be attended to by human actors, given their strictly limited attentional capacity, and one function of selective attention is to allow the cognitive system to process specific information adequately, from a very complex and diverse world (Kahneman & Treisman, 1984). It is clear that systematic selection of information may be an important source of bias in social judgements.

Recently, a number of findings from different paradigms have begun to show that affectively polarized objects are attended to with high priority.

In line with the above-mentioned speculations about the adaptive character of the evaluative response, one function of the evaluative response might be to direct the organism's vigilance towards opportunities and dangers in the environment. Below, I commence by briefly reviewing relevant findings.

Another frequently discussed mechanism by which evaluations can exert their influence is affective priming (Bower, 1991; Fazio et al., 1986; Forgas, 1994): The activation of an evaluative attitude may raise the accessibility of bits of information in memory that share the same evaluation. Thereby, attitude-congruent information in memory might become more readily available to subsequent information-processing, biasing the judgemental process. The major focus of the present chapter is on this proposed affective-priming mechanism.

Affective priming is really an effect, rather than a mechanism. As will be seen, there are in fact different mechanisms which may give rise to the effect. The effect is demonstrated by means of an experimental paradigm adapted from semantic priming (Neely, 1991). Subjects are presented evaluatively polarized target and prime stimuli. In a given trial, subjects may see a valenced word-target (e.g., aggressive), preceded by a valenced word-prime (e.g., rose). Subjects are typically asked to respond only to the target; for example, by classifying it as positive or negative in meaning. When prime and target agree in evaluation (e.g., death aggressive), performance is often facilitated: responses to targets occur faster and with fewer errors than when prime and target disagree in evaluation (e.g., rose aggressive).

Affective priming studies provide a simple model of the unintentional influence of a first evaluative response (to the prime) on subsequent processing (of the target). In this fashion, the paradigm has been used by Dovidio, Evans, and Tyler (1986) and Perdue et al. (1990) to account for racial stereotypes and ingroup bias, respectively. Perdue et al. (1990), for example, argue that the positive affective tone of ingroup designators such as the word-primes "us" and "we" may be activated automatically upon exposure to such words and, through the spread of that activation in a semantic network, "may bias the retrieval of evaluatively congruent material from semantic memory, in an automatic process apparently outside the awareness of the perceiver" (Perdue et al., 1990, p. 483).

In addition, since the affective-priming paradigm has been adapted from so-called semantic priming (Neely, 1991), it can profit from the detailed task- and process-analyses that have been performed in that field. Thereby, affective priming studies have been able to address many of the controversial characteristics of the evaluative response: its possibly automatic, spontaneous character, its possible primacy before cognitive analysis of the stimulus (Zajonc, 1980), and its possibly unconditional and ubiquitous character (Bargh, 1994; Pratto, 1994).

AFFECT AND ATTENTION

In Fazio's (1989) attitude theory, attitudes are seen as object-evaluation associations stored in memory. As any association, the strength of this particular association can vary and determines the likelihood that the evaluation will be activated upon one's encountering the attitude object.

The concept of varying associative strength defines the attitude–nonattitude continuum (Fazio, 1989). At the non-attitude end of the continuum reside objects for which no *a priori* evaluations are stored in memory. At the upper end of the continuum is the case of well-learned association. The association between the attitude object and the evaluation may become so strong that the evaluation is capable of being activated automatically from memory on mere observation of the attitude object. Thus, Fazio does not consider the evaluative response to be unconditional, but rather an automatic evaluative response is restricted to attitude objects with high attitude accessibility.

In Fazio's approach, attitude accessibility, as defined by association strength, is either measured as the speed with which subjects are capable of evaluating an attitude object, or it is experimentally manipulated by measures that temporarily increase the association strength. For example, repeated explicit evaluations of the attitude object are likely to strengthen, at least temporarily, the object–evaluation link.

Affect-evoking Objects Attract Attention

Using both operationalizations of attitude accessibility, Roskos-Ewoldsen and Fazio (1992) found that of a display of six equally familiar objects, presented as pictures, those associated with accessible attitudes were noticed and reported more frequently upon brief presentation (1500 ms) of the display.

In two additional experiments in this series, the subjects' task did not require the scanning of the display. In one experiment, subjects were to perform a number–letter discrimination task. Pictures of attitude objects surrounded the target number or letter, and subjects were asked to ignore these distractors. Nevertheless, when later asked to recall as many distractors as possible, recall probability increased as a function of attitude accessibility, providing indirect evidence for the assumption that attitude-evoking objects had attracted and received more attention than attitude objects with low attitude accessibility.

A more direct test of this hypothesis was provided in a final, fourth experiment. Again, subjects saw displays of six pictures. In each trial, two target objects were named, and the subjects' task was to search for the targets in the display. Subjects were told that the targets could appear in only three positions fixed throughout the experiment. The remaining three positions never held a target, and subjects were well advised to ignore the pictures in these positions, if at all possible. Nevertheless, visual search for targets took longer if the distractor positions were taken by objects associated with high rather than low attitude accessibility, indicating a selective-attention failure so that subjects involuntarily expended some attention on attitude-evoking objects.

Does Negative Information Attract Attention?

While Roskos-Ewoldsen and Fazio (1992) argued that the possible attention-attracting property of attitudes serves the functional purpose of making perceivers aware of objects with possible hedonic (positive or negative) consequences, Pratto and John (1991) proposed that people automatically evaluate perceived stimuli so that attention can be allocated to *negatively* evaluated stimuli. A similar negativity effect for facial expressions has been postulated by Hansen and Hansen (1988). As argued by Pratto (1994), the negativity effect, termed automatic vigilance, may make the human observer aware of threats and dangers in the environment that require fast responses. Related negativity effects are also well known in impression formation, where they refer to the observation that negative stimuli often have higher impact than positive stimuli of the same intensity on social judgements and approach–avoidance behaviour (Peeters & Czapinski, 1990; Skowronski & Carlston, 1989).

Pratto and John (1991) presented positively and negatively evaluated adjectives, denoting personality traits, in different colours. Subjects' task was to name the colour. This task is adapted from the classical Stroop interference task (MacLeod, 1991), in which the words themselves may denote colours. For example, the word "red" may be presented in green. Colour-naming latencies are larger if the word denotes a colour that differs from the colour in which the word is presented, suggesting that word meaning is processed and cannot be completely ignored.

Interestingly, in the present case, colour-naming latencies were larger for negative than for positive traits. In three studies, valence of the trait adjectives, regardless of extremity of evaluation, word length, word frequency, or expected frequency of the trait, was the best predictor of response times. Pratto and John argue, by analogy with Stroop interference (MacLeod, 1991), that both colour and valence are processed, and that the irrelevant negative personality traits capture attention that is diverted from the colour naming task. In line with the assumption that negative personality traits attracted attention, greater incidental learning could be demonstrated in Pratto and John's (1991) Experiment 2 for negative personality traits than for positive traits.

Subsequent research demonstrated that the effect on colour-naming latencies was obtained even when subjects were forwarned (Pratto, 1994). However, in an attempt to include a baseline of neutral words, interference with colour-naming was obtained for both positive and negative words

(Pratto, 1994) relative to neutral words equivalent in word length, word frequency, and extremity of evaluation. As argued by Pratto (1994), this result may have been a consequence of a particular attention-attracting potency of words related to sex, romance and babies, which were present in the list of positive words. When such words were excluded in a second experiment, the negativity effect again emerged. In conflict with the Pratto and John (1991) results, Rothermund, Wentura, and Bak (1995) found a positivity effect for personality traits such that positive traits interfered more with colour-naming than negative traits.

Affect and Attention: Summary

Both Roskos-Ewoldsen and Fazio (1992) and Pratto and John (1991) have provided evidence for an effect of affective aspects of stimulus material on the allocation of attention. Both approaches are based on quite different paradigms and materials. For example, while the pictures used by Roskos-Ewoldsen and Fazio showed mostly positively evaluated objects, Pratto and John used personality adjectives that were positive as often as negative. It is therefore perhaps not surprising that the patterns of results are quite different: Roskos-Ewoldsen and Fazio observed the allocation of attention to be moderated by attitude acessibility, but found no clear relationship with valence (positive vs. negative). In contrast, Pratto and John found that negative words appeared to divert attention more strongly than positive words, i.e. a clear valence effect, whereas the allocation of attention was not a function of the extremity of the evaluation, which is usually highly correlated with accessibility.

Experiments have shown that intention and strategies can modulate effects in selective attention studies (e.g., Greenwald & Rosenberg, 1978; Logan, Zbrodoff, & Williamson, 1984), and subject strategies may be responsible for the differences between the paradigms of Roskos-Ewoldsen and Fazio (1992) and Pratto and John (1991) and for the differences within paradigms (cf. Rothermund, Wentura, & Bak, 1995). For example, as argued by Johnson and Weisz (1994), subjects are likely to notice that mostly positive and negative words occur in the studies by Pratto and John (1991), and subjects' processing may reflect a strategic component in reaction to this composition of the stimulus set.

AFFECTIVE PRIMING: BASIC FINDINGS

Pratto and John (1991) propose that incoming stimuli are evaluated automatically, and that negative information is then allocated attention. As we have seen, the evidence from selective-attention studies, reviewed above, is not, however, conclusive with respect to the proposed automatic character of the evaluating process. In Fazio's (1989) theory, evaluation is not automatic but occurs spontaneously only to the extent to which objects are associated with accessible attitudes.

In cognitive psychology, much of the evidence on automatic and controlled processes comes from priming experiments. In so-called semantic priming, the subjects' task is to respond to a target word; for example, by pronouncing it. The target is preceded by a prime word that is to be ignored. When prime and target are associated (e.g., bread and butter) performance is usually facilitated: responses to targets are faster and more often correct. The interval between onset of prime and onset of target is called the *stimulus onset asynchrony (SOA)*.

In priming studies, the controllability of automatic processes is usually inferred from the effects of SOA. Semantic priming effects that occur at SOAs of less than 300 ms are usually attributed to automatic processes (Neely, 1977; Posner & Snyder, 1975; Ratcliff & McKoon, 1981), most often in the form of spreading activation as elaborated below. At longer SOAs, attentional and strategic factors come into play. It is for these reasons that affective priming studies have often manipulated SOA.

Affective priming studies investigate whether the response to targets is facilitated if the target (e.g., friendly) is preceded by a prime of the same evaluation (e.g., love) that is not necessarily associated or related in meaning to the target. As discussed in the Introduction, the affective priming paradigm provides a simple model of the involuntary influence of a first evaluative response (to the prime) on subsequent processing (of the target) as may contribute to racial stereotypes (Dovidio, Evans, & Tyler, 1986), ingroup bias (Perdue *et al.*, 1990), and the halo error (Greenwald & Banaji, 1995; Klauer, 1991). Furthermore, by adapting task- and processing-analyses from semantic priming, affective priming studies have been able to address many of the controversial issues surrounding the nature of the alleged evaluative response, as discussed below. A final advantage of the affective priming paradigm is methodological: by contrasting performance on evaluatively congruent prime–target pairs (prime and target both positive, or both negative) with incongruent pairs (one positive, the other negative), the affective priming effect does not rely on comparisons of different sets of words (such as comparison of negative vs. positive words, as in negativity effects). The same words enter congruent as well as incongruent prime–target pairs. It is therefore unlikely that *uncontrolled* aspects of the words (familiarity, informational diagnosticity, extremity, etc.) can explain affective priming effects if they occur.

The Studies by Fazio *et al.* (1986)

The first set of studies to demonstrate affective priming effects were conducted by Fazio and colleagues (1986). As in many subsequent studies, these studies employed an evaluative decision task, in which decision-makers judge the affective connotation (positive vs. negative) of an evaluatively polarized target word. Targets were 10 clearly positive and 10 clearly negative adjectives. Prime words were attitude objects. There was also a baseline condition, in which primes were letter strings such as BBB.

In Experiment I, a list of 70 attitude objects had to be evaluated in a first phase of the experiment, the attitude-assessment phase. On the basis of each subject's evaluation latencies, positive and negative attitude objects with high and low attitude accessibility were collected. A total of 16 primes were selected. In the second phase of the experiment, the priming phase, primes were presented for 200 ms, followed after 100 ms by the target, and thus, SOA was 300 ms. Subjects were told to memorize the prime word and to judge the evaluation of the target word. After the evaluative decision on the target word, they were required to recite the memorized prime word.

For primes with a strong object-evaluation association, a priming effect was shown as an interaction of prime and target valence, so that affectively congruent prime-target pairs were responded to faster than affectively incongruent prime–target pairs. Compared to the baseline condition, in which primes were letter strings, there was about as much facilitation (in the order of 35 ms) for congruent pairs as there was inhibition for incongruent pairs. Interestingly, no priming effect emerged for primes associated with low attitude accessibility. This pattern of findings was expected on the basis of Fazio's (1989) theory, which restricts a spontaneous evaluation to attitude objects with high attitude accessibility.

In Experiment II, SOA was varied as a within-subjects factor at two levels, 300 ms and 1000 ms. The same pattern of results as in the first experiment was found at the short SOA, whereas no priming effects emerged at the longer SOA. Thus, priming effects were found with SOA 300 ms for high-accessibility primes. By analogy with semantic priming (Neely, 1991), as discussed above, the short SOA suggests that the evaluative processes involved in affective priming are automatic processes. In this experiment, facilitation dominated: there was facilitation in the order of 37 ms for targets preceded by congruent rather than neutral primes, but no significant facilitation or inhibition for incongruent prime–target pairs.

In Experiment III, finally, attitude accessibility was manipulated experimentally by having subjects repeatedly express their attitudes. Positive and negative attitude objects had been selected on the basis of previous evaluation data for high agreement about their valence between judges. The results paralleled that of Experiment II. At SOA 300 ms in particular, the size of the affective priming effect was found to be a function of attitude accessibility, so that primes for which subjects had repeatedly expressed their attitude, induced a stronger priming effect than control primes. Again, only facilitation for congruent pairs was found ($M = 74$ ms). A smaller, though significant, priming effect was, however, also observed for the control primes associated with lower attitude accessibility (again dominated by facilitation of $M = 43$ ms for congruent pairs). Presumably, the preselection of prime words with high evaluative consistency resulted in a set of stronger attitudes than realized in the previous experiments.

Replications and Extensions of the Fazio *et al.* (1986) Results

The Role of Attitude Accessibility

Since the Fazio *et al.* (1986) paper, a number of studies have confirmed and extended the basic results in different directions. Replicating the Fazio *et al.* results at SOA 300 ms, Bargh *et al.* (1992) found the affective priming effect for primes with high attitude accessibility, but not for low-accessibility primes. Apart from primes with high and low attitude accessibility, a third category of prime words was also realized. These primes were characterized by mean evaluation latencies in the middle range of the mean latency distribution (medium accessibility) as well as highly consistent positive or negative evaluations. A reliable priming effect was also induced by this kind of prime. While there was facilitation for targets preceded by affectively congruent rather than neutral primes in the studies by Fazio *et al.* (1986), the Bargh *et al.* (1992) data appear to be dominated by inhibition for incongruent prime–target pairs (in the order of 40–80 ms).

In a second experiment, Bargh *et al.* (1992) eliminated the immediately prior attitude-assessment task from the paradigm. A delay of 2 days was interpolated between the first phase of the experiment, in which prime words were selected, and the priming study itself. The priming effects for fast and consistent attitude objects were again observed and, interestingly, the interaction with prime type was no longer significant. In fact, even the attitude objects with low accessibility now gave rise to a marginally significant priming effect. The finding that attitude accessibility, as indexed by evaluation latency, plays a less pronounced role when the attitude assessment phase and the priming phase are separated in time, was further corroborated by Chaiken and Bargh (1993). Again, inhibition prevailed over facilitation in the composition of the priming effects.

The finding that priming effects are modulated by the presence of an independent first phase of the experiment is difficult to interpret. It is certainly not easily reconciled with the notion that presentation of the prime instigates an automatic, unconditional spread of activation that facilitates processing of a related target; a notion that is now being challenged even in the context of semantic priming (e.g., Smith, Besner, & Myoshi, 1994; Smith, Theodor, & Franklin, 1983). In particular, the finding is reminiscent of findings suggesting that strategies induced by different threshold-setting tasks can influence subsequent masked semantic priming (Carr & Dagenbach, 1990; Dagenbach, Carr, & Wilhelmsen, 1989).

Although it is tempting to infer a strategic component induced by the prior attitude assessment task, the conclusion may be premature. The smaller effect of attitude accessibility in the delay condition may simply reflect lack of stability of the latency measure of attitude accessibility. If the rank orders of attitude objects in terms of evaluation latency are not highly stable over a delay of 2 days, then different attitude objects are selected on the basis of attitude assessments that precede the priming task with vs. without delay. Since, according to Fazio, the *current* attitude accessibility is the decisive factor, a smaller effect of the *past* accessibility can be accommodated easily as reflecting temporal differences in accessibility rather than differences in the processes underlying the priming effect.

In a third experiment, finally, Bargh *et al.* (1992) eliminated the requirement to memorize and recite the prime word, a requirement that is somewhat unusual in the context of priming studies. Priming effects (SOA 300 ms) were found for high- and low-accessibility prime words, and they were stronger for the high-accessibility prime words. Whether or not subjects were required to memorize the prime word did not moderate these effects.

Wentura (1994) provided an independent replication of the Fazio *et al.* (1986) results at SOA 300 ms. Hermans, de Houwer, and Eelen (1994) used pictures as primes and targets selected for evaluative extremity. Employing otherwise similar procedures to Fazio *et al.* (1986), they found a priming effect at SOA 300 ms, but not at SOA 1000 ms. A subsequent attempt to extend the affective priming effect to smells as primes failed to reveal reliable priming (Hermans, 1996).

The Effects of a Concurrent Load

If, as some argue, the affective priming effect relies on automatic evaluative processes (Bargh, 1994; Pratto, 1994), a number of predictions can be inferred from the proposed automaticity: the priming effect should be quite general and unconditional; in addition it should not be effortful, that is, impose a load on limited-capacity mental resources. Hermans (1996) tested this latter prediction by comparing conditions with and without concurrent load. The load task was to remember and articulate continuously a small set of digits concurrently with a trial of the affective priming experiment. Primes and targets were substantives and adjectives, respectively, selected for evaluative extremity. Using an SOA of 300 ms and a within-subjects manipulation of the load factor, the basic priming effect was, however, not obtained even in the condition without concurrent load. In a second experiment, primes were selected for each subject individually, and in a third experiment, the load factor was manipulated between subjects. In both the latter experiments, the basic affective priming effect could again not be replicated even in the conditions without concurrent load, casting some doubt on the robustness of the basic affective priming effect. Only after SOA was shortened to 150 ms did the basic effect occur again in two final experiments of this series of five (the effects of SOA are discussed more fully below). The priming effect was not diminished under the concurrent load. Maintaining and articulating digit loads is traditionally considered to load the so-called phonological loop in Baddeley's (1986) model of working memory. The phonological loop is a component of working memory responsible for maintaining and manipulating small amounts of phonological, speech-related material. Although it is difficult to reason from null findings in a situation which is characterized by low statistical power (an interaction of the priming effect and the load factor is to be detected), it seems plausible that the phonological loop should not be involved in the making of affective priming effects.

Primes Selected on the Basis of Evaluation Norms

If the affective priming effect relies on a spontaneous evaluative response, by which any incoming stimulus is immediately classified as good or bad (Bargh, 1994; Pratto, 1994), then the effect should be quite general and unconditional. For example, it should be possible to obtain it with any evaluatively polarized word, regardless of whether or not the word is a noun and thus denotes an attitude object. From the attitude-accessibility perspective, affective priming that is based on the strength of an object–evaluation association (Fazio *et al.*, 1986) is also expected to occur for any prime word with strongly associated affective connotation.

A number of researchers have worked with prime words selected on the basis of evaluation norms. Stimulus words with high positive or negative evaluations, as indexed in normative studies, are likely to possess a strong word-evaluation association. Greenwald and co-workers (e.g., Draine & Greenwald, 1995; Greenwald, Klinger, & Liu, 1989; Greenwald, Klinger, & Schuh, 1995) employ evaluatively polarized words selected from the Belleza, Greenwald, and Banaji (1986) norms, which include verbs and adjectives. In some of Herman's (1996) experiments, primes (nouns) were selected on the basis of a separate normative study (Hermans & de Houwer, 1994). Klauer and co-workers (Klauer, Roßnagel, & Musch, 1995, 1997) compiled large sets of positive and negative adjectives selected from the lower and upper 10% of the distribution of evaluation ratings from several sets of norms (Hager & Hasselhorn, 1994). In their studies, a new random sample of primes and targets is drawn from these item pools for each subject, thereby avoiding a possible language-as-fixed-effect fallacy (Clark, 1973). The language-as-fixed-effect fallacy refers to the possibility that effects are generated by a few unusual items in a fixed stimulus set and do not generalize to the intended population of stimuli.

With SOA 500 ms and visible (as opposed to masked) primes, Greenwald, Klinger, and Liu (1989) reported an affective priming effect in two of three experiments. With SOAs ranging between 250 ms and 300 ms, on the other hand, Greenwald, Klinger, and Schuh (1995) failed to find a priming effect for visible primes in an extensive series of experiments, again casting some doubt on the generality of the affective priming effect. Results for masked primes are reviewed separately below.

The Role of SOA

One reason for the failure to obtain priming in these studies may have been related to the choice of SOAs. Klauer, Roßnagel, and Musch (1997) varied SOA between subjects and found reliable affective priming effects only for short SOA (0 ms and 100 ms), but not for SOAs longer than 100 ms, as shown in Figure 3.1, or for a negative SOA (−100 ms: the target preceded the prime). In particular, at moderately long SOAs of 200 ms and 600 ms, there was no evidence for affective priming, a result that is in line with the Greenwald, Klinger, and Schuh (1995) results. The findings of this SOA study have been corroborated by Hermans (1996) by means of a within-subjects manipulation

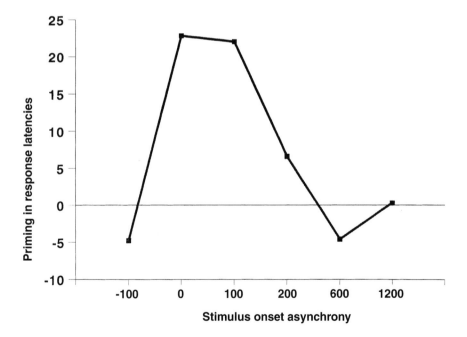

Figure 3.1 Affective priming effects as a function of stimulus onset asynchrony (SOA) (results from Klauer, Roßnagel, & Musch, 1997)

of SOA. Priming was obtained for short non-negative SOA (0 ms and 150 ms), but not for longer SOAs (300 ms and 450 ms), or for a negative SOA (–150 ms). Since a baseline of neutral word-primes was included in this study, it was possible to compare the effects of affective congruency and incongruency to the neutral baseline. Interestingly, the priming effect at SOA 0 ms reflected inhibition for affectively incongruent prime–target pairs rather than facilitation for congruent pairs.

There are many procedural differences between the studies in the tradition of Fazio *et al.* (1986) on the one hand, and the studies by Greenwald and co-workers and those by Klauer, Roßnagel, and Musch (1997) and Hermans (1996) on the other hand, and thus, it is difficult to pinpoint the cause of the discrepancies in the results. Greenwald, Kluger, and Schuh (1995) surmise the following:

> Of the various procedural differences between the present and previous studies, one that may explain this difference in findings is the present use of self-initiated trials and, following self-initiation, a fixed brief interval to onset of the prime–target sequence. This procedure was implemented with the aim of maximizing subjects' ability to attend to the stimuli. In retrospect, it may have worked too well. Other research indicates that attentional focus can suppress automatic activation (see reviews by Greenwald & Banaji, 1995; Mandler, 1994) (p. 38).

Although the studies by Klauer, Roßnagel, and Musch (1997) did not use self-initiation of trials, each trial began with a 3 s countdown, followed by a fixation point and a fixed brief interval to onset of the prime–target sequence, to maximize subjects' ability to attend to the stimuli. Similar measures were also taken by Hermans (1996).

Summary

This review of the literature reveals the following:

- Affective priming effects in the evaluative decision task are found for attitude objects with high attitude accessibility at an SOA of 300 ms, but not at 1000 ms.
- At the 300 ms SOA, priming effects can also be obtained for attitude objects selected for high agreement between judges with respect to valence (positive vs. negative).
- When attitude accessibility is assessed or experimentally manipulated immediately prior to the priming study itself, there is a moderating role of attitude accessibility, so that priming increases with increased accessibility. The moderating role may, however, be reduced or eliminated if the assessment of accessibility is separated in time from the priming study itself (but see above for interpretational problems with this result).

- Affective priming effects are also observed when primes are selected from normative studies on the basis of evaluative extremity and are not restricted to the category of nouns, although, for reasons currently unknown, the priming effects tend to occur reliably only for short SOAs (0 ms and 100 ms), but not for longer SOAs under these conditions.

Explanations for these priming effects have traditionally been adapted from explanations for semantic priming effects. In the following section, such explanations will be reviewed. An alternative account that is adapted from another related paradigm, i.e. Stroop-like interference tasks, will also be considered along with further relevant data.

EXPLANATIONS OF AFFECTIVE PRIMING EFFECTS

Explanations Adapted from Semantic Priming

In the previous section, it was shown that some progress has been made in specifying the conditions under which the affective priming effect occurs reliably. For the social psychologist, the effect is interesting as a model of how a first evaluative response unintentionally colours subsequent processing as well as a tool to studying properties of the evaluative response. For this purpose, it is essential to gain some insight into the processes that cause the affective priming effect. By adapting the detailed task- and process-analyses that have been performed in semantic priming, a rather rich set of possible theoretical mechanisms is obtained and discussed in the literature. The different mechanisms have different implications with respect to the controversial characteristics of the evaluative response, notably its controllability, and antecedent and consequent conditions. For this reason, some effort has been directed towards determining which mechanisms contribute to the observed priming effects.

Many explanations of affective priming effects advance mechanisms similar to those proposed for semantic priming. Following Neely's (1991) review of semantic priming, the explanations can be classified into automatic-spreading-activation accounts, expectancy-based mechanisms, and post-lexical mechanisms. A second, orthogonal distinction is whether the mechanism affects the ease of recognizing the target stimulus, or whether it merely affects the ease of extracting its affective connotation. In the first case, the mechanism will be termed a *stimulus-level* mechanism; in the second, an *evaluative-response* mechanism.

The mechanisms considered in the following should not be considered mutually exclusive. Rather, different processes may operate in concert to produce a complex pattern of results as suggested in current accounts of semantic priming effects (Neely, 1991).

Spreading Activation

Bower (1991), Fazio *et al.* (1986), and Murphy and Zajonc (1993) all propose similar evaluative-response mechanisms that can be couched in terms of automatic spreading activation. Roughly speaking, the evaluation of the prime stimulus is activated automatically and very quickly upon its presentation. If prime and target disagree in evaluation, the evaluative response to the prime interferes with that to the target, whereas if prime and target agree in evaluation, the evaluative response to the target is augmented: affective priming is thereby expected for any kind of task that is based on the evaluative response to the target.

The same authors also admit the possibility of a spreading-activation account at the *stimulus-level.* According to this account, activation in the node of priming word spreads to nodes linked to it directly or via intermediate nodes in a vast semantic network (Hermans *et al.*, 1994). Thereby, the time required for the activation levels to exceed recognition threshold in the activated nodes is reduced. If the spread of activation is assumed to be unlimited in capacity (Posner & Snyder, 1975), and if it is assumed that nodes of words with equal affective connotation are all linked directly or via intermediate nodes (Bower, 1991), affective priming is obtained.

Whether evaluative-response mechanism or stimulus-level account, spreading activation is assumed (a) to occur without a person's awareness or intent, and (b) to be fast-acting (Posner & Snyder, 1975; Neely, 1991). Therefore, the mechanisms employing spreading activation can explain priming with short SOAs. If the activation is assumed to be short-lived, the reduction of affective priming at longer SOAs can also be explained (Murphy & Zajonc, 1993). A moderating effect of attitude accessibility defined as the strength of the object–evaluation association is also very naturally accommodated. On the other hand, since spreading activation can explain only facilitation by related primes, the tentative findings of inhibition by unrelated primes reported above are problematic for the spreading-activation account. The pattern of facilitation and inhibition is in itself not firmly established, however, because of debate as to the appropriate realization of a baseline condition of neutral primes (Bargh *et al.*, 1992; Fazio *et al.*, 1986).

Several authors have argued against spreading-activation explanations at the stimulus-level on theoretical grounds (Bargh *et al.*, 1996; Hermans, Baeyens, & Eelen, 1995). At issue is the assumption of unlimited capacity of spreading activation. Since the number of positive and negative concepts in memory is large, a limited quantity of activation would run out in a so-called cue overload or fanning effect (Anderson & Bower, 1973) and fail to produce facilitation for every affectively related word. In fact, affective priming effects can, however, be obtained even when target words are randomly sampled from large pools of positive and negative words (Klauer, Roßnagel, & Musch, 1997), so that a spreading-activation mechanism of limited capacity seems unlikely. When the experiment involves only a few targets that are presented repeatedly, as has been the case in the tradition of the Fazio *et al.* (1986) paradigm, a modified spreading-activation account of limited capacity may, however, be possible.

Spreading-activation accounts are attractive because they are consistent with the proposed automatic character of the evaluative response and its influence on subsequent processing. In addition, the stimulus-level version implies a highly general effect of spontaneous evaluations on almost any kind of subsequent processing, whereas under the evaluative-response mechanism that influence is restricted to subsequent *evaluative* responses and judgements based on them.

Expectancy

Unlike spreading activation, expectancy is a mechanism that is assumed to be under the subject's control. Expectancy-based mechanisms assume that subjects actively form an expectancy set upon presentation of the prime that consists of potential targets in the case of stimulus-level accounts, or of the predicted evaluation of the target in the case of evaluative-response mechanisms. For example, subjects may be biased to believe that evaluatively polarized primes will be followed by evaluatively consistent targets. Thus, departing from, say, a positive prime they may bias the expected response "positive".

As was the case for spreading-activation accounts, expectancy mechanisms at the stimulus-level seem less likely, because prime and target need not be systematically related other than by affective congruency. Thus, there is little basis, in general, on which to form a small expectancy set of potential *targets* departing from the prime. Again, when only a few targets occur repeatedly in a given experiment, small expectancy sets as subsets of the target set might, however, be formed, on the basis of affective congruency.

Unlike automatic-spreading activation, expectancy-based mechanisms are assumed (a) to be under the subject's strategic and intentional control, and (b) to be relatively slow-acting (Neely, 1991; Posner & Snyder, 1975). In the context of affective priming, an explicit, though untested, assumption is in fact that an SOA of 300 ms is "too brief an interval to permit subjects to develop an active expectancy or response strategy regarding the target adjective that follows; such conscious and flexible expectancies require at least 500 ms to develop and to influence responses in priming tasks" (Bargh, *et al.*, 1992, p. 894; cf., Fazio *et al.*, 1986; Hermans, de Houwer & Eelen, 1994).

Expectancy and List-context Effects

The 300 ms threshold has been a central assumption in interpreting affective priming effects: Since affective priming effects are obtained with an SOA of

300 ms and smaller SOAs, they must rely on automatic processes rather than on active strategies on the part of the subject. The 300 ms threshold is based on the temporal characteristics of list-context effects such as the relatedness proportion effect in semantic priming. The relatedness proportion refers to the proportion of semantically related word-primes and word-targets. The well-known relatedness proportion effect is the phenomenon that the magnitude of semantic priming effects increases as the relatedness proportion increases. The effect is obtained at prime-target SOAs longer than 500 ms (de Groot, 1984; den Heyer, 1985; den Heyer, Briand, & Dannenbring, 1983; Neely, Keefe, & Ross, 1989; and others), and is decreased or eliminated at prime-target SOAs of 250 ms or less (de Groot, 1984; den Heyer, Briand, & Dannenbring, 1983; Stolz & Neely, 1995). It is assumed to reflect the operation of slow-acting, controlled processes in the form of expectancy-based strategies or postlexical mechanisms (discussed below).

The 300 ms threshold, derived by analogy from the semantic priming results, may be too high a threshold for the operation of strategies in the affective priming paradigm. A number of researchers have argued that affective information may be more quickly activated than the kind of semantic information upon which semantic priming is based (e.g., Bargh et al., 1989; Zajonc, 1980). Klauer, Roßagel, & Musch (1997) attempted an explicit test based on the analogy with the semantic priming paradigm and with the relatedness proportion effect in particular.

In the context of affective priming, the proportion of evaluatively consistent prime–target pairs can be varied. Similar to the relatedness proportion, the consistency proportion (CP) can thus be considered. A high CP is given if mostly evaluatively consistent prime–target pairs (both prime and target positive or both negative) are presented. Conversely, the CP is low if mostly inconsistent pairs (one of prime and target positive, the other negative) are shown. When there are as many consistent as inconsistent pairs, CP is 50%, which is the level realized in most studies. A *CP effect* would be given if the size of affecting priming effects increased with increasing CP.

A possible CP effect would flow most naturally from an expectancy-based evaluative-response mechanism: subjects may use the prime to predict the evaluation of the target. They would do so on the basis of their impression of the proportion of evaluatively consistent, relative to inconsistent, pairs: When CP is high (low), the evaluation of the target is likely to be the same as (the opposite of) that of the prime. Subjects may use their predictions to prepare for the expected response to the target. For example, responders might be biased toward the key-press that is more likely to follow the prime given the CP. The evaluative decision would thereby be facilitated if the decision-maker's prediction is met.

In several experiments, we varied both SOA (0 ms, 200 ms, 1200 ms) and CP (0.25, 0.50, 0.75) between subjects. Figures 3.2 and 3.3 show the major

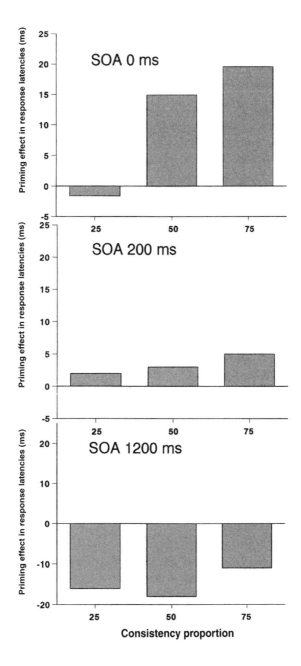

Figure 3.2   Affective priming effects in response latencies as a function of consistency proportioning. SOA = stimulus onset asynchrony

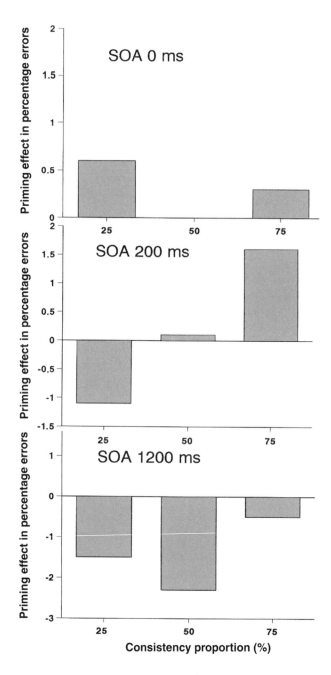

Figure 3.3 Affective priming effects in percentage errors as a function of consistency proportion. SOA = stimulus onset asynchrony

results. A consistency proportion effect emerged in the latency data (see Figure 3.2). As shown in the uppermost panel, the effect was strongest at SOA 0 ms, i.e., with simultaneous presentation of prime and target, whereas at longer SOAs, the effect was not found. At SOA 200 ms, a CP effect occurred in the error data, however, as shown in the middle panel of Figure 3.3. At SOA 1200 ms, where traditional wisdom would expect the strongest CP effect (Neely, 1991), both latency and error data were dominated by reversed priming effects, irrespective of CP; that is, responses to targets preceded by evaluatively inconsistent rather than consistent primes were facilitated.

This pattern of finding runs contrary to what had been expected on the basis of the analogy that is often drawn between semantic priming and affective priming. It suggests that strategic factors operate in affective priming even when prime and target are presented simultaneously. Thus, the 300 ms threshold for the operation of active strategies may be wrong.

The particular strategy underlying the CP effect is, however, probably not an expectancy-based response strategy. It is unlikely that subjects first encode the prime and then generate an expectation about the likely response to the target when prime and target are presented simultaneously. Neither can the effect be explained by slow-acting postlexical relatedness-checking mechanisms (Neely, 1991; see below). Thus, some other kind of mechanism than those considered in the context of semantic priming must be at work. One possibility is a sequential effect (Greenwald, Draine, & Abrams, 1996) as discussed by Klauer, Roßnagel, and Musch (1997). Another possibility is discussed below.

Postlexical Mechanisms

A final, somewhat heterogeneous, class of mechanisms considered for semantic priming has been termed "postlexical" (Neely, 1991). Typically, prime and target are assumed to be evaluated for relatedness or familiarity (de Groot, 1984; Neely & Keefe, 1989; Ratcliff & McKoon, 1981). An impression of relatedness or familiarity, as the case may be, may bias subsequent decisions. For example, subjects may be biased toward "yes" responses in binary decision tasks.

In the context of affective priming, Klauer and Stern (1992) have proposed a postlexical, evaluative-response mechanism. According to Klauer and Stern, the affective connotation of prime and target will be accessed automatically and quickly and will be evaluated equally fast for evaluative consistency. In this model, information about the evaluative consistency of a given pair of words is thus available quickly and may bias subsequent responses. In particular, evaluative consistency is assumed to give rise to a feeling of plausibility that may facilitate making an affirmative response even on the basis of only preliminary evidence, whereas a feeling of implausibility in the case of evaluative inconsistency may lead the person to reconsider and reconfirm the available evidence before responding positively, and vice versa for negative responses. This model thus predicts affective priming in most tasks requiring a response to the target; responses such as pronouncing presented words are classified as (implicitly) affirmative unless avoidance or rejection of targets is explicitly required.

The model can explain affective priming with short SOAs, and it can accommodate the absence of priming at longer SOAs, if it is assumed that prime and target are no longer processed as a pair, given long SOAs, but as distinct events. To the extent to which the activation of the evaluation of the prime is a function of attitude accessibility, a moderating role of accessibility can be explained. To account for the CP effect, it would have to be assumed that the association of evaluative consistency with plausibility is sensitive to the list-context, so that in a list with mostly inconsistent pairs, evaluative *inconsistency* will eventually become associated with a feeling of plausibility in a possibly implicit learning process.

Recently, Wentura (1996) has performed an explicit test of this model, using the lexical decision task. In that task, targets comprise both words and non-words. The subjects' task is to respond "yes" if the target is a word and "no" otherwise. If affective (in)consistency of prime and target biases subjects toward the ("no"-)"yes"-response in this binary decision task, affective priming effects for word-targets are expected and were in fact obtained. In an ingenious subsequent experiment, the assignment of "yes"-responses to words and non-words was varied. For the "word = yes"-condition, the affective priming effect emerged, whereas the data pattern was *reversed* for the "word = no"-condition. Thus, "no"-responses to word-targets preceded by evaluatively inconsistent (rather than consistent) primes were now made faster. The effects were only marginally significant, however. Analogous results were reported by Klauer and Stern (1992) using a different task.

Like spreading-activation models at the stimulus-level, the postlexical model is attractive in that it predicts affective priming in a wide variety of tasks including those that do not involve an explicit evaluative component such as the lexical decision task. As illustrated by the Wentura (1996) study, it is even more flexible than spreading activation in that it may also predict reversed priming effects under certain circumstances.

An Explanation Adapted from the Stroop Paradigm

Although, as we have seen, affective priming has most often been likened to semantic priming, a more appropriate point of reference may be given by Stroop-like selective attention paradigms. For example, in the "flanker" task (Eriksen & Eriksen, 1974), there are two response sets of stimuli; people are presented with a row of letters and asked to concentrate attention on the letter in the centre and to ignore simultaneously presented flanker letters on both sides of it. They are instructed to press one response key if the centre letter belongs to one set of targets (e.g., A and B) and another response key if the centre letter comes from another set of targets (e.g., C and D). Although subjects are instructed to ignore flanker letters, their response times show that they cannot do so completely. Specifically, flankers that belong to the same response set as the centre letter (e.g., BAB) speed the response, but flankers from the wrong response set (e.g., CAC) slow the response.

In the evaluative decision task, there are also two response sets, i.e., the set of positive words and the set of negative words. The evaluative decision task requires subjects to respond differently to words from these sets. Irrelevant flankers, which correspond to the prime words in this analogy, interfere with making the response to the target if flanker and target stem from different response sets, that is, if both are affectively inconsistent in the present case.

There are a number of similarities between the pattern of findings obtained with the evaluative decision task and the findings obtained with Stroop paradigms. In Stroop analogues, as in the evaluative decision task, effects are typically found only for short SOAs (MacLeod, 1991), but not for long SOAs. In addition, list-context effects such as the CP effect occur with short SOAs and even with simultaneous presentation of distractor (prime) and target (MacLeod, 1991). Finally, relative to neutral baseline conditions, both facilitation and inhibition are observed as in the evaluative decision task (although, as has been said, there is a debate concerning the appropriate baseline prime in affective priming).

Logan and Zbrodoff (1979; see also Logan, 1980, and cf., Cohen, Dunbar, & McClelland, 1990) have proposed an explanation of Stroop effects that can be readily adapted to the evaluative decision task. According to Logan and Zbrodoff, the decision-maker's current state of evidence bearing on the evaluative decision is expressed as a weighted sum of the evidence available about the *affective connotation* of the target and that of the prime. Weights that represent automatic processing are fixed in magnitude and sign, whereas additional weights that represent attending to primes and targets may vary in magnitude and sign according to the current strategy to allow a flexible blending of information.

Dividing attention between prime and target amounts to computing and assigning weights to each through an act of attention. The weights would have the same sign (both positive), when consistent prime–target pairs were more frequent, and opposite signs, positive for target, negative for prime, when inconsistent prime–target pairs were more frequent, accounting for the CP effect (Logan & Zbrodoff, 1979). The evaluation of the prime might be processed automatically as well and receive additional weight in the decision process.

Thus, as in models of semantic priming, the eventual decision is an additive outcome of both automatic and attentional processes. Since prime and target are processed in parallel, however, the attentional component can be effective even with simultaneous presentation of primes and targets.

Departing from the Stroop hypothesis, Wentura (1996) looked for a very specific sequential effect that is characteristically found in experiments on Stroop tasks as a kind of signature of Stroop interference in affective priming. Specifically, evaluative inconsistency of prime and target in trial $n-1$ should result in an inhibition of the response to the target in trial n if the target is affectively congruent with the prime of trial $n-1$ (MacLeod, 1991). This prediction was confirmed in an ingenious experiment using the evaluative decision task, lending strong support to Stroop interference as one mechanism contributing to the making of the affective priming effect.

In this as well as in other theoretical accounts of Stroop analogues, interference presupposes an asymmetry in relative speed of processing or, alternatively, in automaticity of processing between two competing stimuli (Posner & Snyder, 1975). An irrelevant stimulus has the potential of interfering with target stimuli if it is processed faster or at least as fast as the target. Analogously, according to the automaticity view, a conflicting dimension requiring less or at most the same amount of attentional processing resources as the target dimension interferes with reporting that dimension. Both relative speed of processing and automaticity can easily accommodate a moderating role of attitude accessibility, defined as the strength of the object–evaluation association.

Absolute levels of automaticity and speed of processing may also explain why effects analogous to those of affective priming are often not found for dimensions other than evaluation. For example, Hermans (1996) reports no priming for size decisions (small vs. large) and symmetry decisions (symmetrical vs. asymmetrical) when primes are congruent rather than incongruent on these physical dimensions. Size and symmetry may not be strongly associated with the objects in memory, and therefore may fail to be activated spontaneously upon presentation of primes to produce Stroop-like interference. For gender decisions on Christian names, on the other hand, Draine and Greenwald (1995) report similar priming effects as for evaluative decisions on evaluatively polarized words. Gender is usually strongly associated with most Christian names.

Summary

Existing explanations for affective priming effects in the evaluative decision task were reviewed and evaluated on empirical and theoretical grounds. Each mechanism was discussed in a stimulus-level variant as well as in an evaluative-response variant. A distinction was drawn between:

- Spreading-activation accounts.
- Expectancy-based mechanisms.
- Postlexical mechanisms.

A CP effect was reported to show that strategic components in affective priming are effective below an SOA of 300 ms and even with simultaneous presentation of primes and targets. Neither spreading-activation accounts nor expectancy-based mechanisms can fully explain the pattern of findings. The postlexical model of Klauer and Stern (1992) could, however, be adapted to account for the data considered so far.

Prompted by the temporal characteristics of the CP effect, the relationship to another class of related paradigms, Stroop-like tasks, was explored in some depth. Theories advanced to account for Stroop interference can be readily adapted to the affective priming paradigm. They succeed in explaining the reviewed data, including the CP effect, in a simple fashion. The account in terms of Stroop-like response interference is restricted to tasks based on *evaluative* responses to the targets, however.

Both theories adapted from semantic priming as well as theories of Stroop interference assume that processing reflects a mix of automatic and strategic components. Given that strategic components have been found in affective priming with simultaneous presentation of primes and targets, there is, however, little direct evidence to support the contribution of an automatic process. Such evidence could be obtained from studies involving masked primes as well as from studies using tasks other than the evaluative decision task. I review results from both types of studies in the following two sections.

AFFECTIVE PRIMING WITH MASKED STIMULI

The existence of an automatic component in affective priming is strongly suggested by findings of priming effects when primes are presented under conditions that prevent awareness of the presence of the prime words. Greenwald, Klinger, and Liu (1989) report three experiments in which primes were masked dichoptically by presentation of a random letter-fragment pattern to the dominant eye, either rapidly following the prime (Experiment 1) or simultaneously with the prime (Experiments 2 and 3). The effectiveness of the masking procedure was demonstrated by the subjects' inability to discriminate the left vs. right position of a test series of words viewed under the same masking conditions as the prime stimuli in the priming task. In all three experiments, significant masked priming effects were nevertheless obtained. Hermans (1996), on the other hand, failed to obtain affective priming in three studies for different kinds of stimuli (pictures and words) and masking procedures including those successfully employed previously by Greenwald, Klinger, and Liu (1989).

Studies of unconscious cognition often examine effects of marginally perceptible stimuli on actions the subject is instructed to perform (direct effects), while concurrently observing uninstructed (indirect) effects that are interpreted as likely indicators of unconscious semantic activation (Greenwald & Draine, in press). For example, in the experiments by Greenwald, Klinger, and Liu (1992), the direct effect is assessed by the position-discrimination task, whereas indirect effects of prime words were the priming effects.

The interpretation of a given set of data as demonstrating unconscious processing of prime words is beset by several methodological and logical difficulties. To demonstrate the absence of direct effects, it is necessary to accept a null hypothesis, which is problematic statistically (Reingold & Merikle, 1988). In addition, it has been argued that both direct and indirect measures may be influenced by conscious as well as unconscious stimulus effects (Greenwald, Klinger, & Schuh, 1995), rendering any pattern of data difficult to interpret. Some minimal assumptions about the sensitivity of direct and indirect measures for conscious stimulus effects are necessary (Reingold & Merikle, 1988).

Recently, Greenwald, Klinger, & Schuh (1995) have proposed a new method to overcome some of these problems in demonstrating unconscious processing. At the heart of the method is a regression analysis, in which an indirect measure is regressed on a comparable direct measure.

Using the new method, Greenwald, Klinger, & Schuh (1995) failed to obtain evidence for masked affective priming with SOAs between 250 ms and 300 ms. Rather, there were some indications of priming only to the extent to which there was also evidence for direct effects, indicating that priming depended upon some amount of conscious processing of the primes.

With a smaller SOA of 67 ms and masked primes presented for 17 ms or 33 ms, Draine and Greenwald (in press) did, however, obtain evidence for masked affective priming. In these studies, indirect effects were assessed by a measure of affective priming effects in the error data (latencies had been experimentally constrained to fall within a narrow experimenter-defined response window, i.e., a time band that occurred earlier than subjects would ordinarily respond). Direct effects were assessed by subjects' ability to discriminate between prime words and letter strings of alternating Xs and Gs viewed under the same conditions as those used in the priming task.

The latter results suggest that the desired pattern of indirect effects without direct effects may be given for affective priming with short SOA, pointing to an automatic component in the making of affective priming effects in the evaluative decision task. As has been said, however, the conclusion relies on a number of substantive assumptions. There is also a statistical problem with the new method proposed by Greenwald, Klinger, and Schuh (1995) that makes necessary some modifications of the statistical analyses (Klauer, Draine, & Greenwald, 1997).

If the results obtained with the new regression method can be consolidated by more appropriate statistical analyses, however, the findings reported by

Draine and Greenwald (in press) in particular suggest that there may be activation of the affective connotation of prime words, even when awareness and indeed perceptibility of prime words is low.

AFFECTIVE PRIMING WITH OTHER TASKS

A number of studies have employed other tasks than the evaluative decision task introduced by Fazio *et al.* (1986). One purpose has been to explore the generality of the affective priming effect (Bargh, 1994). In particular, an important question is whether affective priming occurs even when subjects are not required to evaluate the stimuli. Based on detailed task analyses in the domain of semantic priming, different tasks have also been used to test hypotheses about the mechanisms underlying the affective priming effect. A third category of studies using tasks other than the evaluative decision aims at establishing affective priming as a causal factor in social psychological phenomena such as stereotyping and judgemental biases.

In the context of affective priming, the lexical decision task removes the association of subjects' responses with the affective connotation of the target that is present in the evaluative decision task, thereby rendering evaluative-response mechanisms based on spreading activation expectancy, as well as on the Stroop analogy, ineffective. Both the lexical decision task and the pronunciation task have, furthermore, also been argued to make the evaluative aspects of the stimulus material less obtrusive, thereby lowering the probability of active strategies based on the evaluative contents of stimulus words.

The Lexical Decision Task

Using the lexical decision task, and SOAs of 50 ms, 500 ms, and 1250 ms, Hill and Kemp-Wheeler (1989) found a facilitative effect of negative primes, relative to neutral word primes, on lexical decisions about negative targets. One limitation of this study is that only negative and neutral words were used. Thus, the crucial prime-valence × target-valence interaction that defines affective priming cannot be shown. For example, it is possible, in principle, that the same effect of prime type would have been observed on *positive* targets if any had been realized. Affective priming requires the effect of prime type to be moderated by target valence, however. Wentura (1996), on the other hand, also reports affective priming in the lexical decision task in a study modelled more closely after the Fazio *et al.* (1986) paradigm.

As discussed above, Wentura (1996) has provided suggestive evidence for the involvement of a postlexical relatedness-checking mechanism in affective priming with the lexical decision task. This is also compatible with the following findings. With masked presentation of primes, Kemp-Wheeler and Hill

(1992) obtained only mixed evidence for affective priming. Presenting primes which are rendered difficult to detect presumably makes the use of postlexical checking mechanisms impossible. Similarly, Casaer (1993) failed to find affective priming effects in a single-presentation lexical-decision task, in which stimuli are presented one by one and a lexical decision has to be made for each stimulus. Like priming with masked primes, the single presentation lexical decision task has been argued to rely only on automatic processes (McNamara & Altarriba, 1988; Shelton & Martin, 1992).

The Pronunciation Task

Several studies have looked at affective priming in the pronunciation task. In the context of semantic priming, a number of findings suggest that the pronunciation task may be a relatively pure gauge of the contribution of spreading activation when SOA is short (Neely, 1991).

Hermans, de Houwer and Eelen (1994) used the pronunciation task in an affective priming study with SOA 300 ms that otherwise closely followed the tradition of Fazio *et al.* (1986) (but without the memory word instruction for primes and without attitude accessibility as an experimental factor). Primes (20 nouns and 10 non-word letter strings such as BBB) and targets (30 adjectives) were selected on the basis of evaluation norms, and so there was no first phase of attitude assessment in this study. A priming effect emerged. Relative to the baseline of non-word primes, there were approximately equal amounts of facilitation by congruent primes and inhibition by incongruent primes. Recall that spreading activation predicts only facilitation, so that the presence of inhibition implies the operation of additional processes. As has been said, the appropriateness of non-word letter strings as a neutral baseline condition is contested, however.

Similar results were reported by Bargh *et al.* (1996). In three studies, they consistently found affective priming in the pronunciation task. Priming occurred for primes associated with low and high attitude accessibility alike, whether accessibility was determined in a first attitude assessment phase of the study (Experiment 1), or on the basis of normative data (Experiments 2 and 3). In their Experiment 3, a different set of targets was chosen. Nouns rather than adjectives were used, and they were selected to be only moderately positive and negative according to the Bellezza, Greenwald and Banaji (1986) norms. Bargh *et al.* (1996) do not report mean latencies for targets preceded by neutral (letter-string) primes. Thus, their priming effects cannot be decomposed into facilitative and inhibitive components.

In a subsequent study, Hermans (1996) varied SOA with levels −150 ms, 0 ms, 150 ms, 300 ms and 400 ms within subjects. Affective priming effects were found at none of these SOA levels. In an additional attempt to replicate the priming effect in pronunciation, Hermans (1996) used fewer SOA levels, 150 ms, 300 ms and 1000 ms, and obtained a tendency for an overall affective priming effect. In individual tests, the priming effect was significant at 150 ms.

The studies by Hermans, de Houwer and Eelens (1996), Hermans (1996), and Bargh *et al.* (1996), like many studies in the context of affective priming, use small pools of prime and target words, which are then presented repeatedly. Apart from possible language-as-fixed effect fallacies (Clark, 1973), the repeated presentation of the same words may support the use of expectancy strategies or postlexical checking and mechanisms, as considered above. The roles of target- and prime-set size were explicitly addressed in a recent study in our own laboratory.

The pronunciation task and large pools of strongly positive and strongly negative adjectives were used. Different sets of targets and primes were selected for each subject from these pools. Target-set size as well as prime-set size were varied between subjects in three and two steps, respectively. The target set could consist of one positive and one negative adjective, or of five positive and five negative adjectives, or of 50 positive and 50 negative adjectives, in which case the subject never saw the same target twice. Orthogonally, the prime set could consist of either five positive and five negative adjectives, or 50 positive and 50 negative adjectives. Target set and prime set were always disjoint, that is, they contained different words. Presentation of prime-target pairs closely followed the Bargh *et al.* (1996) procedures; in particular, SOA was 300 ms. Nevertheless, there were no priming effects in terms of response latencies in any of the six experimental groups of 30 subjects each.

While Bargh *et al.* (1996) report that there were no incorrect responses in their experiment, a few pronunciation errors were made by most subjects in our studies. An analysis of the error data did reveal some evidence for affective priming, moderated by target set size. When target set size was small ($n = 2$), there was affective priming. As target set size increased, priming effects in the error data decreased.

Miscellaneous Other Tasks

Affective priming effects and related effects have also been observed in a number of other tasks (e.g., Dovidio, Evans, & Tyler, 1986; Klauer & Stern, 1992; Niedenthal, 1990; Perdue *et al.*, 1990; Wyer & Srull, 1980). Many of these have been concerned with demonstrating the importance of affective priming as a mechanism in causing judgemental biases in the context of racial stereotypes, ingroup bias and halo errors, as discussed in the introduction.

Murphy and Zajonc (1993; cf. Murphy, Monahan, & Zajonc, 1995) used slides of angry and happy faces as negative and positive primes, respectively, in an often-cited series of experiments. These were presented for a duration of either 4 ms or 2000 ms, immediately followed by an unfamiliar Chinese ideograph. The subjects' task was to judge the likeability of the ideograph. The judgements were found to be influenced by the affective primes when presentation was suboptimal (4 ms) even though subjects claimed not to have been aware of the primes. When primes were presented for 2000 ms, on the other hand, the affective priming of the ratings of targets was eliminated.

The pattern of findings is clearly in line with the SOA results obtained with more standard paradigms. Having used neutral targets, the present studies may, however, be more appropriately classified as evaluative-conditioning studies rather than as affective-priming studies, as discussed in the introduction. They describe situations in which affect from one source is transferred to another, previously neutral, source, rather than a situation in which processing is facilitated by the presentation of preceding irrelevant, but affectively congruent, material. An interesting open question is whether evaluative conditioning itself contributes to affective priming effects.

SUMMARY AND CONCLUSIONS

A traditional assumption in social psychology has been that evaluation is a conscious judgemental process based on the implications of descriptive information. Anderson's (1974) information integration theory is probably the most explicit example of these approaches. In contrast, recent work in social cognition suggests that all incoming information is automatically classified as good vs. bad at a preconscious level, suggesting extensive evaluative processes that occur outside of awareness, with minimal effort, and in the absence of deliberate attempts to form evaluative judgements. This has important implications for the role of evaluative processes, the role of consciousness, the nature of judgement and a host of related issues that are important for social psychological theorizing about attitudes, person perception and stereotyping. It is also argued that these preconscious processes influence the allocation of attention, the encoding and storage of information, the construal of the immediate situation and, via this construal, individuals' behaviour.

These claims require careful examination, and in recent years a number of simple paradigms have been adapted from cognitive psychology to the study of evaluative processes. In particular, selective-attention studies and priming studies have been performed using evaluatively polarized stimuli. Results have often been taken to suggest the operation of an automatic evaluation process, sometimes termed the evaluative response, by which any incoming stimulus is quickly and spontaneously evaluated as good or bad (Bargh, 1994; Pratto, 1994). Others have assumed the spontaneous evaluation to occur only to the extent to which the object–evaluation association is strong (Fazio et al., 1986). This controversy has important conceptual implications for the general issues raised above and for the nature of attitudes in particular.

In this paper, I have reviewed data and theory for affective priming effects. Priming effects have been found in different studies using somewhat different procedures and different material. Studies employing the evaluative decision task have found affective priming effects at short SOAs, but not at long SOAs, although results differ in the size of the SOAs at which priming is still obtained reliably. The size of the affective priming effect is moderated by attitude accessibility, if attitude accessibility is assessed or manipulated immediately prior to the priming study.

In a review of theoretical accounts of affective priming, different mechanisms were discussed. Expectancy-based mechanisms, in which subjects form an expectancy about targets departing from the prime, were rendered unlikely by the finding of a consistency proportion effect at short SOA and indeed with simultaneous presentation of primes and targets. The CP effect, suggesting a strategic component operative even at very short SOAs, questions the assumption frequently met in the affective priming literature that an SOA of 300 ms is too brief an interval to permit subjects to employ an active strategy. Thereby, it also renders suspect any claim of automaticity of affective priming, based on short SOA.

A stronger case for an automatic process in the making of affective priming effects in the evaluative decision task stems from studies using masked primes. Presumably, strategic elements are minimized when perceptibility of and awareness of the primes are prevented. A new regression method, developed by Greenwald, Klinger, and Schuh (1995), holds great promise in securing unconscious processing of the affective connotation of primes. Recent data obtained with that method indicate that at least at very short SOAs below 100 ms, an automatic process may contribute to affective priming in the evaluative decision task (Draine & Greenwald, 1995; Greenwald, Draine, & Abrams, 1995).

In the context of semantic priming, the pronunciation task with short SOA has been argued to provide a particularly pure operationalization of spreading activation. Spreading activation at the stimulus level has, however, been questioned on theoretical grounds as a possible explanation of affective priming as discussed more fully above. The reason is that the sets of positive and negative concepts stored in memory are simply too large to make a spread of activation from one member to all other members of the set plausible. A modified spreading-activation account may be possible, however, for affective priming studies that use only small sets of primes and targets viewed repeatedly by subjects.

A number of studies have employed the pronunciation task and have found only mixed evidence for affective priming effects. Given the potential theoretical relevance of an affective priming effect in the pronunciation task, further research to identify the crucial differences between studies showing effects and those revealing no or little priming is highly desirable.

The temporal characteristics of the CP effect in affective priming prompted the argument that a more appropriate point of reference than the semantic priming paradigm may be the Stroop task and related tasks. An explanation of Stroop interference in Stroop analogues was adapted to affective priming in the evaluative decision task and was found to accommodate the major findings quite well. The assumption that affective priming should be likened to Stroop interference rather than to semantic priming immediately leads to a wealth of additional hypotheses based on the robust empirical findings associated with Stroop analogues (MacLeod, 1991). Wentura (1996) has taken a successful first step in examining such hypotheses as discussed above.

Where does all this leave us in terms of the ubiquitous and unconditional evaluative response and its hypothesized far-reaching influence? The different lines of research discussed in this chapter converge on the conclusion that a possible evaluative response may be of rather smaller importance than has initially been thought: the evaluative response appears to be effective for only a short time, as suggested by the SOA results, and its influence appears to be very easily disrupted by almost any kind of subsequent processing. Thus, as discussed by Devine (1989) in the context of racial stereotypes, it seems likely that people can easily correct for spontaneous, but in the present case rather fragile and weak, judgemental and behavioural tendencies induced by the evaluative response through subsequent controlled processing (cf. Murphy & Zajonc, 1993).

From an evolutionary point of view, the adaptive function of the evaluative response has been argued to be to recognize opportunities and threats in the environment. On the other hand, one of the major evolutionary achievements of the human race has been argued to be the ability to ignore the immediate hedonic consequences of given situations and to act instead according to long-term goals. Following this line of reasoning, it is equally adaptive that the evaluative response, if it occurs, is quickly suppressed, if immediate action is not required.

ACKNOWLEDGEMENT

Preparation of this chapter was supported by grants K1 614/4–1 and K1 614/4–2 from the Deutsche Forschungsgemeinschaft to the author.

REFERENCES

Anderson, N. H. (1974). Information integration theory: A brief survey. In D. H. Krantz, R. C. Atkinson, R. D. Luce & P. Suppes (Eds), *Contemporary Developments in Mathematical Psychology*. San Francisco, CA: Freeman.

Anderson, J. R., & Bower, G. H. (1973). *Human Associative Memory*. Washington, DC: V. H. Winston.

Arnold, M. B. (1960). *Emotion and Personality* (Vol. 1): *Psychological Aspects*. New York: Columbia University Press.

Baddeley, A. D. (1986). *Working Memory*. Oxford: Oxford University Press.

Bargh, J. A. (1994). The four horsemen of automaticity: Awareness, intention, efficiency, and control in social cognition. In R. S. Wyer & T. K. Srull (Eds), *Handbook of Social Cognition* (Vol. 1, pp. 1–40). Hillsdale, NJ: Erlbaum.

Bargh, J. A., Chaiken, Sh., Govender, R., & Pratto, F. (1992). The generality of the automatic attitude activation effect. *Journal of Personality and Social Psychology*, **62**, 893–912.

Bargh, J. A., Chaiken, Sh., Raymond, P., & Hymes, C. (1996). The automatic evaluation effect: Unconditional automatic attitude activation with a pronunciation task. *Journal of Experimental Social Psychology*, **32**, 104–128.

Bargh, J. A., Litt, J., Pratto, F., & Spielman, L. A. (1989). On the preconscious evaluation of social stimuli. In A. E. Bennett & K. M. McConkey (Eds), *Cognition on Individual and Social Contexts* (pp. 357–70). Amsterdam: Elsevier.

Bellezza, F. S., Greenwald, A. G., & Banaji, M. R. (1986). Words high and low in pleasantness as rated by male and female college students. *Behavior Research Methods, Instruments, & Computers*, **18**, 299–303.

Bower, G. H. (1991). Mood congruity of social judgments. In J. Forgas (Ed.), *Emotion and Social Judgments* (pp. 31–53). Oxford: Pergamon.

Carr, Th. H., & Dagenbach, D. (1990). Semantic priming and repetition priming from masked words: Evidence for a center-surround attentional mechanism in perceptual recognition. *Journal of Experimental Psychology: Learning, Memory, and Cognition*, **16**, 341–50.

Casaer, S. (1993). *Emotional Priming: Evidence from a Lexical Decision Task*. Poster presented at the Xth General Meeting of the European Association of Experimental Social Psychology. Lisbon: Cosmos.

Chaiken, S. & Bargh, J. A. (1993). Occurrence versus moderation of the automatic attitude activation effect: Reply to Fazio. *Journal of Personality and Social Psychology*, **64**, 759–65.

Clark, H. (1973). The language-as-fixed-effect fallacy: A critique of language statistics in psychological research. *Journal of Verbal Learning and Verbal Behaviour*, **12**, 335–9.

Cohen, J. D., Dunbar, K., & McClelland, J. L. (1990). On the control of automatic processes: A parallel distributed processing account of the Stroop effect. *Psychological Review*, **97**, 332–361.

Dagenbach, D., Carr, T. H., & Wilhelmsen, A. (1989). Task-induced strategies and near-threshold priming: Conscious effects on unconscious perception. *Journal of Memory and Language*, **28**, 412–43.

de Groot, A. M. B. (1984). Primed lexical decision: Combined effects of the proportion of related prime-target pairs and the stimulus-onset asynchrony of prime and target. *Quarterly Journal of Experimental Psychology*, **36A**, 253–80.

de Houwer, J., Baeyens, F., & Eelen, P. (1994). Verbal evaluative conditioning with undetected US presentation. *Behaviour Research and Therapy*, **32**, 629–33.

den Heyer, K. (1985). On the nature of the proportion effect in semantic priming. *Acta Psychologica*, **60**, 25–38.

den Heyer, K., Briand, K., & Dannenbring, G. (1983). Strategic factors in a lexical decision task: Evidence for automatic and attention-driven processes. *Memory & Cognition*, **11**, 374–81.

Devine, P. G. (1989). Stereotypes and prejudice: Their automatic and controlled components. *Journal of Personality and Social Psychology,* **56**, 5–18.

Dovidio, J. F., Evans, N., & Tyler, R. B. (1986). Racial stereotypes: The contents of their cognitive representations. *Journal of Experimental Social Psychology,* **22**, 22–37.

Draine, S. C., & Greenwald, A. G. (in press). Replicable unconscious semantic priming. *Journal of Experimental Psychology: General.*

Eriksen, B. A., & Eriksen, C. W. (1974). Effects of noise letters upon the identification of a target letter in a nonsearch task. *Perception and Psychophysics,* **16**, 143–9.

Fazio, R. H. (1989). On the power and functionality of attitudes: The role of attitude accessibility. In A. R. Pratkanis, S. J. Breckler & A. G. Greenwald (Eds), *Attitude Structure and Function.* Hillsdale, NJ: Erlbaum.

Fazio, R. H., Sanbonmatsu, D. M., Powell, M. C., & Kardes, F. R. (1986). On the automatic activation of attitudes. *Journal of Personality and Social Psychology,* **50**, 229–38.

Forgas, J. P. (1994). The role of emotion in social judgments: An introductory review and an Affect Infusion Model (AIM). *European Journal of Social Psychology,* **24**, 1–24.

Greenwald, A. G., & Banaji, M. R. (1995). Implicit social cognition: Attitudes, self-esteem, and stereotypes. *Psychological Review,* **102**, 4–27.

Greenwald, A. G., & Draine, S. C. (in press). Do subliminal stimuli enter the mind unnoticed? Tests with a new method. In J. Cohen & J. Schooler (Eds), *25th Carnegie Symposium on Cognition: Scientific Approaches to the Question of Consciousness* (pp. 83–108). Hillsdale, NJ: Erlbaum.

Greenwald, A. G., Draine, S. C., & Abrams, R. L. (1996). Three cognitive markers of unconscious semantic activation. *Science,* **273**, 1699–1702.

Greenwald, A. G., Klinger, M. R., & Liu, Th. J. (1989). Unconscious processing of dichoptically masked words. *Memory & Cognition,* **17**, 35–47.

Greenwald, A. G., Klinger, M. R., & Schuh, E. (1995). Activation by marginally perceptible ("subliminal") stimuli: Dissociation of unconscious from conscious cognition. *Journal of Experimental Psychology: General,* **124**, 22–42.

Greenwald, A. G., & Rosenberg, K. E. (1978). Sequential effects of distracting stimuli in a selective attention reaction time task. In J. Requin (Ed.), *Attention and Performance* (Vol. VII, pp. 487–504). Hillsdale, NJ: Erlbaum.

Hager, W., & Hasselhorn, M. (1994). *Handbuch deutschsprachiger Wortnormen* (Handbook of German word norms). Göttingen: Hogrefe.

Hansen, C. F., & Hansen, R. D. (1988). Finding the face in the crowd: An anger superiority effect. *Journal of Personality and Social Psychology,* **54**, 917–24.

Heider, F. (1944). Social perception and phenomenal causality. *Psychological Review,* **51**, 358–78.

Heider, F. (1958). *The Psychology of Interpersonal Relations.* New York: Wiley.

Hermans, D. (1996). Automatische stimulusevaluatie. Een experimentele analyse van de voorwaarden voor evaluatieve stimulusdiscriminatie aan de hand van het affectieve-primingparadigma (Automatic stimulus evaluation. An experimental analysis of the preconditions for evaluative stimulus discrimination using an affective priming paradigm). Unpublished doctoral dissertation: University of Leuven.

Hermans, D., Baeyens, F., & Eelen, P. (1995). Odours as affective processing context for word evaluation: A case of non-associative cross-modal affective priming. Unpublished manuscript.

Hermans, D., & de Houwer, J. (1994). Affective and subjective familiarity ratings of 740 Dutch words. *Psychologica Belgica,* **34**, 115–39.

Hermans, D., de Houwer, J., & Eelen, P. (1994). The affective priming effect: Automatic activation of evaluative information in memory. *Cognition and Emotion*, **8**, 515–33.

Hill, A. B., & Kemp-Wheeler, S. M. (1989). The influence of context on lexical decision time for emotional and non-emotional words. *Current Psychology: Research and Review*, **8**, 219–27.

Johnson, M. K., & Weisz, C. (1994). Comments on unconscious processing: Finding emotion in the cognitive stream. In P. M. Niedenthal & Sh. Kitayama (Eds), *The Heart's Eye* (pp. 145–64). New York: Academic Press.

Kahneman, D., & Treisman, A. (1984). Changing views of attention and automaticity. In R. Parasuranam, & D. R. Davis (Eds), *Varieties of Attention* (pp. 29–61). San Diego, CA: Academic Press.

Kemp-Wheeler, S. M., & Hill, A. B. (1992). Semantic and emotional priming below objective detection threshold. *Cognition and Emotion*, **6**, 113–28.

Klauer, K. C. (1991). Einstellungen: *Der Einfluß der affektiven Komponente auf das kognitive Urteilen* (Attitudes: The Influence of the Affective Component on Cognitive Judgments). Göttingen: Hogrefe.

Klauer, K. C., Draine, S. C. & Greenwald, A. G. (1997). An unbiased errors-invariables approach to detecting unconscious cognition (manuscript submitted for publication).

Klauer, K. C., Roßnagel, C., & Musch, J. (1995). Arbeitsbericht zum Projekt Affektiven Priming (Research report for the project Affective Priming). Unpublished manuscript.

Klauer, K. C., Roßnagel, C., & Musch, J. (1997). List-context effects in evaluative priming. *Journal of Experimental Psychology: Learning, Memory and Cognition*, **23**, 246–55.

Klauer, K. C., & Stern, E. (1992). How attitudes guide memory-based judgments: A two-process model. *Journal of Experimental Social Psychology*, **28**, 186–206.

Krech, D., Crutchfield, R. S., & Ballachey, E. L. (1962). *Individual in Society*. New York: McGraw-Hill.

Krosnick, J. A., Betz, A. L., Jussim, L. J., & Lynn, A. R. (1992). Subliminal conditioning of attitudes. *Personality and Social Psychology Bulletin*, **18**, 155–62.

Lazarus, R. S. (1966). *Psychological Stress and the Coping Process*. New York: McGraw-Hill.

Lazarus, R. S. (1991). *Emotion and Adaptation*. New York: Oxford University Press.

Logan, G. D. (1980). Attention and automaticity in Stroop and priming tasks: Theory and data. *Cognitive Psychology*, **12**, 523–53.

Logan, G. D., & Zbrodoff, N. J. (1979). When it helps to be misled: Facilitative effects of increasing the frequency of conflicting stimuli in a Stroop-like task. *Memory and Cognition*, **7**, 166–74.

Logan, G. D., Zbrodoff, N. J., Williamson, J. (1984). Strategies in the color–word Stroop task. *Bulletin of the Psychonomic Society*, **22**, 135–8.

Lord, C. G., Ross, L., & Lepper, M. R. (1979). Biased assimilation and attitude polarization: The effects of prior theories on subsequently considered evidence. *Journal of Personality and Social Psychology*, **37**, 2098–2109.

MacLeod, C. M. (1991). Half a century of research on the Stroop effect: An integrative review. *Psychological Bulletin*, **109**, 163–203.

Mandler, G. (1994). Hypermnesia, incubation, and mind-popping: On remembering without really trying. In C. Umiltà and M. Moscovitch (Eds), *Attention and Performance, XV: Conscious and Nonconscious Information Processing* (pp. 3–33). Cambridge, MA: MIT Press.

Martin, L., & Levey, A. B. (1978). Evaluative conditioning. *Advances in Behavioral Research and Therapy*, **1**, 57–102.

McNamara, T. P., & Altarriba, J. (1988). Depth of spreading activation revisited: semantic mediated priming occurs in lexical decisions. *Journal of Memory and Language*, **27**, 545–59.

Murphy, S. T., Monahan, J. L., & Zajonc, R. B. (1995). Additivity of nonconscious affect: Combined effects of priming and exposure. *Journal of Personality and Social Psychology*, **69**, 589–602.

Murphy, S. T. & Zajonc, R. B. (1993). Affect, cognition, and awareness: Affective priming with optimal and suboptimal stimulus exposure. *Journal of Personality and Social Psychology*, **64**, 723–39.

Neely, J. H. (1977). Semantic priming and retrieval from lexical memory: Roles of inhibitionless spreading activation and limited capacity attention. *Journal of Experimental Psychology, General*, **106**, 226–54.

Neely, J. H. (1991). Semantic priming effects in visual word recognition: A selective review of current findings and theories. In D. Besner & G. Humphreys (Eds), *Basic Processes in Reading: Visual Word Recognition* (pp. 264–337). Hillsdale, NJ: Erlbaum.

Neely, J. H., & Keefe, D. E. (1989). Semantic context effects on visual word processing: A hybrid prospective/retrospective processing theory. In G. H. Bower (Ed.), *The Psychology of Learning and Motivation: Advances in Research and Theory* (Vol. 24, pp. 207–48). New York: Academic Press.

Neely, J. H., Keefe, D. E., & Ross, K. L. (1989). Semantic priming in the lexical decision task: Roles of prospective prime-generated expectancies and retrospective semantic matching. *Journal of Experimental Psychology: Learning, Memory, and Cognition*, **15**, 1003–19.

Niedenthal, P. M. (1990). Implicit perception of affective information. *Journal of Experimental Social Psychology*, **26**, 505–27.

Nisbett, R. E., & Wilson, T. (1977). The halo effect: Evidence for unconscious alteration of judgments. *Journal of Personality and Social Psychology*, **35**, 250–56.

Ortony, A., & Turner, T. J. (1990). What's basic about basic emotions? *Psychological Review*, **97**, 315–31.

Osgood, C. E., & Suci, G. J. (1955). Factor analysis of meaning. *Journal of Experimental Psychology*, **50**, 325–38

Osgood, C. E., Suci, G., & Tannenbaum, P. H. (1957). *The Measurement of Meaning*. Urbana, IL: University of Illinois Press.

Peeters, G., & Czapinski, J. (1990). Positive-negative asymmetry in evaluations: The distinction between affective and informational effects. In W. Stroebe & M. Hewstone (Eds), *European Review of Social Psychology*, (Vol. 1, pp. 33–60). Chichester: Wiley.

Perdue, C. W., Dovidio, J. F., Gurtman, M. B., & Tyler, R. B. (1990). Us and them: Social categorization and the process of intergroup bias. *Journal of Personality and Social Psychology*, **59**, 475–86.

Posner, M. I., & Snyder, C. (1975). Attention and cognitive control. In R. L. Solso (Ed.), *Information Processing and Cognition: The Loyola Symposium* (pp. 55–85). Hillsdale, NJ: Erlbaum.

Pratto, F. (1994). Consciousness and automatic evaluation. In P. M. Niedenthal & Sh. Kitayama (Eds), *The Heart's Eye* (pp. 115–43). New York: Academic Press.

Pratto, F., & John, O. P. (1991). Automatic vigilance: The attention-grabbing power of negative social information. *Journal of Personality and Social Psychology*, **61**, 380–91.

Ratcliff, R., & McKoon, G. (1981).   Automatic and strategic components of priming in recognition. *Journal of Verbal Learning and Behavior*, **20**(74), 204–15.

Reingold, E. M., & Merikle, P. M. (1988).   Using direct and indirect measures to study perception without awareness. *Perception and Psychophysics,* **44**, 563–75.

Roskos-Ewoldsen, D. R., & Fazio, R. H. (1992).   On the orienting value of attitudes: Attitude accessibility as a determinant of an object's attraction of visual attention. *Journal of Personality and Social Psychology,* **63**, 198–211.

Rothermund, K., Wentura, D., & Bak, P. (1995).   Verschiebung valenzbezogener Aufmersamkeitsasymmetrien in Abhängigkeit vom Handlungskontext: Bericht über ein Experiment (Shifts in valnence-related asymmetries in attention as a function of action context: Report of an experiment). *Trierer Psychologische Berichte,* **22**(4).

Scherer, K. R. (1988).   Criteria for emotion-antecedent appraisal: A review. In V. Hamilton, B. H. Bower & H. Frijda (Eds), *Cognitive Perspectives on Emotion and Motivation* (pp. 89–126). Dordrecht: Kluwer.

Shelton, J. R., & Martin, R. C. (1992).   How semantic is automatic semantic priming? *Journal of Experimental Psychology: Learning, Memory, and Cognition*, **18**, 1191–1210.

Skowronski, J. J., & Carlston, D. E. (1989).   Negativity and extremity biases in impression formation: A review of explanations. *Psychological Bulletin,* **105**, 131–42.

Smith, M. C., Besner, D., Myoshi, H. (1994).   New limits to automaticity: Context modulates semantic priming. *Journal of Experimental Psychology,* **20**, 104–15.

Smith, M. C., Theodor, L., & Franklin, P. E. (1983).   The relationship between contextual facilitation and depth of processing. *Journal of Experimental Psychology: Learning, Memory, and Cognition,* **9**, 697–712.

Staats, A. W., & Staats, C. K. (1958).   Attitudes established by classical conditioning. *Journal of Abnormal and Social Psychology,* **57**, 37–40.

Staats, C. K., & Staats, A. W. (1957).   Meaning established by classical conditioning. *Journal of Experimental Psychology,* **54**, 74–80.

Stolz, J. H., & Neely, J. H. (1995).   When target degradation does and does not enhance semantic context effects in word recognition. *Journal of Experimental Psychology,* **21**, 596–611.

Wentura, D. (1996).   The "meddling-in" of affective information: Evidence for negative priming and implicit judgment tendencies in the affective priming paradigm. Unpublished manuscript.

Wetzel, C. G., Wilson, T. D., & Kort, J. (1981).   The halo effect revisited: forewarned is not forearmed. *Journal of Experimental Social Psychology,* **17**, 427–39.

Wyer, R. S., & Srull, T. K. (1980).   The processing of social stimulus information: A conceptual integration. In R. Hastie, T. M. Ostrom, E. B. Ebbesen, R. S. Wyer, D. L. Hamilton, & D. E. Carlston (Eds), *Person Memory: The Cognitive Basis of Social Perception*. Hillsdale, NJ: Erlbaum.

Zajonc, R. B. (1980).   Feeling and thinking: Preferences need no inferences. *American Psychologist,* **39**, 117–24.

Zillig, M. (1928).   Einstellung und Aussage (Attitude and Proposition). *Zeitschrift für Psychologie,* **106**, 58–106.

Chapter 4

Hindsight Bias: Impaired Memory or Biased Reconstruction?

Dagmar Stahlberg
University of Mannheim
Anne Maass
University of Padua

ABSTRACT

The hindsight bias is the tendency for people to believe falsely that they would have predicted the outcome of an event, once the outcome is known. Although there is a rich literature on hindsight distortions, the underlying mechanisms are not yet fully understood. The present paper addresses the question of whether hindsight distortions represent the results of memory impairment or biased reconstruction processes. The majority of studies presented support the biased reconstruction view. Nevertheless, memory impairment processes cannot be ruled out as an explanation of hindsight bias when certain conditions are met, such as an existing coherent knowledge structure.

Nel balletto dei sondaggi solo l'incertezza è certa [In the dance of the election polls only the uncertainty is certain] (Headline of *La Repubblica*, the day *before* the 1993 local elections)

Il Veneto bianco adesso non c'è più: Cronaca del crollo annunciato [The White (Christian-Democratic) Veneto no longer exists: Chronicle of the announced collapse] (Headline of *La Nuova*, the day *after* the same election)

In hindsight, the journalists cited above had no doubt that the Christian-Democratic party of Italy *had* to collapse in the 1993 elections after almost

---

European Review of Social Psychology, Volume 8. Edited by Wolfgang Stroebe and Miles Hewstone.
© 1998 John Wiley & Sons Ltd.

five decades of continuous power, despite the fact that they apparently had experienced great uncertainty only 3 days earlier. In hindsight, there is little doubt that a particular youngster *had* to become a juvenile delinquent, that a certain marriage *had* to end in divorce, or that a given experiment *had* to produce this and no other result. Apparently, people consider events predictable and sometimes even inevitable once they have occurred. It was Fischhoff and his collaborators (e.g., Fischhoff, 1975; Fischhoff & Beyth, 1975) who first investigated this interesting phenomenon which has since been labelled *hindsight bias* or the *knew-it-all-along* effect. Hawkins and Hastie (1990) have defined the hindsight bias as "a projection of new knowledge into the past accompanied by a denial that the outcome information has influenced judgment" (p. 311).

In a classic experiment, Fischhoff and Beyth (1975) asked their subjects to estimate the likelihood of various outcomes of a visit of President Nixon to the Soviet Union shortly before the visit. After the visit, subjects were asked to recall their previous estimates as correctly as possible. Results showed that if a subject believed that an outcome had actually occurred (for example based on newspaper reports), they exaggerated their previous estimates. If they thought that the outcome had not occurred, they recalled lower estimates than they had given on the pretest. Since then, hindsight biases have been reported very reliably in the literature and have been obtained both in the laboratory and in the field (for overviews, see Christensen-Szalanski & Willham, 1991; Hawkins & Hastie, 1990). Moreover, the hindsight bias seems to be a very robust phenomenon that cannot easily be suppressed. For example, subjects were largely unable to ignore outcome information even when they were carefully informed about the effect, when they were asked to try hard not to fall prey to this bias, or when they were promised rewards for avoiding the bias (see Fischhoff, 1977; Hawkins & Hastie, 1990; Wood, 1978).

STANDARD RESEARCH PARADIGMS

The hindsight bias has been investigated in two distinct research paradigms. In the so-called *memory design* (see, e.g., Fischhoff & Beyth, 1975, study cited above; also Fischhoff, 1977, Experiment 1), subjects make predictions about an event; experimental subjects subsequently receive information about the real or alleged outcome while control subjects do not receive such information. Both groups are then asked to recall their original predictions. In a modified within-subjects design, the experimenter may include a series of trials and provide outcome feedback only for some of them.

In contrast, in the so-called *hypothetical design* (e.g., Fischhoff, 1975), some subjects judge the probability of an outcome without receiving any outcome information (foresight subjects), whereas others first learn about the actual or alleged outcome and are then instructed to indicate their judgments "as if they had not known the outcome". An example of this latter design is a well-known study by Fischhoff (1975) in which subjects received information about rather complex and obscure psychological or historical cases (such as the British–Gurkha war in Nepal) and were asked to judge the likelihood of a series of different outcomes. Subjects in the hindsight condition greatly over-estimated the probability of what they believed to be the actual outcomes. Both paradigms have yielded similar results, although hindsight distortions tend to be stronger in the hypothetical than in the memory design.

PREVIOUS THEORETICAL EXPLANATIONS

Memory Impairment

Although there is a rich literature on hindsight distortions, the underlying mechanisms are not yet fully understood. Fischhoff's original explanation, here referred to as *immediate assimilation hypothesis*, states that memory for the original prediction is altered by subsequent outcome information. When learning about the actual or alleged outcome, the person reinterprets the original evidence in the light of the outcome knowledge, thereby inadvertently modifying what had been previously stored in memory. Subsequent outcome knowledge is integrated on-line into the existing knowledge structure, resulting in a permanent modification of the person's prior representation of the event.

It is interesting to note that Loftus (1979; Loftus & Hoffman, 1989) has proposed a strikingly similar explanation for a related phenomenon, namely the fact that witnesses receiving misleading information about a previously observed event show poorer memory. Curiously, the two research areas, hindsight bias and misleading postevent information, have developed in almost complete isolation from each other, despite the fact that there is a striking resemblance between the two phenomena, the respective experimental paradigms, as well as the dominant theoretical accounts. Loftus's *destructive actualization hypothesis* states that the original memory trace is automatically updated when misleading subsequent information is encountered. Incoming information about a given issue becomes integrated into the existing memory structure, such that the original information is either substituted by or merged with the new information. Similar to Fischhoff's hypothesis, the key idea of Loftus's model is that memory for the original information is permanently altered by subsequent information.

Other variants of the memory impairment hypothesis have located the origin of hindsight biases in the retrieval stage (see the *selective retrieval hypothesis*, Morton, Hammersley, & Bekerian, 1985; Slovic & Fischhoff, 1977; the *dual memory traces model*, Hell et al., 1988). According to the selective retrieval hypothesis, for example, known outcomes serve as retrieval cues for relevant case material. Once an outcome has been learned, information congruent with this outcome will become highly accessible, whereas incongruent information cannot be retrieved with the same ease. Although these approaches focus on different stages, they share the idea that outcome knowledge impairs memory for previous judgments by either altering or erasing existing memory traces or by rendering them less accessible.

Motivational Explanation

From a social psychological point of view, more interesting approaches to explain hindsight distortions are based on the assumption that these distortions are driven by motivation, including: need for control (Campbell & Tesser, 1983); need for cognition (Verplanken & Pieters, 1988); self-relevance (Mark & Mellor, 1991); and, most importantly, self-presentational concerns (Campbell & Tesser, 1983). According to the latter approach, people are motivated to make others believe that their predictions were close to the actual outcome in an attempt to maintain a high level of public self-esteem. Contrary to the memory impairment hypothesis, this explanation interprets hindsight distortions as adjustments during the response generation state. Since empirical evidence for motivational underpinnings of the knew-it-all-along effect is rather weak (see Arkes, 1991; Christensen-Szalanski & Willham, 1991; for reviews, see also Pohl, 1993; Stahlberg, 1994) we will largely ignore this type of model.

AN ALTERNATIVE INTERPRETATION: BIASED RECONSTRUCTION

What we will offer here is an alternative account that is loosely based on McCloskey and Zaragoza's *response bias hypothesis*. McCloskey and Zaragoza's (1985a, 1985b, 1989) model was originally developed within the realm of eyewitness testimony research in order to account for the fact that witnesses receiving misleading information about a previously observed event show poorer memory for the event. Just like the hindsight bias, the misleading information effect was originally attributed to memory impairment (see Loftus, 1975, 1979; Loftus & Loftus, 1980): The memory trace for the original information was supposed to be modified, overwritten, or made less accessible by later (misleading) information. However, this interpretation was subsequently challenged by McCloskey and Zaragoza (1985a, b) who have offered the following account: rather than altering existing memory traces, the new information may simply be used as a point of reference by those who cannot remember the original information and are therefore forced to guess.

According to the response bias view, some people will correctly remember the original information and are likely to report it. Others will have forgotten the original information but if they remember the post-event information they will use it as a rational basis for guessing, as they have no reason to doubt its veridicality. Consequently, misleading information does not alter the original representation but only serves as an anchor to those perceivers who are unable to retrieve the original information.

The debate over whether the misleading information effect is attributable to memory impairment or judgment bias has since led to one of the most interesting and lively controversies in contemporary memory psychology (e.g. Belli, 1989; Loftus & Hoffman, 1989; Loftus, Schooler, & Wagenaar, 1985; McCloskey & Zaragoza, 1985a, b; Tversky & Tuchin, 1989; Zaragoza & Mc-Closkey, 1989; for an overview, see Koehnken, 1987).

We will argue here that McCloskey and Zaragoza's (1985a, b) response bias view may offer a valuable alternative to Fischhoff's (1975) automatic assimilation view of hindsight distortions in much the same way as it offers an alternative to Loftus' (1975, 1979) account of the misleading information effect. Parallels between the hindsight bias and the misleading information paradigms are obvious. Both lines of research pursue the question of whether information stored in memory might be less accessible after being confronted with inconsistent new information. Furthermore, the experimental designs of both research traditions show strong similarities (see Figure 4.1 for an

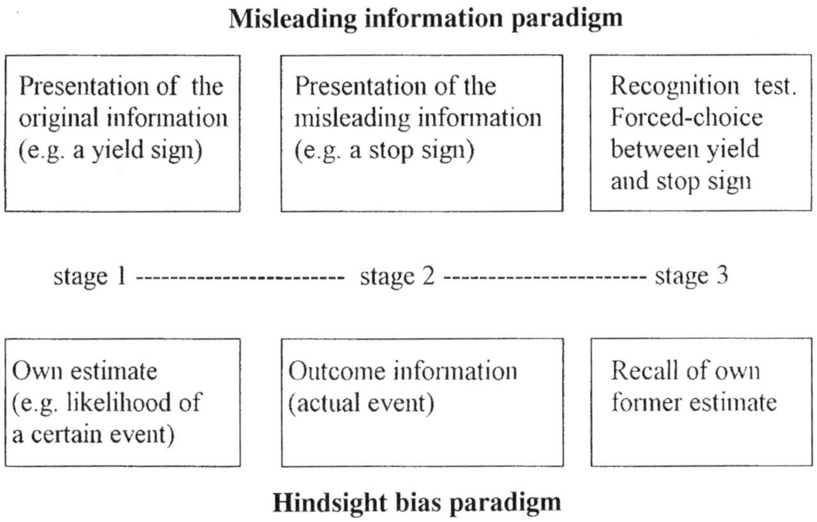

Misleading information paradigm

Presentation of the original information (e.g. a yield sign)	Presentation of the misleading information (e.g. a stop sign)	Recognition test. Forced-choice between yield and stop sign

stage 1 ------------------------ stage 2 ---------------------- stage 3

Own estimate (e.g. likelihood of a certain event)	Outcome information (actual event)	Recall of own former estimate

Hindsight bias paradigm

Figure 4.1   Overview of the misleading information and the hindsight-bias design

overview). In a first experimental stage the relevant information has to be given a chance to be stored in memory (observation of an event/giving own estimates). In the second stage the misleading/outcome information is presented and in the third stage the memory for the original information is tested. Beside these parallels, there are also important differences between the two experimental designs that require some adaptations of the response bias view.

Whereas in the misleading information paradigm the original information is presented by the experimenter, in hindsight bias studies the original estimates are self-generated by the subjects. Encoding of the original information/estimate might therefore be uncertain in the misleading information paradigm but not in the hindsight bias design. A second difference lies in the psychological quality of the misleading/outcome information: misleading information is presented unobtrusively without the subjects being aware of its misleading nature. More importantly, as both sets of information describe the same facts, only one set can be correct. Subjects who are aware of the inconsistency of information are normally excluded from further analysis. This situation is completely different concerning the outcome information given in hindsight studies. It is explicitly labeled as the correct information. But this does not necessarily imply a contradiction, even when own estimates lie far away from the actual outcomes. In some areas some people can be very certain that their estimates or predictions of events are very likely to be incorrect. The degree to which an inconsistency is perceived between one's own predictions and actual outcomes is therefore a consequence of hypotheses or meta-cognitions about the discrepancy between the two cognitions. These meta-cognitions are therefore assumed to play an important role in the reconstruction of one's own estimates that cannot be recalled, as will be described below.

Taking into account these differences between the two research paradigms, we formulated the following adaptation of the McCloskey and Zaragoza model to hindsight bias research. First of all, we assume that people are assumed either to have remembered or to have forgotten their original judgments. Those that do remember their original estimates are likely to reproduce them. Those that have forgotten them are forced to guess and, in the presence of outcome information, are likely to utilize this information as an anchor, assuming that their estimates must have been somewhere in the proximity of the true outcome. But since people are generally overly optimistic about their capacities (Greenwald, 1980), they will locate their presumed prior estimates closer to the real outcome than it had actually been, resulting in the hindsight bias (see also Figure 4.2 for a summary of the model).

At this point it is necessary to stress that the assumptions underlying the biased reconstruction view are here formulated in their most simple form. Of course, one might argue that memory for the original judgment might not be an all-or-nothing phenomenon. Rather, memory traces for the original judgments might be more or less strong. Biased reconstruction in its pure form

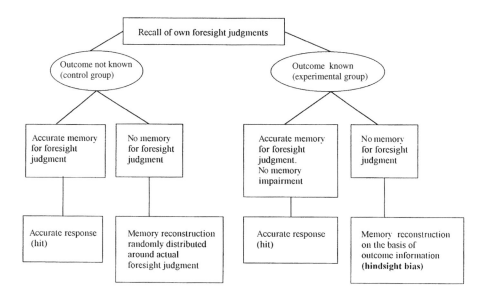

Figure 4.2   A model of biased recognition to explain hindsight bias

might only apply to pieces of information that are clearly below a certain threshold of recollection. Sometimes, however, people may possess vague memories for their own judgments, for example they might remember a certain "confidence interval" in which their original judgment was probably placed. In these cases the recalled judgment might be the product of retrieval processes and reconstructional processes at the same time. We will come back to this point when we discuss the limits of the biased reconstruction approach.

On the other hand, a distinction between a memory-impairment and a biased reconstruction explanation might not be as easy as it is assumed here for the sake of simplicity and clarity of the basic hypotheses. On the one hand, judgmental or reconstruction processes are obviously also mostly memory-based: for example, in our approach meta-cognitions stored in memory are assumed to lead the reconstruction of one's own estimates relative to the actual outcome. On the other hand, the term *memory-impairment view* has only been loosely sketched in the hindsight bias research (see the idea of immediate assimilation, Fischhoff, 1975). Researchers who studied the misinformation effect in eyewitnesses even doubted whether it could be formulated precisely on the basis of the current knowledge:

> *Memory impairment* could refer to a weakening of memory traces, or a clouding of memory, or an intrinsic impoverishment of memory. It could refer to what an earlier generation of psychologists called "unlearning" . . . or what a later generation called "disintegration" of features . . . Whatever the mechanisms, its

fading involves things that we currently cannot see or touch but can only infer from behavior (Loftus & Hoffman, 1989, p. 101).

In our research we have tried to find such behavioral indicators that might allow us to disentangle memory impairment processes and biased reconstruction processes.

Comparing Memory Impairment and Biased Reconstruction

In order to decide which of the above models can account most efficiently for the hindsight phenomenon, it is important to identify those predictions that are unique to each explanation. Memory impairment and biased reconstruction differ in multiple ways from each other. Generally speaking, the former refers to largely automatic memory processes that intervene between initial estimate and response generation (this is also true for the selective retrieval hypothesis and for the dual memory traces model), whereas the latter refers to deliberate judgment processes that operate only at the response generation stage.

This difference has two important implications. First of all, the memory impairment model predicts that outcome knowledge (or misleading postevent information in the testimony case) will impede memory for the original information, resulting in a reduced *hit rate*. Correct recall will therefore be lower in experimental conditions in which outcome knowledge is provided than in no-feedback control conditions. According to the biased reconstruction view, in contrast, outcome feedback should not affect the person's ability to correctly recall his/her initial estimates, resulting in comparable hit rates for experimental and no-feedback control conditions. Only those that have meanwhile forgotten their initial estimates are expected to be influenced by outcome feedback.

The second important difference between the two models is the role of *meta-cognitive considerations*. The assumption of meta-cognitive processes might bring social psychology back into hindsight bias research because they allow for variables of the social context to influence the strength of the bias. If, for example, there is a high social consensus that a certain actual outcome was extremely unlikely, a person might think that he/she would never have predicted such an outcome and might therefore only produce a very small hindsight bias (or even a reversed hindsight bias, see below). Meta-cognitive processes are central in biased reconstruction but irrelevant in memory impairment, where memory traces are thought to be updated automatically. Following the logic of biased reconstruction, hindsight distortions will only occur when the person has reasons to believe that his/her initial estimate must have been close to the true outcome. In most cases people are supposed to make this self-serving assumption (see above). However, although considered the default process, this will not always be the case. Hindsight distortions are predicted to disappear or even to reverse whenever meta-cognitive beliefs suggest that the original prediction must have been distant from the true outcome. Before representing research that was explicitly designed to test these differential predictions, we will briefly review previous findings that cannot easily be accounted for by the theoretical explanations developed by Fischhoff and others but for which the biased reconstruction perspective can offer a parsimonious account.

EVIDENCE FOR BIASED RECONSTRUCTION IN PAST RESEARCH

The biased reconstruction explanation can account for a number of past findings that were puzzling to previous explanations. First of all, hindsight distortions have generally been found to emerge more forcefully in the hypothetical than in the memory design (Campbell & Tesser, 1983; Fischhoff, 1997). This is quite consistent with a reconstruction approach that assumes that hindsight bias is only due to those subjects that have forgotten their previous estimates and are therefore forced to guess. Some subjects in the memory design will remember their previous estimates correctly but correct recall is, by definition, impossible in the hypothetical design, so that all subjects are potentially subject to hindsight distortion. Statistically speaking, the difference in hindsight bias between the two paradigms is entirely attributable to differential hit rates and should indeed disappear when hits are partialled out (a hypothesis that is currently being tested by the authors). The same argument can also explain why hindsight biases generally diminish in all those situations that enhance the strength of the memory traces for the initial estimates, such as shorter time intervals (see Hell *et al.*, 1988).

Another finding that is perfectly coherent with the active reconstruction perspective (but difficult to reconcile with the idea of automatic assimilation as well as the other memory-based explanations of the bias, such as the selective retrieval hypothesis and the dual traces model) is the fact that hindsight distortions are radically reduced when the experimentally provided outcome feedback is subsequently discredited (Hasher, Attig, & Alba, 1981) or when alternative potential outcomes are brought to attention (Arkes *et al.*, 1988; Davies, 1992, 1993; Slovic & Fischhoff, 1977).

Also, reversed hindsight effects have occasionally been observed in the literature, all of which refers to events of low probability that were apparently experienced as highly surprising (Hoch & Loewenstein, 1989; Mazursky & Ofir, 1990; Verplanken & Pieters, 1988; Wendt, 1993). When encountering such surprising events, people should believe that they would never have predicted the outcome and should consequently exaggerate the distance between estimate and outcome feedback in line with this meta-cognition. A similar argument can be made for Wasserman, Lempert, and Hastie's (1991) finding, that the hindsight bias in the Gurkha war case was radically reduced when the (fictitious) outcome was attributable to an unpredictable cause (weather conditions) rather than a predictable one (military supremacy). Again, meta-cognitive considerations can easily explain why people show little bias when they believe that they would not have been able to make correct predictions. It is, indeed, this emphasis on meta-cognitive thoughts that is one of the central advantages of the active reconstruction approach.

TESTING BIASED RECONSTRUCTION AGAINST MEMORY IMPAIRMENT

Although biased reconstruction seems to offer a parsimonious account for many findings in the hindsight literature, none of these findings constitutes an explicit comparative test. We will therefore report some of the results obtained within a larger research project which was explicitly designed to test biased reconstruction against memory impairment accounts.

Does Feedback Affect Hit Rates?

The first question for which biased reconstruction and memory impairment make different predictions is the accuracy of recall. Both models assume that hindsight distortions will occur, but the memory impairment hypothesis states that outcome information *per se* interferes with recall accuracy by erasing or modifying existing memory traces, whereas the biased reconstruction approach predicts that outcome feedback will not damage memory traces but only be utilized in those cases in which the original information has been forgotten, for whatever reason. In other words, the memory impairment view predicts a deterioration in memory due to feedback, and hence lower hit rates for experimental items for which outcome information is available than for no-feedback control items. Contrary to this, the biased reconstruction view predicts equal hit rates for experimental and control items.

In one of our studies (Stahlberg *et al.*, 1995, Experiment 2), subjects first made predictions on a series of almanac questions (e.g. "What percentage of German households have a television?"). After a 30 minute interval, they received fictitious outcome information that was either above or below their initial predictions, or they received no outcome information (the feedback factor was a within-subjects factor in all experimental designs presented here; six to eight items were presented in each experimental condition). Subsequently they were asked to reproduce their previous predictions as accurately as possible. Both shifts in estimates as well as hit rates were considered. As can be seen in Table 4.1, subjects showed reliable hindsight distortions by

Table 4.1 Mean pre–post differences in percentage estimates and mean hit rates as a function of feedback. (From Stahlberg *et al.*, 1995a, Experiment 2, reproduced with permission)

Type of feedback	Pre–post differences	Hit rates
Above	2.54[a]	2.17
	(4.49)	(1.58)
None	–2.91[b]	2.11
	(5.82)	(0.83)
Below	–5.85[c]	2.05
	(5.43)	(1.16)

Means with different superscripts differ reliably from each other; *t*-Test, $p < 0.05$.
Hit rates can vary between 0 and 6 (6 items per condition).
Standard deviations are given in parentheses.

shifting their estimates toward the alleged outcome, but their hit rates were unaffected by outcome feedback, suggesting that memory was not impaired by alleged outcome information. Thus, hindsight distortions occurred but they were not attributable to the fact that outcome information may have damaged existing memory traces. This finding (which has received support from additional studies by Dehn & Erdfelder, 1992, 1996; Erdfelder, 1992; Erdfelder & Buchner, 1995; Pohl, 1993; Tammeo, 1995) confirms the biased reconstruction view but argues against a memory impairment perspective.

THE ROLE OF OUTCOME INFORMATION: IS IT MERGED WITH PREVIOUS KNOWLEDGE OR USED AS AN ANCHOR?

Proponents of the memory impairment vs. biased reconstruction positions not only differ in their beliefs about the memory-damaging potential of outcome information, but also assign different roles to this variable. According to the memory impairment view, the outcome information will either overwrite the existing memory trace (in which case the outcome information will substitute the initial estimate) or else be merged with the existing trace (in which case initial estimate and outcome information will be merged into an intermediate judgment). As a result, the subjects exposed to outcome feedback ought to mistakenly locate their initial estimate anywhere between their initial estimate and the outcome feedback (including the value of the outcome). Predictions are very different from a biased reconstruction perspective: here the outcome information will be used as an anchor for guessing by those that do not remember their previous estimate. Reconstructed estimates will therefore vary around the outcome information taking values either below or beyond the presumed outcome.

In order to test the different predictions, we (Stahlberg *et al.*, 1995b) have developed a modified research design. Subjects are initially asked to make percentage estimates on a series of survey findings. One week later, they receive outcome information about the "true" survey results on some of the items (experimental items), while no such information is provided for control items. Up to this point the design is identical to the classic hindsight bias design. The difference lies in the dependent variable. Rather than asking subjects to recall their previous estimate freely, they are asked to *recognize* their previous estimate between two alternative responses provided by the experimenter, supposedly in order to facilitate the subject's task. Subjects are told that one of the two alternatives may have been their previous estimate; if they recognize their previous estimate among the two alternatives, they are asked to mark it; but if they believe that neither of the two alternatives corresponds to the previous estimate, they are asked to freely reproduce it.

Importantly, one of the two alternatives is located half-way between the subject's initial estimate and the outcome information, the other beyond the outcome information (from the perspective of the initial estimate). We will refer to the former as "between" alternative, and to the latter as "beyond" alternative. The critical feature of the design is that the two alternatives are located at the same distance from the alleged outcome, as can be seen in Figure 4.3.

If outcome feedback is merged with the initial impression, as predicted by the memory impairment view, then subjects should predominantly choose the "between" alternative on those items for which the outcome is known. Hence, "between" choices should be much more frequent on experimental than on control items. In contrast, the reconstruction approach would predict that the "between" and "beyond" alternatives be chosen with approximately

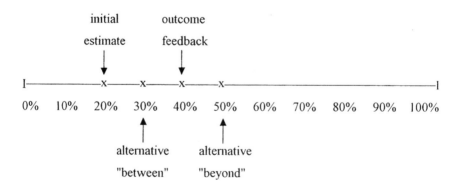

Figure 4.3 Example for response alternatives provided in Stahlberg *et al.*'s (1995b) paradigm

equal likelihood, as they are equally distant from the outcome feedback. Importantly, the relation of "between" to "beyond" choices ought to be the same for control and experimental items. This implies that the hindsight bias should actually disappear under these conditions, as responses to experimental and control items should be the same.

The results contradict the predictions of the memory impairment perspective. As can be seen in Table 4.2, choices of the "between" alternative slightly outnumbered those of the "beyond" alternative but this pattern was identical for experimental and control items, providing no evidence for *merging* of outcome feedback and initial estimate on experimental items ($\varepsilon^2 \times 100 < 0.01\%$). The fact that the "between" alternative was favored overall may simply have been due to the fact that the "between" value was generally located close to the scale midpoint and, as such, more acceptable. The same study also provided further support for the fact that hit rates are not influenced by outcome information ($\varepsilon^2 \times 100 = 0.45\%$). In line with the reconstruction view (but in contradiction to the memory impairment view), outcome feedback did not affect the subjects' ability to recall their previous estimates.

It is quite obvious that the memory impairment explanation encounters great difficulties in accounting for the above data sets, whereas the reconstruction approach remains a strong candidate. At the same time, none of the studies reported so far provide unequivocal evidence for the reconstruction approach, as null effects were predicted (and found) from the biased reconstruction perspective. Furthermore, one can argue (as one of the reviewers of this chapter proposed) that the null results for the preference of the "between" alternative may merely be the consequence of random choice when two alternatives are offered by the experimenters. Therefore, to strengthen the argument for the biased reconstruction position we will proceed by reporting experiments planned to provide a more explicit test of the reconstruction processes that are hypothesized to operate according to this approach.

Table 4.2 Mean preferences for "between" over "beyond"—alternative and mean hit rates on experimental and control items. (From Stahlberg *et al.*, 1995b)

	Preference for "between" over "beyond"	Hit rates
Experimental items	0.89	1.53
	(0.98)	(1.27)
Control items	1.03	1.56
	(1.13)	(1.34)

Mean preferences for "between" alternative can vary from –8 to 8.
Hit rates can vary from 0 to 8 (8 items per condition).
Standard deviations are given in parentheses.

THE ROLE OF META-COGNITION

As outlined earlier, biased reconstruction and memory impairment differ with regard to their emphasis on meta-cognitive considerations. If outcome information is assimilated into the existing knowledge structure in an automatic fashion, there is little reason to believe that meta-cognitive processes should play a relevant role. The biased reconstruction view, in contrast, argues that people will make some more or less explicit assumptions about how close or distant their original estimate may have been from the true outcome. It is exactly this subjective assumption that determines the direction and magnitude of the hindsight bias.

In most cases people will tend to overestimate their ability to correctly predict events: their overly optimistic beliefs constitute the *default* assumption, which is responsible for the fact that hindsight distortions occur so frequently. But there are significant exceptions to this rule. At times, people will assume that their predictive abilities may have been rather poor and that their estimates must have been rather distant from the "true" outcome (see previous review of reversed hindsight effects, Hoch & Loewenstein, 1989; Mazursky, & Ofir, 1990; Verplanken & Pieters, 1988; Wendt, 1993).

Stahlberg and Eller (1992) have experimentally manipulated assumptions about how close estimates may have been to the actual outcome. As in previous experiments, subjects were asked to make a series of predictions about survey-type questions (e.g., "What percentage of adults would sacrifice income in order to gain spare time?"). Subsequently, they received feedback about their alleged predictive abilities. Depending on the condition, subjects were either told that their predictions had, for the most part, been highly accurate or rather poor (generally far away from the actual outcomes, generally too high or too low). Subsequently, subjects received outcome feedback for some items that either exceeded or remained below their initial estimates (experimental items), while no feedback was provided for control items.

The biased reconstruction approach predicts that subjects would show a marked hindsight bias when believing that their predictions had been rather accurate but not when thinking that their predictions had been generally poor, too high or too low. At the same time, there is no reason to assume that hit rates would differ, either as a function of outcome feedback or as a function of assumed predictive ability.

The results support the latter hypothesis: neither the knowledge of the "true" outcome nor the alleged predictive ability affected the hit rates (see Table 4.3b). Note, however, that there was a non-significant trend for hits to be more frequent on no-feedback control items ($M = 1.35$) than on experimental items ($M = 1.09$). One can therefore not exclude with certainty that memory processes may have contributed to the results, in addition to the proposed reconstruction processes. We will come back to this issue below.

Turning to differences between actual and recalled estimates, the results show that hindsight distortions were most pronounced when subjects believed that they had been quite accurate in their predictions (see Table 4.3a). In this case, they shifted their recalled estimates reliably in the direction of what they thought was the actual outcome. Although hindsight shifts were much weaker in the remaining conditions, they did not disappear completely. Even when subjects had reason to doubt their predictive abilities ("poor, too low or too high" prediction conditions), they still recalled higher estimates in the high than in the low outcome feedback condition. Thus, in line with the biased reconstruction model, the stronger hindsight bias was found when people believed that their previous estimates were located close to the actual outcome. Yet, believing that one's predictions must have been rather distant from the "true" outcome did not entirely eliminate the hindsight bias. This suggests that intentional reconstruction based on beliefs about one's own predictive abilities is not the *only* process operating in hindsight distortions. In line with other authors (Fischhoff, 1975; Fischhoff & Beyth, 1975; Hawkins

Table 4.3 Mean pre–post differences in percentage estimates and hit rates as a function of alleged predictive ability and outcome feedback. (From Stahlberg & Eller, 1992)

Type of outcome feedback	Alleged predictive ability[1]	
	Good	Poor
(a) Pre–post differences		
Higher	6.11[a]	3.60[a]
	(3.64)	(5.21)
None	1.08[b]	–1.63[ab]
	(3.13)	(5.50)
Lower	–6.19[c]	–3.19[b]
	(3.60)	(4.45)
(b) Hit rates[2]		
Higher	0.83	1.27
	(0.92)	(1.08)
None	1.33	1.35
	(1.41)	(1.25)
Lower	0.89	1.05
	(0.90)	(1.28)

[1] Within each "predictive ability" condition, means that do not share the same superscript differ reliably from each other, t-test, $p < 0.05$.
Standard deviations are given in parentheses.
[2] Hit rates can vary between 0 and 6 (6 items per condition).
Standard deviations are given in parentheses.

and Hastie, 1990) we therefore suspect that automatic anchoring processes are operating in addition to intentional reconstruction mechanisms. Thus subjects may inadvertently use the outcome knowledge as an anchor when reconstructing their estimates, even when they have little confidence in their predictive abilities. Importantly, such automatic anchoring represents an unintentional *judgment* process that should not be confused with automatic memory processes such as assimilation.

AUTOMATIC ANCHORING EFFECTS

With reference to Tversky and Kahneman's (1982) anchoring-and-adjustment hypothesis, we suggest that people often use comparison values (in our case outcome knowledge) as anchors when making their judgments, adjusting for presumed differences between anchor and own estimate. Typically, such adjustments are insufficient, as demonstrated, among others, by a classical experiment by Tversky and Kahneman (1982), in which subjects were asked to estimate the percentage of African states in the United Nations. Before making their estimates, a random number from 1 to 100 was generated through the use of a wheel of fortune. Subsequently, subjects were asked to turn the wheel until it reached the number that, in their opinion, corresponded to the percentage of African states in the United Nations. As predicted, subjects used the random number as anchor and showed insufficient adjustments, providing a low estimate (25%) when the randomly generated anchor was low (10) but a high estimate (45%) when the anchor was high (65).

In order to investigate whether such involuntary anchoring mechanisms are also operating in hindsight distortions, Stahlberg and Eckert (1994) conducted an experiment in which the outcome feedback was discredited. Hasher, Attig, and Alba (1981) had earlier observed that the hindsight bias diminished when outcome feedback was subsequently discredited as "wrong". Stahlberg and Eckert's experiment followed the same logic but, contrary to Hasher, Attig, and Alba's study, subjects in the present design were warned that outcome feedback was incorrect *before* receiving information about the "true" outcome. In the critical condition, they were informed that the values listed as "true" outcome were actually wrong, owing to a mistake in the transcription of the results, and they were therefore instructed to cross out the inaccurate feedback data before proceeding with their task. Thus, contrary to Hasher, Attig, and Alba's study, one can rule out that memory was altered by outcome knowledge before people were aware that outcome feedback was perfectly invalid.

On the one hand, if hindsight distortions are entirely based on conscious reconstruction guided by assumptions about one's predictive ability, then hindsight distortions should be completely eliminated when people learn that the outcome information is invalid. Logically, "wrong" outcome information should be perfectly useless as a means for reconstructing one's estimates. On the other hand, if hindsight biases are driven by both conscious reconstruction and automatic anchoring processes in Tversky and Kahneman's sense, then hindsight distortions can still be expected, albeit in reduced magnitude.

The findings are presented in Table 4.4. Subjects showed reliable hindsight distortions, regardless of whether outcome feedback was valid or not. Compared with no-feedback control items, subjects in both accuracy conditions recalled higher previous estimates when outcome feedback exceeded their prior estimates and lower estimates when outcome feedback fell short of their prior estimates. At the same time, hindsight biases were reliably stronger when outcome information was valid than when it was not, as demonstrated by a significant interaction between type and accuracy of feedback. As in all previous studies, no differences in hit rates emerged between the conditions.

In summary, these results suggest that automatic anchoring effects are operating in addition to intentional reconstruction processes in hindsight bias. These results nicely parallel those obtained by Tversky and Kahneman (1982). Subjects in Tversky and Kahneman's study tended to use random

Table 4.4 Mean pre–post differences in percentage estimates and mean hit rates as a function of type and alleged accuracy of outcome feedback. (From Stahlberg & Eckert, 1994)

Type of outcome feedback	Alleged accuracy of outcome feedback	
	Correct	Wrong
(a) Pre–post differences		
Higher	4.98 (6.21)	2.89 (6.06)
None	−1.73 (6.09)	
Lower	−6.81 (5.12)	−5.06 (5.87)
(b) Hit rates		
Higher	1.25 (1.17)	1.23 (1.03)
None	1.03 (0.89)	
Lower	1.15 (1.02)	1.25 (1.07)

Standard deviations are given in parentheses.
Hit rates can vary between 0 and 6 (6 items per condition).

numbers as anchors when making decisions under uncertainty, whereas our subjects used such information even when it was explicitly labelled as wrong. Although none of our subjects would probably consider this a rational strategy, they inadvertently used the outcome feedback as an anchor, despite the fact that they were fully aware of the diagnostic uselessness of such information.

Two features of this pattern of results seem of particular theoretical relevance. First, these results are supportive of automatic anchoring, rather than automatic assimilation of outcome information into memory. Just as in the previously cited experiments, the analysis of correct recall revealed no evidence for memory impairment, suggesting that memory processes are not implicated here. Second, the data pattern suggest a dual process in which intentional reconstruction and automatic anchoring contribute independently. The fact that hindsight distortions occur, even when the outcome feedback is discredited *a priori*, suggests that the anchoring-and-adjustment heuristic plays a significant role. The fact that hindsight distortions are considerably more pronounced when the feedback is considered valid, suggests that intentional reconstruction contributes above and beyond automatic anchoring.

Taken together, these findings suggest that hindsight biases are attributable to erroneous judgment processes rather than memory impairment. At the same time, they show that our initial assumptions were too simplistic and that biased reconstruction derives from two distinct biases that may be operating at different levels of awareness. On the one hand, subjects tend to locate their estimates close to the outcome because they are generally overly optimistic about their predictive abilities. On the other hand, they inadvertently (and probably automatically) use the outcome information as an anchor when reconstructing their previous estimates.

IMPLICATIONS FOR INDIVIDUAL VS. GROUP JUDGMENTS

The reinterpretation of hindsight phenomena as judgment rather than memory bias also allows some speculations about which factors will enhance and which factors will reduce the likelihood of hindsight distortions. If hindsight distortions are due to erroneous judgments on those items that cannot be retrieved from memory, then any factor that increases the likelihood of correct recall should automatically reduce the impact of biased reconstruction, and hence the magnitude of the hindsight bias. Among the many factors that are likely to improve memorization are increased elaboration at encoding, shorter retention intervals, and encoding specificity, but also individual characteristics such as mnemonic capacity or motivation, or structural variables related to the social settings in which judgments are made. One such factor, which we have investigated in the research by Stahlberg *et al.* (1995a, Experiment 2) already mentioned, concerns the difference between group and individual judgments. Subjects in this study provided probability estimates for a series of questions, either individually or in small groups. They subsequently received fictitious outcome information that was either above or below their initial predictions, or no feedback was provided (control items). They were then asked to reproduce their previous predictions (again, either individually or in groups).

From an applied point of view, it is relevant to know whether groups are just as likely as individuals to fall prey to hindsight distortions, considering that particularly important decisions in politics, industry, education, and law are generally made by small groups rather than by individuals. From a theoretical point of view, the comparison is interesting because the biased reconstruction model allows specific predictions about individual–group differences. If outcome knowledge affects only those items that can no longer be retrieved from memory, then groups may be less susceptible to hindsight distortions because they enjoy at least two recall advantages compared to individuals: first, group decisions generally take more time and require more (and possibly deeper) processing than individual decisions, thereby facilitating encoding of the original predictions; second, there is a greater likelihood that at least one group member will recall the previous judgment correctly, thus reducing the memory task for the other group members to the easier task of recognition, compared to the free recall task for all subjects in the individual judgment condition (see Steiner, 1972). As a result of both processes, groups should encounter fewer difficulties than individuals in recalling their initial estimates. This should indirectly affect the magnitude of the hindsight bias. Taken together, differences between groups and individuals should emerge mainly on correct recall rates and should only indirectly affect the degree of hindsight distortions.

Indeed, results do show that groups ($M = 3.00$) showed reliably better hit rates than individuals ($M = 2.11$), regardless of outcome feedback (see Table 4.5b). Looking at the pre–post differences reported in Table 4.5a, it becomes clear that hindsight distortions occur under both individual and group judgment conditions but that the magnitude is reduced when decisions are made in groups. Interestingly, our analyses also suggest that both differential hit rates and differential hindsight distortions are mainly due to the greater elaboration at encoding in the group condition. When time to reach the initial decision is partialled out, differences between individual and group decisions practically disappear.

Although groups are by no means immune to hindsight distortions, they seem to have better access to their previous estimates than individuals because more time and effort goes into reaching the initial decisions.

If the better performance of groups is indeed attributable to their recall advantage, then the superiority of groups over individuals should disappear when asked to make hypothetical decisions ("as if they did not know the outcome"—see hypothetical design). Recall is, by definition, irrelevant in hypothetical decisions, suggesting that memory-enhancing strategies will be

Table 4.5 Mean pre–post differences in percentage estimates and mean hit rates as a function of individual vs. group judgment condition and feedback. (From Stahlberg *et al.*, 1995a, Experiment 2, reproduced with permission)

Type of feedback	Judgment condition	
	Individual	Group
(a) Pre–post differences		
Above	2.54	3.43
	(4.49)	(3.51)
None	−2.91	−1.08
	(5.82)	(3.68)
Below	−5.85	−2.18
	(5.43)	(3.76)
(b) Hit rates		
Above	2.17	2.78
	(1.58)	(1.06)
None	2.11	3.22
	(0.83)	(1.47)
Below	2.06	3.00
	(1.16)	(1.57)

Standard deviations are given in parentheses.
Hit rates can vary between 0 and 6 (6 items per condition).

ineffective in this case. In order to test this possibility, we (Stahlberg *et al.*, 1995a, Experiment 1) asked individuals and groups to make hypothetical predictions in the presence or absence of outcome knowledge and obtained reliable hindsight distortions that emerged to an approximately equal extent in the individual and group condition.

To sum up, the results of the two studies confirm the predictions of the biased reconstruction approach, while the data pattern seems inconsistent with a memory impairment perspective (for a detailed discussion, see Stahlberg *et al.*, 1995a). They also provide an illustration of the fact that the biased reconstruction interpretation may be useful when trying to identify those social settings that are most conducive to unbiased judgments.

CRITICAL EVALUATION: HOW PERVASIVE IS ACTIVE RECONSTRUCTION?

All the data reported so far point in the same direction. They converge in showing that the biased reconstruction interpretation offers a valuable and parsimonious alternative to the memory impairment perspective. In particular, four observations emerge from the above studies that argue for biased reconstruction rather than memory impairment.

First, throughout all studies conducted within this research project, there was no single instance in which outcome feedback affected hit rates in a reliable way. Only in one experiment (Stahlberg & Eller, 1992) was there a non-significant trend for hits to be more frequent on no-feedback control items than on experimental items. Thus, outcome knowledge apparently did *not* interfere with correct recall, as argued by the biased reconstruction view (but contrary to what would be predicted by advocates of the memory impairment explanation). Along the same lines, results from a modified research paradigm in which subjects had to recognize their previous estimates from two alternative choices (Stahlberg *et al.*, 1995b) provided no evidence that outcome information was merged with the previous estimate. Apparently, outcome knowledge neither interferes with nor is merged with previous information.

Second, although outcome information had no reliable effects on hits in any of our studies, it generally produced reliable hindsight distortions consistent with the alleged outcome (higher estimates when feedback exceeded the prior judgment, and lower estimates when feedback fell short of prior judgment). This suggests that reconstructive processes only come into play when initial estimates cannot be retrieved otherwise.

Third, evidence in support of the biased reconstruction view refers to the powerful role of meta-cognitive processes. As predicted, hindsight distortions were most pronounced when people had reason to believe that their initial estimates must have been very close to the actual outcome. Yet, the hindsight bias was not entirely eliminated when people were made to doubt their predictive abilities. This latter finding forced us to revise the original formulation and to acknowledge the potential role of automatic anchoring and adjustment processes, in which people inadvertently use the outcome as anchor regardless of explicit meta-cognitive beliefs about their predictive accuracy. In other words, automatic anchoring appears to contribute above and beyond intentional reconstruction.

Finally, the application of the model to an applied question, namely the relative susceptibility of groups vs. individuals to hindsight distortions, proved useful. As a whole, the present research project provided strong and consistent support for the biased reconstruction interpretation. Recently, this interpretation has also been supported by studies using multinomial modeling (for an overview, see Erdfelder & Buchner, 1995). Does this mean that memory impairment should be banished once and for all from the list of explanations that are competing to account for the hindsight bias? We don't think so.

Although our own research program provides considerable support for the active reconstruction view, it does so under specific circumstances and in a specific paradigm. Note that all of the above studies employed a similar research paradigm, a similar procedure, and similar experimental material. In particular, in all of the above studies research participants made foresight and/or hindsight estimates on largely uninvolving trivial questions in what is generally referred to as the *almanac paradigm*. As far as almanac questions are concerned, the biased reconstruction approach might dominate the task to recall one's own former judgments, because here the process of remembering the relevant information stored in memory might economically be conceptualized as the all-or-nothing process mentioned above. On the contrary, vague memories predisposed to distortion by later outcome information may be more likely with more complex judgmental tasks.

Almanac questions undoubtedly constitute one type of problem for which people show reliable hindsight effects, but it is not the only one. Other authors have presented considerably more complex social or historical cases, such as Fischhoff (1975) when he asked subjects to judge the likelihood of different outcomes in the war between the Gurkhas and the British in Nepal. The question then arises whether the active reconstruction approach can equally well account for hindsight biases on such complex tasks, or whether other processes such as automatic assimilation may come into play.

One hypothesis that we have recently started to investigate is that active reconstruction and memory impairment may not offer mutually exclusive explanations (as has generally been assumed in the literature) but that they may have distinct areas of application. Both memory and reconstructive processes may play a role in hindsight bias but they may be operating under specific conditions, have distinct realms of application and operate within specific boundaries.

In particular, we argue that the outcome information (or misleading post-event information in the eyewitness area) will be integrated into or merged with previous knowledge only if there is a coherent knowledge structure in which the new information can be integrated, if originally memorized and new information represent stimuli that can be merged, and if people are motivated to do so. In other words, we suggest that immediate assimilation of new information in Fischhoff's terms, or up-dating of existing memory traces in Loftus's terms, will occur only if specific conditions are met.

If immediate assimilation requires the existence of a knowledge structure in which the new information can be integrated then the almanac paradigm (in which subjects make frequency estimates about trivial and perfectly uninteresting survey questions), it may not offer the optimal conditions. Imagine that subjects are asked, "What percentage of families have at least two children?" or "What percentage of households have more than 3 cars?" and are subsequently told that the "real" percentage deviates substantially from their own guesses (e.g., 23% rather than 56%). It is difficult to imagine in which knowledge structure this new information could possibly be integrated. This is quite different from experimental paradigms such as Fischhoff's (1975) well-known Gurkha war study, where subjects made estimates about ambiguous historical or psychological cases for which they had received a rich and complex set of information that could lead to multiple outcomes, including a Gurkha victory, a British victory, or a peace treaty. Outcome feedback was partially consistent and partially inconsistent with the previously received information about the case, which made it possible to accommodate any of the possible outcomes into the existing knowledge structure. It is therefore conceivable that for such complex case studies, outcome information is indeed merged with previous knowledge, resulting in memory impairment, whereas reconstructive processes may prevail on almanac-type tasks.

In addition, the prevalence of automatic assimilation or reconstruction may depend on the processing goal. In most situations, people may spontaneously integrate new information on-line into what they already know about an issue (see Hastie & Park's, 1986, distinction between on-line and memory-based judgments), but memory instructions may undermine the subject's natural tendency to integrate outcome knowledge.

There is a third criterion that will not be discussed in this context: stimulus features of original and new information must be such that they can potentially be merged into a meaningful compromise. Our own studies (asking likelihood or percentage estimates) met this criterion, but there are many studies, especially in the eyewitness literature, where old and new pieces of information are distinct and mutually exclusive entities that can substitute for each other but cannot be merged (such as *hammer* and *wrench* in Zaragoza and McCloskey's research program). We suspect that assimilation processes are unlikely to occur unless stimulus features are potentially mergeable and unless the dependent variable allows for a blended representation (continuously varying measures like percentage estimates or categories that incorporate a blended representation, such as the color turquoise as a potential blend between blue and green).

Taking all this into consideration, we hypothesize that automatic assimilation will only occur under specific conditions, namely when there is a coherent and sufficiently complex knowledge structure that may accommodate the outcome (or post-event) information and when people are not prevented from on-line processing.

We first tested this prediction in a study in which subjects were encouraged either to develop a coherent cognitive representation of a target person or simply to memorize detailed information. All subjects received a series of complex case histories indicative of social or psychological problems (unemployment, suicide, divorce, etc.). This information was accompanied by instructions either to form a coherent impression about the target person, or else to remember detailed information about each case for a subsequent memory test. Research by Hamilton, Katz, and Leirer (1980) has shown that

impression formation instructions generally lead to more organized knowledge structures than mere instructions to memorize detailed information. To
strengthen the manipulation further, the case information was presented
either as a continuous text, which was assumed to encourage impression
formation, or as isolated bits of information that were presented one at a time.
Importantly, subjects in the two conditions received exactly the same information and had to make the same probability estimates about each case, but
processing goals varied so as to encourage either the formation of a coherent
impression or the memorization of isolated facts.

Subjects subsequently received information about the "true" likelihood
that was either above or below their previous estimate, or they received no
such information (control items). As in the previously reported study by
Stahlberg *et al.* (1995b), subjects were asked to recognize their previous estimates from two response alternatives (*between* previous estimate and outcome feedback or *beyond* outcome feedback) or else to freely recall their
previous estimate if they thought it was not among the two alternatives.

On the one hand, if subjects assimilated the outcome information into their
previous knowledge structure, then (a) in accurately recalling their previous
estimates they should encounter greater difficulties on experimental than on
control items (indicative of memory impairment) and (b) they should show a
greater preference for the *between* alternative (indicative of merging) on
experimental than on control items. On the other hand, biased reconstruction
should not result in differential memory deficits or in differential preference
for the *between* alternative on experimental vs. control items. The results
(reported in Table 4.6) tend to support both views, but under different conditions. Under impression formation instructions, the pattern of results was
indicative of assimilation and memory impairment: subjects with outcome
feedback preferred the alternative that best represented a memory blend
lying in between their original estimates and the "true" likelihood, and they
also tended to have fewer correct memories than under no-feedback conditions. Opposite to this, reconstructive processes seemed to operate under
memory instructions: there was no preference for the memory alternative that
was conceptualized as a blend between original estimates and feedback and
there was no reduction in the hit rates due to the outcome information (for
similar findings, see Pohl & Gawlik, 1995).

If this preliminary data set receives support in future studies, this would
suggest that the hindsight phenomenon is not driven by a single process but
that both automatic assimilation and active reconstruction contribute to
erroneous hindsight judgments. This implies that memory impairment and
response bias may not be quite as contradictory as they have appeared
throughout the debate on misleading postevent information in the eyewitness
area. Rather than being mutually exclusive, they seem to have distinct areas
of application, with different conditions promoting one or the other process

Table 4.6 Relative preference of "between" over "beyond"-alternative and mean hit rates as a function of outcome feedback and processing goal (impression formation vs. memory)

Type of feedback	Condition		
	Impression formation		Memory
Relative preference for "between" and "beyond" ("between" minus "beyond")			
Higher	1.25	>	0.08
Lower	1.19	>	0.66
None	0.81	=	0.72
Hits			
Higher	0.19	>	0.56
Lower	0.19	>	0.50
None	0.31	=	0.44

(although the exact conditions conducive to memory impairment vs. biased reconstruction have still to be identified). This also implies the interesting possibility that seemingly identical phenomena (such as hindsight bias and susceptibility to misleading information) may result from distinct underlying processes.

CONCLUSION

All in all, the research reported here suggests that hindsight distortions are in large part a (biased) judgment rather than a memory phenomenon, and that memory processes become relevant only under specific circumstances. Beyond the specific contribution to understanding the hindsight phenomenon, the present research project also demonstrates that two apparently unrelated areas, hindsight bias and eyewitness identification after misleading information, have much more in common than the separate development of these two areas would suggest. This is one of many interesting cases in which fields develop in complete isolation over long time periods despite the fact that they are investigating similar problems that are part of a more general phenomenon. Indeed, Hawkins and Hastie (1990) have argued that there are a number of additional phenomena, including perseverance and the reconstruction of personal histories, that may well be part of this same larger picture. Our own research illustrates that the heated debate on misleading information in eyewitness testimony can profitably be applied to the hindsight bias area, and that hindsight researchers can, on the one hand, learn a great deal from this debate and, on the other hand, might offer interesting contributions to this controversy.

ACKNOWLEDGEMENT

This research was in part supported by a grant from the Deutsche For-schungsgemeinschaft (Grant No. Fr 472/6-1). During the preparation of this paper, the second author was supported by a grant from the Alexander von Humboldt-Stiftung while visiting the University of Kiel in Summer 1995. We are grateful to Dieter Frey for his helpful comments on a former draft of this paper.

REFERENCES

Arkes, H. R. (1991).   Costs and benefits of judgment errors: Implications for debias-ing. *Psychological Bulletin*, **110**, 486–98.
Arkes, H. R., Faust, D., Guilmette, T. J., & Hart, K. (1988).   Eliminating the hindsight bias. *Journal of Applied Psychology*, **73**, 305–7.
Belli, R. F. (1989).   Influences of misleading postevent information: Misinformation interference and acceptance. *Journal of Experimental Psychology: General*, **118**, 72–85.
Campbell, J. D., & Tesser, A. (1983).   Motivational interpretations of hindsight bias: An individual difference analysis. *Journal of Personality*, **51**, 605–20.
Christensen-Szalanski, J. J. J., & Fobian Willham, C. (1991).   The hindsight bias: A meta-analysis. *Organizational Behavior and Human Decision Processes*, **48**, 147–68.
Davies, M. F. (1992).   Field dependence and hindsight bias: Cognitive restructuring and the generation of reasons. *Journal of Research in Personality*, **26**, 58–74.
Davies, M. F. (1993).   Field dependence and hindsight bias: Output interference in the generation of reasons. *Journal of Research in Personality*, **27**, 222–37.
Dehn, D., & Erdfelder, E. (1992).   *Hindsight Bias: Bloß ein Artefakt des Aggregierens über Individuen*. Report 34, Tagung experimentell arbeitender Psychologen, Osnabrück.
Dehn, D., & Erdfelder, E. (1996).   What kind of bias is the hindsight bias? Un-published manuscript, Saarbrücken.
Erdfelder, E. (1992).   *Multinominiale Modelle zum Hindsight-Bias-Paradigma*. Re-port 34, Tagung experimentell arbeitender Psychologen, Osnabrück.
Erdfelder, E., & Buchner, A. (1995).   Decomposing the hindsight bias: A processing tree model for separating recollection and reconstruction biases in hindsight (Man-uscript submitted for publication).
Fischhoff, B. (1975).   Hindsight ≠ foresight: The effect of outcome knowledge on judgment under uncertainty. *Journal of Experimental Psychology: Human Perfor-mance and Perception*, **1**, 288–99.
Fischhoff, B. (1977).   Perceived informativeness of facts. *Journal of Experimental Psychology: Human Perceptions and Performance*, **3**, 349–58.
Fischhoff, B., & Beyth, R. (1975).   "I knew it would happen". Remembered proba-bilities of once-future things. *Organizational Behaviour and Human Performance*, **13**, 1–16.
Greenwald, A. G. (1980).   The totalitarian ego: Fabrication and revision of personal history. *American Psychologist*, **35**, 603–18.

Hamilton, D. L., Katz, L. B., & Leirer, V. O. (1980). Organizational processes in impression formation. In R. Hastie, T. M. Ostrom, E. B. Ebbesen, R. S. Wyer, Jr, D. L. Hamilton & D. E. Carlston (Eds), *Person Memory: The Cognitive Basis of Social Perception*. Hillsdale, NJ: Erlbaum.

Hasher, L., Attig, M. S., & Alba, J. W. (1981). I knew it all along: Or did I? *Journal of Verbal Learning and Verbal Behavior*, **20**, 86–96.

Hastie, R., & Park, B. (1986). The relationship between memory and judgment depends on whether the judgment task is memory-based or on-line. *Psychological Review*, **93**, 258–68.

Hawkins, S. A., & Hastie, R. (1990). Hindsight: Biased judgments of past events after the outcomes are known. *Psychological Bulletin*, **107**, 311–27.

Hell, W., Gigerenzer, G., Gauggel, S., Mall, M., & Müller, M. (1988). Hindsight bias: An interaction of automatic and motivational factors? *Memory and Cognition*, **16**, 533–8.

Hoch, S. J., & Loewenstein, G. F. (1989). Outcome feedback: Hindsight and information. *Journal of Experimental Psychology*, **15**, 605–19.

Köhnken, G. (1987). Nachträgliche Informationen und die Erinnerung komplexer Sachverhalte—Empirische Befunde und theoretische Kontroversen. *Psychologische Rundschau*, **38**, 190–203.

Loftus, E. F. (1975). Leading questions and the eyewitness report. *Cognitive Psychology*, **7**, 560–72.

Loftus, E. F. (1979). *Eyewitness Testimony*. Cambridge, MA: Harvard University Press.

Loftus, E. F., & Hoffmann, H. G. (1989). Misinformation and memory: The creation of new memories. *Journal of Experimental Psychology: General*, **118**, 100–104.

Loftus, E. F., & Loftus, G. R. (1980). On the permanence of stored information in the human brain. *American Psychologist*, **35**, 409–20.

Loftus, E. F., Schooler, J. W., & Wagenaar, W. A. (1985). The fate of memory: Comment on McCloskey & Zaragoza. *Journal of Experimental Psychology: General*, **114**, 375–80.

Mark, M. M., & Mellor, S. (1991). Effect of self-relevance of an event on hindsight-bias: The foreseeability of a layout. *Journal of Applied Psychology*, **76**, 569–77.

Mazursky, D., & Ofir, C. (1990). "I could never have expected it to happen": The reversal of the hindsight bias. *Organizational Behavior and Human Decision Processes*, **46**, 20–33.

McCloskey, M., & Zaragoza, M. (1985a). Misleading postevent information and memory for events: Arguments and evidence against memory impairment hypotheses. *Journal of Experimental Psychology: General*, **114**, 1–16.

McCloskey, M., & Zaragoza, M. (1985b). Postevent information and memory: Reply to Loftus, Schooler, and Wagenaar. *Journal of Experimental Psychology: General*, **114**, 381–7.

McCloskey, M., & Zaragoza, M. (1989). Misleading postevent information and the memory impairment hypothesis: Comment on Belli and reply to Tversky and Tuchin. *Journal of Experimental Psychology: General*, **118**, 92–9.

Morton, J., Hammersley, R. H., & Bekerian, D. A. (1985). Headed records: A model for memory and its failures. *Cognition*, **20**, 1–23.

Pohl, R. F. (1993). Der Rückschau-Fehler: Ein Modell zur Analyse und Erklärung systematisch verfälschter Erinnerungen. Habilitationsschrift (unpublished), Trier, Germany.

Pohl, R. F., & Gawlik, B. (1995). Hindsight bias and the misinformation effect: Separating blended recollections from other recollection types. *Memory*, **3**, 21–55.

Slovic, P., & Fischhoff, B. (1977).   On the psychology of experimental surprises. *Journal of Experimental Psychology: Human Perception and Performance, 3*, 544–51.

Stahlberg, D. (1994).   Der Knew-it-all-along Effekt—Eine urteilsthoeretische Erklärung. Habilitationsschrift (unpublished), Kiel, Germany.

Stahlberg, D., & Eller, F. (1992).   *Hindsight-Effekte—Belege für ein Antwortten-denzmodell.* Report 34, Tagung experimentell arbeitender Psychologen, Osnabrück.

Stahlberg, D., & Eckert, H. (1994).   *Hindsight-Effekte—bewußte Rekonstruktion und automatische Verankerung.* Report 35, Tagung experimentell arbeitender Psychologinnen und Psychologen, Munich.

Stahlberg, D., Eller, F., Frey, D., & Maass, A. (1995a).   We knew it all along: Hindsight bias in groups. *Organizational Behavior and Human Decision Processes,* **63**, 46–58.

Stahlberg, D., Eller, F., Frey, D., & Maass, A. (1995b).   Hindsight-bias: Memory impairment or response bias? Unpublished manuscript, Kiel, Germany.

Steiner, I. D. (1972).   *Group Process and Productivity.* New York: Academic Press.

Tammeo, B. (1995).   Senno di poi: alterazione della memora a distorzione sistematica della risposta? (Hindsight bias: Memory alteration or systematic response distortion?) Unpublished Master's Thesis, Padua University, Italy.

Tversky, A., & Kahneman, D. (1982).   Judgment under uncertainty: Heuristics and biases. *Science,* **185**, 1124–31.

Tversky, B., & Tuchin, M. (1989).   A reconciliation of the evidence on eyewitness testimony: Comments on McCloskey and Zaragoza. *Journal of Experimental Psychology: General,* **118**, 86–91.

Verplanken, B., & Pieters, R. G. M. (1988).   Individual differences in reversed hindsight bias: I never thought something like Chernobyl would happen. Did I? *Journal of Behavioral Decision Making, 1*, 131–47.

Wassermann, D., Lempert, R. O., & Hastie, R. (1991).   Hindsight and causality. *Personality and Social Psychology Bulletin, 17*, 30–35.

Wendt, D. (1993).   Kein Hindsight Bias ("Knew-it-all-along-Effekt") bei den Landtagswahlen in Schleswig-Holstein 1988 und 1992. *Zeitschrift für Sozialpsychologie,* **24**, 273–9.

Wood, G. (1978).   The "knew-it-all-along" effect. *Journal of Experimental Psychology: Human Perception Performance, 4*, 345–53.

Zaragoza, M. S., & McCloskey, M. (1989).   Misleading and postevent information and the memory impairment hypothesis: Comment on Belli and reply to Tversky and Tuchin. *Journal of Experimental Psychology: General,* **118**, 92–9.

Chapter 5

Cognitive and Social Consequences of the Need for Cognitive Closure

Donna M. Webster
Winthrop University
Arie W. Kruglanski
University of Maryland, College Park

ABSTRACT

This paper reviews research on the antecedent conditions and the cognitive and social consequences of the need for cognitive closure (Kruglanski, 1989). This particular need is conceived of as a desire for definite knowledge on some issue and the eschewal of confusion and ambiguity. It is considered proportionate in magnitude to the perceived benefits of closure and the costs of lacking closure. Those benefits and costs, in turn, are assumed to vary situationally and also represent stable individual differences in the tendency to value closure. The consequences of the need for closure are assumed to derive from two general tendencies, those of *urgency* and *permanence*, respectively. The urgency tendency refers to the inclination to attain closure without delay, and to "seize" on early information potentially leading to closure. The permanence tendency refers to the inclination to maintain closure for as long as possible, hence to "freeze" on present closure and safeguard future closure. Those dual tendencies are shown to impact a broad variety of social psychological phenomena on intrapersonal, interpersonal and group levels of analysis.

The construction of knowledge is a fundamental human activity indispensable for our everyday functioning. Its products are myriad and they provide the basis for most reasoned decisions and intelligent actions. Even the simplest, most mundane tasks (ordering a meal at a restaurant, conversing with a

European Review of Social Psychology, Volume 8. Edited by Wolfgang Stroebe and Miles Hewstone.
© 1998 John Wiley & Sons Ltd.

colleague) require multiple on-line judgments, and in this sense the continuous formation of novel knowledge. The understanding of processes involved
in knowledge construction is thus a major task for any science concerned with
the explanation of human behavior.

Constructing knowledge is an inherently interpersonal undertaking, as
various social entities (other people, the media, books or newspapers) may be
the ends of constructive endeavors or the sources of information, that is,
means toward constructive ends. The process itself may be involved and
intricate at times, requiring an access of information from memory or the
environment, the evaluation of competing alternatives and the integration of
disparate pieces of information into coherent wholes. These activities may
pose considerable demands on resource allocation, hence they may require
appreciable motivation to get under way.

Specifically, individuals may be motivated to possess knowledge on some
topics more than on others, hence they may focus their constructive efforts in
those particular domains. The reasons for such preferences may relate to the
valence of the information about a given concern or to the possibility that it
provides *definite* information, required for some purpose. Thus, an individual
may prefer to *know that* he/she has won the lottery, since this means that a
windfall of money is imminent, whereas the administrator of the prize may
desire to *know what* the winning numbers are so that appropriate payment
may be made. The former case, of *knowledge that* (something desirable is the
case) has been referred to (Kruglanski, 1989) as a need for a specific closure,
indicating a directional motivational bias toward the desirable conclusion.
The latter case, of *knowledge what* (the case may be, desirable or not) has
been referred to as the need for a non-specific closure connoting a non-
directional motivational bias, or a preference for *any* firm answer, compared
to confusion or ambiguity. Of course, a preference for *any* answer ultimately
leads to the adoption of *some* answer; this need not reflect a preference for
such an answer's specific features, however, but merely its capability of providing closure simply because of its presence. This, in turn, may depend on the
"answer's" chronic accessibility (as in the case of prevalent stereotypes), its
situational activation (as in priming), or its appearance early in the informational sequence (as in primacy effects). According to the present conception,
all such cases (discussed subsequently) wherein an answer is adopted simply
because of it "being there" reflect a non-directional rather than a directional
need for closure.

It is also of interest that, whereas directional motivational biases have
received extensive attention in the social psychological literature (e.g. see
Kunda, 1990, for a review), non-directional biases have been accorded markedly less research emphasis. In an attempt to address this void, this chapter
examines non-directional need for closure effects on the knowledge construction process, focusing in particular on the social-psychological

consequences that the motivated epistemic process may mediate. We begin with a brief discussion of the need for closure, its essential characteristics and its antecedents.

THE NEED FOR CLOSURE CONTINUUM

The need for cognitive closure is conceptualized as potentially variable across situations and persons. Thus, individuals may desire clear-cut answers in many circumstances, whereas in other contexts they may be less interested in closure or may prefer to *avoid* it all together. Similarly, some individuals may possess a chronic desire for closure (perhaps because of the order and stability it promises), while others may tend to prefer the freedom inherent in a lack of closure. In other words, individuals' degrees of motivation toward closure may be represented on a continuum ranging from a high need for closure to a high need to avoid closure. An individual high on the need *for* closure may render snap judgments based on inconclusive evidence and act in a closed-minded manner, refusing to entertain alternative views. A person high on the need to avoid closure may enjoy the freedom associated with ambiguity and may prefer to suspend judgment, generating alternatives to any potential conclusion. The effects of the closure-motivation are assumed to be mono-tonic along the continuum. Thus, the higher (vs. lower) the degree of the closure-motivation, the higher (vs. lower) the degree of the motivational effect, irrespective of where on the continuum the two comparison points might lie.

ANTECEDENTS OF THE CLOSURE-MOTIVATION

The antecedent conditions of the closure-motivation are assumed to be pro-portionate to the perceived costs or benefits of possessing closure. Those costs and benefits may vary according to contextual factors or result from chronic individual differences.

Situational Determinants

A potential benefit of possessing closure may be the ability to act once a judgment was made. Thus, the need for closure should be heightened in circumstances where action was particularly valued (e.g., when members of a work group must complete some task quickly). An alternative benefit of possessing closure is that it frees an individual from the necessity to engage in continued information processing. Thus, in cases when information process-ing is perceived as costly (e.g., when an individual is fatigued or when the processing task is dull), need for closure should be correspondingly heightened.

Potential costs of possessing closure are assumed to lower the need for closure and raise the need to avoid closure. Under certain circumstances closure may appear detrimental (e.g., due to concerns about judgmental errors, or because closure threatens personal freedom and narrows one's range of options). Thus, heightened need to avoid closure and an accompanying desire to suspend judgment may often arise when concerns about decision accuracy are high or when judgmental flexibility is subjectively important to the individual.

It is of interest to note that the concern with accuracy or the fear of invalidity (Kruglanski & Freund, 1983) need not invariably usher in open-mindedness or prompt the eschewal of closure. If a particular closure appeared unquestionably valid (e.g. because of the indubitable credentials of its source), the desire for accuracy may increase the tendency to adopt it rather than prompting an open-mindedness to new concepts and information. Thus, the relation between accuracy concerns and the need for closure is *contingent* rather than absolute. Such concerns may lower the need for closure only where no obviously correct opinion existed, but where it did, it might induce closed-mindedness instead.

The need for closure notion may seem related to several influential concepts in the social cognition literature. One prominent such construct is the notion of "elaboration likelihood" introduced by Petty and Cacioppo (e.g. 1986). According to these authors (ibid., p. 128), "Elaboration in a persuasion context (means) the extent to which a person thinks about the issue-relevant arguments contained in a message". Elaboration likelihood is thought to depend upon motivational as well as ability factors and it essentially involves careful consideration of the arguments, and the consequent derivation of ". . . an overall evaluation of, or attitude toward, the recommendation" (ibid.). A motivation to engage in extensive elaboration may seem to connote an avoidance of closure, yet the overall purpose of elaboration is the ultimate attainment of closure, i.e. "An overall evaluation . . . or attitude". Furthermore, an absence of elaboration need not necessarily denote the attainment of closure, for it could mean instead the dwindling of an interest in the topic, and its abandonment without forming a clear-cut opinion. In short, whereas high need for closure probably denotes a low elaboration likelihood, low elaboration likelihood does not necessarily signify a high need for closure, neither does high elaboration likelihood betoken an avoidance of closure.

"Involvement", another seemingly relevant construct to the need for closure, has been typically operationalized by attitude-change theorists (Chaiken, Liberman, & Eagly, 1989; Petty & Cacioppo, 1986; Petty, 1994) as a concern about the accuracy of one's attitude. In those circumstances, its relation to need for closure is akin to the concern for accuracy (or the fear of invalidity) discussed above. It is noted in passing that although "involvement" has been typically identified with the accuracy motivation, this need not be so necessarily. For example, an individual might be issue-involved for esteem-related reasons, in which case involvement may induce a defensive or an impression management motivation (Chaiken, Liberman, & Eagly, 1989), i.e. a need for a directional closure in present terminology. Finally, the individual could be involved in an issue because of a strong desire for (non-directional) closure, in fact, and an intolerance of ambiguity about it. These complications were recognized (Eagly & Chaiken, 1993, p. 288), leading them to conclude that, "Involvement is not one but several constructs and . . . different types of involvement may exert differing effects on information processing, attitude change and its persistence". In fact, it may be more useful to think about "involvement" as a *magnitude* of motivation rather than a particular motivational type. In those terms, involvement *per se* is no longer expected to yield unique cognitive effects. Rather, it should be necessary to specify further the type of involvement, the quality of the motivation in regard to an issue. To illustrate this point, Sorrentino et al. (1988) found the high personal involvement induced *certainty-orientated* individuals to be *less careful* or systematic in processing of message arguments, whereas it made *uncertainty-orientated* individuals *more* careful.

Individual Differences

It is also possible that there exist stable individual differences in the extent to which persons cherish closure. Those differences may derive from a variety of sources, including norms, and socialization practices that differ in the extent to which judgmental confidence, orderliness and clarity are culturally appreciated (Hofstede, 1980). Individuals growing up in cultures placing high value on those attributes may develop a stronger need for closure than individuals where they are de-emphasized or regarded negatively. Potentially, too, specific family dynamics (with a given culture) may induce a stable need for closure in young children, e.g. where inconsistencies in parental actions and pronouncements may at once undermine closure and evoke anxiety. Also, situations where considerable uncertainty is associated with highly negative potential outcomes (e.g. growing up in a war-zone where one's very life and that of one's family and relatives is perennially at risk) might render uncertainty particularly aversive, hence instilling a need for closure.

Historical Background

Individual differences in the proclivity toward closed-mindedness have commanded prior conceptual and empirical attention by major personality and social psychologists. Thus, Freud (1923) traced the openness to new experience to a successful development during the oral period, giving rise to a sense of basic trust. By contrast, a basic distrust originating in an oral fixation was thought to promote closed-mindedness. *Intolerance of ambiguity* was described by Frenkel-Brunswik (1949) and Eysenck (1954) as a perceptual-cognitive rigidity and emotional ambivalence. Rokeach (1960) investigated the antecedents and consequences of closed and open belief systems, with particular reference to their impact on the attitudes toward new information. Kagan (1972) maintained that uncertainty resolution is a primary determinant of behavior and Sorrentino recently carried out impressive research on cer-tainty and uncertainty orientations, defining the extent to which a person "likes to stick to familiar events and traditional beliefs" (Sorrentino & Short, 1986, p. 400) vs. striving to "integrate new events or beliefs into already existing belief systems" (ibid, p. 399). Finally, the present distinction between closed-mindedness and open-mindedness is shared by the Openness factor of the Big Five (McCrae and Costa, 1985).

Undoubtedly, the need for closure construct is similar in some respects to those prior notions, but it is also distinct from them in rather consequential ways. The primary similarity is that those earlier concepts, too, bear on the issue of a prejudiced disposition, and on the tendency to be rejecting and impervious in regard to new ideas or experiences. This commonality notwith-standing, however, the prior notions were mostly dynamic in character, referred to broad personality topologies, were linked to particular belief-contents (e.g. the closed and open belief systems discussed by Rokeach differed fundamentally in the contents of their basic premises), were often treated as *cognitive* rather than *motivational* (Sorrentino & Short, 1986) and often stressed the dysfunctional nature of uncertainty avoidance (for discus-sion, see Kruglanski & Webster, 1996). The present conceptual framework is broader by comparison, encompassing as it does situational as well as individual-difference factors, and shunning commitment to any particular cir-cumstances in the psychosexual development (Adorno et al., 1950; Eysenck, 1954; Rokeach, 1960; Sorrentino & Short, 1986) or any particular contents of belief systems (Rokeach, 1960).

Empirical Relations with Related Constructs

The above differences and commonalities suggests that the need for closure should exhibit low to moderate correlations with several kindred constructs. Webster's and Kruglanski's (1994) psychometric work on the need for closure scale yields evidence consistent with this expectation. Specifically, the correla-tion between need for closure and the F scale (Sanford *et al.*, 1950) was 0.26. That between need for closure and intolerance of ambiguity (Frenkel-Brunswik, 1949) was 0.29, and that between need for closure and dogmatism (Rokeach, 1960) was 0.28.

Other empirical relations are of interest. Thus, it is noteworthy that the need for closure is not significantly related to intelligence ($r = -0.17$). Furthermore, it is only slightly (and negatively) related to the "need for cognition" ($r = -0.28$) (Cacioppo & Petty, 1982), defined as the extent to which "one engages in and enjoys thinking". This seems quite reasonable: although the possession of closure obviates the necessity to think further, one may refrain from thinking without necessarily attaining closure.

Of paramount importance is our assumption that diverse need for closure sources should be *functionally equivalent* with respect to theoretically relevant phenomena. Thus, we would expect similar, theoretically hypothesized, effects of need for closure to emerge irrespective of the particular source of this motivation or the way it has been operationally defined. Empirical evidence for such a convergence is considered in what follows.

CONSEQUENCES OF THE NEED FOR CLOSURE: THE URGENCY AND PERMANENCE TENDENCIES

The need for closure may affect information processing activities involved in the construction of knowledge. First, it may instill an *urgency* tendency, that is, a desire to attain closure quickly. This may result in quick "seizing" upon judgmentally relevant cues (Kruglanski & Webster, 1996). Furthermore, it may instigate a *permanence* tendency, that is, a desire to preserve past knowledge or to safeguard future knowledge; this may result in a "freezing" upon prior judgments (Kruglanski & Freund, 1983). Collectively, those tendencies may affect information processing and indirectly impact a wide array of social-psychological processes that information processing may mediate. Empirical demonstrations of such effects are considered next.

KNOWLEDGE FORMATION EFFECTS

Extent of Information Processing

The amount of information processed *en route* to a judgment may be affected jointly by the urgency and permanence tendencies. Specifically, individuals experiencing a need for closure may process less information and generate fewer competing hypotheses prior to reaching a judgment because of their propensity to "seize" upon early information and quickly "freeze" on judgments it implies, thus closing their minds to further relevant information.

One manifestation of the "seizing" and "freezing" sequence is restriction of the informational search prior to making a decision. This process was examined in a study by Webster, Richter, and Kruglanski (1996) where need for closure was operationalized in terms of mental fatigue. Specifically, fatigue was expected to raise the need for closure, as tired individuals should seek closure to avoid further information processing that may appear as laborious, hence costly to those persons. Psychology students took part in an impression formation task in which they played a personnel-manager faced with a hiring decision. Students were randomly assigned to complete the task either before or after a normal class period or following a final examination. Those conditions were designed to produce low and high degrees of mental fatigue, respectively. Manipulation checks provided evidence that: (a) the fatigue induction was successful (that is, participants tested either before or after a normal class exhibited a lower degree of fatigue than those tested after the final examination); and (b) fatigue varied positively with a need for closure. As part of the impression formation task, participants were presented with a list of materials "often used in the evaluation of job applicants" and were asked to indicate which of those items they would like to review prior to making their own evaluations of the candidate. The list consisted of a variety of relevant items, including resume, references, transcripts and a personal statement, and indicated the number of pages involved for each document. Participants were asked to check off those items they wanted to review. As expected, individuals experiencing a relatively high (vs. low) need for closure requested significantly fewer pages of relevant information prior to forming their impression of the job candidate. Furthermore, when some participants were held accountable for their judgments (a manipulation designed to lower their need for closure) they requested significantly more pages of information than those not held accountable.

The extent of information processed *en route* to knowledge-formation was also examined in an experiment by Mayseless and Kruglanski (1987, Study 2). Participants identified barely visible digits appearing on a tachistoscopic screen. Need for closure was heightened for some participants by informing them that mental concentration and intelligence are positively correlated with the ability to form "unambiguous, clear-cut opinions". Those instructions were designed to heighten the need for closure by enhancing the perceived value of closure. The need to avoid closure was aroused in other participants by accuracy instructions and the promise of extra experimental credits for correctly identifying 9 out of 10 digits. Those instructions were designed to increase participants' tolerance of ambiguity and their propensity to entertain various possibilities regarding a digit's identity. A neutral control condition was also included in which no motivational induction was attempted. All participants were given the opportunity to operate the tachistoscope an unlimited number of times. Results indicated that, as expected, the extent of informational search (defined as the number of times participants operated the tachistoscope) was lowest in the need-for-closure condition, intermediate in the control condition and highest in the need-to-avoid-closure condition.

Hypothesis Generation

The "seizing" and "freezing" tendencies evoked by the need for closure may affect not only the processing of external stimulus information, but also the processing of internal stimulus information (i.e., information stored in memory). This possibility was assessed in an experiment on hypothesis generation conducted by Mayseless and Kruglanski (1987, Study 3). Participants were shown photos of parts of common objects such as a comb or a toothbrush that were enlarged and taken from unusual angles so as to disguise their true identity. On each of several trials, participants listed as many hypotheses as possible concerning an object's identity and finally selected what they deemed as the most likely identity. Need for closure was aroused in some subjects by stressing that clear-cut opinions are related to intelligence and mental concentration. Need to avoid closure was induced in other participants by informing them that mental concentration and intelligence are related to correct visual recognition. A neutral condition was also included. As expected, results indicated that participants in the need-to-avoid-closure condition generated *more* hypotheses on the average compared to the neutral control condition, while participants in the need-for-closure condition generated *fewer* hypotheses on average than the control group.

Subjective Confidence

One consequence of reduced generation and consideration of hypotheses prior to the formation of judgments may be the attainment of greater judgmental confidence. If individuals under need for closure are less aware of competing judgmental possibilities, they may be more confident in the judgment they ultimately form. Indeed, elevated confidence of subjects experiencing need for closure has been observed in studies that operationalized the closure-motivation in a variety of ways, including stressing the value of clear-cut opinions (Mayseless & Kruglanski, 1987), time pressure (Kruglanski & Webster, 1991), dullness of task (Webster, 1993) and difficulty of information processing (Kruglanski, Webster, & Klem, 1993). Those findings suggest that attainment of certain views is possible in the absence of relatively extensive information processing. In fact, our research demonstrates that *paradoxically*, the restriction of information-processing under heightened need for closure may often go hand-in-hand with elevated confidence.

Type of Information Sought

The reduction of hypothesis-generation under need for closure (Mayseless & Kruglanski, 1987, Study 3) may affect the *type* in addition to the *amount* of information sought prior to making a judgment. This notion was examined in a study (Kruglanski & Mayseless, 1988) that required participants to evaluate whether or not a target person belonged in a given professional category. Individuals under a need for closure were expected to prefer prototypical information about the category, as their main concern might be determining whether the target fits that particular possibility. Individuals experiencing a need to avoid closure were expected to prefer diagnostic information (Trope & Bassok, 1983) capable of discriminating among different possibilities regarding the target's professional affiliation. Indeed, the results indicated that participants under need for closure were more likely to seek information about prototypical features of the professional category, while participants under need to avoid closure were more likely to ask for diagnostic information.

CUE UTILIZATION

A general propensity to base judgments on early cues and to under-adjust such judgments in the light of later relevant information may be prompted by the urgency and permanence tendencies evoked by the closure-motivation: Specifically, the "seizing" tendency should dispose persons to quickly utilize early cues toward the formation of initial judgments, whereas the "freezing" tendency should dispose them to fixate and perseverate on those particular judgments.

Primacy Effects in Impression Formation

A prime example of such effects is the "primacy effect" in impression formation (Asch, 1946) which concerns the tendency to base social impressions on early information, to the relative neglect of later information. If this effect reflects the "seizing" and "freezing" tendencies, it should be exaggerated under high (vs. low) need for closure. Indeed, this prediction has been supported in a variety of studies. The effect was demonstrated first in an experiment by Kruglanski and Freund (1983, Study 1). In this study, need for closure was heightened for some participants via time-pressure designed to highlight the *benefits* of early closure, and reduced for other participants via accountability instructions designed to highlight the *costs* of premature closure. As expected, the magnitude of the primacy effect varied positively with time pressure and negatively with accountability. This effect was replicated in several studies that operationalized the need for closure in disparate ways, including (again) time-pressure (Freund, Kruglanski, & Schpitzajzen, 1985; Heaton & Kruglanski, 1991), requests for global impressions (Freund, Kruglanski, & Schpitzajzen, 1985), mental fatigue (Webster, Richter, & Kruglanski, 1996), and scores on the Need for Closure Scale (Webster & Kruglanski, 1994).

Anchoring Effects

Another example of the inclination to rely on early cues when forming judgments may be reflected in the classic anchoring and insufficient adjustment effect (Tversky & Kahneman, 1974). Here, individuals asked to assess the probability of some event, given a starting point, will use the starting point as an anchor and then adjust their judgment. The resulting final judgment tends to be biased in the direction of the anchor. This anchoring phenomenon seems to represent a special case of cue-utilization and should, therefore, be appropriately affected by the need for closure. A study designed to test this notion (Kruglanski & Freund, 1983, Study 2) demonstrated that probability estimates were more likely to reflect the anchoring tendency under high need for closure (manipulated via time pressure) and less likely to do so under a need to avoid closure (manipulated via evaluation apprehension).

The Correspondence Bias

The tendency to over-utilize early cues and fail to adjust appropriately in light of further information may also underlie the correspondence bias in social perception (Jones, 1979). This prevalent bias involves the propensity to over-estimate the role of dispositional as opposed to situational causes for an actor's behavior. The effect was originally demonstrated in a study by Jones and Harris (1967) that required participants to judge the true attitude of a target person after reading an opinion-essay allegedly prepared by the target under either free-choice or no-choice conditions. Even when participants learned that the target was given no choice in determining the contents of the essay, they still estimated that his/her attitude corresponded to the one expressed in the essay.

Various theorists (e.g., Jones, 1979; Quattrone, 1982; Gilbert, Pelham, & Krull, 1988) have considered the possible role that the anchoring and insufficient adjustment process may play in effecting this particular bias. Specifically, when subjects are asked to judge the target's true attitude, the most salient piece of evidence is the behavior that has occurred (i.e., the opinion endorsed in the essay). This may directly bring to mind the assumption that the behavior corresponds to the writer's attitude. This initial hypothesis may serve as an anchor that is subsequently adjusted in the course of a "controlled" process that involves the consideration of less salient evidence (e.g., that the writer was situationally constrained). Because such adjustment is typically insufficient (Tversky & Kahneman, 1974), the final attitude attribution would be biased in the direction of the anchor (i.e., the initial dispositional hypothesis).

This controlled adjustment process may require substantial cognitive resources and effort. Indeed, evidence suggests that the correspondence bias is enhanced when the individual's cognitive capabilities are reduced (Gilbert, Pelham, & Krull, 1988). If adjustment requires significant cognitive effort, however, it should be appropriately affected by motivation to expend the effort. Research by Tetlock (1985) suggests that this may be so. Specifically, Tetlock found that the correspondence bias was reduced when participants were made to feel accountable for their judgments. It seems, then, that accountability concerns may motivate subjects to become more active and discriminating information processors, leading to greater adjustment of the initial hypothesis and lowering the bias in the final judgment.

The foregoing findings are consistent with the idea that, in a manner similar to that seen with the primacy and anchoring effects, the correspondence bias involves a tendency to rely on early hypotheses or estimates while neglecting further information. Thus, the bias may also be appropriately affected by the need for closure. This possibility was tested in a series of experiments by Webster (1993). Subjects completed a typical attitude-attribution task in which they estimated a target's attitude after hearing her deliver a speech criticizing student exchange programs. The speech was allegedly prepared under high- or low-choice conditions. The need for closure was manipulated via perceived task attractiveness. Specifically, perceptions of the attitude-attribution task were varied by comparing this initial task to a subsequent, expected task. In some conditions, the subsequent task was very appealing (watching a comedy video), and prompted subjects to view the initial attitude attribution task as unattractive by comparison. In other conditions, the subsequent task was rather unappealing (watching a video of a lecture on multivariate statistics) and prompted subjects to perceive the initial task as attractive by comparison. Finally, in a control condition, the subsequent task was portrayed as very similar to the initial one, leading subjects to perceive it as equivalent to it, and moderate in attractiveness.

Manipulation checks suggested that these task attractiveness conditions were successful in producing the corresponding differences in need for closure. Specifically, need for closure was highest in the unattractive task condition, lowest in the attractive task condition and intermediate in the neutral control condition. Most importantly, the correspondence bias appeared to be influenced by the need for closure in the expected manner. Specifically, this bias was enhanced in the unattractive task condition relative to the control condition and reduced in the attractive task condition, relative to the control condition. Those results were replicated in a second study, where need for closure was operationalized via scores on the Need for Closure Scale (Webster & Kruglanski, 1994). Finally, in a third study the pattern of results was reversed when initial cues implied a situational rather than a dispositional attribution. Specifically, individuals under high need for closure were less likely to make dispositional attributions while those under low need for closure were more likely to do so, when both were compared to the control condition. This suggests that need for closure effects are essentially content-free, and it is the order of the cues (i.e. their appearance early vs. late in the sequence) rather than their particular substance (implying a dispositional vs. a situational attribution) that is critical.

KNOWLEDGE UTILIZATION EFFECTS

Stereotypic Judgments

The findings reviewed so far suggest that as a result of the joint "seizing" and "freezing" tendencies, individuals experiencing a high (vs. low) need for closure rely more on information encountered early as opposed to later in the knowledge-construction sequence, as such information affords quick closure. A related possibility is that individuals under need for closure will "seize" on judgmentally relevant information readily accessible in memory and "freeze" upon judgments it implies, rather than processing extensive case-specific information which may delay closure. Thus, need for closure may lead individuals to over-utilize chronically accessible stereotypes, prejudices or pre-existing attitudes when forming judgments, to a relative neglect of case-specific or individuating information. This possibility was first tested in an experiment by Kruglanski and Freund (1983) that examined the impact of ethnic stereotypes about the academic competence of Ashkenazi and Sephardi Jews in Israel on the assignment of grades for a literary composition. Findings indicated that these stereotypes were more likely to influence grade-assignments when the evaluators were under high need for closure (manipulated via time pressure) as compared to low need for closure (manipulated via accountability concerns).

In subsequent similar research, time-pressure was found to increase reliance on gender stereotypes (Jamieson & Zanna, 1989). Specifically, subjects known to hold negative attitudes about women in management were more likely to devalue the resumés of female (vs. male) applicants for a management position when placed under high (vs. low) time pressure. This effect occurred even though pretesting indicated that the information presented on the male and female resumés was essentially equivalent. Those findings support the notion that need for closure leads to reliance on pre-existing knowledge structures to the relative neglect of case-specific information.

Recently, Dijksterhuis et al. (1996) found that such a tendency to rely on stereotypes has important effects on memory as well as judgment. In that research, dispositional need for closure was assessed via the Dutch version of the Need for Closure Scale (Cratylus, 1995). In one study, Dutch undergraduates were presented with behavioral information about a negatively valenced group of soccer hooligans and were asked to form an impression of this group. Participants high in need for closure recalled relatively more stereotype-consistent information, whereas participants low in need for closure recalled more stereotype-inconsistent information. Furthermore, participants high in need for closure judged the target group more stereotypically and perceived it as more homogeneous compared to participants low in need for closure. Those results were replicated in a second study, where the target-group was positively valenced, consisting of nurses.

Construct Accessibility Effects

This tendency of individuals experiencing a high need for closure to base judgments on pre-existing stereotypes occurs presumably because these are readily accessible in memory and provide a means of reaching closure quickly. This assumption received a direct test in a study by Ford and Kruglanski (1995) based on a priming paradigm developed by Higgins, Rholes, and Jones (1977). Subjects who scored either high or low on the Need for Closure Scale (Webster & Kruglanski, 1994) received one of two primes during a memory task: either the negatively valenced adjective "reckless" or the positively valenced adjective "adventurous". They then performed an impression formation task that required them to characterize a target person with a single word after reading behavioral information about the target that was ambiguous with respect to the adventurous/reckless distinction. Results indicated that subjects high (vs. low) on a dispositional need for closure tended to characterize the target more in terms suggesting recklessness in the negative prime condition and adventurousness in the positive prime condition. Thus consistent with the "seizing" and "freezing" notion, subjects high on need for closure exhibited stronger effects of priming than subjects low on this need. Similar results were reported by Thompson *et al.* (1994).

In summary, research reviewed above supports a broad variety of hypotheses concerning intrapersonal effects of the need for closure consistent with the "seizing" and "freezing" notions related to the urgency and permanence tendencies this motivation may evoke. A listing of those hypotheses and their empirical tests is given in Table 5.1.

INTERPERSONAL CONSEQUENCES OF THE CLOSURE-MOTIVATION

In studies reviewed thus far, need for closure was found to effect a curtailment in information processing, resulting in various biases in social judgment. It seems reasonable that the closure-motivation may also affect interpersonal processes, as processing information about one's interaction partners is an important part of social interaction. Evidence supporting this notion is considered subsequently.

Table 5.1 Intrapersonal consequences of "seizing" and "freezing" under heightened need for closure. A listing of hypotheses and relevant research

Hypotheses	Research
1. Need for closure effects a restriction of information processing	Webster, Richter, and Kruglanski (1996) Mayseless and Kruglanski (1987, study 2)
2. Need for closure restricts hypothesis generation	Mayseless and Kruglanski (1987, study 3)
3. Need for closure augments subjective confidence in a judgment	Mayseless and Kruglanski (1987) Kruglanski and Webster (1991) Webster (1993) Kruglanski, Webster, and Klem (1993)
4. Need for closure induces a preference for prototypic (vs. diagnostic) information	Kruglanski and Mayseless (1988)
5. Need for closure effects an over-utilization of early or readily accessible cues	Kruglanski and Freund (1983) Freund, Kruglanski, and Schpitzajzen (1985) Jamieson and Zanna (1989) Webster, Richter, and Kruglanski (1996) Webster and Kruglanski (1994) Ford and Kruglanski (1995) Thompson et al. (1994)
6. Need for closure increases the recall of stereotype-consistent vs. inconsistent features and of stereotypic judgments of a group	Dijksterhuis et al. (1996)

Perspective Taking and Empathy

The "urgency" and "permanence" tendencies prompted by need for closure influence information processing and may therefore be expected to affect interpersonal processes that involve the exchange of information. A relevant domain of phenomena in this connection are interpersonal processes involving perspective taking and empathy.

Perspective taking is an aspect of empathy discussed by Davis (1983) that involves an ability to see things from another person's vantage point. Empathic concern is another aspect of empathy referring to the extent to which we may express compassion, sympathy or caring for someone (Davis, 1983). Perspective taking is likely to affect empathic concern, as we are more likely to feel concern for others if we understand their situation or appreciate their predicament.

It seems reasonable to assume that the taking of another person's perspective may require substantial cognitive effort, as the first thing that comes to mind is typically one's own perspective. If so, perspective taking may require correction and adjustment, both of which necessitate cognitive labor. This may be especially true if one is trying to take the perspective of a dissimilar person who holds a very different viewpoint. If need for closure reduces an individual's tendency to put forth mental effort in processing information, it may be expected to reduce perspective taking and empathic concern when relating to a person with a dissimilar perspective. Those ideas were examined in two recent studies conducted by Webster, Findley, and Irvin (1995).

In this research, need for closure was operationalized in terms of mental fatigue. Participants in the high fatigue condition were given a difficult proof-reading and reading comprehension task. Those under low fatigue were given an uncomplicated reading task and they reported being considerably less fatigued than individuals in the high fatigue condition. Manipulation checks also confirmed that fatigued (vs. non-fatigued) participants experienced a higher need for closure. After participants completed the fatigue portion of the study, they completed a social perception experiment that involved read-ing information allegedly provided by another participant in a previous study. The participants' task was to form impressions of that participant.

The target information depicted a negative social experience. Half the sub-jects read a description in which the target reported suffering from chronic shyness, as well as feelings of disappointment and dejection after a specific failed attempt to socialize at a party. The remaining subjects read the same description except for the fact that the target now reported feeling guilty and agitated after the social failure. The first variation described affect common among individuals with a chronic actual/ideal self-discrepancy (Higgins, 1987), whose emotional problems stem from not fulfilling their wishes and desires. The second variation described affect typical of people with a chronic actual/ought self-discrepancy (Higgins, 1987) whose emotional problems stem from failing to meet their perceived duties and obligations. These two varia-tions were used to manipulate similarity, as participants were pre-selected on the basis of possessing one or the other chronic self-discrepancy. More specifi-cally, the participants read about a target who either expressed thoughts and feelings similar to how they might feel in the same situation, or about some-one who expressed thoughts and feelings different from how they might feel.

After having read the description, participants responded to several ques-tions. First, they evaluated the appropriateness of the target's response to the incident. This was designed to assess perspective taking. In addition, they were asked to indicate the extent to which they felt compassionate, sympa-thetic, tender, warm, and softhearted with respect to the target. These ques-tions were adapted from a measure designed by Batson et al. (1983) to assess empathic concern. Manipulation checks confirmed that the similarity manipu-lation was successful and that there were no significant differences in this regard as a function of the type of discrepancy.

Analyses of the main dependent variables indicated, first, that perceived appropriateness of the response (reflecting perspective taking) was reduced by fatigue when the target was dissimilar to the participant. This condition represented a case when perspective taking would require cognitive effort which fatigued perceivers (assumed to experience need for closure) apparently did not make. No significant differences in perspective taking due to fatigue occurred when the target and the participant were similar. An identical pattern of findings emerged for the measure of empathic concern. Less empathic concern was reported by fatigued subjects when the target was dissimilar, while no significant differences in empathic concern occurred when he/she was similar to the participant. Those data are summarized in Table 5.2.

If perspective taking and empathic concern for dissimilar targets was reduced by the need for closure, lowering the need for closure should reverse this effect. A second study tested this possibility. In this study, need for closure was expected to be diminished if individuals expected to be outcome-dependent on the target, since past research demonstrates that outcome dependency motivates people to make accurate judgments (e.g., Erber & Fiske, 1984) and accuracy concerns seem to lower the need for closure (Mayseless & Kruglanski, 1987).

The procedure of the second study was highly similar to that of the first, but an outcome-dependency manipulation was added. Half the subjects believed they would be interacting with the target in the future as part of a peer support program; the remaining participants did not have this expectation. The relevant findings are displayed in Table 5.3. They indicate that non-

Table 5.2 Mean perspective taking and empathic concern as a function of perceived similarity and mental fatigue

	Similarity	
	Similar	Dissimilar
Perspective taking (perceived appropriateness of target's response)		
Mentally fatigued	4.47 (SD = 1.36)	2.94 (SD = 1.57)
Not mentally fatigued	4.88 (SD = 1.26)	3.94 (SD = 1.24)
Empathic concern		
Mentally fatigued	3.81 (SD = 1.34)	2.43 (SD = 1.04)
Not mentally fatigued	4.29 (SD = 1.04)	3.90 (SD = 1.31)

SD = standard deviation.

Table 5.3 Mean perspective taking and empathic concern as a function of perceived similarity (S) mental fatigue and outcome dependency

	Similarity	
	Similar	Dissimilar
Perspective taking (perceived appropriateness of target's response)		
Not outcome-dependent		
Mentally fatigued	4.64 (SD = 1.43)	3.30 (SD = 1.55)
Not mentally fatigued	5.00 (SD = 1.00)	4.40 (SD = 1.09)
Outcome-dependent		
Mentally fatigued	5.00 (SD = 1.04)	4.58 (SD = 1.51)
Not mentally fatigued	5.17 (SD = 1.14)	4.85 (SD = 1.34)
Empathic concern		
Not outcome-dependent		
Mentally fatigued	4.29 (SD = 1.31)	2.83 (SD = 1.35)
Not mentally fatigued	4.09 (SD = 1.57)	3.93 (SD = 1.18)
Outcome-dependent		
Mentally fatigued	4.60 (SD = 1.11)	4.50 (SD = 1.62)
Not mentally fatigued	4.56 (SD = 1.46)	4.34 (SD = 1.31)

SD = standard deviation.

outcome-dependent participants behaved pretty much as did subjects in Study 1. Fatigued (vs. non-fatigued) perceivers rated the target's response as significantly less appropriate when target–perceiver perspectives were dissimilar. No comparable differences emerged when target–perceiver perspectives were similar. Analyses of the empathic concern data revealed the same general pattern. Fatigued (vs. non-fatigued) perceivers rated the target's response as significantly less appropriate when target–perceiver perspectives were dissimilar, yet no such differences emerged when target–perceiver perspectives were similar.

A very different data-pattern emerged in the outcome-dependent condition (see Table 5.3), where no fatigue effects appeared on either perspective taking or emphatic concern. It seems that despite their fatigue, outcome-dependent participants were quite capable of taking the target's perspective and consequently experiencing empathic concern even when target's perspective was dissimilar from their own. These findings are consistent with the notion that the empathic deficits owing to fatigue are at least in part motivational in nature (i.e. related to the need for closure that fatigue may induce).

Appropriate manipulation check items confirmed that reported need for closure was indeed higher for perceivers under fatigue. Also in accord with expectation, reported need for closure was significantly lower for perceivers in the outcome-dependent condition. These findings are consistent with the notion that outcome dependency reduced the need for closure and, thus, increased perspective taking and empathic concern when target-subject perspectives were dissimilar. Further analysis (Baron & Kenny, 1986) suggested that the effects of need for closure on empathic concern were mediated by perspective taking. Those findings are consistent with the possibility that the "seizing and freezing" on one's own perspective may play an important role in such a distinctly interpersonal phenomenon as empathy.

Interpersonal Communication and Rapport

If need for closure induces the tendency to seek permanent knowledge and avoid the recurrence of ambiguity, it should foster a bias toward general, trans-situationally stable knowledge. Accordingly, people under a heightened need for closure should prefer abstract descriptions and category labels over concrete (hence situationally specific) depictions (Mikulincer, Yinon, and Kabili, 1991; Boudreau, Baron, and Oliver, 1992). Such abstraction bias may exert considerable influence on interpersonal communication, and on interpersonal rapport such communication may mediate.

We often acquire knowledge by formulating questions and directing them at others who then provide us with informative answers. Recent work by Semin, Rubini and Fiedler (1995) indicates that the abstractness level of questions influences the locus of causal origin for answers. Specifically, questions formulated with action verbs (e.g., to help, to write) cue the logical subject of a question as the causal origin for answers. Questions formulated with state verbs (e.g., to love, to like) cue the logical object of a question as the causal origin for answers. Thus, if asked a question such as, "Why do you own a dog?" we are prompted to respond by referring to ourselves (the subject of the question) as the causal agent of the answer, e.g., "Because I enjoy the companionship". If we are asked "Why do you like dogs?" we are prompted to respond by referring to the object itself, e.g., "Because dogs are good companions". One interesting implication of this effect is that individuals might feel they disclose more about themselves when asked questions formulated with action-verbs as opposed to state-verbs. As a consequence, they might feel closer and friendlier toward the interviewer, which could invite reciprocal friendliness on his/her part. By contrast, the more abstract the question, the greater the interpersonal distance created between collocutors.

Semin, Rubini, and Fiedler (1995) also found that the abstractness level of the questions tends to be matched by the abstractness of the answers. Thus, the more abstractly formulated questions tend to elicit also the more abstract answers. Such a drift toward abstraction might increase felt interpersonal distance and feelings of estrangement in and of itself, apart from any possible effects due to implicit causality. After all, abstractness implies generality and deindividuation, hence it may well depersonalize the interaction and render it more distant and less friendly.

Those notions were supported in a recent series of studies by Rubini and Kruglanski (1996). In the first experiment, participants under high need for closure (induced via ambient noise) selected questions characterized by a higher level of abstractness than questions selected by low-need-for-closure participants. In a second study, questions selected by participants under high need for closure were found to elicit more abstract answers from respondents, and ones focused more on the logical object (vs. the subject) of the question. Also, respondents reported lesser felt friendliness toward the interviewer whose questions were more (vs. less) abstract. Finally, in a third study the results of the previous two experiments were replicated in a free interaction context. In that research interviewers under high (vs. low) need for closure asked more abstract questions, which elicited more abstract answers focused more on the logical object (vs. subject) of the question, and consequently elicited lesser felt friendliness between the interviewee and the interviewer. Thus, the permanence-tendency induced by the need for closure may affect the level of linguistic abstractness, and in doing so may imbue the nascent social relations among conversation partners.

Persuadability

Beyond its induction of a preference for abstract, broadly generalizable knowledge, the permanence tendency induced by the closure-motivation may manifest itself in a predilection toward consensual judgments unlikely to be challenged by members of one's reference group. This desire for consensus may affect an individual's behavior during an interpersonal encounter that involves a persuasive attempt. This possibility was investigated in a series of studies conducted by Kruglanski, Webster, and Klem (1993). Participants in this research were required to discuss a legal case with another mock-juror (actually an experimental accomplice). Half the participants received prior information regarding the case, allowing them to form a confident opinion about it, while the remaining participants did not receive sufficient information to form a confident opinion. The need for closure was operationalized via scores on the Need for Closure Scale (Webster & Kruglanski, 1994) or via ambient noise. In each case, participants under high (vs. low) need for closure reported a greater desire to attain consensus with their partner. However, the manner in which they attempted to reach agreement varied as a function of the informational condition. If given adequate informational resources to form a prior opinion, high- vs. low-need-for-closure subjects declared a greater preference for an easily persuadable partner and were themselves more resistant to the partner's persuasive attempts. Apparently, they aspired to attain consensus via a "change other" strategy (Festinger, 1950) of exerting pressure on the partner so that his/her opinion would come to match their own. By contrast, in the absence of adequate informational resources high (vs. low) need-for-closure subjects expressed a greater preference for a persuasive partner and were themselves more receptive to the partner's persuasive attempts. Presumably, they sought to attain consensus via a "change self" strategy (Festinger, 1950) of modifying their own opinion to match their partner's.

EFFECTS ON GROUP INTERACTION

Rejection of Opinion Deviates

Failure to satisfy the consensus strivings through either the "change-self" or the "change-other" strategy may result in frustration and negative affect directed at opinion-dissenters whose idiosyncratic views impede the attainment of consensus. Heightened need for closure that augments consensus strivings may, therefore, lead to greater derogation and rejection of opinion deviates. This possibility was investigated in a series of studies by Kruglanski and Webster (1991). In the first study, groups of Tel-Aviv scouts were presented with a decision regarding the location of their annual 2-week "working camp". Two choices were presented, although the preference of the group members was known in advance. One member of each group was asked to play the role of either conformist or deviant and argue for either the consensual or the unpopular choice, respectively. Need for closure was manipulated by time-pressure. Specifically, the confederate expressed the (dissenting or conforming) viewpoint at one of three times: in the *objectively early* condition, he/she did so near the start of the discussion; in the *objectively late* condition, near the expected deadline; and in the *subjective early* condition, at the same temporal point as in the *objectively late* condition but, as the deadline was postponed in this condition, participants had as much time at their disposal (from occurrence of dissent till deadline) as did those in the *objectively early* condition. Manipulation checks suggested, as expected, that need for closure was proportionate to the discussion-time subjects believed they had remaining when the confederate's view was expressed.

The main dependent variable was the magnitude of evaluative shifts toward the confederate following the discussion. No significant differences in evaluative shifts as a function of timing emerged in regard to the conformist. The evaluative shifts toward the deviant were substantially more dramatic and corresponded to timing of the opinion expression in becoming progressively more negative with increasing proximity of the deadline. Specifically, whereas no significant evaluative-shift toward the deviant occurred in the *early* condition, such shifts occurred in both the *subjectively early* and *objectively late* conditions, the latter being significantly more pronounced than the former.

Those findings were replicated in an additional experiment (Kruglanski & Webster, 1991, Study 2) which operationalized the need for closure in terms of ambient noise. Groups of university students in favor of drug testing were asked to reach consensus on a case involving compulsory drug testing of athletes. Two confederates participated in the group discussions and rotated the enactment of roles. Specifically, one confederate enacted the role of conformist and argued the majority viewpoint in favor of testing; the other enacted the deviant role and argued the minority viewpoint against testing.

If working in a noisy environment raises the need for closure by making information processing more costly, greater rejection of the deviate should occur in the noisy (vs. quiet) conditions. This prediction was confirmed, as ratings of the deviant were significantly lower in the noise vs. no-noise condition. To examine the possibility that greater rejection of the deviate occurred under noise due to noise-induced irritation rather than due to need for closure, another study was conducted that replicated Study 2, but included an additional experimental variation. Specifically, in some conditions subjects were given the option of reaching closure by formally excluding the deviate from the decision-making process. These subjects were allowed to form their decision by *majority rule* rather than by *consensus*. Results indicated that rejection of the deviate occurred only in the *noise/consensus rule* condition, where the deviant frustrated other group members' desire for collective closure. No comparable rejection occurred in the *noise/majority rule* condition, presumably because collective closure was satisfied via the allowable majority rule. Consistent with this interpretation, in an additional study a conformist who vocally endorsed the consensual view was evaluated *more positively* in fact under noise vs. no-noise conditions. Thus, it seems that noise-induced need for closure may instill a striving for consensus manifest in the rejection of opinion deviants and the adulation of conformists.

Task-orientation and Cooperation

The "seizing" and "freezing" tendencies assumed to be induced by the need for closure may have other interesting consequences for members of problem-solving groups. Based on prior work (Ford & Kruglanski, 1995; Thompson *et al.*, 1994), it appears that "seizing" would encourage defining the situation in terms of the most accessible goal construct. It seems plausible to assume that, even though members of problem-solving groups may enact a variety of social-emotional behaviors (aimed at favorable self-presentation, maintenance of group morale, or subtle manipulation of other members' attitudes) the *most accessible* definition of the group goal would be the official one in terms of task performance. If group members with a high need for closure indeed "seize" on the most accessible situational definition, which then comes to dominate their subsequent activities, under situational conditions expected to arouse this motivation such as time-pressure, and/or for persons for whom this motivation is dispositionally high, the relative tendency to emphasize task-relevant vs. socio-emotional aspects of the interaction should increase. Moreover, the permanence-tendency-based inclination to seek consensus might encourage group members under high (vs. low) need for closure to exhibit greater cooperativeness with each other.

Those hypotheses were tested in a recent study by De Grada *et al.* (1996). Volunteer participants, students at the University of Rome, role-played the members of a corporate committee deciding the division of a monetary award among meritorious employees. Two participants in each group were high, and two were low on the need for closure, as assessed by the Italian version of the Need for Closure Scale (Pierro *et al.*, 1995). Following an initial phase, half the groups were placed under time-pressure whereas the remaining half carried out their activities without pressure. The entire interaction sequence was video-taped and analyzed according to the Interaction Process Analysis (IPA) (Bales, 1950, 1970), and the Systematic Multiple Level Observation of Groups (SYMLOG) (Bales & Cohen, 1979; Polley, 1987; 1989a, 1989b). In accordance with expectations it was found that high-need-for-closure individuals placed under time-pressure exhibited: (a) a lower proportion of socio-emotive, relative to task-orientated, behaviors; (b) a greater degree of cooperativeness than did low-need-for-closure individuals or high-need-for-closure individuals under no time-pressure. It is noted in passing that this study was the only one so far in which an individual difference measure of the need for closure was contrasted with a situational induction of this motivation. The potential implications of an interaction between these two variables, obtained in the foregoing research, are of considerable interest and will be discussed later.

INTERGROUP EFFECTS

Linguistic Intergroup Bias

As Rubini's and Kruglanski's (1996) results demonstrate the need-for-closure-based tendency toward permanence may induce a bias in favor of abstract (vs. concrete) linguistic categories. The permanence tendency may, moreover, foster a preference for consensual knowledge, unlikely to be challenged in the future by significant members of one's group (Kruglanski & Webster, 1991; Kruglanski, Webster, & Klem, 1993). Those inclinations may have intriguing consequences for a phenomenon known as the *linguistic intergroup bias* (LIB) (Maass & Arcuri, 1992; Maass & Stahlberg, 1993; Maass *et al.*, 1989, 1995).

The LIB involves a tendency for individuals to describe positive ingroup and negative outgroup behaviors in relatively abstract terms, implying that the behavior represents a stable characteristic of the actor. Conversely, negative ingroup and positive outgroup behaviors are typically described in relatively concrete terms, implying situational specificity, hence externality to the actor. The underlying mechanisms of the LIB could be both expectancy-based and motivational (Maass & Stahlberg, 1993). First, because the stereotype of the ingroup is typically positive and that of the outgroup is often negative, positive behaviors of the ingroup and negative behaviors of the outgroup are easily assimilated to the stereotype, and described in general terms. However, negative ingroup and positive outgroup behaviors are inconsistent with the corresponding stereotypes and therefore tend to be perceived as unique and situationally specific. Thus, expectancies regarding prototypical behaviors of the ingroup and outgroup may play a role in the LIB.

A motivational basis of the effect may be that abstract descriptions of positive ingroup and negative outgroup behaviors serve to portray the former favorably and the latter unfavorably. Similarly, concrete descriptions of negative ingroup behaviors minimize their significance as evidence for corresponding group characteristics, as do concrete depictions of positive outgroup behaviors. In other words, those linguistic tendencies serve to protect the perception that the ingroup is superior to the outgroup.

The need for closure may constitute another motivational variable relevant to the abstraction-level of linguistic descriptions. The desire for trans-situational consistency evoked by permanence strivings should work to increase the abstraction level of all descriptions across the board, that is, including positive and negative behaviors of both ingroups and outgroups. However, the desire for consensus, also evoked by permanence strivings, may enhance the significance of the ingroup as a source of motivational gratification (of consensus strivings), thereby raising the propensity for ingroup protectiveness.

How might the tendencies toward abstraction and ingroup protectiveness interact? They should work in concert for positive ingroup and negative outgroup behaviors converging on the same outcome: enhanced abstractness-level of linguistic descriptors. Those tendencies should be in conflict, however, for negative ingroup and positive outgroup behaviors. Specifically, the general abstraction tendency should be at odds with the preference for concrete descriptors necessary for ingroup protection. Thus, differences in abstraction due to need for closure should be reduced or eliminated for such descriptions. Those ideas were examined in two studies conducted by Webster, Kruglanski, and Pattison (1997).

In Study 1, participants previously classified as high or low in dispositional need for closure (Webster & Kruglanski, 1994) were selected to take part in an experiment described as an investigation of impression formation. Ingroup vs. outgroup status of a target person was operationalized in terms of his/her endorsement of the "pro-choice" vs. the "pro-life" stance on abortion. Specifically, an ingroup status was defined when the participant and the alleged target had the same position on abortion, and an outgroup status when their positions differed. The ingroup or the outgroup target disclosed two behavioral items of information about him/herself and the participants' task was to describe those behaviors in their own terms. Participants read information about a target person who was identified as an ingroup or an outgroup member and who engaged in a negative or a positive behavior (persuading a friend to cheat, or lending money to a friend in need).

Results, summarized in Table 5.4, indicated that individuals high (vs. low) in need for closure adopted a significantly higher level of abstraction when describing positive ingroup and negative outgroup behaviors, while such differences in abstraction were non-significant for negative ingroup behaviors and positive outgroup behaviors. Those findings support the hypothesis that the permanence-tendency produced by elevations in the closure-motivation leads to a general propensity toward abstractness and a more specific tendency toward ingroup protectionism. Those tendencies sometimes work in concert (i.e., for positive behaviors of the ingroup and negative ones of the outgroup), leading to greater abstraction in descriptions for those high (vs. low) in need for closure. At other times (i.e., for negative behaviors of the ingroup and positive behaviors of the outgroup) the tendencies may conflict, leading to diminished differences in abstraction as a function of the closure-motivation.

Table 5.4 Linguistic abstraction of behavioral descriptions as a function of behavior valence. Target group membership and dispositional need for closure

	Positive behavior		Negative behavior	
	Ingroup member	Outgroup member	Ingroup member	Outgroup member
Dispositional need for closure				
High	3.461 (SD = 0.927)	2.364 (SD = 0.694)	2.677 (SD = 0.726)	3.489 (SD = 0.799)
Low	2.490 (SD = 0.929)	2.039 (SD = 0.807)	2.152 (SD = 0.867)	2.514 (SD = 0.838)

The higher the figure, the higher the level of linguistic abstraction. SD = standard deviation.

These notions were subjected to further test in a second study that induced a need for closure via a situational manipulation involving ambient noise (Webster, Kruglanski, & Pattison, 1997, Study 2). Participants working in a noisy (vs. quiet) environment were expected to experience a greater need for closure, as closure would free them of the subjectively costly task of continuing to process information under difficult (noisy) conditions. Indeed, manipulation checks suggest that individuals in the noisy (vs. quiet) environment felt a greater need for closure. Furthermore, linguistic abstraction was greater for subjects in the noisy (vs. quiet) environment for descriptions of positive ingroup and negative outgroup behavior (see Table 5.5). Those differences were eliminated for negative ingroup and positive outgroup behavior, thus replicating the pattern of findings observed in Study 1.

In summary, the need for closure notion affords a variety of hypotheses on significant interpersonal, group and intergroup phenomena. A listing of those hypotheses and the relevant empirical research is given in Table 5.6.

SEPARATING THE "SEIZING" AND "FREEZING" TENDENCIES: THE POINT OF BELIEF CRYSTALLIZATION

The bulk of the early research on the need for closure (e.g., the "cue-utilization" work by Kruglanski & Freund, 1983; Jamieson & Zanna, 1989; Webster, 1993) examined the joint consequences of "seizing" and "freezing" upon judgments implied by accessible cues. That work did not allow the separation of urgency and permanence effects, both presumably induced under a heightened need for closure. More recent in origin is work focused uniquely on permanence-effects manifest in consensus and consistency strivings (Kruglanski & Webster, 1991; Webster, Kruglanski, & Pattison, 1997;

Table 5.5 Linguistic abstraction of behavioral descriptions as a function of behavior valence. Target group membership and dispositional need for closure

	Positive behavior		Negative behavior	
	Ingroup member	Outgroup member	Ingroup member	Outgroup member
Environmental noise condition				
Noise	3.521 (SD = 0.743)	2.654 (SD = 0.661)	2.49 (SD = 0.940)	3.526 (SD = 0.775)
No-noise	2.70 (SD = 0.798)	2.462 (SD = 0.794)	2.322 (SD = 0.876)	2.60 (SD = 0.784)

The higher the figure, the higher the level of linguistic abstraction. SD = standard deviation.

Table 5.6 Interpersonal group-level and intergroup consequences of the need for cognitive closure. A listing of hypotheses and relevant research

Hypotheses	Research
Interpersonal hypotheses	
1. Need for closure reduces perspective taking and empathy to dissimilar others	Webster, Findley, and Irvin (1995)
2. Need for closure increases abstractness of questions and answers, promotes an object-focus and breeds estrangement in the question–answer paradigm	Rubini and Kruglanski (1996)
3. Need for closure reduces persuadability in the case of firm prior opinions and enhances persuadability in the absence of such opinions	Kruglanski, Webster, and Klem (1993)
Group-level hypotheses	
4. Need for closure increases the desire for consensus in a group	Kruglanski, Webster, and Klem (1993)
5. Need for closure increases the tendency to reject opinion deviates	Kruglanski and Webster (1991)
6. Need for closure increases the tendency toward task-orientation relative to socio-emotional orientation	De Grada *et al.* (1996)
7. Need for closure increases the tendency toward cooperation with others in a group	De Grada *et al.* (1996)
Inter-group hypothesis	
8. Need for closure induces the linguistic intergroup bias (LIB) in a group for positive ingroup and negative outgroup behaviors, but not for negative ingroup and positive outgroup behaviors	Webster, Kruglanski, and Pattison (1997)

Rubini & Kruglanski, 1996). An essential question, however, concerns the boundary conditions that may demarcate the urgency from the permanence tendencies. One promising such boundary condition appears the point of *belief-crystallization*, i.e., the time-interval during which a hesitant conjecture is transformed into an assured opinion. It seems plausible that, prior to that point, increasing the need for closure should prompt increased "seizing" upon, and in this sense open-mindedness to, information potentially leading to closure, whereas following this point, increasing need for closure should manifest itself in "freezing" upon one's extant opinions, and relative closed-mindedness to subsequent information.

Consistent with those notions are findings of Kruglanski, Webster, and Klem (1993) mentioned earlier where subjects under high (vs. low) need for closure who did not receive prior information allowing them to form an assured opinion manifested open-mindedness to, or "seizing" upon, information and arguments provided by the persuasive communicator, whereas high- (vs. low)-need-for-closure subjects in possession of relevant prior information manifested closed-mindedness to the persuasive communicator's arguments, or "freezing" on their prior opinions. As a consequence, in the absence of prior information-base, high- (vs. low)-need-for-closure subjects were more persuadable, whereas in the presence of such a base they were more resistant to persuasion (see Table 5.7).

The notion that initial confidence in an opinion may represent a boundary condition for operation of the urgency vs. the permanence tendencies was tested in an additional set of studies by Kruglanski, Peri, and Zakai (1991). Participants in this research were presented with five series of drawings. All series contained either two or four standard drawings on a given topic ("man", "woman", or "tree") each drawn by a different person, and a criterion drawing on a different topic (invariably, "house") drawn by *one* of the persons who had prepared the standard drawing. The participants' objective was to identify for each series the particular standard drawing of the person

Table 5.7 Mean pre-to-post-discussion verdict shifts[1] and time spent in discussion[2] as a function of need for closure and informational base[3] (From Kruglanski, Webster, and Klem 1993), with permission

	Informational base	
	Present	Absent
Experiment 1: Environmental noise condition		
Noise	1.48/6.99	4.64/3.89
	(2.02)/(0.80)	(1.59)/(1.53)
No-noise	3.04/6.25	3.23/5.67
	(1.63)/(1.21)	(1.74)/(1.36)
Experiment 2: Dispositional need for closure		
High	1.50/7.32	4.10/4.20
	(0.75)/(0.37)	(1.37)/(1.35)
Low	3.46/5.60	2.30/6.47
	(1.71)/(1.60)	(1.49)/(0.52)

[1] Given on the left.
[2] Given on the right (in minutes).
[3] Standard deviations given in parentheses.

responsible for the criteria drawing. The time allotted for this task was 3 minutes. Participants stated their interim judgment after 1 minute and during the remaining 2 minutes were allowed to engage in information search concerning alleged other subjects' responses. This was accomplished by having subjects turn over some (or all) of the standard drawings, which bore on their backs the percentages of previous subjects choosing them as the correct answers.

Participants' initial confidence was manipulated via the number of choice alternatives with which they were presented. In the high-confidence condition, participants chose from between two standard drawings, whereas in the low-confidence condition they did so from among four drawings. Appropriate checks verified that this confidence manipulation had the intended effect.

The need for closure was manipulated differently in the two experiments. Based on pilot data we knew that the novel experimental task is somewhat confusing to subjects and that it therefore induces a relatively high base level of the need for closure. Rather than elevating it further via experimental manipulations, we decided to lower it instead in the appropriate conditions. In one study, we did so by providing subjects with clear criteria for assessing the drawings' similarity (specifically, in terms of the drawing's size and location on page, its linear quality, its degree of elaboration and the presence/absence of a depth dimension). In the second study we did so by inducing a fear of invalidity in some of our subjects, namely by telling them that mistaken judgments would be punished by a loss of points.

We were interested in two aspects of the information search, its speed of initiation, and its extent, that is, the number of drawings subjects turned over. If low confidence typifies the pre-crystallization phase, and high confidence the post-crystallization phase—and if, moreover, need for closure produces "seizing" in the former phase and "freezing" in the latter—it should exert opposite effects on our dependent variables at the two confidence-levels: in the low confidence condition, high vs. low need for closure should induce "seizing", manifested in a relatively hurried commencement of the informational search and its relatively ample extent. By contrast, in the high-confidence condition high vs. low need for closure should induce "freezing", manifested in relatively late commencement and limited extent of the information search. That is exactly what happened, suggesting, once again, that initial confidence in an opinion may constitute a boundary condition separating the urgency tendency responsible for "seizing" from the permanence tendency underlying "freezing". The relevant results are summarized in Table 5.8.

GENERAL DISCUSSION

This chapter considered the nature, antecedents and consequences of the need for cognitive closure, a motivational variable thought to impact the

Table 5.8 Mean numbers of drawings turned over[1] and latency of turning over the first drawing[2] as a function of need for closure and confidence level[3] (from Kruglanski, Peri, & Zakai (1991), with permission

	Confidence level	
	High	Low
Experiment 1: Need for closure		
High	2.62/65.11 (1.49)/(31.66)	3.60/39.79 (1.75)/(41.66)
Low	3.94/37.01 (1.42)/(34.46)	3.00/47.84 (1.87)/(44.84)
Experiment 2: Need for closure		
High	2.50/60.39 (1.68)/(38.36)	3.52/33.67 (1.75)/(39.77)
Low	4.37/19.47 (1.44)/(33.73)	2.82/49.01 (1.65)/(39.53)

[1] Given on the left.
[2] Given on the right.
[3] Standard deviations given in parentheses.

fundamental human process of knowledge construction. This need was conceptualized as involving a desire for decisive knowledge as opposed to confusion or uncertainty and as deriving from situational or personality factors that influence the subjective costs or benefits of possessing cognitive closure.

Empirical evidence regarding the broad range of effects exerted by the closure-motivation was reviewed and those effects were conceptualized as stemming from two general tendencies: an urgency tendency, involving the desire to attain closure quickly (referred to as "seizing") and a permanence tendency, involving the desire to maintain closure once achieved (referred to as "freezing"). Operating jointly, those tendencies may be at the base of a wide variety of social-cognitive effects including: (a) less extensive information processing and hypothesis generation (Webster, Richter, & Kruglanski, 1996; Mayseless & Kruglanski, 1987); (b) elevated judgmental confidence (e.g., Mayseless & Kruglanski, 1987; Kruglanski & Webster, 1991; Kruglanski, Webster, & Klem, 1993); (c) greater preference for prototypical rather than diagnostic evidence (Kruglanski & Mayseless, 1988); (d) greater utilization of judgmental cues (Kruglanski & Freund, 1983; Freund, Kruglanski, & Schpitzajzen, 1985; Heaton & Kruglanski, 1991; Webster, 1993); (e) greater reliance on pre-existing knowledge structures (Kruglanski & Freund, 1983; Jamieson & Zanna, 1989); and (f) greater effects of primes on subsequent judgments (Ford & Kruglanski, 1995; Thompson *et al.*, 1994).

Because knowledge construction processes affected by the urgency and permanence tendencies typically take place in social contexts, those tendencies may indirectly effect a variety of interpersonal, group-level or intergroup-level consequences, including: (a) lowered perspective taking and empathic concern for dissimilar others (Webster, Findley, & Irvin, 1995); (b) greater linguistic abstraction in interpersonal communication (Webster, Kruglanski, & Pattison, 1997; Rubini and Kruglanski, 1996) leading, in turn, to greater feelings of estrangement and interpersonal distance between collocutors; (c) greater desire for consensus in groups (Kruglanski, Webster, & Klem, 1993); and (d) increased rejection of opinion deviates who may block consensus (Kruglanski & Webster, 1991); (e) greater tendency to be task-oriented (vs. socio-emotional) and cooperative in problem-solving groups.

It is important to stress that the effects described above obtained across a broad variety of conditions that highlight the benefits of closure. Those included factors as diverse as time pressure, ambient noise, mental fatigue, and dullness of information processing, among others. Furthermore, circumstances thought to lower the need for closure by highlighting its costs, including conditions involving accountability, evaluation apprehension or accuracy concerns, produced the opposite effects in many cases. Finally, several of the effects resulting from situational manipulations were replicated when need for closure was operationalized in terms of scores on the Need for Closure Scale (Cratylus, 1995; Pierro *et al.*, 1995; Webster & Kruglanski, 1994), suggesting that the closure-motivation represents a stable personality dimension in addition to being the product of situational factors.

Although these results are encouraging, they are not without alternative interpretations. The major ones of those are considered in what follows.

MOTIVATION VS. COGNITIVE CAPACITY

Briefer extent of information processing, or the reliance on accessible cues need not reflect a motivation for closure, but rather may be the result of a depletion in cognitive capacity due to the various situational constraints, like time pressure, noise or fatigue, whereby need for closure was manipulated in our various studies. To consider this issue, it is well to delineate first the possible ways whereby capacity and motivation may interface. Our own assumption is that, as far as formation of judgments is concerned, cognitive capacity and motivation are related multiplicatively. That is, at least some degrees of capacity and motivation are required for a judgmental activity to take place. Setting either to zero will undermine it, and no amount of increment in the remaining one should suffice to override the deficit. Granted some capacity and motivation, however, the relation between the two could be compensatory. Reduction in capacity may be offset by an increment in motivation, and vice versa. According to this interpretation, our situational manipulations did not exhaust capacity altogether (i.e. did not set it to zero). As we have seen, our accountability and accuracy instructions attenuated the effects of such situational demands as time pressure, mental fatigue, or noise, quite consistently (e.g. Kruglanski & Freund, 1983; Kruglanski, Webster, & Klem, 1993; Webster, Richter, & Kruglanski, 1996). It appears, then, that when sufficiently motivated to the contrary, participants are perfectly capable of overcoming the effects of various situational constraints on information processing, at least at the magnitudes at which these constraints are typically manipulated in social psychology experiments.

Granted the putative multiplicative relation between capacity and motivation, two logical possibilities suggest themselves. In one, the two are independent of each other and in the second they are causally related. The independence hypothesis states that capacity reduction *per se* (e.g. stemming from organismic energy depletion or situational demands) does not have any motivational consequences, even though it may be compensated for by added motivation. This is analogous to the case in which the deflation of bicycle tires may be compensated for by enhanced pedaling effort, even though it does not cause it as such.

By contrast, the causality hypothesis suggests that the depletion of cognitive capacity does have distinct motivational consequences, in fact, as it induces the desire to expend as little effort as possible on the requisite judgment. This motivation assumes the form of the need for cognitive closure, that is, the desire for confidence and clarity obviating the need for further processing. Indeed, our position is that the various effects of our situational-constraint manipulations were due not to capacity reduction as such but rather to the motivational state such reduction might have engendered. The evidence for this claim is manifold. First, note that our situational manipulations had a variety of motivational consequences. Specifically, they induced a specific pattern of preferences and affective reactions to various social stimuli. Thus, in research by Kruglanski, Webster and Klem (1993), participants with a firm opinion on a topic placed in a noisy (vs. quiet) environment *preferred* non-persuasive, non-dominant discussion partners, whereas participants lacking a firm opinion preferred self-assured and persuasive partners when placed under noise. In research by Kruglanski and Webster (1991), group members placed under time pressure or in a noisy environment tended more to reject the opinion deviates in the group and to extol the conformists, whose actions seemed to facilitate the formation of consensus or the forging of a closure-affording social reality.

Importantly, the capacity-restriction concept seems incapable of explaining such patterns of interpersonal preferences or evaluations because the notion of cognitive capacity, as such, is devoid of implications as to affect or preferences. On the other hand, a motivational construct (such as the need for closure) readily implies preferences and affective expressions, as functions of the extent to which the motivational end is advanced or thwarted in a given situation. Thus, the clear motivational effects of situational demands are inconsistent with the independence assumption, whereby those demands have purely cognitive effects.

Also inconsistent with the independence hypothesis is the finding that participants exhibit higher judgmental confidence when placed under situational constraints vs. the absence of such constraints. The independence assumption seems to suggest just the contrary, specifically that a reduction of capacity without a compensatory increase in motivation should effect a decline rather than a rise in confidence. Yet it is found that participants report the highest confidence precisely where their capacity is most severely challenged (e.g., by noise, time-pressure or fatigue) and without the introduction of a compensatory motivation (e.g., Kruglanski, Webster, & Klem, 1993; Webster, 1993; Webster, Kruglanski, & Pattison, 1997).

One might object by pointing out that situational demands may impair cognitive capacity and may induce a motivational state without the two being necessarily related. At least the observed cognitive or judgmental effects could stem from capacity restrictions, as such rather constituting the indirect evidence for an induced motivation. Some evidence against this contention was obtained in recent research (Kruglanski, Webster, & Klem, 1993; Webster, 1993) wherein the *judgmental* effects of specific situational demands (e.g. noise) were rendered non-significant once the motivation for closure was controlled statistically via a multiple regression procedure (Baron & Kenny, 1986). This suggests that the cognitive effects of situational demands were in fact mediated by (rather than being independent of) the need for closure.

Last, but not least important, numerous effects of the situational constraints imposed in our research were replicated by means of our individual-difference measure of the need for closure. Note that numerous items on this particular scale (namely 26 of the 42 such items) have distinctly motivational phrasing (e.g., including expressions like "I like", "I enjoy", "hate", "dislike", or "prefer"). It is thus unlikely that scores on this measure reflect a cognitive capacity restriction of some sort. All in all, then, it appears that the entire data pattern yielded by our research program is more compatible with a motivational rather than a cognitive capacity restriction interpretation.

"CLOSURE" OR "SIMPLE STRUCTURE"?

Recently, Neuberg, Judice, and West (1997) criticized need-for-closure research on the grounds that it instead reflects a desire for simple structure assessed via the Personal Need for Structure scale (Neuberg & Newsom, 1993). Although Neuberg, Judice, and West (1997) never acknowledge it,

however, the Personal Need for Structure scale (PNS) was originally developed by Thompson, Naccarratto, and Parker (1992) to operationalize the
need for closure (for discussion, see Kruglanski *et al.*, in press). Two issues
arise in this context: (a) Whether the term "structure" or "closure" better
captures the empirical domain addressed by the relevant research; (b)
whether such research taps a desire for "simplicity" or for "closure". We
consider both in turn.

Early on (cf. Kruglanski & Freund, 1983), the motivational construct pres-
ently at issue was labeled the "need for structure", and it was subsequently
renamed as the "need for closure" (Kruglanski, 1989). This semantic shift was
prompted by the realization that the latter term captures our conceptual
intent more precisely than does the former. Specifically, James Drever's *Dictionary of Psychology* (1963, p. 40) comments on the Gestalt theoretic origins
of the term "closure" and defines it as the "subjective closing of gaps (in
percepts, memories and actions), or the completion of incomplete forms, so as
to constitute wholes". Conceptually, this sounds very akin to our own phrasing in terms of a "firm answer" to a question, i.e. "a complete form" as
opposed to "confusion and ambiguity", analogous to a gap.

By contrast, Drever (1963, p. 280) defined "structure" as "the composition
and arrangement of component parts, and organization of a complex whole,
(defined) with reference to the positional and functional interdependence of
(the) parts . . .". Clearly, this is not the meaning we intended to convey, hence
the term "closure" seemed considerably more felicitous given the phenomena
we purported to address.

Moreover, given the definition of "structure" in terms of a complex whole,
the term "simple structure" (Neuberg & Newsom, 1993; Neuberg, Judice, &
West, 1997) seems a bit of an oxymoron. Nor do findings obtained with the
PNS seem to reflect "structure" in the sense above. Such findings included:
greater tendency of persons with high (vs. low) PNS scores to engage in
gender stereotyping (Neuberg & Newsom, 1993; Study 4); to base impressions
of a given group's intelligence on relatively global indices (number of anagrams solved) rather than taking into account the fine-grained information as
to the anagrams' difficulty level (Schaller *et al.*, 1995); to form spontaneous
trait inferences (Moscowitz, 1993); to assimilate judgments to primed constructs (Thompson *et al.*, 1994); and to be less likely to change beliefs when
confronted with new information (Rice *et al.*, 1991).

None of those results speak much to the "composition and arrangement of
component parts, and organization of a complex whole" (Drever, 1963,
p. 280). By contrast, they seem quite compatible with the present theorizing
about the need for closure (see also Kruglanski & Webster, 1996). Specifically, the tendencies to judge people stereotypically, to assimilate judgments
to primed constructs, to engage in spontaneous trait-inferences, or base impressions upon global or coarse-grained rather than fine-grained information

correspond to the *urgency* tendency assumed to characterize persons under heightened need for closure and their inclination to "seize" upon closure quickly. Primed constructs (Thompson *et al.*, 1994) or chronically accessible stereotypes (Neuberg & Newsom, 1993, Study 4) afford such quick judgments, hence they are "seized" upon under high need for closure. The urgency tendency also implies the inclination to rely more upon global vs. fine-grained information (Schaller *et al.*, 1995) because they may be processed more readily, affording quicker closure. Finally, the resistance to belief-change in the light of new information (Rice *et al.*, 1991) is explicable in terms of the second major tendency postulated by need for closure theory, namely that toward *permanence*, giving rise to the inclination to preserve, or "freeze" on, past closure.

Thus, recent findings with the PNS seem more appropriately interpretable in terms of the need for closure rather than that for "structure". Neither is it altogether clear that they reflect a craving for "simplicity", as Neuberg and colleagues emphasize. For instance, the tendencies to form stereotypes, or spontaneous inferences, to assimilate judgments to primed constructs, or to resist the influence of new information, do not seem to reflect simplicity, as the stereotypes, primed constructs, spontaneous inferences or prior beliefs could in fact be quite complex rather than simple. The one study directly addressing simplicity concerned the tendency of high- (vs. low)-PNS individuals to sort pieces of information into fewer groupings (Neuberg & Newsom, 1993, Study 3), yielding a lower complexity score according to Scott's H index. Note, however, that such a tendency may well be confounded here with the extent of information processing that multiple vs. reduced number of groupings may require. It is quite possible, in other words, that high-PNS participants' alleged tendency to exhibit a desire for "simplicity" might instead reflect a tendency to arrive at closure *urgently*. The findings to date are quite compatible with both interpretations, and the "urgency hypothesis", since it accounts for a broader range of relevant findings, enjoys the advantage of parsimony. Further research may well be required to determine whether a desire for simplicity has an independent existence, or whether simplicity is appealing primarily as a way of rapidly reaching closure.

HOW MIGHT NEED FOR CLOSURE SOURCES COMBINE?

Another issue in need of further exploration concerns the way the various sources of need for closure may combine to determine the overall level of this motivation. We have generally assumed that they combine additively, but have found in recent work that they may do so interactively (De Grada *et al.*, 1996). As reported earlier, in that particular research persons with high (vs. low) scores on the Italian version of the Need for Closure Scale (Pierro *et al.*,

1995), and put under time-pressure vs. no-pressure exhibited: (a) a lower proportion of socio-emotive relative to task-oriented behaviors; and (b) a greater degree of cooperativeness. How might one interpret such interactive effects? Two possibilities come to mind. One is a *threshold* hypothesis, whereby a given magnitude of need for closure needs to be reached for need for closure effects to be revealed. According to this hypothesis, the reason for the obtained interaction in the De Grada *et al.* (1996) research was that the threshold magnitude of need for closure was only reached where both sources of the closure motivation, i.e. the personality disposition, and the situational manipulation, were present. A major implication of this hypothesis is that increasing time-pressure, and/or selecting participants with more extreme (high and low) scores would ultimately result in a statistical main effect of those variables replacing the currently found interaction.

A second possibility suggests a *sensitivity* hypothesis, whereby only persons with a high predisposition toward closure would react to situational pressures toward closure attainment. According to such an interpretation, for example, prior findings that time-pressure may reduce the amount of social-emotional behavior exhibited by group members (Isenberg, 1981; Kelly & McGrath, 1985) might be restricted to persons with a high dispositional need for closure that for some unknown reason happened to be over-represented in the relevant research samples. Furthermore, research where dispositional need for closure yielded significant effects in the absence of situational manipulations (e.g., Kruglanski & Webster, 1991; Kruglanski, Webster, & Klem, 1993) may have incorporated situational conditions (e.g., the sheer requirement to render *some* judgment!) likely to activate such a need. Be it however it may, the interaction of a dispositional need for closure and time-pressure in DeGrada *et al.*'s (1996) work is intriguing and worthy of further systematic exploration.

To conclude, even though a number of challenging issues remain for further work, the extra convergence of empirical findings across multiple operationalizations and social psychological phenomena supports the present conceptualization of the need for cognitive closure, its antecedent conditions and its consequences. Because of its widely ramifying implications and the ubiquitous conditions that may arouse it, the need for closure represents an epistemic motivation of considerable relevance to many domains of social psychology. Particularly promising is the implication that an essentially intrapersonal approach, based on notions of motivated social cognition (Kruglanski, 1996), may serve to illuminate multiple phenomena on interpersonal (e.g. communication and persuasion) and group (attitudes toward deviates, members of ingroups or outgroups, stereotyping) levels of analysis. Although it may reside in the knower's "head", motivated social cognition appears powerfully impacted by the social context, which it may substantially influence in return.

ACKNOWLEDGEMENTS

Work on this article was supported by National Science Foundation Grant SBR 9417422, National Institute of Mental Health Grant 1RO1 MH 52578) and Research Scientist Award KO5 MH 01213 to Arie Kruglanski.

REFERENCES

Adorno, T. W., Frenkel-Brunswik, I., Levinson, D. J. & Sanford, R. N. (1950). *The Authoritarian Personality*. New York: Harper and Brothers.

Asch, S. E. (1946). Forming impressions of personality. *Journal of Abnormal and Social Psychology,* **41**, 258–90.

Bales, R. F. (1950). *Interaction Process Analysis, A Method for the Study of Small Groups*. Reading, MA: Addison-Wesley.

Bales, R. F. (1970). *Personality and Interpersonal Behavior*. New York: Holt, Rinehart and Winston.

Bales, R. F. & Cohen, S. P. (1979). *SYMLOG: A System for the Multiple Level Observation of Groups*. New York: Free Press.

Baron, R. M. & Kenny, D. A. (1986). The moderator–mediator variable distinction in social psychological research: Conceptual strategies and statistical considerations. *Journal of Personality and Social Psychology,* **51**, 1173–82.

Batson, C. D., O'Quinn, K., Fultz, J., Vanderplas, U., & Isen, A. U. (1983). Influence of self-reported distress and empathy on egoistic versus altruistic motivation to help. *Journal of Personality and Social Psychology,* **45**, 706–18.

Boudreau, L. A., Baron, R., & Oliver, P. V. (1992). Effects of expected communication target expertise and timing of set on trait use in person description. *Personality and Social Psychology Bulletin,* **18**, 447–52.

Cacioppo, J. T., & Petty, R. E. (1982). The need for cognition. *Journal of Personality and Social Pychology,* **42**, 116–31.

Chaiken, S., Liberman, A., & Eagly, A. H. (1989). Heuristic versus systematic information processing within and beyond the persuasion context. In J. S. Uleman & J. A. Baragh (Eds), *Unintended Thought: Limits of Awareness, Intention and Control* (pp. 212–52). New York: Guilford.

Cratylus (1995). *Need for Closure (Nederlandse versie)*. Amsterdam: Vrije Universiteit, Vakgroep Social Psychologie.

Davis, M. H. (1983). Measuring individual differences in empathy: Evidence for a multidimensional approach. *Journal of Personality and Social Psychology,* **44**, 113–26.

De Grada, E., Kruglanski, A. W., Mannetti, L., & Pierro, A. (1996). Motivated cognition and group interaction: Need for closure effects on task orientation, interpersonal affect and social relations (under editorial review).

Dijksterhuis, A. P., Van Knippenberg, A. D., Kruglanski, A. W., & Schaper, C. (1996). Motivated social cognition: Need for closure effects on memory and judgment. *Journal of Experimental Social Psychology,* **32**, 254–70.

Drever, J. (1963). *A Dictionary of Psychology*. Baltimore, MA: Penguin.

Eagly, A.H., & Chaiken, S. (1993). *The Psychology of Attitudes*. San Diego, CA: Harcourt Brace Jovanovich.

Erber, R., & Fiske, S. T. (1984).   Outcome dependency and attention to inconsistent information. *Journal of Personality and Social Psychology*, **47**, 709–26.

Eysenck, H. J. (1954).   *The Psychology of Politics*. New York: Praeger.

Festinger, L. (1950).   Informal social communication. *Psychological Review*, **57**, 271–82.

Ford, T. E., & Kruglanski, A. W. (1995).   Effects of epistemic motivations on the use of accessible constructs in social judgment. *Personality and Social Psychology Bulletin*, **21**, 950–62.

Frenkel-Brunswik, E. (1949).   Intolerance of ambiguity as emotional and perceptual personality variable. *Journal of Personality*, **18**, 108–43.

Freud, S. (1923).   The ego and the id. In J. Strachey (Ed. And Trans.), *Standard Edition of the Complete Psychological works of Sigmund Freud* (pp. 171–225). London: Hogarth Press.

Freund, T., Kruglanski, A. W., & Schpitzajzen, A. (1985).   The freezing and unfreezing of impressional primacy: Effects of the need for structure and the fear of invalidity. *Personality and Social Psychology Bulletin*, **11**, 479–87.

Gilbert, D. T., Pelham, B. W., & Krull, D. S. (1988).   On cognitive busyness: When person perceivers meet persons perceived. *Journal of Personality and Social Psychology*, **54**, 733–40.

Heaton, A., & Kruglanski, A. W. (1991).   Person perception by introverts and extraverts under time pressure: Need for closure effects. *Personality and Social Psychology Bulletin*, **17**, 161–5.

Higgins, E. T., Rholes, W. S., & Jones, C. R. (1977).   Category accessibility and impression formation. *Journal of Experimental Social Psychology*, **13**, 141–54.

Higgins, E. T. (1987).   Self-discrepancy: A theory relating self and self affect. *Psychological Review*, **94**, 319–40.

Hofstede, G. (1980).   *Culture's Consequences: International Differences in Work-related Values*. Beverly Hills, CA: Sage.

Isenberg, D. J. (1981).   Some effects of time-pressure on vertical structure and decision making accuracy in small groups. *Organizational Behavior and Human Performance*, **27**, 119–34.

Jamieson, D. W., & Zanna, M. P. (1989).   Need for structure in attitude formation and expression. In A. Pratkanis, S. Breckler & A. G. Greenwald (Eds), *Attitude Structure and Function*. Hillsdale, NJ: Erlbaum.

Jones, E. E. (1979).   The rocky road from acts to dispositions. *American Psychologist*, **34**, 107–17.

Jones, E. E., & Harris, V. A. (1967).   The attribution of attitudes. *Journal of Experimental Social Psychology*, **3**, 1–24.

Kagan, J. (1972).   Motives and development. *Journal of Personality and Social Psychology*, **22**, 51–66.

Kelly, J., & McGrath, J. E. (1985).   Effects of time limits and task types on task performance and interaction of four-person groups. *Journal of Personality and Social Psychology*, **49**, 395–407.

Kruglanski, A. W. (1996).   Motivated social cognition: Principles of the interface. In E. T. Higgins & A. W. Kruglanski (Eds), *Social Psychology: A Handbook of Basic Principles* (pp. 493–520). New York: Guilford.

Kruglanski, A. W. (1989).   *Lay Epistemics and Human Knowledge: Cognitive and Motivational Bases*. New York: Plenum.

Kruglanski, A. W., & Freund, T. (1983).   The freezing and un-freezing of lay-inferences: Effects on impressional primacy, ethnic stereotyping and numerical anchoring. *Journal of Experimental Social Psychology*, **19**, 448–68.

Kruglanski, A. W., & Mayseless, O. (1988). Contextual effects in hypothesis testing: The role of competing alternatives and epistemic motivations. *Social Cognition*, **6**, 1–21.

Kruglanski, A. W., & Webster, D. M. (1981). Group members' reactions to opinion deviates and conformists at varying degrees of proximity to decision deadline and of environmental noise. *Journal of Personality and Social Psychology*, **61**, 212–25.

Kruglanski, A. W., & Webster, D. M. (1996). Motivated closing of the mind: Seizing and freezing. *Psychological Review*, **103**, 263–83.

Kruglanski, A. W., Peri, N., & Zakai, D. (1991). Interactive effects of need for closure and initial confidence on social information seeking. *Social Cognition*, **9**, 127–48.

Kruglanski, A. W., Webster, D. M., & Klem, A. (1993). Motivated resistance and openness to persuasion in the presence or absence of prior information. *Journal of Personality and Social Psychology*, **64**, 861–76.

Kruglanski, A. W., Atash, N., De Grada, E., Mannetti, L., Pierro, A., & Webster, D. M. (1997). Psychological theory testing versus psychometric nay saying: Need for closure scale and the Neuberg *et al.* critique. *Journal of Personality and Social Psychology*, **73**, 1005–1016.

Kunda, Z. (1990). The case for motivated reasoning. *Psychological Bulletin*, **108**(3), 480–98.

Maass, A., & Arcuri, L. (1992). The role of language in the persistence of stereotypes. In G. Semin & K. Fiedler (Eds), *Language, Interaction and Social Cognition* (pp. 129–43). Newbury Park, CA: Sage.

Maass, A., & Stahlberg, D. (1993). The linguistic intergroup bias: The role of differential expectancies and in-group protective motivation. Paper presented at the conference of EAESP, Lisbon, September.

Maass, A., Salvi, D., Arcuri, L. & Semin, G. (1989). Language use in intergroup contexts: The linguistic intergroup bias. *Journal of Personality and Social Psychology*, **57**, 981–93.

Maass, A., Milesi, A., Zabbini, S., & Stahlberg, D. (1995). The linguistic intergroup bias: Differential expectancies or in-group protection? *Journal of Personality and Social Psychology*, **68**, 116–26.

Mayseless, O., & Kruglanski, A. W. (1987). What makes you so sure? Effects of epistemic motivations on judgmental confidence. *Organizational Behavior and Human Decision Processes*, **39**, 162–83.

McCrae, R. R., & Costa, P. T. Jr (1985). Openness to experience. In R. Hogan & W. H. Jones (Eds), *Perspectives in Personality* (pp. 145–72). Greenwich, CT: JAI Press.

Mikulincer, M., Yinon, A., & Kabili, D. (1991). Epistemic needs and learned helplessness. *European Journal of Personality*, **5**, 249–58.

Moscowitz, G. B. (1993). Individual differences in social categorization: The influence of Personal Need for Structure on spontaneous trait inferences. *Journal of Personality and Social Psychology*, **65**, 132–42.

Neuberg, S. L., & Newsom, J. T. (1993). Personal Need for Structure: Individual differences in the desire for simple structure. *Journal of Personality and Social Psychology*, **65**, 113–31.

Neuberg, S. L., Judice, T. N., & West, S. (1997). What the Need for Closure Scale measures and what it does not: Toward differentiating among related epistemic motives. *Journal of Personality and Social Psychology* **72**, 1396–1412.

Petty, R. E. (1994). Two routes to persuasion: State of the art. In G. d'Ydewalle, P. Eelen & P. Bertelson (Eds), *Current Advances in Psychological Science: An International Perspective*. Hillsdale, NJ: Erlbaum.

Petty, R. E., & Cacioppo, J. T. (1986).   The elaboration likelihood model of persuasion. In L. Berkowitz (Ed.), *Advances in Experimental Social Psychology* (Vol. 19, pp. 123–205). New York: Academic Press.

Pierro, A., Mannetti, L., Converso, D. Garsia, V., Miglietta, A., Ravenna, M., & Rubini, M. (1995).   Caratteristiche strutturali della versione italiana della scala di bisogno di chiusura cognitiva (di Webster e Kruglanski). *Testing, Psicometria, Metodologia*, **2**, 125–41.

Polley, R. B. (1987).   The dimensions of interpersonal behavior: A method for improving rating scales. *Social Psychology Quarterly*, **50**, 72–82.

Polley, R. B. (1989a).   On the dimensionality of interpersonal behavior: A reply to Lustig. *Small Group Behavior*, **20**, 270–78.

Polley, R. B. (1989b).   Operationalizing Levinian field theory. In E. J. Lawler & B. Markowski (Eds), *Advances in Group Process: Theory and Method* (pp. 205–27). Greenwich, CT: JAI Press.

Quattrone, G. A. (1982).   Overattribution and unit formation: When behavior engulfs the person. *Journal of Personality and Social Psychology*, **42**, 593–607.

Rice, G. E., Okun, M. A., Farren, D. E., & Christiansen, J. G. (1991).   *Older Adults' Processing of Texts Containing Information which Contradicts their Erroneous Beliefs about Osteoarthritis* (Tech. Rep. No. 2). Adult Development and Aging Program, Arizona State University.

Rokeach, M. (1960).   *The Open and Closed Mind*. New York: Basic Books.

Rubini, M., & Kruglanski, A. W. (1997).   Brief encounters ending in estrangement: Motivated language-use and interpersonal rapport in the question–answer paradigm, *Journal of Personality and Social Psychology*, **72** (5), 1047–1060.

Sanford, R. N., Adorno, E., Frenkel-Brunswik, E., & Levinson, D. J. (1950).   The measurement of implicit antidemocratic trends. In E. Adorno, E. Frenkel-Brunswik, D. J. Levinson, & R. N. Sanford (Eds), *The Authoritarian Personality* (pp. 222–79). New York: Harper and Row.

Schaller, M., Boyd, C., Yohannes, J., & O'Brien, M. (1995).   The prejudiced personality revisited: Personal need for structure and formation of erroneous group stereotypes. *Journal of Personality and Social Psychology*, **68**, 544–55.

Semin, G. R., & Fiedler, K. (1988).   The cognitive functions of linguistic categories in describing persons: Social cognition and language. *Journal of Personality and Social Psychology*, **54**, 558–68.

Semin, G. R., Rubini, M., & Fiedler, K. (1995).   The answer is in the Question: The Effect of Verb Causality upon Locus of Explanation. *Personality and Social Psychology Bulletin*, **21**, 834–41.

Sorrentino, R. M., & Short, J. C. (1986).   Uncertainty orientation, motivation and cognition. In R. M. Sorrentino & E. T. Higgins (Eds), *Handbook of Motivation and Cognition: Foundations of Social Behavior* (Vol. 1, pp. 379–403). New York: Guilford.

Sorrentino, R. M., Bobocel, D. R., Gitta, M. Z., Olson, J. M., & Hewitt, E. L. (1988). Uncertainty and persuasion: Individual differences in the effects of personal relevance on social judgments. *Journal of Personality and Social Psychology*, **55**, 357–71.

Tetlock, P. E. (1985).   Accountability: A social check on the fundamental attribution error. *Social Psychology Quarterly*, **48**, 227–36.

Thompson, M. M., Naccarato, M. E., & Parker, K. H. (1992).   Measuring cognitive needs: The development and validation of the Personal Need for Structure (PNS) and Personal Fear of Invalidity (PFI) Measures. Unpublished manuscript, University of Waterloo.

Thompson, E. P., Roman, R. J., Moscovitz, G. B., Chaiken, S., & Bargh, J. A. (1994). Accuracy motivation attenuates covert priming: The systematic reprocessing of social information. *Journal of Personality and Social Psychology, 66*, 474–89.

Trope, Y., & Bassok, M. (1983). Information gathering strategies in hypothesis testing. *Journal of Experimental Social Psychology, 19*, 560–76.

Tversky, A., & Kahneman, D. (1974). Judgment under uncertainty: Heuristics and biases. *Science, 185*, 1124–31.

Webster, D. M. (1993). Motivated augmentation and reduction of the overattribution bias. *Journal of Personality and Social Psychology, 65*(2), 261–71.

Webster, D. M., Findley, C., & Irvin, J. (1995). Motivational antecedents of interpersonal apathy: Effects of fatigue and accountability on empathic responding. Unpublished manuscript, University of Florida, Gainesville.

Webster, D. M., & Kruglanski, A. W. (1994). Individual differences in need for cognitive closure. *Journal of Personality and Social Psychology, 67*(6), 1049–62.

Webster, D. M., Richter, L., & Kruglanski, A. W. (1996). On leaping to conclusions when feeling tired: Mental fatigue effects on impressional primacy. *Journal of Experimental Social Psychology, 32*, 181–95.

Webster, D. M., Kruglanski, A. W., & Pattison, D. A. (1997). Motivated language use in intergroup contexts: Need for closure effects on the linguistic intergroup bias. *Journal of Personality and Social Psychology, 72*, 1122–31.

Chapter 6

The Context/Comparison Model of Social Influence: Mechanisms, Structure, and Linkages that Underlie Indirect Attitude Change

William D. Crano and Eusebio M. Alvaro
University of Arizona

ABSTRACT

This chapter details the development of the context/comparison model, applied to the analysis of indirect minority influence. The model assumes that minorities generally cannot affect strongly established beliefs. When ingroup, however, the persuasive minority evokes leniency in its message targets. While change is resisted, the ingroup minority's message is elaborated, and the minority itself is not derogated. Such a pattern introduces an imbalance into the attitude structure, and beliefs proximate to the focal attitude may be affected. Research involving norm formation and established attitudes yields results consistent with these expectations, and highlights the cognitive underpinnings of such indirect changes.

The study of attitudes and social influence is a dominant feature of social psychology, and has been so from the field's inception. In one of psychology's first experiments, Triplett (1898) examined the effects of the mere presence of others on performance, and his concern with social influence has been shared by the field from that time forward. In the empirical works and theoretical disputations of prominent scholars who have shaped the landscape of today's

European Review of Social Psychology, Volume 8. Edited by Wolfgang Stroebe and Miles Hewstone.
© 1998 John Wiley & Sons Ltd.

social psychology—Allport (1935), Asch (1951), Campbell (1961, 1963), Festinger (1953, 1957), Moscovici (1980, 1985), and Sherif (1935), among others—we find the constant analysis, reanalysis, and dissection of moderators and mediators of attitudes and social influence. Arguably, Allport's observation that attitudes are social psychology's "most distinctive and indispensable concept" is as true today as it was more than 60 years ago (Allport, 1935, p. 798), and the factors that affect social influence remain of intense concern (Eagly & Chaiken, 1993; Petty & Krosnick, 1995).

A major innovator in today's study of attitudes and social influence is Serge Moscovici, whose investigations on the persuasive power of the minority helped to reinvigorate the field (cf. Moscovici, 1976, 1980, 1985; Moscovici, Lage, & Naffrechoux, 1969). Moscovici's work has led not only to a new focus on minority influence but, paradoxically, to a renewed interest in the factors that affect the capacity of the *majority* to persuade. Moscovici portrayed his original work as a reaction against a dominant paradigm in social psychology in which majority-inspired concerns with maintaining the status quo were the prime motivators of critical treatments and measures. He maintained that the minority also could wield influence, and that the factors that affected minority persuasion merited serious consideration. The field has been responsive to his assertions. As a result of these pioneering efforts, interest in minority influence has attained an enthusiastic pitch in social psychology, and few today question the source or locus of this activity (cf. Brewer & Crano, 1994; Levine & Russo, 1987; Moscovici, Mucchi-Faina, & Maass, 1994; Mugny & Pérez, 1991). This chapter is concerned with some of the issues that have arisen as a consequence of Moscovici's creative insight and that remain unresolved in the face of vigorous inquiry. It does not focus in other than oblique ways on the question of whether or not disparate processes are responsible for minority and majority influence (cf. Kruglanski & Mackie, 1990), but rather details a theoretical model that helps organize many of the diverse themes that have evolved since Moscovici's seminal work, and that points to questions still in need of resolution. This chapter is a summary of work in progress—for the model is still evolving—and a prescription for the future of a field that has yet to consolidate its rich empirical database.

THE CONTEXT/COMPARISON MODEL

The context/comparison model (CCM) is a theoretical system that offers a means of integrating and understanding minority *and* majority influence (cf. Alvaro & Crano, 1997; Crano, 1994; Crano & Hannula-Bral, 1994). It is based on considerations of the cognitive processes that sustain attitude development and change. The model derives from converging evidence from research on intergroup relations, social comparison, dual process models of persuasion, and small-group decision making. It was developed to delineate the factors that affect the likelihood that an influence source will prevail in a persuasion context. Originally, the CCM held that the success or failure of an attempt at social influence was dependent on the interplay of the minority/majority status of source and target, the source's status as ingroup or outgroup to the target, and the subjective or objective nature of the issue under consideration. Recent research (Alvaro & Crano, 1997) requires that two additional components be factored into the predictive equation, the self-relevance of the attitude object (Crano, 1995), and the proximity of the influence source's position to that of the target. The CCM assumes different reactions to social influence as a consequence of the centrality of the targeted belief. Let us consider first those situations that involve low-vested issues (beliefs that are not central to the target) or on which no belief exists, as in contexts involving norm- or attitude-formation.

SETTINGS INVOLVING WEAK OR UNVESTED ATTITUDES OR NORM FORMATION

Minority Effects

The CCM assumes that ingroup minorities enjoy a persuasive *advantage* relative to the majority or outgroup minorities when attempting to influence norm formation (the development of a response rule in a novel setting) or to change weakly held or unvested attitudes. This perhaps unexpected advantage is thought to occur as a consequence of minority group members' distinctiveness, their capacity to stimulate divergent thought and message elaboration, and the positive regard they evoke as a consequence of their ingroup association with the influence target (cf. Alvaro & Crano, 1996; Legrenzi *et al.*, 1991; McGuire & McGuire, 1988; Martin, 1988, 1992; Nemeth, 1986; Nemeth & Kwan, 1987; Nemeth *et al.*, 1990; Turner *et al.*, 1987). An ingroup minority's distinctiveness leads its targets to attend to, and elaborate, its message. This elaboration is accompanied by little defensive counter-argumentation given the unvested nature of the ill-formed attitude or norm. Enhanced elaboration without counter-argument heightens message impact. If the communication is of reasonable strength, change is expected (cf. Petty & Cacioppo, 1986a, b). There is little resistance to influence in such a situation, because there is no established position to defend and no resistance to being identified with the (ingroup) minority's position. Enhanced elaboration can be a two-edged sword, however; when a weak message is proffered, elaboration may result in no change, or in contrast.

As an ingroup, the minority is not likely to be derogated, for to derogate a member of one's own reference group is in some ways to derogate oneself

178 WILLIAM D. CRANO AND EUSEBIO M. ALVARO

(Abrams & Hogg, 1990; Hogg & Abrams, 1988; Kelley, 1952; Kelly, 1990; Maass, Clark, & Haberkorn, 1982; Turner, 1991; Turner *et al.*, 1987). Further, considerable research on the perception of belief solidarity suggests that members of a group typically perceive ingroup members' beliefs as more variable than those of the outgroup, which is viewed as being more monolithic in its positions (Jones, Wood, & Quattrone, 1981; Quattrone, 1986; Quattrone & Jones, 1980). As such, ingroup attitude variations on all but the most critical issues of group identity may not be seen as a danger to be avoided, but rather as a natural concomitant of group life. Accordingly, minority positions taken by members within the group may not be adjudged threatening or particularly unexpected, but rather as part and parcel of being a member of a group, to be considered and appraised. This position is consistent with Marques' research on the "black sheep" effect (Marques, Robalo, & Rocha, 1992; Marques & Yzerbyt, 1988; Marques, Yzerbyt, & Leyens, 1988), which suggests greater derogation of an ingroup opinion deviant only when the critical disagreement calls perceivers' social identities into question. On less central issues, the minority position does not lead to source derogation or message rejection (see also Trost, Maass, & Kenrick, 1992).

To maximize the predictive power of the model, the form of the belief under influence pressure (or the judgment context, in our terms) also requires consideration. In the CCM, greater susceptibility to ingroup influence is assumed on issues involving subjective beliefs (attitudes and opinions, rather than objective judgments or matters of fact). This assumption (cf. Crano & Hannula-Bral, 1994) is based on converging evidence from disparate realms of psychological theory and research, including social comparison theory (Gorenflo & Crano, 1989; Olson, Ellis, & Zanna, 1983) and decision-making in small groups (Kaplan, 1987, 1989; Rugs & Kaplan, 1993; Laughlin, Chandler, & Shupe, 1995; Laughlin & Ellis, 1986).

Majority Effects

The same processes that determine minority influence suggest different outcomes when sources of majority status are at issue. Such sources are not distinctive, and thus are less likely to stimulate elaboration. The persuasive quality of the majority's communication is not a critical consideration because its pronouncements are not scrutinized carefully. In the absence of elaboration, lasting change (or conversion, in Moscovici's terms) will not occur. This is not to suggest that the majority lacks the power to coerce and thereby force compliance. However, majority interests often are not clear in circumstances involving issues on which no strong position has been established, or in which a novel response norm is being formed, and so majority coercion seems unlikely. The majority is expected to have little influence in the absence of some indication that the "appropriate" beliefs or actions are critical if one is to preserve membership in the group, whose denial is the central threat the group can levy.

Similar considerations hold in contexts involving the formation of novel response norms, in which a generalized method of responding or cognizing is propounded by the influence source, not a specific belief or behavior (cf., Crano, 1970; Sherif, 1935). In such contexts, it is the response blueprint or generalized response schemata that must be assimilated and internalized if the norm is to guide future actions or beliefs. In the absence of elaboration, there is little chance of internalization. Majority pressure thus appears a relatively ineffective method of inducing internalized response norms given the lack of elaboration thought to characterize recipients' responses to the majority's message.

Outgroup minorities are almost never capable of persuasion unless the issue is one on which no prior attitude is held. Even in this circumstance, the minority might fail if the suggested modification is antithetical to the well-being of the ingroup (Mackie, Worth, & Asuncion, 1990).

SETTINGS INVOLVING VESTED OR CENTRAL ATTITUDES

Minority Effects

In contexts involving the staple of social influence research, the modification of established beliefs, the underlying change dynamics described by the CCM are identical to those already detailed—but the outcome of the process is decidedly different. When established or vested beliefs are the target of minority change pressure, the target's reluctance to be associated with the minority position must also be considered (Pérez & Mugny, 1990; Pérez, Papastamou, & Mugny, 1995). In many influence contexts minority status is defined in terms of belief congruence or incongruence—the minority source is a minority precisely because it holds a belief at variance with that of the plurality of its reference group. In all, or most, other ways, the ingroup minority and the majority are identical. While there may be a reluctance on the part of the majority member to be identified with the deviant position, unless the issue is one that questions a fundamental feature of group identity there also is strong reluctance to derogate other ingroup members, even though they espouse deviant positions (Kelley, 1952). In a situation of this type, the source and target enter into a tacit understanding that we have labeled the *leniency contract* (Alvaro & Crano, 1996, 1997), which stipulates that the deviant message be processed and elaborated with little counter-argument or source derogation. Such a response pattern is the standard recipe for attitude change (Brewer & Crano, 1994; Hovland, Janis, & Kelley, 1953; Petty & Cacioppo,

1986a). However, an important counterweight of the leniency contract is the implicit understanding that no change will ensue in response to the communication. It is by this stratagem that the deviant message can be processed and considered open-mindedly, with little defensiveness or hostility. In the interactive system created by the contract, change is repudiated to avoid close identification with the minority position (Pérez & Mugny, 1990). This process avoids the threat of direct change, but it renders the target susceptible to indirect attitude change, which we define as a change of beliefs that are closely related to the focal issue. Recall that as part of the contract, cognitive defenses are not raised in response to the ingroup minority's message. The message is processed, and its information thereby gains entry into the belief system. If inconsistent with established attitudes, this elaborated information will prove troublesome, as prior research has shown (Gruder et al., 1978; Homer & Kahle, 1990; Pratkanis et al., 1988). This earlier research suggests that a persuasive message that is processed or elaborated will exert a long-term effect on beliefs even if it is discredited immediately after it is read. In the context of minority influence, we expand on these findings to suggest that processing a message without counter-argument or derogation will introduce stress or imbalance into the belief system, which cannot be eased by a change in the focal attitude, for to change the focal attitude would violate the terms of the contract. However, imbalance can be relieved by altering allied beliefs that are proximal to the focal attitude in the target's belief configuration. Such alteration is expressed as indirect attitude change.

This process does not occur with outgroup minority influence sources. Counter-argument and source derogation effectively defuse the impact of the outgroup's information, thereby blocking entry of the counter-attitudinal testimony into the belief system. Change pressure is minimized, no imbalance created, and the outgroup minority is rendered impotent as a source of change. Of course, one can conceive of situations in which the outgroup's message may be elaborated, and then processes similar to those expected in ingroup persuasion may occur, but such circumstances represent the exception rather than the rule.

Majority Effects

Prior research suggests that the majority is most influential in public settings, when the social categorization of source and target is identical, the issue is cast as subjective, and measurement is immediate (Wood et al., 1994). Under these conditions, positive evaluation of the ingroup majority may lessen the tendency to counter-argue, leading to direct, if not well-elaborated, change. Or, as Moscovici (1985) suggests, change may be a result of compliance to social pressure. Such change typically is restricted to the focal issue—it does not spread to related beliefs because it is not the outcome of elaboration and internalization.

The CCM's interpretation of majority influence on established attitudes stresses the normative power of the majority and its power to levy sanctions and to reward. As such, it is consistent with Moscovici's views. The model assumes that the majority can impose substantial social pressure by monitoring responses and threatening punishment or expulsion from the group for non-compliance, by emphasizing solidarity, or by coming under attack and thereby compelling members to come to the support of an imperiled source of social identity. These factors can motivate group members to comply with the majority, thereby altering reported beliefs or actions so as to become consistent with the majority's requirements. Such change is not the result of intense message elaboration, but an instrumental action taken to defuse social pressure, lend support, or show solidarity. As such, it will not persist, neither will it spread to related beliefs.

The CCM holds that the majority can cause lasting change (conversion), but this requires that receivers elaborate its message. Elaboration may be prompted by self-interest, as shown in the work of Baker and Petty (1994) and de Dreu and de Vries (1993, Study 2), whose persuasive messages involved the tripling of college tuition or implementing senior comprehensives, respectively, issues almost certain to engage the undergraduate student. Under conditions of high self-interest, elaboration is expected (Crano, 1995), and in both studies resulted in majority influence. Mackie's (1987) work also supports the CCM's elaboration thesis. In her studies, the majority had direct and indirect effects when the experimental arrangements promoted elaboration. When conditions inhibited elaboration, indirect change was not evident. When majority-induced change is not the result of elaboration, but of social pressure (Moscovici, 1985) or the need to attain or maintain group solidarity (Turner, 1991), change will neither persist nor affect related beliefs. If majority membership is not salient or important, then even the limited form of influence (compliance, vs. conversion) will not occur. The CCM thus explains successful and unsuccessful majority influence, and locates the source of success in the target's regard (or lack of regard) for the majority and the self-relevance of the issues under consideration.

To recapitulate, the CCM is based on message elaboration. An ingroup minority stimulates elaboration and attenuates counter-argument and source derogation. A benevolent reaction to a source coupled with attention to its message without concomitant counter-argumentation ordinarily leads to direct attitude change. Owing to a reluctance to identify with the source's position, direct change is resisted, but actively processing a counter-attitudinal message produces an imbalance in the attitude configuration, and change on indirectly implicated attitudes may occur to defuse change pressures. Majority sources typically do not stimulate elaboration, and as such, will not produce lasting change. If conditions (e.g., high self-relevance) foster elaboration, resulting changes may have lasting and far-reaching impact.

A REPRESENTATIVE EXPERIMENT ON NORM FORMATION

In an initial test of the CCM, Crano and Hannula-Bral (1994) investigated the impact of majorities and minorities on the establishment of a novel response norm, a study in the tradition of Sherif's (1935) autokinetic research. Respondents, all students of the same university, completed a minimal groups procedure in which they were informed that they fell into the majority or minority on the basis of their responses to a short inventory of (irrelevant) questions (Tajfel *et al.*, 1971). They also learned the (majority or minority) status of their alleged response partner. Then, in isolation, they made a series of judgments via computer terminal of a series of obscure factual items drawn from Pettigrew's (1958) category width scale. After each judgment, information flashed on their computer terminals disclosed the judgment made by their partner. This "other" respondent was an experimental artifice, a computer program designed to provide estimates which, on average, were two scale units greater than those of the respondent. The study's intent was to determine if this consistent (apparent) overestimation would cause respondents to form response norms that tended toward higher estimates on subsequent trials. The items were substantively independent, so the information provided on one had no implications for succeeding items. The constant upward pressure on responses was the critical source of influence.

The task was characterized for half the participants as involving objective judgments, while the remainder were told that although a correct answer was feasible, the items were so obscure as to be largely subjective. Experimental participants responded in concert with their custom-designed confederate for 15 trials, always responding before learning the partner's estimate. Then they made five private estimates, without information from the influence source. In addition to experimental participants, responses of a group of control subjects who received no information from any source also were obtained.

Analysis of experimental vs. control subjects' responses revealed that the computerized confederates had considerable impact. As shown in Figure 6.1, which combines five trials in each response block, the influence sources affected public responses (the first three response blocks), and the influence persisted on the private judgments (block 4), which were made in the absence of information from the response partner. The analysis demonstrates an impressive treatment effect on responses. As inferred from control responses, participants' natural inclination was to lower estimates over trials. The treatment overcame and reversed this tendency.

Having established that the treatment operated as planned, we may determine which independent variables affected responses. Analysis of experimental participants revealed that the source that had been designated as being of minority status had greater influence in both public and private response

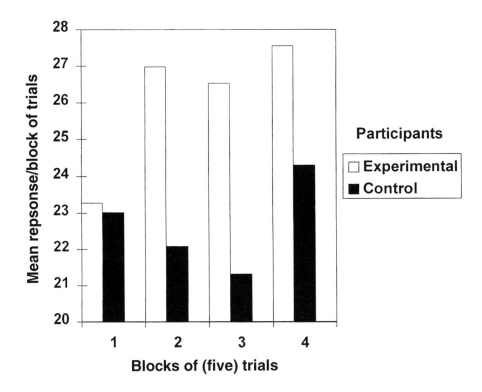

Figure 6.1 Mean judgments of experimental and control participants across blocks of public (blocks 1–3) and private (block 4) response trials (each block represents the average of five responses)

sessions. As predicted, estimates of participants paired with a minority source were substantially greater (i.e., in accord with the observations of the influence source) than those of subjects paired with the majority source. Furthermore, this minority influence effect persisted even when the source was effectively removed from the setting in the private response session. Evidently, source status mattered. When forming a new response norm, respondents were more influenced by minority than majority influence sources.

Source and participant status interacted with the subjective–objective task manipulation. Consistent with predictions, targets of minority status were more influenced than majority subjects by similar (in this case, minority) sources when the task was described as involving subjective judgments. On objective judgments, participants of majority status were more influenced by dissimilar (i.e., minority) sources. These influence differences persisted even when the source had been effectively removed from the judgment context.

These findings strongly support the CCM. The model predicts the persuasive superiority of a minority influence source when the task involves the formation of a novel response norm. In this case, the norm was one of overestimation—of generating estimates considerably higher than those of an uninfluenced control sample (Figure 6.1) or a group exposed to a source of majority status. In the analysis of experimental respondents' estimates, the significant main effect of source demonstrates the persuasive superiority of the minority source and confirms this feature of the model. The CCM also predicts an enhancement of minority persuasive superiority as a consequence of the subjective or objective nature of the judgment task, and this expectation, too, was confirmed.

Interestingly, the majority source had little impact in any circumstance. There are two reasons for this lack of effect. In this context, the majority source would not have motivated participants to attend to its message. Inattention is fatal in norm formation; without attention, the norm is never learned. Further, majority effects were seriously attenuated because the source's estimate, which constituted the persuasive communication, was always delivered *after* participants had made their judgments. If the majority's impact is seen principally on direct judgments, then the design of this experiment mitigated against any affect because its influence was always delivered after the naive participants had made their judgments.

These results suggest that the CCM is a plausible predictive device in contexts involving the formation of novel response norms. But does the model operate as well when established attitudes are at issue, and the concern involves their change, rather than norm formation? In these circumstances, the CCM suggests the relevance of indirect influence, whose consideration forms the core of the remainder of this chapter.

INDIRECT INFLUENCE

A long-held theoretical proposition supported amply by primary empirical investigation and consolidated in the important meta-analysis of Wood *et al.* (1994) is that minority influence occurs primarily on *indirect* measures. However, "indirect" influence has taken on different meanings in social psychology. For some, it refers to a change of attitudes that are related, but not identical, to the focal beliefs directly addressed in a persuasive communication (e.g., Aebischer, Hewstone, & Henderson, 1984; Alvaro & Crano, 1996, 1997; de Dreu & de Vries, 1993; Pérez & Mugny, 1987, 1990). This is the most indirect conceptualization of indirect influence. It offers a stiff challenge to the theorist to understand and establish the underlying determinants of change. However, solution of the puzzle posed by this view of indirect influence offers the promise of important theoretical advance.

Indirect influence also has been conceptualized in terms of "latent" vs. "manifest" judgments of perceptual stimuli (e.g., Moscovici & Personnaz, 1980, 1991; Personnaz, 1981). The latent–manifest distinction is useful in answering the query, "Are participants reporting their perceptions honestly, without regard to possible problems of experimenter demand or subject acquiescence?" (Festinger, 1953). Research on the social influence of perception (Moscovici & Personnaz, 1980; Personnaz & Personnaz, 1994) suggests that fundamental perceptual processes may be amenable to social influence. Although controversial (cf., Doms & van Avermaet, 1980; Sorrentino, King, & Leo, 1980), findings from the "blue/green" studies have interesting implications for the theoretical perspective outlined in this chapter. Three results from this literature support the view that change on indirect issues is a relatively unconscious process: Moscovici and Personnaz (1980) report that targets of minority influence who modified their latent perceptions generally were unaware of these changes. Further, even as targets became aware of their perceptual changes, they tended to see them as self-initiated, not as the result of social influence (Personnaz, 1981). Finally, minority influence appears to lead to increased *attention* to the object of judgment (Personnaz & Personnaz, 1994), consistent with the CCM's assumption that information from a minority is more distinctive, and thus more likely to be elaborated. All three of these "auxiliary" findings complement the theoretical bases of the CCM.

Personnaz and Personnaz (1994) rightly contend that perceptual research is relevant to considerations of belief change because perceptual norms represent forms of strongly internalized beliefs. Even so, given social psychology's long-standing affair of the heart with attitude change, it is not surprising that indirect attitude influence in reaction to minority persuasion has been an issue of most intense interest. The findings of Wood *et al.* (1994) imply that understanding indirect influence is central to understanding minority influence, and thus, we will provide a detailed consideration of studies whose principal focus is indirect attitude change.

An early social influence experiment with important implications for indirect change was performed by Nemeth and Brilmayer (1987), who assessed influence in a mock-jury setting. In this series, jurors appeared to be uninfluenced when confronted by a consistent minority arguing for a particular judgment in a court case. In our terms, Nemeth and Brilmayer (1987) presented no evidence of direct minority influence. However, indirect change may be inferred, because jurors who had faced the consistent minority were found to decide in ways consonant with the minority's position when later called to render judgments on similar cases.

Working with the more obvious "attitude" issue of abortion, Mugny and Pérez (1991) also found strong indirect influence effects. In their study, participants were presented a counter-attitudinal message favoring abortion (the direct issue), and their attitudes toward both abortion and birth control (the linked, indirect issue) were assessed. The pro-abortion message induced more liberal attitudes toward contraception, even though contraception was never mentioned in the persuasive communication. Mugny and Pérez's (1991) interpretation of their results is consistent with that developed in research on perceptual phenomena. They explained indirect influence in terms of Moscovici's (1980, 1985) concept of validation, whereby targets concentrate their cognitive activity on the content of a source's message and then infer the principles on which the position is based. They reasoned that direct influence failed owing to targets' desires to avoid identification with the minority. The identification obstacle is removed in indirect influence because the minority source is not directly associated with the position on the indirect issue. The principles inferred from the minority's position on the issue at hand are applied to the related issue, resulting in indirect change.

De Dreu and de Vries (1993, Study 2) further document the capacity of minorities to elicit indirect change on a topic (student achievement and grant eligibility) related to a focal issue of a persuasive communication (introduction of admission exams). Their study was based on the idea that people activate different cognitive processes when elaborating majority- and minority-based messages. Drawing on Nemeth's distinction between divergent and convergent thinking (Nemeth, 1986; Nemeth & Kwan, 1987), the authors suggest that a minority's information is processed systematically rather than heuristically, and this more elaborated processing style promotes divergent thinking which, in turn, fosters indirect change (de Dreu & de Vries, 1993, 1996; de Vries *et al.*, 1996; Eagly & Chaiken, 1993).

Although all of these studies support the argument that minorities exert influence indirectly, more specific conclusions regarding the mechanisms underlying indirect change are hampered by a number of unresolved issues. The first regards targets' perceptions of majority and minority sources. As Nemeth and Brilmayer (1987) did not include a majority condition, it cannot be determined whether a majority would have stimulated similar responses. Pérez and Mugny (1987) included both majority and minority source conditions, but they utilized gender to differentiate ingroups (females) from outgroups (males). While this was obviously appropriate in their experimental context, it also is true that males have been used frequently in persuasion to represent the majority, and females the minority. Thus, it is unclear whether participants were responding to the majority/minority status of the information sources, or their group status. De Dreu and de Vries (1993) made an explicit numeric identification of the minority group. The fact that source and targets were college students favors an interpretation of the minority as ingroup, but the ingroup/outgroup nature of the minority was not addressed explicitly. As such, interpreting the effects of minority status is somewhat problematic in this study. In all the studies described, the same question recurs: what are the qualities of an information source that cause indirect influence? We assume that a minority is more likely than the majority to stimulate indirect change. Is it necessary that the minority be ingroup? From our research, the conclusion that only ingroup (vs. outgroup) minorities have much chance of activating indirect change appears inescapable, but the issue remains moot.

A second issue that must be addressed in any discussion of indirect influence is the identification of the indirect attitude object. Nemeth and Brilmayer (1987) used case similarity as indicative of issue relationship, but similarity was not established in any rigorous manner. Pérez and Mugny (1987) utilized obviously linked attitude issues, abortion and contraception; however, there is concern that the link may be too obvious. Moreover, the link—obvious as it may be—was never assessed empirically. De Dreu and de Vries (1993) report a substantial correlation between focal and indirect attitude issues; however, the authors do not establish whether or not the study's participants consciously recognized the relationship between issues. To meet Festinger's (1953) recommendation that private acceptance and public compliance be differentiated, it is important that the connection between linked focal and indirect issues be relatively opaque. Only in such circumstances, which mimic the "blue/green" studies of the perceptual after-image paradigm, can we be assured that indirect changes are not merely instrumental actions undertaken consciously to defuse the discomfort of disagreement with a source of an attitudinally inconsistent message, or to help confirm an esteemed experimenter's expectations (cf., Cook *et al.*, 1970; Harris & Rosenthal, 1985).

A last concern raised by these studies is that, while the theoretical explanations of indirect influence generally focus on the content and processes of the target's cognitions, the investigations themselves generally lack any measures of cognitive activity beyond attitude change. Of the aforementioned studies, only de Dreu and de Vries (1993) measured theoretically derived internal mechanisms proposed to be responsible for direct and indirect change. And, while the role attributed to cognitive processing in this study is well addressed in the authors' theoretical rationale, it is not clear that their results support it. The authors propose that convergent and/or divergent thinking is differentially engaged as a result of majority or minority support for persuasive arguments, but utilize an operationalization of convergent processing that appears ill-suited to the theoretical construct. Specifically, convergent processing is operationalized as the ratio of positive-to-negative arguments developed in a thought-listing task—an operationalization that has long been employed as an indicator of message strength, but not convergent thought (cf., Petty & Cacioppo, 1986a).

A REPRESENTATIVE STUDY OF INDIRECT INFLUENCE

Concerns of this type led us to conduct research (cf., Alvaro & Crano, 1996, 1997) in which the link between the direct and indirect issues was established empirically. To qualify as an indirectly linked attitude, four criteria were imposed: participants' evaluations of the critical (focal and indirect) issues were required to be significantly correlated; the relationship could not appear necessary on any logical basis; the relationship between linked (focal and indirect) attitude objects could not be readily accessible; and the objects must be proximal in multidimensional space.

To discover attitudes that met these criteria, Alvaro and Crano (1997) asked participants to indicate their attitudes on a number of issues of contemporary concern (e.g., gun control, homosexuals in the military, abortion, tuition, etc.). Analysis disclosed that attitudes toward gun control and gays in the military were strongly correlated ($r = 0.42$). However, they do not appear logically interdependent. A second study was conducted to test the utility of these same attitude objects. In this extension, participants estimated the probability that a change in one of their attitudes would prompt a change in another. The format of all items was as follows:

> If you changed your mind regarding your position on HOMOSEXUALS IN THE MILITARY, what is the probability that you would also change your position on ABORTION?
> PROBABILITY = ——————————— [Probabilities could range from 0 to 100%.]

All 15 possible pairs of attitude objects were constructed from the six critical items.

Consistent with the first study's result, the correlation between the critical attitude objects (gun control and gays in the military) remained strong ($r = 0.40$). Analysis of the probability of change measure suggested that participants did not perceive much connection between the critical attitude objects: the mean estimated probability of a change in attitudes toward gun control given a change in beliefs regarding homosexuals in the military was only 10.78%. These probability of change judgments served as similarity estimates in a multidimensional scaling (MDS) analysis, which produced an interpretable two-dimensional configuration. More importantly, the analysis disclosed strong proximity between participants' attitudes toward gays in the military and gun control in the space that characterized the overall configuration of attitudes. Only attitudes toward birth control and abortion were linked more closely, a result anticipated by Pérez and Mugny (1987, 1990). It is important to note that correlation does not necessarily imply proximity in multidimensional space. Some attitude objects (e.g., gun control and birth control) that were strongly correlated ($r = 0.45$) were not proximate.

The results of these analyses satisfy the criteria suggested to establish linkage. As shown, there was a strong correlation between the two critical attitude objects, and the MDS established the proximity of the objects in multidimensional (cognitive) space, despite participants' lack of awareness of the link. It is in this fashion that linkages between attitude objects should be established. To rely only on correlational evidence is dangerous, as shown in the analysis of the gun control–birth control link, which disclosed strong correlation but low proximity in multidimensional space. To rely only on logic is also dangerous, in that it opens the door to possible effects or demand, problems with which the field has wrestled from the time of Asch (1951) and Festinger (1953).

The MDS findings were used as the basis of a series of experiments, all of which took a similar form. In these experiments, all participants read and responded to a persuasive message after having disclosed their attitudes on a number of issues (cf., Alvaro & Crano, 1997, for detailed description of this series). Measures of attitude change, cognitive responses, and source evaluation were taken after message presentation. In the first experiment of this series, the focal issue concerned allowing homosexuals in the military, then a topic of high salience in the USA. Analysis revealed that source variations had no direct effect on pretest–post-test attitude change. However, substantial change was noted on participants' attitudes toward gun control, an issue the MDS analysis had shown to be strongly linked to the focal issue. Analysis on the indirect attitude object revealed that participants who received a conservative-leaning, counter-attitudinal (homosexuals in the military) message from the ingroup minority changed their attitudes on gun control in a conservative direction, consistent with the persuasive message, when judgments were characterized as being subjective (vs. objective). As shown in Figure 6.2, no other group formed by the factorial combination of source × judgment type evidenced any change on the indirect attitude object.

Variations on source evaluation and message elaboration complement the indirect attitude change results. Participants exposed to the ingroup minority generated more positive thoughts, and fewer counter-arguments, than those whose identical persuasive message was attributed to a source of outgroup minority or (ingroup) majority status. Further, the ingroup minority was evaluated more positively than either of the other groups. Consistent with the expectations of the leniency contract, analysis disclosed that the evaluation of the ingroup minority was not affected by the consistency or inconsistency of its message with receivers' attitudes. This was not true in the case of the majority source. When the majority's message was contrary to targets' beliefs, evaluations of the majority suffered accordingly.

These findings are completely compatible with theory-based expectations, but there is no question that they also are exceptional. To determine the robustness of the results, a conceptual replication of the first experiment was undertaken. This replication followed the same format as the first, except that the focal and indirect issues were reversed. As before, preliminary study documented the link between the critical issues, homosexuals in the military and gun control. In this second study, following an extensive pretest, a

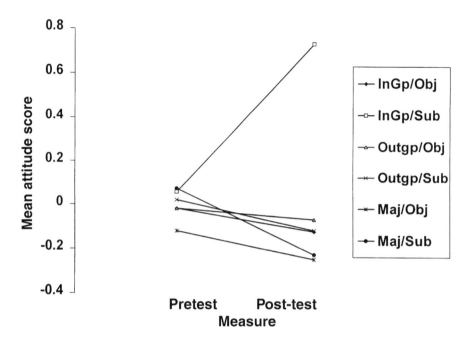

Figure 6.2 Standardized pretest to post-test attitude change on the indirect attitude (gun control) as a function of source (Maj = majority source, InGp = ingroup/minority, and OutGp = outgroup/minority) and task type (Obj = objective, and Sub = subjective)

strongly conservative message arguing the futility and inadvisability of gun control was delivered, and measures were taken of participants' reactions on a set of attitude objects, including the critical indirect measure. Consistent with the first experiment, analysis revealed no apparent effect on the focal attitude. In no condition did participants change in a way that indicated agreement with the anti-gun control message. However, those who received the conservative counter-attitudinal position on gun control that was delivered by a source of ingroup minority status changed their attitudes toward allowing homosexuals in the military, thus manifesting indirect change. These respondents became less positive toward this policy than they had been before exposure to the gun control message. As in the first experiment, the cognitive response analysis revealed that those exposed to an attitudinally inconsistent message from an ingroup minority did not derogate the source and did not counter-argue its message. These findings replicate the first experiment's results. They are compatible with, and predicted by, the CCM, and confirm the model as a useful predictive device. In addition, the findings point to issues whose consideration is mandatory if continued progress is to be made. Their review occupies the remainder of this chapter.

STRUCTURAL CONSIDERATIONS

Social psychology has long been concerned with between-attitude relationships, and the effect that change pressure on one belief might have on another. Early examples of social psychological focus on attitude linkages include such noteworthy contributions as congruity theory (Osgood & Tannenbaum, 1955), belief congruence (Rokeach & Rothman, 1965), and symbolic psychologic (Abelson & Rosenberg, 1958). It would appear that any consideration of between-attitude consistency requires consideration of attitude structure, which has to do with the manner in which attitudes are associated, and the dynamic interaction of the components of such an associative network when one or another is put under change pressure. Let us consider some of the implications of this view.

Network Models

Associative network models of attitudes (Fink & Kaplowitz, 1993; Judd et al., 1991; Judd & Krosnick, 1989) propose that attitudes are stored as nodes in long-term memory and organized into associative networks. The functioning of the network is similar to Anderson's (1983) model of memory. Conceptualizing between-attitude relationships in this manner fosters the view of attitude structures as having dynamic properties. As such, a change in one attitude should affect other attitudes within the network. Ultimately, following this approach, assessment of system-wide changes in attitudes may become possible. Only a handful of empirical studies have been conducted on this issue (e.g., Judd & Krosnick, 1989; Judd et al., 1991; Tourangeau et al., 1989; Tourangeau, Rasinski, & D'Andrade, 1991), but results hold promise for future research on indirect influence.

The results of these earlier studies suggest that strong attitudes may lead to more robust indirect change effects than weak attitudes. Strong attitudes are generally more extreme, and more powerfully linked with other, associated, beliefs (Petty & Krosnick, 1995). At the same time, they are more difficult to change, especially by minority groups (Trost, Maass, & Kenrick, 1992). Applying change pressure to a strong attitude, then, may result in strong resistance to direct change, but given the enhanced linkages with other beliefs that characterize strong attitudes, such pressure may spread to related attitudes, thereby facilitating indirect change.

Many conclusions relevant for indirect influence can be drawn from these studies. First, attitudes appear to be organized in networks. As such, priming one may facilitate access to other, linked, beliefs. Second, activating an attitude increases its extremity (strength), and as extremity increases, so too does accessibility. In consequence, influence applied to an attitude may have implications for change on linked beliefs, with stronger, more accessible attitudes associated with the more efficient spread of effect on linked beliefs.

Maximizing Indirect Change

These possibilities suggest that there are a number of controllable features of a persuasion setting that might be used to maximize indirect change effects. The first requirement for lasting influence is that targets elaborate the minority's position rather than focusing entirely on the relational elements that are part and parcel of the persuasion context. Moreover, this elaboration must not be accompanied by strong counter-argument. Elaboration of message content renders the critical attitude accessible, along with the (indirect) beliefs with which it is linked. Accessing a specific attitude structure primes the pathways to linked beliefs that reside within the same associative network, and these related attitudes are themselves activated.

To illustrate the relevance of these considerations for indirect influence, consider the two issues utilized by Alvaro and Crano (1997)—homosexuals in the military and gun control. In our view, participants' consideration of a minority-authored message against homosexuals in the military activated targets' cognitions and evaluations of homosexuals in the military *and* their (linked) attitudes toward gun control. Given the linkage, which had been established via correlational and MDS analysis, predicted changes on the indirect attitude object were obtained when the focal issue was brought under persuasive attack. In the follow-on study in which the attitude objects were reversed—that is, gun control became the topic of persuasion, and homosexuals in the military the indirect object—the identical pattern of indirect change obtained.

As with Petty and Cacioppo's (1986a, b, 1990) dual process model of attitude change, the CCM lays heavy stress on the quality of persuasive messages. If the context is such that it evokes elaboration of ingroup minority's persuasive communication—and the conditions necessary to promote elaboration have been detailed by the CCM—then any factor that detracts from the impact of a message of high quality will diminish indirect change. By this logic, messages of low strength would inhibit not only direct change, but indirect effects as well.

Many other variables that have been considered in minority influence research might be evaluated in terms of their power to affect message elaboration, and consequent indirect change. Distraction is one obvious example. Clearly, if an individual is distracted from elaborating a strong message, the persuasive power of the communication will be attenuated. A host of factors may serve as distractors from message content. Psychologization, for example, would draw one's focus from message content to source characteristics, and in consequence diminish not only direct influence but indirect effects as well (cf., Mugny *et al.*, 1984; Papastamou, 1986; Papastamou & Mugny, 1990). Similarly, inconsistency in a minority's message presentation strategy would detract from the persuasive power of the message, because as the minority's "script" changed from one presentation to another, the inconsistency would detract from message impact (or would attenuate message strength in Petty and Cacioppo's terms). It is conceivable that the importance of what Moscovici and his colleagues have dubbed behavioral style may reside in its capacity to enhance elaboration (cf. Moscovici, 1994; Moscovici, Lage, & Naffrechoux, 1969; Moscovici & Lage, 1978; Moscovici & Mugny, 1983). Much the same can be said of the distinction between rigidity and consistency drawn by Nemeth, Swedlund, and Kanki (1974), who demonstrated that while a minority's rigid adherence to the "party line" was not persuasive, a consistent adherence to a position was influential. If a rigid presentation can be dismissed as unreasonable, then the relevance of message quality again is suggested. One need not process a message that is illegitimate or unreasonable.

This same general interpretation can be made of the position of Wood *et al.* (1994) that minority communications that succeed in persuading typically are viewed by targets as feasible, if not particularly consistent with established beliefs. Feasibility implies a certain reasonableness of position, even though the position is at odds with one's own. This stress on feasibility is consistent with Papastamou and Mugny's (1990) view that the minority's position must be "coherent". Research by Mugny (1982) that suggested the persuasive utility of contextualizing minorities as innovators rather than deviants also is consistent with Wood's—and our—reasoning if we interpret feasibility, coherence, or innovation as suggesting legitimacy, which by our logic fosters elaborated processing. In a similar vein, Gerard (1985) proposed that minorities must be seen as holding a credible or reasonable position if they are to persuade. This view coincides with Mugny's (1982, 1984) that minority-supplied information must have a "certain legitimacy at its base". Viewing a message as feasible or legitimate fosters attention to the minority's position and lessens the likelihood of counter-argument.

Studies of double minorities (Clark & Maass, 1988; Maass, Clark, & Haberkorn, 1982) also may be interpreted from this perspective. This research has demonstrated consistently that double minorities are at a major persuasive disadvantage when compared with single minorities. For our perspective, it is important to note that studies typically operationlize double minorities as stigmatized individuals advocating positions that are contrary to their targets' beliefs, whereas single minorities simply advocate belief-discrepant positions, but are not stigmatized. Usually, the issue advocated by the double minority serves its self-interest. As such, attention is focused on trustworthiness, a source variable, rather than to message content.

Minorities achieve highest indirect influence when targets can attend to message content rather than relational factors. The lack of social power or threat inherent in *ingroup* minority status frees targets to consider the minority position rather than focus on the message source. Any elements of the persuasion context that cause attention to be directed away from the source's position may negate social influence. In sum, any factor that suggests to the target that the minority's position is invalid or untenable, unfeasible or illogical, will detract from message processing, and thereby attenuate indirect influence. Adopting this message-elaboration orientation to the analysis of indirect minority influence has the potential to organize a host of heretofore disconnected research themes, and thereby add to our capacity for progress.

The most optimal circumstances for indirect change involve strong communications (i.e., feasible, reasonable, coherent, etc.) delivered by credible sources directed toward change of strong attitudes that are (or become) highly accessible *and* not likely to change. In such a circumstance, attitudes strongly linked to the message-activated belief are vulnerable to (indirect) change in a direction consistent with the thrust of the persuasive communication. The lack of strong defenses raised to defend linked indirect attitudes, coupled with their association with the focal attitude, renders indirect change most probable. It is precisely these circumstances that prevailed in the research of Alvaro and Crano (1997), and that appear to have fostered the change of attitudes on objects that were not even addressed in the persuasive communication.

Indirect Influence in the Absence of Direct Change

Why would attitudes on an issue related to the target belief change in the absence of direct change? When envisioned as a change in one attitude eliciting changes in linked beliefs, spreading activation is nothing new; however, indirect change in the absence of direct change is somewhat more counterintuitive and—of greater concern—insufficiently accounted for by the literature on minority influence. Let us consider the issue in detail. A counter-attitudinal message presented by an ingroup minority may not be sufficient to change an established position. But, owing to relational demands, the target may well attend to the arguments offered by the ingroup (deviant) source. On a conscious level, this "leniency" may be felt a sufficient boon to a fellow ingroup member to mitigate the need for further accommodation. As is well established, the minority lacks the power to compel more extensive and overt changes. In combination, the feeling that one had "done enough", coupled with the minority's lack of coercive power, might be thought as signaling the termination of influence possibilities. However, in the process of accommodation, or responding politely to a fellow group member, the content of the message has been processed, and other attitudes within the structure have been activated. If, following Gilbert, information unhindered by counter-argumentation is perceived as true, then this "true" information, which has gained access to the target's attitude network, must be integrated with other components of the structure (cf., Gilbert, 1991; Gilbert, Tafarodi, & Malone, 1993). Thus, below a conscious level, related attitudes may be modified so as to accommodate the new information. By integrating the new "true" information into the network of beliefs, some measure of structural consistency is maintained.

The processes discussed to this point relate to relatively short-term change processes. Let us assume for the moment that indirect change does occur, in the absence of direct change. What are the likely structural/cognitive adjustments that might occur as a consequence of such a pattern over the medium or long term? We envisage three likely possibilities.

First, the indirect changes might be reversed because of their inconsistency with the unchanged focal attitude, and the general inertia of the associative network. In this case, the indirect attitude would return to its original state. Such a reversal in the "indirect" attitude would restore consistency to the attitude network. The likelihood of such a reversal may depend upon the relative strength of the two linked beliefs. It seems a reasonable hypothesis that the stronger the link between attitudes, the less likely is such a reversion of the indirect attitude.

A second possibility is that the attitude structure will be organized so that the newly-changed indirect attitude falls into a different cluster of beliefs. This pattern is feasible if we accept the proposal of Tourangeau et al. (1989, 1991) that attitudes are organized in clusters owing to shared similarities. If indirect change results in an attitude that is different in kind, not merely in polarization, then a rearrangement of the attitudes that had formerly resided in the same network seems indicated. Thus, a change in the indirect attitude toward gun control without a concomitant direct change on the related issue of gays in the military may result in cognitive reorganization such that the two issues become disassociated. Follow-up studies of the correlation and multidimensional structure of treated focal and indirect beliefs would help establish the manner in which this potential reaction to indirect change might operate.

The most intriguing possibility is that changes in "related" (indirect) attitudes, with the passage of time, come to change the focal attitude in a direction congruent with the newly established evaluation of the indirect object. The structural analysis of indirect change put forward here explains delayed (focal) attitude change, a common feature of the minority influence literature (cf., Wood et al., 1994), in a novel fashion. Consider the possibility that minority-inspired delayed influence (which we term a reverse sleeper effect) on the focal issue is the result of the following process: initially, the attention to focal message content stimulates indirect influence—linked attitudes change in a manner consistent with that described throughout this presentation; over time, the attitude system restores consistency between the newly-changed belief and the focal issue by inspiring change in the initial (i.e., the focal) attitude. Later, when attitudes are remeasured, results indicate that the original attitude has been modified in the direction of the original persuasive message. Consistent with contemporary interpretations, one is led to conclude that minority influence can occur, but only with the passage of time. The CCM provides an explanation of the manner in which such time-dependent change is brought about.

SUMMARY AND CONCLUSIONS

Attitude has been a central concern from the earliest days of social psychology's existence as a scholarly, scientific enterprise. Throughout our long and constructive history, attitudes typically have been studied as isolated cognitive events. Although everyone understood that individual beliefs did not exist *in vacuo*, our central research paradigms were constructed as if they did. This resolute neglect of the obvious has proved costly. In the short run, the price often is not great. If one is concerned with the impacts of different variables on attitude formation and change, then considering attitudes as isolated cognitive events with few linkages to other beliefs may not be damaging. In the long run, this approach has resulted in a conceptualization of attitude that is impoverished at best, and misleading at worst. The time has come to begin to act on the inescapable conclusion that mental events are interconnected, and that such linkages may have profound implications for understanding. This acknowledgement creates an important and necessary foundation for progress. Just as Fischer's *F*-test allowed us to move from one-variable-at-a-time analyses, and thus to begin to explore the interactions between and among variables, a consideration of the interconnected nature of our beliefs allows us to develop a more veridical picture of the manner in which social cognitive systems operate.

We hold that the stronger the linkage among beliefs within a given network (which may include a very few to hundreds of beliefs), the more likely are interactions among them. Pressuring one belief in a highly polarized and accessible attitude structure seems certain to have implications for other, linked attitudes that comprise the structure. Whether similar attitude interactions occur in less polarized or less accessible structures remains to be seen. Unfortunately, the means of addressing issues of even this level of complexity are far from apparent. We have not yet developed the methodological skills to enable a facile investigation of the antecedents and consequences of an interactive, structural approach to attitude. At present, we are left with the sometimes awkward application of extant techniques which are molded or commissioned in unusual ways to meet investigative needs. Thus, while we acknowledge the interactive nature of attitudes, we do not as yet possess the methodological tools necessary to investigate this presumption. Whether one wishes to develop techniques to establish the strength and extent of linkages within associative networks, or to develop theoretical models that allow us to understand the implications of strongly and weakly linked attitudes for focal and indirect change, the point is that such work is long overdue. It should start now. It is our hope that this chapter has emphasized the urgency of this prescription, and provided the encouragement necessary for researchers to begin this journey.

ACKNOWLEDGEMENT

This chapter was supported by NSF grant # SBR-9396057 to the first author, for which we are most grateful.

REFERENCES

Abelson, R. P., & Rosenberg, M. J. (1958). Symbolic psychologic: A model of attitudinal cognition. *Behavioral Science, 3*, 1–13.

Abrams, D., & Hogg, M. A. (Eds) (1990). *Social Identity Theory: Constructive and Critical Advances*. New York: Harvester Wheatsheaf.

Aebischer, V., Hewstone, M., & Henderson, M. (1984). Minority influence and musical preference: Innovation by conversion not coercion. *European Journal of Social Psychology, 14*, 23–33.

Allport, G. W. (1935). Attitudes in C. Murchinson (Ed.), *Handbook of Social Psychology* (Vol. 2). Worchester, MA: Clark University Press.

Alvaro, E. M., & Crano, W. D. (1996). Cognitive responses to minority or majority-based communications: Factors that underlie minority influence. *British Journal of Social Psychology, 35*, 105–21.

Alvaro, E. M., & Crano, W. D. (1997). Indirect minority influence: Evidence for leniency in source evaluation and counterargumentation. *Journal of Personality and Social Psychology, 72*, 949–964.

Anderson, J. R. (1983). *The Architecture of Cognition*. Cambridge, MA: Harvard University Press.

Asch, S. E. (1951). Effects of group pressure upon the modification and distortion of judgment. In H. Guetzkow (Ed.), *Groups, Leadership, and Men*. Pittsburgh, PA: Carnegie Press.

Baker, S. M., & Petty, R. F. (1994). Majority and minority influence: Source-position imbalance as a determinant of message scrutiny. *Journal of Personality and Social Psychology, 67*, 5–19.

Brewer, M. B., & Crano, W. D. (1994). *Social Psychology*. Minneapolis and St Paul, MN: West.

Campbell, D. T. (1961). Conformity in psychology's theories of acquired behavioral dispositions. In I. A. Berg & B. M. Bass (Eds), *Conformity and Deviation*. New York: Harper.

Campbell, D. T. (1963). Social attitudes and other acquired behavioral dispositions. In S. Koch (Ed.), *Psychology: A Study of a Science* (Vol. 6), *Investigations of Man as Socius*. New York: McGraw-Hill.

Clark, R. D. III, & Maass, A. (1988). Social categorization in minority influence. The case of homosexuality. *European Journal of Social Psychology, 18*, 347–64.

Cook, T. D., Bean, J. R., Calder, B. J., Frey, R., Krovetz, M. L., & Reisman, S. R. (1970). Demand characteristics and three conceptions of the frequently deceived subject. *Journal of Personality and Social Psychology*, **14**, 185–94.

Crano, W. D. (1970). Effects of sex, response order, and expertise in conformity: A dispositional approach. *Sociometry*, **33**, 239–52.

Crano, W. D. (1994). Context, comparison, and change: Methodological and theoretical contributions to a theory of minority (and majority) influence. In S. Moscovici, A. Mucchi-Faina & A. Maass (Eds), *Minority Influence* (pp. 17–46). Chicago, IL: Nelson-Hall.

Crano, W. D. (1995). Components of vested interest and attitude-behavior consistency. In R. E. Petty & J. A. Krosnick (Eds), *Attitude Strength: Antecedents and Consequences*. The Ohio State University series in attitudes and persuasion (Vol. 4). Hillsdale, NJ: Erlbaum.

Crano, W. D., & Hannula-Bral, K. A. (1994). Context/categorization model of social influence: Minority and majority influence in the formation of a novel response norm. *Journal of Experimental Social Psychology*, **30**, 247–76.

de Dreu, C. K. W., & de Vries, N. K. (1993). Numerical support, information processing and attitude change. *European Journal of Social Psychology*, **23**, 647–62.

de Dreu, C. K. W. & de Vries, N. K. (1996). Differential processing and attitude change following majority versus minority arguments. *British Journal of Social Psychology*, **35**, 77–90.

de Vries, N. K., de Dreu, C. K. W., Gordijn, E., & Schuurman, M. (1996). Majority and minority influence: A dual-role interpretation. In W. Stroebe & M. Hewstone (Eds) *European Review of Social Psychology* (vol. 7, pp. 145–192) Chichester: Wiley.

Doms, M., & van Avermaet, E. (1980). Majority influence, minority influence, and conversion behavior: A replication. *Journal of Experimental Social Psychology*, **16**, 283–92.

Eagly, A. H., & Chaiken, S. (1993). The Psychology of Attitudes. Fort Worth, TX: Harcourt Brace Jovanovich.

Festinger, L. (1953). An analysis of compliance behavior. In M. Sherif & M. O. Wilson (Eds), *Group Relations at the Crossroads*. New York: Harper.

Festinger, L. (1957). *A Theory of Cognitive Dissonance*. Evanston, IL: Row, Peterson.

Fink, E. L., & Kaplowitz, S. A. (1993). Oscillation in beliefs and cognitive networks. In G. A. Barnett & W. Richards (Eds), *Progress in Communication Sciences* (Vol. 12, pp. 247–72). Norwood, NJ: Ablex.

Gerard, H. B. (1985). When and how the minority prevails. In S. Moscovici, G. Mugny, & E. van Avermaet (Eds), *Perspectives on Minority Influence* (pp. 171–86). Cambridge, MA: Cambridge University Press.

Gilbert, D. T. (1991). How mentals systems believe. *American Psychologist*, **46**, 107–19.

Gilbert, D. T., Tafarodi, R. W., & Malone, P. S. (1993). You can't not believe everything you believe. *Journal of Personality and Social Psychology*, **65**, 221–33.

Gorenflo, D. W., & Crano, W. D. (1989). Judgmental subjectivity/objectivity and locus of choice in social comparison. *Journal of Personality and Social Psychology*, **57**, 605–14.

Gruder, C. L., Cook, T. D., Hennigan, K. M., Flay, B. R., Alessi, C., & Halamaj, J. (1978). Empirical tests of the absolute sleeper effect predicted from the discounting cue hypothesis. *Journal of Personality and Social Psychology*, **36**, 1061–74.

Harris, M. J., & Rosenthal, R. (1985). The mediation of interpersonal expectancy effects: 31 meta-analytic studies. *Psychological Bulletin*, **97**, 363–86.

Hogg, M. A., & Abrams, D. (1988). *Social Identifications*. London: Routledge.

Homer, P. M., & Kahle, L. R. (1990). Source expertise, time of source identification, and involvement in persuasion: An elaborative processing perspective. *Journal of Advertising*, **19**, 30–39.

Hovland, C. I., Janis, I. L., & Kelley, H. H. (1953). *Communication and Persuasion*. New Haven, CT: Yale University Press.

Jones, E. E., Wood, G. C., & Quattrone, G. A. (1981). Perceived variability of personal characteristics in ingroups and outgroups: The role of knowledge and evaluation. *Personality and Social Psychology Bulletin*, **7**, 523–8.

Judd, C. M., & Krosnick, J. A. (1989). The structural bases of consistency among political attitudes: Effects of political expertise and attitude importance. In A. R. Pratkanis, S. J. Breckler, & A. G. Greenwald (Eds), *Attitude Structure and Function* (pp. 99–128). Hillsdale, NJ: Erlbaum.

Judd, C. M., Drake, R. A., Downing, J. W., & Krosnick, J. A. (1991). Some dynamic properties of attitude structures: Context-induced response facilitation and polarization. *Journal of Personality and Social Psychology*, **60**, 193–202.

Kaplan, M. F. (1987). The influence process in group decision making. In C. Hendrick (Ed.), *Review of Personality and Social Psychology: Group Processes* (Vol. 8, pp. 189–212). Beverly Hills, CA: Sage.

Kaplan, M. F. (1989). Task, situational, and personal determinants of influence processes in group decision making. *Advances in Group Processes*, **6**, 87–105.

Kelly, C. (1990). Social identity and levels of influence: When a political minority fails. *British Journal of Social Psychology*, **29**, 289–301.

Kelley, H. H. (1952). The two functions of reference groups. In G. E. Swanson, T. M. Newcomb, & E. L. Hartley (Eds), *Readings in Social Psychology* (pp. 410–14). New York: Holt.

Kruglanski, A. W., & Mackie, D. M. (1990). Majority and minority influence: A judgmental process analysis. In W. Stroebe & M. Hewstone (Eds), *European Review of Social Psychology* (Vol. 1). Chichester: Wiley.

Laughlin, P. R., Chandler, J. A., & Shupe, E. I. (1995). Generality of a theory of collective induction: Face-to-face and computer-mediated interaction, amount of potential information, and group versus member choice of evidence. *Organizational Behavior and Human Decision Processes*, **63**, 98–111.

Laughlin, P. R., & Ellis, A. L. (1986). Demonstrability and social combination processes on mathematical intellective tasks. *Journal of Experimental Social Psychology*, **22**, 177–89.

Legrenzi, P., Butera, F., Mugny, G., & Pérez, J. A. (1991). Majority and minority influence in inductive reasoning: A preliminary study. *European Journal of Social Psychology*, **21**, 359–63.

Levine, J. M., & Russo, E. M. (1987). Majority and minority influence. In C. Hendrick (Eds.), *Review of Personality and Social Psychology: Group Processes* (Vol. 8), Newbury Park, CA: Sage.

Maass, A., Clark, R. D., & Haberkorn, G. (1982). The effects of differential ascribed category membership and norms on minority influence. *European Journal of Social Psychology*, **12**, 89–104.

Mackie, D. M. (1987). Systematic and nonsystematic processing of majority and minority persuasive communications. *Journal of Personality and Social Psychology*, **53**, 41–52.

Mackie, D. M., Worth, L. T., & Asuncion, A. G. (1990). Processing of persuasive ingroup messages. *Journal of Personality and Social Psychology*, **58**, 812–22.

Marques, J. M., Robalo, E. M., & Rocha, S. A. (1992). In-group bias and the "black sheep" effect: Assessing the impact of social identification and perceived variability on group judgments. *European Journal of Social Psychology,* **18**, 287–92.

Marques, J. M., & Yzerbyt, V. Y. (1988). The black sheep effect: Judgment extremity towards in-group members in inter- and intra-group situations. *European Journal of Social Psychology,* **18**, 287–92.

Marques, J. M., Yzerbyt, V. Y., & Leyens, J-P. (1988). The "black sheep effect": Extremity of judgments towards in-group members as a function of group identification. *European Journal of Social Psychology,* **18**, 1–16.

Martin, R. (1988). In-group and out-group minorities: Differential impact upon public and private response. *European Journal of Social Psychology,* **18**, 39–52.

Martin, R. (1992). The effects of ingroup–outgroup membership on minority influence when group membership is determined by a trivial categorization. *Social Behavior and Personality,* **20**, 131–42.

McGuire, W. J., & McGuire, C. V. (1988). Content and process in the experience of self. In L. Berkowitz (Ed.), *Advances in Experimental Social Psychology* (Vol. 21, pp. 97–143). San Diego, CA: Academic Press.

Moscovici, S. (1976). *Social Influence and Social Change.* New York: Academic Press.

Moscovici, S. (1980). Toward a theory of conversion behavior. In L. Berkowitz (Ed.), *Advances in Experimental Social Psychology* (Vol. 13, pp. 209–39). New York: Academic Press.

Moscovici, S. (1985). Innovation and minority influence. In G. Lindzey & E. Aronson (Eds), *The Handbook of Social Psychology* (Vol. 2, 3rd edn, pp. 347–412). New York: Random House.

Moscovici, S. (1994). Three concepts: Minority, conflict, and behavioral style. In S. Moscovici, A. Mucchi-Faina, & A. Maass (Eds), *Minority Influence* (pp. 233–252). Chicago, IL: Nelson-Hall.

Moscovici, S., & Lage, E. (1978). Studies in social influence: III. Majority versus minority influence in a context of original judgments. *European Journal of Social Psychology,* **8**, 349–65.

Moscovici, S., Lage, E., & Naffrechoux, M. (1969). Influence of a consistent minority on the responses of a majority in a color perception task. *Sociometry,* **32**, 365–80.

Moscovici, S., Mucchi-Faina, A., & Maass, A. (Eds) (1994). *Minority Influence.* Chicago, IL: Nelson-Hall.

Moscovici, S., & Mugny, G. (1983). Minority influence. In P. B. Paulus (Ed.), *Basic Group Processes* (pp. 41–64). New York: Springer-Verlag.

Moscovici, S., & Personnaz, B. (1980). Studies in social influence: V. Minority influence and conversion behavior in a perceptual task. *Journal of Experimental Social Psychology,* **16**, 270–82.

Moscovici, S., & Personnaz, B. (1991). Studies in social influence: VI. Is Lenin orange or red? Imagery and social influence. *European Journal of Social Psychology,* **21**, 101–18.

Mugny, G. (1982). *The Power of Minorities.* New York: Academic Press.

Mugny, G. (1984). Compliance, conversion, and the Asch paradigm. *European Journal of Social Psychology,* **14**, 353–68.

Mugny, G., Kaiser, C., Papastamou, S., & Pérez, J. (1984). Group relations, identification, and social influence. Special Issue: Intergroup processes. *British Journal of Social Psychology,* **23**, 317–22.

Mugny, G., & Pérez, J. A. (1991). *The Social Psychology of Minority Influence.* Cambridge, MA: Cambridge University Press.

Nemeth, C. J. (1986). Differential contributions of majority and minority influence. *Psychological Review,* **93**, 1–10.

Nemeth, C. J., & Brilmayer, A. G. (1987). Negotiation versus influence. *European Journal of Social Psychology,* **17**, 45–56.

Nemeth, C. J., & Kwan, J. (1987). Minority influence, divergent thinking, and detection of correct solutions. *Journal of Applied Social Psychology,* **17**, 786–97.

Nemeth, C. J., Mayseless, O., Sherman, J., & Brown, Y. (1990). Exposure to dissent and recall of information. *Journal of Personality and Social Psychology,* **58**, 429–37.

Nemeth, C. J., Swedlund, M., & Kanki, B. (1974). Patterning of the minority's responses and their influence on the majority. *European Journal of Social Psychology,* **4**, 53–64.

Olson, J. M., Ellis, R. J., & Zanna, M. P. (1983). Validating objective versus subjective judgments: Interest in social comparison and consistency information. *Personality and Social Psychology Bulletin,* **9**, 427–36.

Osgood, C. E., & Tannenbaum, P. H. (1955). The principle of congruity in the prediction of attitude change. *Psychological Review,* **62**, 42–55.

Papastamou, S. (1986). Psychologization and processes of minority and majority influence. *European Journal of Social Psychology,* **16**, 165–80.

Papastamou, S., & Mugny, G. (1990). Synchronic consistency and psychologization in minority influence. *European Journal of Social Psychology,* **20**, 85–98.

Pérez, J. A., & Mugny, G. (1987). Paradoxical effects of categorization in minority influence: When being an out-group is an advantage. *European Journal of Social Psychology,* **17**, 157–69.

Pérez, J. A., & Mugny, G. (1990). Minority influence: Manifest discrimination and latent influence. In D. Abrams & M. Hogg (Eds), *Social Identity Theory: Constructive and Critical Advances.* London: Harvester Wheatsheaf.

Pérez, J. A., Papastamou, S., & Mugny, G. (1995). "Zeitgeist" and minority influence—Where is the causality? A comment on Clark (1990). *European Journal of Social Psychology,* **25**, 703–10.

Personnaz, B. (1981). Study in social influence using the spectrometer method. Dynamics of the phenomenon of conversion and covertness in perceptual responses. *European Journal of Social Psychology,* **11**, 431–8.

Personnaz, M., & Personnaz, B. (1994). Perception and conversion. In S. Moscovici, A. Mucchi-Faina, & A. Maass (Eds), *Minority Influence* (pp. 165–84). Chicago, IL: Nelson-Hall.

Pettigrew, T. F. (1958). The measurement and correlates of category width as a cognitive variable. *Journal of Personality,* **26**, 532–44.

Petty, R. E., & Cacioppo, J. T. (1986a). *Communication and Persuasion: Central and Peripheral Routes to Attitude Change.* New York: Springer-Verlag.

Petty, R. E., & Cacioppo, J. T. (1986b). The elaboration likelihood model of persuasion. In L. Berkowitz (Ed.), *Advances in Experimental Social Psychology* (Vol. 19, pp. 123–205). New York: Academic Press.

Petty, R. E., & Cacioppo, J. T. (1990). Involvement and persuasion: Tradition versus integration. *Psychological Bulletin,* **107**, 367–75.

Petty, R. E., & Krosnick, J. A. (Eds) (1995). *Attitude Strength: Antecedents and Consequences.* Mahwah, NJ: Erlbaum.

Pratkanis, A. R., Greenwald, A. G., Leippe, M. R., & Baumgardner, M. H. (1988). In search of reliable persuasion effects: III. The sleeper effect is dead. Long live the sleeper effect. *Journal of Personality and Social Psychology,* **54**, 203–18.

Quattrone, G. A. (1986).   On the perception of a group's variability. In S. Worchel & W. G. Austin (Eds), *Psychology of Intergroup Relations* (pp. 24–48). Chicago, IL: Nelson-Hall.

Quattrone, G. A., & Jones, E. E. (1980).   The perception of variability within in-groups: Implications for the law of small numbers. *Journal of Personality and Social Psychology, 38,* 141–52.

Rokeach, M., & Rothman, G. (1965).   The principle of belief congruence and the congruity principle as models of cognitive interaction. *Psychological Review, 72,* 128–42.

Rugs, D., & Kaplan, M. F. (1993).   Effectiveness of informational and normative influences in group decision making depends on the group interactive goal. Special Issue: Social processes in small groups: II. Studying social processes in small groups. *British Journal of Social Psychology, 32,* 147–58.

Sherif, M. (1935).   A study of some social factors in perception. *Archives of Psychology, 27*(187), 1–60.

Sorrentino, R. M., King, G., & Leo, G. (1980).   The influence of the minority on perception: A note on a possible alternative explanation. *Journal of Experimental Social Psychology, 16,* 293–301.

Tajfel, H., Billig, M. G., Bundy, R. P. & Flament, C. (1971).   Social categorization and intergroup behaviour. *European Journal of Social Psychology, 1,* 149–78.

Triplett, N. (1898).   The dynamogenic factors in pacemaking and competition. *American Journal of Psychology, 9,* 507–33.

Tourangeau, R., Rasinski, K. A., Bradburn, N., & D'Andrade, R. (1989).   Belief accessibility and contexts effects in attitude measurement. *Journal of Experimental Social Psychology, 25,* 401–21.

Tourangeau, R., Rasinski, K. A., & D'Andrade, R. (1991).   Attitude structure and belief accessibility. *Journal of Experimental Social Psychology, 27,* 48–75.

Trost, M. R., Maass, A., Kenrick, D. T. (1992).   Minority influence: Personal relevance biases cognitive processes and reverses private acceptance. *Journal of Experimental Social Psychology, 28,* 234–254.

Turner, J. (1991).   *Social Influence.* Pacific Grove, CA: Brooks/Cole.

Turner, J. C., Hogg, M. A., Oakes, P. J., Reicher, S. D., & Wetherell, M. (1987).   *Rediscovering the Social Group: A Self-categorization Theory.* Oxford: Blackwell.

Wood, W., Lundgren, S., Ouellette, J. A., Busceme, S., & Blackstone, T. (1994).   Processes of minority influence: Influence effectiveness and source perceptions. *Psychological Bulletin, 115,* 323–45.

Chapter 7

The Group as a Basis for Emergent Stereotype Consensus

S. Alexander Haslam, John C. Turner, Penelope J. Oakes, Craig McGarty and Katherine J. Reynolds
Australian National University

ABSTRACT

The fact that stereotypes are shared within groups is essential to stereotype definition and operationalization. Nonetheless, stereotype consensus remains under-researched and under-explained. To address this problem we present a theoretical analysis of the process through which stereotype consensus develops. Derived from self-categorization theory, this argues that consensus is produced by shared social identification and the collective co-ordination of perception and behaviour that flows from it. This analysis is examined in a review of relevant research and in studies where dynamic processes of category representation and social influence are shown to contribute to consensual stereotypes of both out-groups and ingroups.

"Dr Hunt . . . has collected all the reliable modern authorities, and demonstrates what every unperverted American *knows*—that the Negro is a different and subordinate species or race. This fundamental *fact*, clearly apprehended and accepted, becomes the starting point for the mental regeneration of our people and the restoration of peace, union and harmony in all sections of our common country" (Van Evrie, 1864, cited in Smith, 1993, p. 10).

The above statement is taken from the preface to an anti-abolitionist tract written at the height of the American Civil War and is included in a recent historical volume which reproduces material relating to the development of

European Review of Social Psychology, Volume 8. Edited by Wolfgang Stroebe and Miles Hewstone.
© 1998 John Wiley & Sons Ltd.

anti-Black stereotypes around the end of the last century. A number of things about the book as a whole are remarkable, but one of the most striking is the repetitive vigour of its contents. Thus the writings of Van Evrie, of which this extract is typical, were not those of someone who was out of step with that part of society for which he presumed to speak, and history suggests that although what he had to say served dramatically to undermine national "union and harmony", it was in a very tangible sense both unifying and harmonizing for the groups he addressed. In short, it is clear that while it divided a nation, the Civil War was a unifying force within the opposed groups and that at its heart were shared beliefs about people—elevated to the status of facts—that served to justify and explain the conflict. So, when Van Evrie referred to "what every unperverted American knows" he was proudly referring to stereotypic beliefs *consensually* held within his ingroup.

Yet despite the apparent centrality of consensus to the expression and force of stereotypes, it is intriguing to note not only that the topic of stereotype consensus has been steadily pushed down the research agenda in the last 60 years, but that efforts have recently been made to bridle its investigation further. This is marked in three inter-related sets of claims: the first, that agreement between people is an irrelevant feature of stereotype definition, the second that stereotype consensus is illusory, and the third that traditional methods for investigating consensus (like the Katz–Braly (1933) checklist) are defective.

The basis of the first and third claims can be found in Ashmore and Del Boca's (1981) influential review, which jettisoned consensus as a definitional feature of stereotypes on the basis of an argument that interest in stereotype consensus had originally emerged only by methodological accident, and that "it seems unwise to tailor conceptual definitions to fit convenient, often used methods" (p. 19; see also Devine & Elliot, 1995, p. 1146). Like others before them (e.g., Brigham, 1971), these reviewers noted that the pattern for investigating stereotypes had been established by Katz and Braly's (1933) development of a method which "implicitly buil[t] consensus into the meaning of the term". This is certainly true, as the method devised by Katz and Braly identified stereotypes by reporting the percentage of subjects who selected the most commonly chosen traits from a given list of 84 to describe various ethnic and national groups. In other words, stereotypes were only identified where there was some degree of consensus in subjects' trait selection. Rejecting this as a methodological constraint, Ashmore and Del Boca proposed that the term stereotype be reserved solely for individual beliefs (to be distinguished from the shared or "cultural stereotypes" identified by the Katz–Braly checklist). Recent reviewers have been even more strident in arguing that the consensus criterion is superfluous and limiting, claiming that because in the final analysis stereotypes "reside in the minds of individuals" it is *as individual beliefs* that they should be studied (Hamilton, Stroessner, & Driscoll, 1994, p. 298; see also Judd & Park, 1993, p. 110).

Studies using checklist methodology have also provided a basis for arguments that stereotype consensus does not actually exist. In particular, Gardner (1993, p. 5, p. 19; see also Taft, 1959) concludes that in these studies "consensus isn't all that great" after noting the "seldom emphasized" fact that only seven of the 120 traits included in the stereotypes originally identified by Katz and Braly (i.e., only 5.8%) were assigned by more than 50% of the subjects. In replications conducted by Gilbert (1951) and Karlins, Coffman, and Walters (1969), comparable values were two out of 84 (2.4%) and five out of 110 (4.6%) respectively. Condor (1990) has developed this critique by implying that researchers may have conspired to overlook consensus-related issues, together with evidence that stereotypes are not widely shared, for fear that such examination would be self-defeating. As she puts it, "Ideas about shared stereotypes . . . are often nothing more than *a priori* assumptions which may function to preclude any further analysis of a potentially contentious issue" (Condor, 1990, p. 237).

Considering these points together, researchers may think themselves well-advised to leave the issue of stereotype consensus well alone, and most have. For not only has the phenomenon been seen as irrelevant and proved hard to isolate empirically but, as a number of commentators have noted (e.g., Brigham, 1971; Leyens, Yzerbyt, & Schadron, 1994), methodologies designed for this purpose do not lend themselves to the analysis of *psychological process* as readily as those which treat stereotypes simply as individual beliefs.

Yet although such a course of action may seem expedient, it is ironic that of all the properties of stereotypes that researchers commonly investigate and seek to explain (e.g., their negativity, their homogeneity, their rigidity), the only feature which is *essential* for them to be studied in the first place is the one to which least attention has been paid. As Stangor and Lange (1994, p. 403) point out, "Despite recent attempts to do away with the consensus criterion . . . it is simply not possible to consider stereotypes without assuming that they are shared, at least to some extent, among individuals". This is because most of the methods that have been developed to study stereotyping are implicitly designed around assumptions that within any group of subjects certain beliefs about groups will prevail over others—that librarians will be thought of as studious rather than loud, old people as passive rather than active, skinheads as vicious rather than gentle. For example, all research which uses stereotype consistency as an independent or dependent variable incorporates such assumptions and this is one of the most common features of stereotyping experiments (e.g., see Rojahn & Pettigrew, 1992; Stangor & McMillan, 1992). In this sense, then, even if researchers choose to ignore it, it remains true that uniformity of belief represents what Thorndike (1977, p. 134) referred to as "the very essence of the stereotype concept" (see also Gardner, Kirby, & Finlay, 1973).

Furthermore, if stereotypes were *not* shared there would be little interest in them in the first place. As Stangor and Lange (1994, p. 403) note, their "precise danger"—and hence the most commonly presented reason for studying them—lies in the fact that groups of people, like Van Evrie and his supporters, tend to respond to members of stigmatized outgroups in *similar* ways (see also Schneider, 1996; Ruscher, Hammer, & Hammer, 1996; Stangor & Schaller, 1996). Anticipating this point, Tajfel (1981, p. 147) argued that the "common adoption [of stereotypes] by large numbers of people who share a social affiliation" was implicated in the two most important questions for stereotyping researchers. These questions concern (i) *why* stereotypes are shared, and (ii) the nature of the links between group membership and the structured psychological activity that underpins stereotype consensus. Yet although Tajfel provided some good answers to the first question, little has been done to go beyond his "hazy blueprint" for research to examine the second (p. 167).

The aim of this chapter is to confront the second of Tajfel's questions directly. Specifically, it argues that stereotype consensus is a product of social identity salience, depersonalization of the self (self-stereotyping) and the *co-ordination of perception and behaviour* that flows from it. Derived from self-categorization theory (Turner, 1982; 1985; Turner *et al.*, 1987), the analysis developed here regards social identity salience as a product of categorization-in-context that consensualizes belief within a given group by: (1) enhancing perceived ingroup homogeneity; (2) providing associated *expectations* of mutual agreement; and (3) producing pressure to *actively reach* consensus through mutual influence (Haslam, 1996, 1997; Oakes, Haslam, & Turner, 1994; Turner, 1991). Evidence for this process and all three of these phenomena is discussed, prior to the presentation of data from studies which link the theoretical analysis of psychological process with measures of stereotype consensus. The chapter concludes that far from being expendable, an understanding of consensus (and of the process through which it is reached) is vital to a full appreciation of the stereotype as a social product and force.

THE RISE AND DEMISE OF THE CONSENSUS ISSUE

For all the debate that has surrounded it, the topic of consensus has rarely been the focus of explicit theorizing on the part of researchers. This is despite it being the case both (a) that measurement of the phenomenon was an implicit feature of the checklist paradigm that dominated the early stereotyping literature, and (b) that variation in consensus across stereotyping and stereotyped groups was a commonly discussed research finding. For example, using the index of stereotype uniformity devised by Katz and Braly (1933), it is clear that the mean level of consensus in Princeton students' stereotypes of

Negroes changed dramatically between 1933 and 1967 (this index, U, is the least number of traits necessary to include 50% of subjects' trait assignments to a given group, where a smaller number is indicative of greater consensus). Stereotypes of Negroes were the most uniform of the 10 elicited by Katz and Braly in 1933 ($U = 4.6$); in Gilbert's (1951) replication they had declined to become the fifth most uniform ($U = 12.0$), and in Karlins, Coffman & Walters, (1969) study they were actually the second least uniform ($U = 12.3$). What factors led to this dramatic decline? Why was it the case that in 1933 84% of subjects agreed that Negroes were "superstitious" and 75% that they were "lazy", but by 1967 agreement was substantially reduced and observed on a completely different attribute ("musical', a trait assigned by 47% of subjects)?

Two hypotheses that might intuitively account for these and other findings were entertained by early researchers (e.g., Schoenfeld, 1942; Taft, 1959; Vinacke, 1956). The first was that consensus reflected a uniform narrowness on the part of subjects—this, in effect, being a corollary of the claim that stereotyping is synonymous with prejudice (as proposed, for example, by Bogardus, 1950; Hyakawa, 1950; Klineberg, 1951). The second, related idea was that consensus arose from a lack of personal contact with a given group, reflecting a common response to widespread ignorance which would be dispelled if perceivers were given the opportunity for intimate acquaintance (cf. the "contract hypothesis", Amir, 1969). Both these hypotheses appealed to researchers, not least because they were consistent with the belief that social (i.e., shared) stereotypes provide an inherently deficient representation of social reality and that their force must therefore be diluted by any form of reality testing.

Yet neither hypothesis was lent any consistent support by empirical research. In particular, a number of studies showed that people shared beliefs about groups that they liked and with which they were very familiar (e.g., Vinacke, 1956). This is most marked in the apparent uniformity of *self*-stereotypes: American students' stereotypes of Americans, for example, were more uniform than stereotypes of the Chinese and Turks in all three phases of the Princeton trilogy (Gilbert, 1951; Karlins, Coffman, & Walters, 1969; Katz & Braly, 1933). Consensus also varied *within* studies that manipulated features of the context in which particular groups were judged but where there was no variation in *a priori* prejudice or familiarity. For example, in a study reported by Diab (1963), 62% of Arab-Moslem subjects described Americans as "rich" when this group was juxtaposed with Russians, but only 36% did so when the implied contrast was with Germans and the English.

In view of such findings, researchers were generally led to reject both "consensus as prejudice" and "consensus as ignorance" hypotheses, but were reluctant to develop alternatives (e.g., Vinacke, 1956; Schoenfeld, 1942; for a review see Haslam, 1997). It seems reasonable to suggest that a number of factors contributed to this predicament. First, as we have seen, the pattern of

results obtained in checklist studies did not lend itself to any simple explanation of consensus. Second, although a more complex analysis might have been
derived from a general theory of stereotyping, the main candidate theory at
the time—that of the Authoritarian personality (after Adorno *et al.*, 1950)—
was ill-equipped for the task because its analysis of stereotyping and prejudice
was explicitly couched in terms of individual differences in predisposition
rather than group similiarities. Third, it is clear that as checklist research
developed, researchers became less interested in stereotype uniformity and
more preoccupied with methodological and measurement issues. So, by the
time that researchers like Brigham (1971), Sigall and Page (1971) and Mc-
Cauley, Stitt, and Segal (1980) were questioning the utility of the Katz–Braly
procedure, its potential to contribute to an understanding of stereotype
consensus was essentially irrelevant. Accordingly, researchers developed
individual-based measures which, although they were methodologically more
refined and more amenable to statistical analysis than the checklist, no longer
afforded much insight into stereotypes as shared beliefs.

In fact all these factors are inter-related, but in summary it seems that the
failure of stereotyping researchers to explain stereotype consensus adequately
can be put down to the array of metatheoretical, theoretical and methodological choices that have guided research development over the past 25 years. An
essential part of our argument is that for progress to be made in understanding the social psychological basis of stereotype consensus, there is a need to
present an alternative to the orthodoxy that prevails at all three of these
levels.

RESURRECTING THE CONSENSUS ISSUE: SELF-CATEGORIZATION THEORY, STEREOTYPING AND SOCIAL INFLUENCE

Social Categories as Variable Representations of Reality

The approach to stereotype consensus developed here represents an application of the analysis of stereotyping and social influence provided by self-
categorization theory (Haslam, 1996, 1997; Oakes, Haslam, & Turner, 1994;
Turner, 1991; Turner & Oakes, 1989). At the heart of our approach to stereotyping is the argument that stereotypes are not inferior representations of
social reality that are used as a basis for perceiving, judging and acting only
when superior, more accurate individualized representations are unavailable
(Oakes & Turner, 1990; Oakes & Reynolds, 1997; Spears & Haslam, 1997).
On the contrary, we argue that stereotypes generally serve to represent
group-based realities apprehended from the perspective of a perceiver's own
salient group membership.

Despite being at odds with the "cognitive miser" metatheory which, in various guises, has informed stereotyping research since its inception (e.g., Allport, 1954; Fiske & Taylor, 1984; Lippmann, 1922), this position is consistent with the views of a number of early stereotyping researchers (e.g., Fishman, 1956; Laviolette & Silvert, 1951; Sherif, 1967; Vinacke, 1956) who rejected arguments that stereotypes were rigid expressions of prejudice associated with an untrained and unsophisticated approach to social life. Their concerns were later taken up by Tajfel (1981), who argued that any cognitive analysis of stereotyping needed to recognize the role which group memberships and social relations played in shaping cognition. A goal of our research over the past 10 or more years has been to develop the intergroup approach to stereotyping advocated by Tajfel within an integrated theoretical analysis supported by a comprehensive empirical program.

It is worth noting at the outset that much of this work has incorporated as a central feature checklist procedures based on those originally devised by Katz and Braly (1933). Of course at one level this strategy can be characterized as regressive insofar as it revives a paradigm that has been roundly maligned by a host of influential reviewers. For example, McCauley, Stitt, and Segal (1980, p. 197) followed other researchers like Brigham (1971, p. 24) and Eysenck and Crown (1948, p. 36) by arguing that checklist methodology was "weak in that (a) it may artificially force stereotyping, (b) . . . it may not represent individual attributions and (c) it offers no possibility of identifying idiosyncratic personal stereotypes". To this list can be added claims that the method obstructs the analysis of psychological process (Brigham, 1971; McCauley & Stitt, 1978) and treats traits as if they mean the same thing to all participants (Condor, 1990). Such criticisms, which foreshadowed more recent analyses (e.g., Devine & Elliot, 1995; Hamilton, Stroessner, & Driscoll, 1994; Judd & Park, 1993), are summarized in McCauley, Stitt, and Segal's (1980) assertion that:

> Psychologists want to know how stereotypes are learned, are changed, and affect behaviour. These questions cannot be studied effectively so long as stereotypes can be measured only in terms of group, or social stereotypes. Stereotypes are held by individuals, and the individual origins and effects of stereotypes can only be guessed at without an individual and preferably quantitative measure (p. 197).

In rejecting the urgings of these critics, our use of checklist procedures is based primarily on the counter-argument that stereotypes are worth investigating only to the extent that they are held by groups and that the *group* origins and effects of stereotypes can only be guessed at without a group-based measure which taps and quantifies their *shared* nature (cf. Oakes, Haslam, & Turner, 1994; Stangor & Lange, 1994; Tajfel, 1981). To date, the checklist is the only procedure which provides such a measure—although, as we note below, we have attempted to refine its use in order to obtain data suitable for inferential statistical analyses pertinent to issues of stereotype homogeneity, favourableness and consensus.

In this regard, we do not disagree that standard checklist responses elicit (or "force") a group-based response, but would argue that it is precisely this response which is most relevant to (and most predictive of) intergroup attitudes and behaviour. Accordingly, this is the response in which we are most interested. And while we also acknowledge that the meaning of individual traits is not fixed, we would note that this also applies to *any* quantitative measure of the sort routinely gathered by stereotyping researchers (e.g., based on rating scales or information recall). The advantage of the checklist method, then, is that its hermeneutic flavour is more transparent and hence more easily becomes a topic for direct investigation: for example, in studies which show how changes in trait meaning are predicted by judgemental context (Asch, 1951; Vinacke, 1956). Finally, we would argue that reviews of research which has relied on checklist methodology suggest that this work *does* provide important—although frequently overlooked—insights into the stereotyping process (indicating, for example, that stereotypes are shaped by comparative context and intergroup relations; e.g., Diab, 1963; Meenes, 1943; cf. Haslam, 1991; Oakes, Haslam, & Turner, 1994).

Details of our full empirical program are presented elsewhere (e.g., Haslam *et al.*, 1996; Oakes & Turner, 1990; Oakes, Haslam, & Turner, 1994; Turner *et al.*, 1994), but in broad terms we have attempted to explore how group formation and the cognitive representation of groups (i.e., stereotypes) are determined by an interaction between the perceiver and social reality rather than by cognitive error. Self-categorization theory assumes that categorization of the self and others occurs at different levels of abstraction, higher levels being more inclusive (cf. Rosch, 1978). For the purposes of theoretical exposition it has also been useful to focus on three levels of the social self-concept: self-categorization at a superordinate *human* level as a human being (in contrast to other species), at an intermediate *social* level as an ingroup member (as distinct from outgroups), and at a subordinate *personal* level as a unique individual (different from other relevant ingroup members). We argue that stereotyping reflects categorization at the social level based on a division of self and others into ingroup and outgroup. Further, we propose that the salience of an ingroup–outgroup (or indeed any other self-nonself) categorization *accentuates* on relevant dimensions the perceived similarities between group members within both categories and the perceived differences between those categories—thereby enhancing the degree to which members of the same social category are perceived to be psychologically interchangeable (Haslam & Turner, 1992; Turner, 1982).

Looking specifically at ingroup–outgroup categories (the social level of self-categorization), it is hypothesized that one crucial determinant of salience is "fit", the degree to which a social categorization matches reality in both its comparative and normative aspects (Oakes, 1987, 1996). Comparative fit is defined by the principle of *meta-contrast* (Turner, 1985), which states that a given set of stimuli is more likely to be categorized as a single entity to the extent that the intraclass differences between those items are seen to be smaller than the interclass differences between those items and others that are included in a given comparative context. So, for example, a Sydneysider and a Canberran are more likely to categorize themselves as "Australians" (and to acknowledge their similarities) when they find themselves in a situation which includes both Australians and non-Australians rather than just Australians (e.g., if they meet overseas rather than at home). The importance of meta-contrast is that it contextualizes categorization by tying it to an on-the-spot judgement of *relative differences*. Normative fit refers to the content aspect of the match between category specifications and the instances being repres-ented. For example, in order to categorize a group of people as Australians rather than Americans, they must not only differ (in attitudes, actions, etc.) from Americans more than from each other (comparative fit), but the nature of this difference must be consistent with a perceiver's content-related expec-tations, beliefs and theories about the categories (e.g., if the perceiver is Australian, Australians should appear to be more happy-go-lucky and less nationalistic).

Importantly, the principles of fit determine category salience in interaction with perceiver readiness (Oakes, Haslam, & Turner, 1994). Individuals do not engage in social encounters by mechanically processing information in a dis-passionate, uninvolved manner to decide matter-of-factly whether a particular group or thing is good or bad. On the contrary, categorization is determined not only by the subjectively perceived features of a stimulus array but also by the prior expectations, goals and theories of perceivers which structure that subjectivity—many of which derive from their group membership (Bar Tal, 1990; Oakes, Haslam, & Turner, 1994; Reicher, 1996; Sherif & Cantril, 1947; Turner & Giles, 1981). In this way a readiness to categorize people in particu-lar ways (e.g., in terms of "race" rather than height, and in terms of particular racial divisions rather than others) is conferred by societies, cultures and ideologies which—through political debate and conflict—collectively instruct and shape perception.

However, to focus for present purposes on the contribution of comparative fit to the categorization process, one of its clear implications, alluded to in the above example, is that as perceivers' comparative context is extended, their salient self-category will include more other people. An Australian comparing him/herself with another Australian will tend to categorize him/herself in terms of personal (or lower level social) identity and accentuate differences between him/herself and that other person (as in Figure 7.1, Case 1). However, if the context is extended to include different others (e.g., some

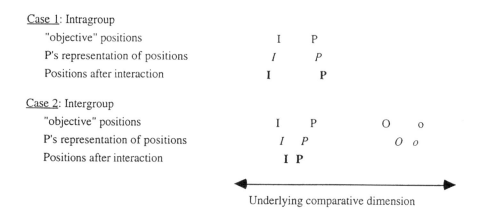

Figure 7.1 A schematic representation of the role of comparative context in defining the categorical relationship between a perceiver and others. P = perceiver; I = "ingroup" member; O and o = salient "outgroup" members (as defined in Case 2). In Case 1, I is defined in terms of personal (or low-level social) identity and differentiated from P but in Case 2, I and P (like O and o) are defined in terms of a shared category membership and represented as more interchangeable with each other. When I's self-prototypicality for P is high (and vice versa, i.e., in Case 2 but not Case 1), this provides a basis for mutual influence and ensuing consensualization of belief on issues relevant to the underlying dimension of comparison

American people), it becomes more appropriate for that person to categorize both him/herself and the other in terms of a higher level social identity, as "us Australians" who are similar to each other and different from "those Americans" (as in Figure 7.1, Case 2).

This analysis is relevant to a number of well-documented stereotyping phenomena. In particular it has been used to account for both (a) variation in perceptions of group homogeneity, and (b) the effects of frame of reference and own position on judgemental accentuation. In relation to the first of these phenomena, one important principle to emerge from the above analysis is that when a given group membership becomes salient for a perceiver, *depersonalization of the self* (the process of self-stereotyping; Turner, 1982) should lead to that group being seen as more homogeneous (Hogg & Turner, 1987a; Simon, Pantaleo, & Mummendey, 1995).

This has been shown in studies examining the effects of group-based interaction (Oakes *et al.*, 1995), minority status (Simon, 1992; Simon & Brown, 1987; Simon & Hamilton, 1994) and political conflict (Kelly, 1989). Significantly, the principle of comparative fit also provides an explanation of the "outgroup homogeneity effect"—the tendency for people to perceive outgroups as more homogeneous and less differentiated than ingroups (e.g., Linville, Salovey, & Fischer, 1986; Park & Judd, 1990). In experimental studies of this phenomenon subjects are typically required to judge ingroups in a (restricted) intragroup context (as in Case 1), but, by definition, they judge outgroups in an (extended) intergroup context. If personal categories become salient in the context of intragroup comparison and social categories become salient in the context of intergroup comparison, then ingroup members should tend to be individuated more than outgroup members when judgement of the ingroup members is made in the absence of a salient intergroup division. It follows, though, that, other things being equal, ingroup homogeneity should be enhanced and the outgroup homogeneity effect should be attenuated, if *both* ingroup and outgroup are judged in an intergroup context (as in Case 2). For this reason we explicitly reject the idea that perception of relative outgroup homogeneity is a cognitive *principle* and instead consider it, like instances of relative *in*group homogeneity (see Simon, 1992), to be a *variable* outcome of a common categorization process (see Haslam *et al.*, 1996; Oakes, Haslam, & Turner, 1994).

This analysis was tested in studies where Australian subjects were asked to assign traits from the Katz–Braly checklist either to an ingroup (Australians) or an outgroup (Americans) and then to estimate the percentage of group members to whom the traits applied (Haslam *et al.*, 1995), where a higher percentage is indicative of greater perceived homogeneity (cf. Park & Judd, 1990). Subjects did this in conditions where only one or both of these groups were judged. As predicted, across conditions where only one group was judged, there was evidence of an outgroup homogeneity effect. In Experiment 1, for example, assigned traits were seen to apply to 75% of Americans but only 57% of Australians. However, where both groups were judged this asymmetry disappeared: here assigned traits were seen to apply to 74% of Americans and 74% of Australians. Similarly, data reported by Bartsch and Judd (1993) as discussed by Haslam and Oakes (1995) and Simon (1995) indicates that when a perceiver's judgemental context is extended by judging an ingroup after, rather than before, an outgroup, perceived variability within the ingroup is reduced. This point has also been confirmed in experiments reported by Doojse *et al.* (in press; see also Doise, Deschamps, & Meyer, 1978; Ellemers & van Knippenberg, 1997; Haslam *et al.*, 1996). Thus, under appropriate conditions, manipulations of comparative context on normatively fitting dimensions can completely eliminate perceived asymmetry in ingroup–outgroup homogeneity.

Along similar lines, other studies demonstrate that perceptions of shared identity, and associated judgements of another person's similarity to the self change as a predictable consequence of extensions to a perceiver's frame of reference. In a series of three studies, Haslam and Turner (1992, see also Haslam & Turner, 1995; Wilder & Thompson, 1988) showed that perceivers judged a common target to be more similar to themselves, and stereotyped the target's group more favourably to the extent that the comparative context made salient other people more different to the target than the subject. So, for example, in Experiment 1 when all subjects were assigned an identity as "slightly pragmatic" they perceived a more pragmatic target to be more similar to themselves in an extended context that referred to other people who were non-pragmatic than in a restricted context including only pragmatic others (as in Figure 7.1). When they had to describe the target's group using a stereotype checklist they were also more likely to do so by assigning positive traits (e.g., "practical") rather than negative ones (e.g., "materialistic") in the extended context. Summary data from Experiment 2, where subjects were all assigned an identity as "borderline idealistic/pragmatic" and had to judge a "slightly idealistic" target are presented in Table 7.1.

These various studies can be seen to make a number of points but, most significantly, they suggest that the process of ingroup–outgroup categorization is structured by, and serves to reflect, ongoing social realities—in particular, the relative interchangeability of social stimuli including the self—as apprehended from a particular perspective (Turner *et al.*, 1994). It is not the case that stereotypes are beliefs associated with immutable representations of "ingroup" and "outgroup" (cf. Judd & Park, 1988; Linville, Salovey, & Fischer, 1986), but rather that the very division of stimuli into particular self and nonself categories is an ongoing reflection of the perceiver's place relative to features of the social world that they confront at any given point in time.

Social Categories as a Basis for Social Action

The above analysis has been directed to the explanation of stereotyping phenomena that are generally studied by looking at the responses of individual, non-interacting stereotypers (e.g., intercategory accentuation and

Table 7.1 Perceived similarity of target and favourableness of the target's group's stereotypic definition as a function of comparative context. From Haslam & Turner, 1992, Experiment 2, reproduced with permission

Measure	Comparative context		
	Restricted range (–1 to +1)	Medium range (–3 to +3)	Extended range (–5 to +5)
Perceived similarity to self (z-scores)	–0.42	–0.04	0.46
Self-target difference	1.82	0.83	0.71
Stereotype favourableness	2.52	2.94	3.42

In all conditions subjects were assigned an identity as "borderline pragmatic/idealistic" (0) and judged a "slightly idealistic" target (–1).
Self-target difference: max = 11, min = 0.
Stereotype favourableness: max = 5.0, min = –5.0.

perceived group homogeneity). However, like most of the prevailing analyses of these same stereotyping phenomena, it would have limited usefulness in moving us towards an explanation of stereotype consensus, were it not for the fact that the dynamic process of self-categorization described above is also assumed to have ongoing consequences for the *active co-ordination* of individuals' perceptions and behaviour. In this respect, a key assertion of self-categorization theory is that shared social self-category membership serves to regulate individual cognitive activity, not only by providing a common perspective on social reality but also by *providing a basis for mutual influence* (Turner, 1987, 1991; see also Hogg & Turner, 1987b; Turner & Oakes, 1989). That is, when people perceive themselves to share group membership with another person in a given context they will both expect to agree with that person on issues relevant to their shared identity, and also be motivated to strive actively to reach agreement on those issues. They should attempt to achieve this through, amongst other things, identifying shared beliefs, specifying frames of reference, articulating background knowledge, clarifying points of disagreement, and exchanging relevant information—in short, through persuasion, negotiation and argument (cf. Reicher, Hopkins, & Condor, 1997a).

The need for such a process derives from the fact that it is not possible to establish the subjective validity and correctness of social beliefs (e.g., stereotypes) simply through individual reality testing—the testing of beliefs by "independent" activity on the part of the perceiver. Indeed, even where it appears to occur, such behaviour is still in fact premised upon previously established shared meanings and norms (Turner, 1987, 1991). So, for example, while numerous stereotyping researchers have argued that the accuracy of stereotypes can be established relative to a benchmark of independently administered "objective" tests of a given social groups' characteristics (e.g., Abate & Berrien, 1967; Schumann, 1966; Judd & Park, 1993), it is clear that these tests, and the researchers' faith in them, are grounded in accepted normative practice (e.g., which accords self-reports or those of clinical psychologists higher status than those of outgroups; for reviews see Oakes, Haslam, & Turner, 1994; Oakes & Reynolds, 1997).

Social reality testing—the testing and validating of one's views in collaboration with others categorized as similar to self in a given context—is therefore a necessary accompaniment to personal reality testing. As Turner (1991) puts it, these are equally important interdependent phases of social cognition. It is precisely through individuals' identification of, and conformity to, contextually shared social norms that their potentially idiosyncratic views become socially potent (e.g., as instruments of social change; Reicher, 1996). This is because it is through this process that individual views are co-ordinated and thereby transformed into shared beliefs. As is clear from the quotation with which this chapter began, these beliefs are no longer experienced as subjective but instead articulate, symbolize and carry forward a common, as-if-objective view (cf. Hardin & Higgins, 1996; Moscovici, 1984). It is, then, precisely because the achievement of consensus transforms stereotypes into subjectively valid beliefs (that are perceived to be objectively valid), that it is so critical to the stereotyping process.

The role of these processes is well documented in treatments of topics other than stereotyping and dates back to famous studies by Asch (1951) and Sherif (1936), which showed the dramatic power of ingroups to regulate and structure individual cognitive activity. It is worth noting too that in a field which has endured pressure at both methodological and metatheoretical levels to become progressively more individualistic, these early studies of conformity and norm formation have probably still to be surpassed as demonstrations of the consensualizing power of ingroups. More recently, though, studies have directly supported self-categorization theory's arguments: (a) that the ability of disagreement with another person to generate subjective uncertainty in a perceiver (i.e., feelings of doubt and of a need for clarification) is contingent on that person being perceived as a member of a relevant ingroup (McGarty *et al.*, 1993; (b) that a person's persuasive impact is similarly predicated on their status as a prototypical ingroup member (Abrams & Hogg, 1990; Haslam, McGarty, & Turner, 1996b; McGarty *et al.*, 1994; Mackie, Worth, & Asuncion, 1990; for a review see Turner, 1991); and (c) that these and related processes are underpinned by categorization-in-context, so that the ability of a person or group to exert positive influence is dependent, *inter alia*, on features of the comparative and normative setting in which they are encountered (David & Turner, 1992, 1996; e.g., as in Figure 1). Recent work by McGarty and Grace (1996) also shows that the drive for consensus is a naturally occurring feature of interacting groups within which a common identity is salient. Furthermore, their studies of group decision-making show that once it is achieved, consensus is taken by the group members as evidence of the objective validity of their beliefs, so that ingroup-favouring responses are no longer a matter of opinion (with which some subjects agree; cf. Tajfel *et al.*, 1971), but rather a matter of fact (with which almost all subjects agree).

CONFRONTING THE CONSENSUS ISSUE

The Analysis of Stereotype Consensus

The arguments developed above lead us to propose that stereotype consensus is a product of self-stereotyping processes which *under conditions of social identity salience* lead people first to *perceive and expect homogeneity* within a relevant ingroup and then to *work actively* to achieve it. In essence, then, we suggest that stereotypes will come to be held consensually when individuals define themselves in terms of a shared social identity and that identity then functions as a basis for interacting with, and reacting to, both the stereotyped and the stereotyping group. As previous work indicates, however, the salience of a given social identity is itself a lawful outcome of the categorization process which gives meaning to social reality by *selectively* structuring the definition of self and others (Oakes, 1996; Oakes, Haslam, & Turner, in press). Accordingly, the preconditions for the emergence of stereotype consensus are expected to be both meaningful and systematic in that they depend upon a given social identity being both accessible and fitting for members of a given group in any given context.

Significantly, then, and in contrast to models of consensus that are implicit in contemporary stereotyping research (see Stangor & Lange, 1994, p. 404), we do not expect that consensus will be reached either (a) because a group of people are simply exposed to similar information (the "common informational input model"; Haslam, 1997) or (b) through a process of mindless conformity. Indeed, it follows from this analysis that stereotype consensus should fail to emerge when perceivers are not acting in terms of a common social identity. This can occur either because lower level (personal) identities are salient or because their behaviour is structured by diverse group memberships and norms. Importantly, though, where lack of consensus is observed because the cognitive activity and behaviour of individuals is shaped by conflicting group memberships (e.g., those for and against a given social policy like emancipation, abortion or gun control), it will tend to be the case that this is predicated both (a) on the salience of lower-level group memberships (in which consensus is high), and (b) on the implicit recognition of a *need for consensus* at a higher level of abstraction (e.g., in society as a whole).

In this sense, the drive for stereotype consensus needs to be understood as part of the political struggle through which groups compete to assert their values at progressively higher levels (Oakes, Haslam, & Turner, 1994, Chapter 8; see also Haslam, 1997). So, even where people actively disagree about the content of stereotypes, we would argue that their disagreement may still be premised upon an assumption that consensus is possible and necessary. Indeed, for us the importance of the process of striving to reach consensus derives largely from the fact that it is this process and the related need to assert and coordinate one's social identifications that underpins most instances of stereotype expression (cf. Doosje & Ellemers, 1997).

Critically too, the above arguments also make it clear that the emergence of consensus must be contingent on a *capacity* for flexibility and change in individuals' beliefs (cf. Tajfel, 1978). The analysis thus builds on our previous work which has demonstrated that such a capacity exists (e.g.., Haslam *et al.*, 1992, 1995; Haslam & Turner, 1992, 1995; for reviews see Oakes, Haslam, & Turner, 1994; Oakes & Turner, 1990), and provides a further counterpoint to arguments that stereotypes are inherently rigid and immutable (after Lippmann, 1922).

The Comparative and Normative Basis of Stereotype Consensus

Before going on to present research of our own which tests the above claims, it is useful first to consider how consistent they are with the findings of previous research. One immediately apparent implication of the analysis is that it in no way suggests that stereotype consensus *should* be universally observed within a given population, unless that population is psychologically galvanized by a social identity that demands a common reaction towards a given stereotyped group. Clearly, this condition has not been explicitly met by the majority of studies which have used Katz–Braly methodology, and so it is hardly surprising that these studies have often revealed low levels of consensus (cf. Gardner, 1993). Indeed, the opportunity for consensus to develop through processes of mutual influence has been conspicuously absent from most, if not all, checklist studies.

Where consensus has been observed, though, it *is* typically associated with a significant intergroup division in relation to which the stereotypers may be assumed to have a reasonably common position. The high consensus amongst Princeton students' stereotypes of Negroes observed in Katz and Braly's original (1933) study, for example, can be understood to have arisen from the fact that those students were all White and presumably had a reasonably common set of norms governing their expectations of, and behaviour towards, Blacks. Clearly, though, it is likely that this common identity was eroded over time as that ingroup became more heterogeneous and divided into more distinct (e.g. racist and non-racist) subgroups. These subgroups would each be expected to endorse different stereotypes and this would obviously contribute to the dramatic reduction in consensus observed by later researchers (e.g., Gilbert, 1951; Karlins, Coffman, & Walters, 1969; see also Devine & Elliot, 1995). A similar analysis would account for the constantly high levels of consensus in stereotypes of Germans and the English over this 34-year period (groups with respect to which Americans as a national entity had significant and unified ongoing international relations) as well as the constantly low levels of consensus in stereotypes of Turks and the Chinese (where no such relations prevailed). The argument is also consistent with evidence that consensus in Americans' self-stereotypes and their stereotypes of the Japanese increased over the course the Second World War (Schoenfeld, 1942).

This analysis of consensus can also be reconciled with recent research by Reicher and his colleagues into the contextual structuring of people's stereotypic views of their own national ingroup (Reicher, 1996; Reicher, Hopkins, & Condor, 1996a, 1996b). Amongst other things, this research demonstrates that members of different political parties in Scotland entertain completely different ideas about what it means to be Scottish, which reflect, and are used to validate and justify, the distinct ideologies and perspectives of those parties. Thus, a member of the Liberal Democrat party remarks, "I don't conceive the

Scottish character as being subject to the kind of narrow nationalism that in my judgement the Scottish National Party promotes", while a Scottish Nationalist argues that, "The trouble with the Scots is that . . . they don't have a political system which reflects the true nature of the Scottish psyche"—that "true nature" being reflected in a sense of community distinct from the emphasis on the self and the individual he considers characteristic of the English.

Given that in the context in which these statements were elicited the beliefs of these politicians were orientated to, and structured by, conflicting group memberships, each associated with competing ideologies and agendas, it is not surprising that the researchers exposed disagreement rather than consensus in stereotypic beliefs. Moreover, we might go further and speculate that if these politicians were to interact with each other in a context where these opposed identities remained salient (e.g., in parliament), their disagreement might become even more pronounced (cf. the phenomenon of group polarization; for relevant discussions, see Wetherell, 1987; Turner, 1987, 1991). On the other hand, though, we would also predict that if they interacted in a context where a common identity became salient (e.g., at a Burns Night), then they would be more likely to articulate similar views, and these might be consensualized further by mutual interaction.

It is worth noting, however, that Reicher and his colleagues frame much of their work in terms of a discourse analytic critique of self-categorization theory (cf. Wetherell & Potter, 1992). Reicher *et al.* (1997b, p. 70), for example, argue that, "The social identity tradition presupposes that the definition of a given group will be unitary and consensually accepted. Everybody will share the same self-stereotype and the same stereotype of other groups" (cf. Condor, 1990). Similarly, they characterize self-categorization theory's approach to social category definition as "essentially passive and cognitive rather than active and strategic" (p. 70).

As the foregoing review makes clear, it is certainly true that self-categorization theorists have devoted less energy to exploring the interactive, negotiated aspects of stereotype development and use than to other aspects of these processes. To some extent this is a response to the agenda set by other research in the field and, as we have indicated, a large part of this chapter's brief is to provide an alternative metatheoretical and methodological agenda. In this respect, Reicher's work makes an important and timely contribution in refocusing some attention on to the political and strategic dimensions of stereotyping, making it clear that the "raw data" upon which perceivers' cognitions work is neither raw nor unproblematic.

Nonetheless, we consider stereotyping to be anything but a "passive and cognitive" process and a large part of our argument is that *no* psychological reality is a universal and consensual *given* (as argued, for example, in criticism of the common informational input model; Haslam, 1997). Instead, like stereotype consensus itself, we see such reality as a collective *accomplishment* that is realized only in *specific* contexts. In this regard, Reicher, Hopkins, and Condor's own words (1997a, p. 101) actually serve as a summary of the position we have attempted to develop thus far (for corollary statements see Haslam, 1997; Oakes, Haslam, & Turner, 1994, Chapter 8; Oakes & Reynolds, 1997):

> In terms of consequences, one way of rephrasing our foregoing argument is to say that the nature of collective action will flow from the definition of social categories: the extent of who forms part of the collective and who the collective acts against will relate to the boundaries of ingroup and outgroup: the direction which the collective takes will relate to the content of group identity and ability to gain influence over the collective will relate to who is prototypical. . . . In short, the definition of social categories becomes the very stuff of politics.

Having said this, one significant point of disagreement with Reicher relates to his argument that trait-based methodologies like the Katz–Braly checklist are ill-equipped to allow researchers to explore the dynamic processes of stereotype development and change. As he sees it, these perpetuate the view that stereotypes are simply fixed-meaning trait descriptions (and nothing more). However, while there is a very real danger that checklist methodology can be reified in this manner, such reification neglects the metatheoretical understanding that underpinned the checklist's development and promulgation as a tool for exploring *shared* beliefs in the context of large-scale social upheaval (for a review see Oakes, Haslam, & Turner, 1994, Chapter 2). It is, then, out of a desire to rekindle precisely such an understanding that our own research has endeavoured to breathe new life into checklist methodology (see Haslam *et al.*, 1996c). Accordingly, a large part of this research has been dedicated to *elaborating* rather than denying the role of stereotypes as contributors to, and explanations of, intergroup relations (e.g., as argued by Oakes, 1987; Oakes & Turner, 1990; Tajfel, 1969; Yzerbyt, 1997).

This point is demonstrated in a study which we conducted to examine contextual variation in Australians' stereotypes of Americans during the course of the 1990 war in the Persian Gulf. The study examined responses to change both (a) over time—against the background of spiralling conflict—and (b) in the configuration of other groups with which Americans were compared. In *restricted-range* conditions reference was made just to Americans, Australians and the British, in *medium-range* conditions, Russians were added to this list, and in *extended-range* conditions both Russians and Iraqis (Haslam *et al.*, 1992). The intention here was to demonstrate the sensitivity of stereotypes to social change and to the stereotyper's frame of reference, under conditions where these variables were manipulated in a more subtle fashion than previous checklist studies.

Like earlier studies using the Katz–Braly paradigm, our results supported conclusions that stereotypes are more flexible than traditionally assumed and that the nature of change is a product of the specific intergroup relations that a given historical and judgemental context makes salient. Here, then, stereotypes of Americans became generally less favourable as the Gulf War progressed, but this deterioration was confined to restricted and medium-range conditions, where reference was not made to Iraq. These findings also supported the more detailed prediction that stereotypes would be least favourable when the comparative context engendered differentiation on self-referentially important dimensions (e.g., pro- or anti-war) and America was clearly identified as an outgroup (a distinction that was presumably clouded by the inclusion of Iraq).

Interestingly, too, subsequent reanalysis of the data from this study suggests that this pattern of results was also reflected in the overall *consensus* in subjects' stereotypes. As can be seen from Table 7.2 the mean level of uniformity in restricted and medium-range conditions at the end of the war was greater than in the other four conditions of the study ($U = 4.78$ and 5.64, respectively). That is, subjects' descriptions of Americans were not only more negative but also more consensual where stereotypes were elicited in the context of a salient ingroup–outgroup division (i.e., in the latter stages of the War where no reference was made to Iraq).

In a more recent study (Haslam *et al.*, 1996c, Experiment 2) use of checklist methodology also allowed us to test directly our assertion that stereotype consensus can be enhanced through a process of conformity to stereotypic ingroup norms. The study employed a three-factor design in which Australian students used the Katz–Braly checklist to assign traits either to Australians or Americans. Importantly though, they did this in the context of feedback about the traits that had previously been selected by either an ingroup

Table 7.2 Favourableness and consensus of American stereotypes during the Gulf War as a function of comparative context and time. From Haslam *et al.*, 1992, reproduced with permission

Measure	Comparative context		
	Restricted range (Australia, UK, USA)	Medium range (+ USSR)	Extended range (+ Iraq)
Stereotype favourableness			
Phase 1 (start of war)	−0.72	−1.50	−2.56
Phase 2 (end of war)	−2.54	−2.14	−1.86
Stereotype consensus (U)			
Phase 1 (start of war)	5.56	6.20	5.08
Phase 2 (end of war)	5.04	4.50	5.58

Stereotype favourableness: max = 5.0, min = −5.0.
U = uniformity (max = 2.5; min = 42).

(comprising unprejudiced students at the same university) or an outgroup (prejudiced people). The feedback itself was either consistent with pre-existing stereotypes (e.g., that Australians are "straightforward", "happy-go-lucky" and "practical", or Americans "extremely nationalistic", "materialistic" and "arrogant") or inconsistent.

We predicted that subjects' selection of traits would be influenced by provision of this feedback so that they would be likely to conform to the normative choices made by the ingroup but would reject those of the outgroup. Importantly, though, we expected that choices would not simply reflect blind conformity to the ingroup position, but that they would be moderated by the meaningfulness of those choices in terms of subjects' normative expectations. Thus, the impact of feedback was expected to lead to greater consensus and more polarized evaluations of the groups where the traits an ingroup selected were stereotype-consistent and those selected by the outgroup were stereotype-inconsistent (i.e., where normative fit was maximized).

These predictions were confirmed both by the general favourableness of selected traits and by the consensus in their selection. As can be seen from the data in Table 7.3, the most dramatic illustration of this was provided by subjects' selection of the trait "extremely nationalistic", an attribute which, on the basis of data from previous studies, could be interpreted as constituting

Table 7.3 Percentage of subjects assigning stereotypic traits as a function of stereotyped group, the source of feedback and the stereotype-consistency of feedback. From Haslam *et al.*, 1996c, Experiment 2, reproduced with permission

Stereotyped group:	Australia				USA			
Feedback source:	Ingroup		Outgroup		Ingroup		Outgroup	
Stereotype-consistency of feedback:	Cons	Incons	Cons	Incons	Cons	Incons	Cons	Incons
Stereotypic Australian traits								
Straightforward	45	59	29	55	7	38	21	13
Happy-go-lucky	41	34	29	38	7	10	7	3
Practical	24	17	29	24	4	10	4	3
Talkative	17	17	14	10	11	66	32	32
Sportsmanlike	52	21	39	38	4	17	4	6
M	35.8	29.6	27.0	33.0	6.6	28.2	13.6	11.4
Stereotypic American traits								
Ext. nationalistic	0	3	0	3	93	38	46	61
Materialistic	14	21	25	17	56	38	36	42
Arrogant	7	14	7	0	26	17	21	16
Ostentatious	7	10	0	3	30	17	29	26
Loud	7	21	7	14	41	48	18	32
M	7.0	13.8	7.8	7.4	49.2	31.6	30.0	35.4
Difference in *M*s*	28.8	15.8	19.2	25.6	42.6	3.4	16.4	24.0

*Signed to reflect stereotypic differentiation.

the "core" of Australians' American stereotype (or the "undisputably pro-totypic" trait). When this trait was selected by fellow ingroup members to describe Americans, virtually all of the subjects (93%) did so themselves, but when that ingroup had selected counter-stereotypic traits (e.g., "straightfor-ward" and "happy-go-lucky") it was assigned by only 38%. However, the very opposite pattern emerged when the outgroup made the same selections: here corresponding levels of assignment were 46% and 61%.

As a means of making the statistical analysis of these effects more rigorous, levels of stereotype consensus were also examined by developing a measure of the degree to which each subject's trait selections contributed to within-condition agreement in assignment. The *consensus co-efficient* (or posterior probability of agreement; P_a) refers to the likelihood that if any one of the traits assigned to a group by a subject was selected at random it would also be selected by another randomly-chosen subject in the same condition. The co-efficient has a value of between 0 (if none of the traits chosen by a subject are chosen by anyone else) and 1 (if all the traits chosen by a subject are chosen by all other subjects). The advantage of this measure is that, unlike Katz and Braly's (1933) measure of uniformity (U), it can be computed for each subject (rather than just each condition) and is therefore amenable to inferential statistical analysis. Consistent with our predictions, consensus in this study was greater when subjects received feedback from an ingroup rather than an outgroup ($P_a = 0.25, 0.19$ respectively) and this main effect was qualified by a significant interaction with the stereotype-consistency of feedback, so that consensus increased when the ingroup provided stereotype-consistent feed-back ($P_a = 0.27$) and reduced when the same feedback was provided by an outgroup ($P_a = 0.16$).

Taken as a whole, the results of the study (which are summarized in Table 7.4) clearly support the assertion that individuals' subjective confidence in the validity of stereotypes—and hence consensus in their expression of them—will tend to be enhanced to the extent that those beliefs are either (a) vali-dated by people with whom, on the basis of a shared social identity, they expect to agree (ingroup members), or (b) rejected by people with whom they expect to disagree (outgroup members; McGarty *et al.*, 1993; Turner, 1991; Turner & Oakes, 1989). The latter finding is particularly relevant to the process of stereotype change as it suggests that when information that contra-dicts a stereotype can be understood to be symptomatic of underlying *social conflict* (i.e., confirming expected disagreement with an outgroup about the nature of social reality), that information may actually serve to *strengthen* (rather than undermine) perceivers' pre-existing beliefs. In this study, then, when subjects were informed that prejudiced people thought that Australians were extremely nationalistic or that Americans were pleasure-loving, they reacted strongly against the message (and its source) and affirmed their initial, opposing beliefs all the more forcefully.

Table 7.4 Favourableness and consensus of stereotypes as a function of stereotyped group, the source of feedback and the stereotype-consistency of feedback. From Haslam et al., 1996c, Experiment 2, reproduced with permission

Stereotyped group:	Australia				USA			
Feedback source:	Ingroup		Outgroup		Ingroup		Outgroup	
Stereotype-consistency of feedback:	Cons	Incons	Cons	Incons	Cons	Incons	Cons	Incons
Measure								
Consensus co-efficient (P_a)	0.21	0.21	0.15	0.21	0.33	0.25	0.18	0.24
Stereotype favourableness	1.62	1.10	0.89	1.24	−2.93	−1.03	−1.46	−1.62

Stereotype favourableness: max = 5.0, min = −5.0.

Significantly too, a previous study in this series also supported our argument that the ability of an ingroup to influence stereotyping is contingent upon the contextual definition of that group (Haslam et al., 1996c, Experiment 1). In this study the source of stereotype-relevant feedback about Americans and Australians was manipulated across three levels: being defined as an outgroup (prejudiced people) or an ingroup (students at the same university as the subjects), or as an ingroup explicitly contrasted with an outgroup (referring to *unprejudiced* students at the same university). On the basis of principles of comparative fit, the contrast of the ingroup with an outgroup (prejudiced people) was expected to make that ingroup identity more salient and thus produce greater conformity to stereotypic ingroup norms. Table 7.5 presents mean levels of stereotypic differentiation as a function of the source of feedback and the feedback's stereotype consistency, an index of the degree to which subjects differentiated between the national groups in a stereotype-consistent manner (e.g., seeing Australians as more sportsmanlike than Americans and less nationalistic). These results support the prediction that the influence of an ingroup is greater—bolstering stereotypes more when it provides stereotype-consistent information and undermining them more

Table 7.5 Stereotypic differentiation as a function of the source of feedback and its stereotype-consistency. From Haslam et al., 1996c, Experiment 1, reproduced with permission

Stereotype-consistency of feedback:	Consistent			Inconsistent		
Feedback source:	In-not-out	In	Out	In-not-out	In	Out
Stereotypic differentiation	14.2[ef]	10.1	6.6[eg]	7.0[fh]	9.2	13.5[gh]

Means with a common superscript letter are significantly different ($p < 0.05$)

when it provides inconsistent feedback—where it is explicitly differentiated from an outgroup. In this they again underline the sensitivity of the influence process (and emergent consensus) to group definition in social context (cf. David & Turner, 1996; as in Figure 7.1).

As well as this, both of these studies provided dramatic evidence against the claim that stereotypes are a manifestation of enduring internal representations of social reality (i.e., with rigid cores and prototypes; cf. Lippmann, 1922). So despite—or rather, we would suggest, *because of*—their use of trait-based methodology, these studies lead us to conclusions that extended those of Reicher and his colleagues. Like them we conclude "that neither the underlying nor the manifest definition of social groups . . . is fixed but rather *both* are socially and contextually negotiated" (Haslam *et al.*, 1996c, p. 27), yet at the same time we are in a position to provide a social psychological analysis of the *basis* for such negotiation and of its likely course and consequences.

The Group-based Dynamics of Stereotype-Consensualization

The above research supports the argument that stereotype consensus is structured by social context and, in particular, is enhanced both (a) by factors which increase the salience of a shared social identity, and (b) by normatively-consistent feedback which builds upon and reinforces that identity. Having said that, most of these studies still have the (non-interacting) individual stereotyper as the primary unit of analysis and in only one (Haslam *et al.*, 1996c, Experiment 2) was stereotype consensus the explicit focus of investigation. In view of the fact that one of the distinctive features of the present analysis is its focus on the ongoing, dynamic role which salient group memberships play in shaping consensus, our most recent research has therefore attempted to confront these aspects of the stereotyping process more directly. The present discussion, however, is intended only to provide an overview of this work, as details are presented elsewhere (Haslam *et al.*, in press).

An initial study in this program involved a relatively straightforward manipulation of social identity salience along the lines of previous studies of perceived group homogeneity (Haslam *et al.*, 1995; see also Doise, Deschamps, & Meyer, 1978; Haslam & Oakes, 1995). Australian subjects were assigned to one of two independent conditions and selected traits from Katz and Braly's original checklist to describe both Americans and Australians. In one condition they described Australians *before* Americans and in the other they described them *after* Americans. On the basis of the principle of comparative fit, we anticipated that when they described Australians, subjects' shared identity (as Australians) would be more salient if they did this after describing Americans, as this would take place in an extended intergroup rather than a restricted intragroup context (as in Figure 7.1). In other words, describing Australians after Americans should enhance self-stereotyping because it would constitute what Doise and Sinclair (1973) refer to as a symbolic intergroup encounter. Accordingly, along lines proposed by Tajfel (1978, pp. 44–5), we expected that there would be greater uniformity of trait selection in the Australian stereotype in the American-then-Australians condition. At the same time the order manipulation was expected to have little impact on the consensus of subjects' American stereotypes as this outgroup would, by definition, always be described in an intergroup context (although this might be less explicit when Americans were rated before Australians). The pattern of results supported both predictions.

The first study therefore goes some way to supporting our argument that, as discussed in relation to the data presented by Reicher and his colleagues, consensus in ingroup stereotypes can be enhanced when those groups are judged in intergroup rather than intragroup contexts. Yet, having said that, even in intergroup contexts the degree of consensus was still only moderate. So, at best, the trait most commonly selected to describe Australians ("sportsmanlike") was assigned by only 60% of subjects and only 65% selected the most commonly chosen American trait ("extremely nationalistic").

Again, though, an important prediction of our analysis is that stereotype consensus should be enhanced through mutual interaction to the extent that this interaction is premised upon a shared social identity relevant to the stereotype. This is because social identity salience should lead to greater mutual influence between group members by promoting perceptions of their interchangeability (following depersonalization and self-stereotyping) and thereby increasing their perceived capacity for mutual validation. To investigate this idea, we conducted a two-phase study in which individuals first used the Katz–Braly checklist to describe either Australians or Americans, and then were assigned to groups of either three or four members and had to perform exactly the same task *collectively*—arriving at their assignments through a process of group discussion. It was predicted that the consensualizing effects of this discussion would be most marked in discussions of the outgroup stereotype, since subjects' own shared identity (as Australians) would be more salient in this intergroup context than in the intragroup context where they only described Australians.

Supporting these predictions, levels of consensus at the individual phase were similar to those of the Australians-then-Americans conditions of the previous study but the consensus in group response was considerably higher, especially when groups described the outgroup (for the American stereotype $U = 3.75$, $P_a = 0.37$, for the Australian stereotype $U = 6.75$, $P_a = 0.19$). It is important to note, too, that in the case of the outgroup stereotype, the degree of postdiscussion stereotype uniformity was very high: on average each of the five most commonly selected traits was assigned by 58% of groups. This study thus demonstrates quite vividly the role which groups play not only in polarizing belief (i.e., making it more extreme, cf. Moscovici & Zavalloni, 1969; Wetherell, 1987) but also in *consensualizing* it.

Two points about this finding are also worth emphasizing at this stage. First, it suggests that stereotype consensus is not chimerical. In contrast to arguments that consensus is a figment of researchers' imaginations (cf. Gardner, 1993; Condor, 1990), it appears that under appropriate circumstances—that is, where premised upon common social identity and validated by group interaction—stereotypic beliefs will come to be highly shared.

Second, given that it is the stereotypic beliefs of commonly identified members of interacting groups that have traditionally been of most interest to researchers (or at least given that such beliefs are typically used to justify their own research; cf. Stangor & Lange, 1994, Tajfel, 1981), it appears that despite the novelty of this experimental finding, it is not one that is especially contrived. Instead, we would argue, it is the persistent focus of researchers on individualized, non-interacting subjects that has contrived to *conceal* this reality. Furthermore, while discourse analysts champion their methodology as one which avoids the individualistic pitfalls of most experimental research (because, amongst other things "this is notoriously bad at exploring dynamics"; Reicher, Hopkins, & Condor, 1997, p. 115), it is clear that it too has contributed to this concealment because it lends itself to the analysis of interpersonal rather than intragroup interactions (i.e., those between a single experimenter and a single subject, rather than those between multiple members of a common social group). In such situations, the salience for a subject of the group membership in which the experimenter is interested will not always be high, and even where it is, the ability (or desire) of the experimenter to validate and reinforce the subject's beliefs will typically be limited.

The foregoing points should not be read as a rejection of the analysis of verbal interaction as a means of throwing light on the process of stereotype consensualization. We would merely argue that this methodology, no less than experimental research, incorporates theoretical assumptions that impact upon the phenomena under investigation (cf. Haslam & Oakes, 1995). Indeed, following the arguments of Reicher and his colleagues, it seemed to us that within the present paradigm, examination of the content of group discussion *would* potentially provide additional information about exactly how social interaction served to consensualize stereotypes in the manner observed.

In a preliminary examination of this idea we tape-recorded and transcribed discussions of four additional groups using the Katz–Braly checklist to collectively describe either Australians or Americans. Examination of the discussion (which led to effects similar to those observed in the previous experimental study), served to confirm a number of the points that we have made so far. First, and most significantly, it is clear that the discussions themselves were vigorous and animated and that subjects were all keen to instigate and participate in a process that would lead to mutual agreement. As we would expect, this was particularly marked in discussion of the American stereotype. There was also evidence that when discussing Australians (in the intragroup context), although there was pressure for agreement, disagreement was less problematic for participants partly because they were able to make sense of this disagreement in terms of meaningful lower-level categorizations (e.g., the differences between rural and urban Australians, or between Southerners and Northerners; cf. Park, Ryan, & Judd, 1992).

Differences in the emergent consensus of American and Australian stereotypes could also be traced to evidence that the precise meaning of the traits was more a topic for negotiation and debate in the intragroup context. Consistent with the observations of Reicher, Hopkins, and Condor (1997a), it appeared that when subjects discussed their own national identity, the precise meaning of terms like "sportsmanlike" and "arrogant" was sometimes quite hard for them to agree on. Significantly, though, there was little evidence of similar confusion when discussing the meaning of these and other terms in relation to Americans. Following the arguments presented earlier, we would suggest that this is because here the intergroup comparative context served to disambiguate the traits by providing subjects with a shared perspective on their meaning-in-context. So, for example, while the meaning of the term "sportsmanlike" might be relatively unclear when Australians are considered alone, we would expect that it would become more clear if Australians were compared with the Chinese (a comparison that might engender a common reaction by making salient issues related to the consumption of performance-enhancing drugs). In contrast, then, to the assumption that ambiguity is a *stable* feature of trait meaning (as argued by critics of checklist methodology), we would argue that, like other aspects of stereotypes, varies lawfully with changes in the context of social categorization.

Although the above studies support our model of emergent consensus, it is clear too that features of their design limit our ability to draw appropriate conclusions from the findings. This is the case primarily because the intragroup–intergroup distinction is confounded with both an ingroup–outgroup division and a number of other potential differences associated with the specific nations that subjects were required to stereotype. Thus, the greater consensus observed in stereotypes of Americans may reflect a generalized (or specific) "outgroup consensus effect" (similar to the "outgroup homogeneity effect"), rather than the fact that this group was judged in an intergroup rather than an intragroup context.

With this issue in mind we conducted a final study which incorporated the two conditions of the previous two studies, but also an additional condition in which the Australian ingroup was judged in an intergroup (not just an intragroup) context. In this additional condition, in both individual and group phases of the study, subjects had to assign traits to Australians *in contrast to Americans*. We reasoned that the task in this additional condition would serve to render subjects' shared social identity (as Australians differentiated from Americans) more salient and that this identity would provide a common perspective for group members prior to interaction and serve as a basis for enhanced mutual influence when they came together as a group. It was therefore expected that in the individual phase of the study there would be greater consensus in this condition than when Australians were judged without reference to Americans but that this difference in consensus would be especially marked subsequent to group discussion. Indeed, it was anticipated that levels of consensus in both phases of this condition would be similar to those observed in descriptions of Americans.

Results again provided clear support for our predictions. In the conditions in which Australians and Americans were judged alone there was an asymmetry in observed levels of consensus following the patterns observed in previous studies—this being particularly pronounced at the group phase of the study (for the American stereotype $U = 3.80$, $P_a = 0.44$, for the Australian stereotype $U = 5.67$, $P_a = 0.28$). However, no such asymmetry was apparent when Australians were described in an intergroup context in contrast to Americans (indeed, levels of consensus here were remarkably similar to those observed in judgements of Americans; $U = 3.80$, $P_a = 0.41$).

This study thus provides strong evidence to substantiate our argument that the emergence of stereotype consensus is not limited to individuals' characterization of outgroups. On the contrary, high levels of consensus will also emerge in beliefs about ingroups to the extent that features of judgemental context lead to those beliefs being framed by, and orchestrated with reference to, a shared social self-categorization. This fact also reconfirms the point that consensus, like perceived group homogeneity, cannot be explained either by antipathy towards the stereotyped group, or by a lack of contact with it, in the manner proposed by both early and more contemporary theorists (e.g., Linville, Salovey, & Fischer, 1986; Vinacke, 1956).

However, two arguments could be presented as alternatives to our claim that the emergence of consensus in this and previous studies is premised upon social identity salience and the process of self-stereotyping. First, it could be argued what these studies demonstrate is simply that consensus emerges as a process of conformity which groups are particularly successful at inducing. In part we agree with this, although we contend such influence arises as a result of rational cognitive activity on the part of perceivers in a quest for social validation of their beliefs, rather than slavish compliance (McGarty *et al.*, 1994; Turner, 1991). Yet what such an analysis lacks is the capacity to explain why conformity varies predictably as a function of the comparative setting within which the group is defined.

Second, it could be argued that consensus is dependent not on the shared social identification of perceivers, but rather on the definition of the target. So the fact that consensus is greater when Australians are judged after Americans or contrasted with them, could reflect the fact that this manipulation makes the definition of that group more focused—for example, by making aspects of Australianess that are irrelevant to comparison with Americans irrelevant to that ingroup stereotype. Again, there is some validity to this point and indeed we have argued that such factors are implicated in the ability of context to disambiguate stimulus meaning. However, because these variables are highly confounded in reality we would also note that it is very difficult to manipulate social identity salience in a way that has no implications for the target of judgement (particularly when that target is an ingroup). Importantly, though, simple variation in stimulus definition (like a simple conformity explanation) cannot account for the interaction effects observed in these studies. If stimulus definition is *all* that is important for emergent consensus then it is not clear why our studies did not simply produce main effects for both target group and experimental phase. However, it is clear that relatively small differences in consensus at the individual phase of both studies blew out into very dramatic differences after group discussion. This suggests that not just group interaction but group identity—as made salient more in some contexts than in others—is having considerable impact on the consensualization process through its ability to structure individual psychological activity.

CONCLUSION

The goal of this chapter has been to develop and test a theoretical anlysis of stereotype consensus—attempting to identify the psychological processes which underpin the emergence of shared beliefs about social groups. In view of the historical centrality of this phenomenon to the field as a whole (after Katz & Braly, 1933), the novelty of this endeavour is interesting in itself, as is the fact that current research trends have led to a denial of both its significance and its very existence. Going against these trends, we believe that the topic of consensus is rather like Cinderella: overlooked and much-maligned, but with an undeniable claim on our attention.

Following self-categorization theory, the analysis we have proposed argues that the critical psychological substrate of stereotype consensus is social identity salience and depersonalization of the self through self-stereotyping. Cognitively, this provides perceivers with a common vantage point, but it also has an ongoing regulatory function in providing the basis for those cognitions to be interactively tested and validated. In effect, then, we propose that stereotype consensus is the emergent product of a dynamic synergy through which the group intersubjectively fashions the cognitions of the individual.

Under this model, the failure of research to uncover consensus can also be traced not to its non-existence, but rather to the reluctance of researchers to study the development of stereotypes in real groups. In this regard it is worth pointing out that in one notable exception to this trend, where Sherif and his colleagues observed the emergent stereotypes of groups of schoolboys in conflict at the Robbers Cave summer camp, they were struck by both the force and the consensual manner in which those stereotypes came to be expressed, noting that, over time, "Negative attitudes and social distance in relation to the outgroup were standardized in both groups" (Sherif *et al.*, 1961; pp. 111–12). Sherif and his colleagues themselves offered only a limited analysis of the processes underpinning this standardization (which they identified as product of "intergroup friction"). However, as Tajfel (1981) subsequently argued, given the clear association of such consensus with the issues of intergroup hatred and violence that are routinely used to justify stereotyping research, this is far less problematic than the failure of the field as a whole to tackle the issues which their research exposed.

Although the work described in this chapter has largely been directed to re-addressing this challenge, it is clear too that its analysis is not only relevant to the stereotyping domain, but is applicable to broader theorizing about the development of all forms of shared meaning and conceptual understanding. Indeed, recently a number of cognitive psychologists have noted that some of the more fundamental questions about the nature of categorization, including that of "why we have the categories we have and not others", need to be addressed by looking *inter alia* at the social psychology of consensus, including factors which contribute to perceivers' shared theories about the world (Barsalou, 1990; Freyd, 1983, 1990; Keil, 1987; McIntyre, 1995; Medin, Wattenmaker, & Hampson, 1987, p. 243, Wisniewski & Medin, 1994).

Within the current framework, we would argue that the answers to such questions are again to be found in the role which relevant group memberships play in orientating and regulating cognition. Evidence to this effect was reported in a recent study by McIntyre (1995), where subjects had to categorize stick figures which varied on multiple dimensions (facial expression, body size and amount of hair) and hence could be categorized in multiple different ways. Subjects were given information about how other people had categorized the figures and half were also given a reason for this strategy, indicating that it was chosen because the variable in question "plays a larger role in their [the source's] social interactions with others". Results indicated that subjects were more likely to use the same strategy as those others to the extent that an explanation for the strategy was provided; however, this effect was restricted to conditions where the source of the strategy and theory was explicitly identified as an ingroup rather than an outgroup (as university students rather than young children). Significantly, too, the source of feedback also affected subjects' consensus in their descriptions of a new figure, so that there was significantly higher intersubject agreement when participants had been given feedback from an ingroup source that was explicitly distinguished from an outgroup (cf. Haslam *et al.*, 1996c, Experiment 1).

One important point that emerges from this study is that learning about the world and how to categorize it meaningfully is not simply a product of raw experience with a given categorical system in the manner argued by a range of cognitive, developmental and social theorists (e.g., Goldstone, 1994, p. 197; Hamilton & Trolier, 1986, p. 154; see Haslam 1997). Instead it is a product of *socially mediated* experience. In order for perceivers to have confidence in the correctness of their beliefs—and therefore use them as a basis for co-ordinated and subjectively meaningful social behaviour—those beliefs need to be validated by other people. Significantly, though, the capacity of others to perform that validating role is itself the product of an act of context-dependent categorization on the part of the perceiver (Turner, 1991; Turner & Oakes, 1989). As McIntyre's study shows, to be informative about reality others have to be categorized as similar to self (i.e., as ingroup members) on a relevant dimension of social comparison, but this and other research discussed above makes it clear that the very same source will have very different status in this regard as comparative and normative context changes (David & Turner, 1992).

For this reason it is just as wrong to suggest that consensus has its basis in raw social experience as to suggest that it is grounded in purely cognitive activity. Indeed, one common (but not inherent) difference between the domains of stereotyping and cognition research is that in stereotyping research social reality and people's categorical relationship to each other tend to be *profoundly negotiable* (and hence *is* so often a topic for negotiation; cf., Reicher, Hopkins, & Condor, 1997a). We would argue that it is largely for this reason that consensus in the former domain can prove so elusive (cf. Gardner, 1993) while in the latter it is so often taken for granted.

Nonetheless, two of the three central points which we want to press home are (1) that consensus *can* be achieved in the social domain and, moreover (2), that the process through which it is achieved is of central relevance to the development and use of stereotypes. We refer to this process as one of *group consensualization* (Haslam, 1996), because we believe that the work discussed here and elsewhere makes it clear (3) that psychological group membership, rather than social pressure or information *per se*, is the basis of stereotype consensus. As such, that consensus is an outcome and expression of an identi-fication process that is capable of mobilizing and motivating group members in a way that independent activity and an individual product never could.

In this regard, it can be seen that over the past 25 years many of the touted developments in stereotyping research have helped the field move away from the need to acknowledge these points and from the realities of stereotypes as dynamic, collective achievements. Yet if one considers again the quotation at the start of this chapter, it is clear that these are the realities that our research questions must address. Reaching answers to those questions is no small goal, but we believe we have shown that progress can now be made in this direction.

ACKNOWLEDGEMENTS

This research was funded by a grant from the Australian Research Council. Many people commented on an earlier draft of this manuscript, but we are particularly indebted to Steve Reicher for a series of very productive discussions about its content.

REFERENCES

Abate, M., & Berrien, F. K. (1967). Validation of stereotypes: Japanese versus American students. *Journal of Personality and Social Psychology,* **7**, 435–8.

Abrams, D., & Hogg, M. A. (1990). Social identification, self-categorization and social influence. In W. Stroebe & M. Hewstone (Eds), *European Review of Social Psychology* (Vol. 1, pp. 195–228). Chichester: Wiley.

Adorno, T. W., Frenkel-Brunswik, E., Levinson, D. J., & Sanford, R. N. (1950). *The Authoritarian Personality.* New York: Harper.

Allport, G. W. (1954). *The Nature of Prejudice.* Cambridge, MA: Addison-Wesley.

Amir, Y. (1969). Contact hypothesis in ethnic relations. *Psychological Bulletin,* **71**, 319–42.

Asch, S. E. (1951). Effects of group pressure upon the modification and distortion of judgements. In H. Guetzkow (Ed.), *Groups, Leadership and Men* (pp. 177–90). Pittsburg, PA: Carnegie Press.

Ashmore, R. D., & Del Boca, F. K. (1981). Conceptual approaches to stereotyping. In D. L. Hamilton (Ed.), *Cognitive Processes in Stereotyping and Intergroup Behaviour.* Hillsdale, NJ: Erlbaum.

Bar-Tal, D. (1990). Israeli–Palestinian conflict: A cognitive analysis. *International Journal of Intercultural Relations,* **14**, 7–29.

Barsalou, L. W. (1990). Access and inference in categorization. *Bulletin of the Psychonomic Society,* **28**, 268–71.

Bartsch, R. A., & Judd, C. M. (1993). Majority–minority status and perceived ingroup variability revisited. *European Journal of Social Psychology,* **23**, 471–85.

Brigham, J. C. (1971). Ethnic stereotypes. *Psychological Bulletin,* **76**, 15–38.

Bogardus, E. S. (1950). Stereotypes versus sociotypes. *Sociological and Social Science Research,* **34**, 286–91.

Condor, S. G. (1990). Social stereotypes and social identity. In D. Abrams & M. A. Hogg (Eds), *Social Identity Theory: Constructive and Critical Advances.* Hemel Hempstead: Harvester Wheatsheaf.

David, B., & Turner, J. C. (1992). Studies in self-categorization and minority conversion. Paper presented at the joint EAESP/SESP meeting, Leuven/Louvain-la-Neuve, Belgium, 15–18 July.

David, B., & Turner, J. C. (1996). Studies in self-categorization and minority conversion: Is being a member of the outgroup an advantage? *British Journal of Social Psychology,* **35**, 179–99.

Diab, L. N. (1963). Factors determining group stereotypes. *Journal of Social Psychology,* **61**, 3–10.

Devine, P. G., & Elliot, A. J. (1995). Are racial stereotypes *really* fading? The Princeton trilogy revisited. *Personality and Social Psychology Bulletin,* **21**, 1139–50.

Doise, W., Deschamps, J. P., & Meyer, G. (1978). The accentuation of intra-category similarities. In H. Tajfel (Ed.), *Differentiation Between Social Groups* (pp. 159–68). London: Academic Press.

Doise, W., & Sinclair, A. (1973). The categorization process in intergroup relations. *European Journal of Social Psychology,* **3**, 145–57.

Doosje, B., & Ellemers, N. (1997). Stereotyping under threat: The role of group identification. In R. Spears, P. J. Oakes, N. Ellemers & S. A. Haslam (Eds), *The Social Psychology of Stereotyping and Group Life.* Oxford: Blackwell.

Doosje, B., Haslam, S. A., Spears, R., Oakes, P. J., & Koomen, W. (in press). The effect of comparative context on central tendency and variability judgements and the evaluation of group characteristics. *European Journal of Social Psychology.*

Ellemers, N., & van Knippenberg, A. (1997). Stereotyping in social context. In R. Spears, P. J. Oakes, N. Ellemers & S. A. Haslam (Eds), *The Social Psychology of Stereotyping and Group Life.* Oxford: Blackwell.

Eysenck, H. J., & Crown, S. (1948). National stereotypes: An experimental and methodological study. *International Journal of Opinion and Attitude Research,* **2**, 26–39.

Fishman, J. A. (1956). An examination of the process and function of social stereotyping. *Journal of Social Psychology,* **43**, 27–64.

Fiske, S. T., & Taylor, S. E. (1984). *Social Cognition.* Reading, MA: Addison-Wesley.

Freyd, J. F. (1983). Shareability: The social psychology of epistemology. *Cognitive Science,* **7**, 191–210.

Freyd, J. F. (1990). Natural selection of shareability? *Behavioural and Brain Sciences,* **13**, 732–4.

Gardner, R. C. (1993). Stereotypes as consensual beliefs. In M. P. Zanna & J. M. Olson (Eds), *The Psychology of Prejudice: The Ontario Symposium* (Vol. 7). Hillsdale, NJ: Erlbaum.

Gardner, R. C., Kirby, D. M., & Finlay, J. C. (1973). Ethnic stereotypes: The significance of consensus. *Canadian Journal of Behavioural Science,* **5**, 4–12.

Gilbert, G. M. (1951). Stereotype persistence and change among college students. *Journal of Abnormal and Social Psychology,* **46**, 245–54.

Goldstone, R. (1994). Influences of categorization on perceptual discrimination. *Journal of Experimental Psychology,* **123**, 178–200.

Hamilton, D. L., & Trolier, T. K. (1986). Stereotypes and stereotyping: An overview of the cognitive approach. In J. F. Dovidio & S. L. Gaertner (Eds), *Prejudice, Discrimination, and Racism.* New York and Orlando, FL: Academic Press.

Hamilton, D. L., Stroessner, S. J., & Driscoll, D. M. (1994). Social cognition and the study of stereotyping. In P. G. Devine, D. L. Hamilton, & T. M. Ostrom (Eds), *Social Cognition: Contributions to Classic Issues in Social Psychology* (pp. 291–321). New York: Springer-Verlag.

Hardin, C., & Higgins, E. T. (1996). Shared reality: How social verification makes the subjective objective. In R. M. Sorrentino & E. T. Higgins (Eds), *Handbook of Motivation and Cognition* (Vol. 3, pp. 28–84). New York: Guilford.

Haslam, S. A. (1991). Social comparative context, self-categorization and stereotyping. Unpublished PhD thesis: Macquarie University.

Haslam, S. A. (1997). Stereotyping and social influence: Foundations of stereotype consensus. In R. Spears, P. J. Oakes, N. Ellemers & S. A. Haslam (Eds), *The Social Psychology of Stereotyping and Group Life.* Oxford: Blackwell.

Haslam, S. A. (1996).   Stereotyping and group consensualization: The role of social influence in emergent stereotype sharedness. Paper presented at the Eleventh General Meeting of the European Association of Experimental Social Psychology. Gmunden, Austria, 13–18 July.

Haslam, S. A., McGarty, C., & Turner, J. C. (1996b).   Salient group memberships and persuasion: The role of shared group memberships in the validation of beliefs. In J. Nye & M. Brower (Eds), *What's Social about Social Cognition? Social Cognition Research in Small Groups* (pp. 29–56). Beverly Hills, CA: Sage.

Haslam, S. A., & Oakes, P. J. (1995).   How context-independent is the outgroup homogeneity effect? A response to Bartsch and Judd. *European Journal of Social Psychology*, **25**, 469–76.

Haslam, S. A., Oakes, P. J., McGarty, C., Turner, J. C., Reynolds, K. J., & Eggins, R. A. (1996c).   Stereotyping and social influence: The mediation of stereotype applicability and sharedness by the views of ingroup and outgroup members. *British Journal of Social Psychology*, **35**, 369–97.

Haslam, S. A., Turner, J. C., Oakes, P. J., Reynolds, K. J., Eggins, R. A., Nolan, M., & Tweedie, J. (in press).   When do stereotypes become really consensual? Investigating the group-based dynamics of the consensualization process. *European Journal of Social Psychology*.

Haslam, S. A., Oakes, P. J., Turner, J. C., & McGarty, C. (1995).   Social categorization and group homogeneity: Changes in the perceived applicability of stereotype content as a function of comparative context and trait favourableness. *British Journal of Social Psychology*, **34**, 139–60.

Haslam, S. A., Oakes, P. J., Turner, J. C., & McGarty, C. (1996).   Social identity, self-categorization and the perceived homogeneity of ingroups and outgroups: The interaction between social motivation and cognition. In R. M. Sorrentino & E. T. Higgins (Eds), *Handbook of Motivation and Cognition* (Vol. 3, pp. 182–222). New York: Guilford.

Haslam, S. A., & Turner, J. C. (1992).   Context-dependent variation in social stereotyping 2: The relationship between frame of reference, self-categorization and accentuation. *European Journal of Social Psychology*, **22**, 251–78.

Haslam, S. A., & Turner, J. C. (1995).   Extremism as a self-categorical basis for polarized judgement. *European Journal of Social Psychology*, **25**, 341–71.

Haslam, S. A., Turner, J. C., Oakes, P. J., McGarty, C., & Hayes, B. K. (1992).   Context-dependent variation in social stereotyping 1: The effects of intergroup relations as mediated by social change and frame of reference. *European Journal of Social Psychology*, **22**, 3–20.

Hogg, M. A., & Turner, J. C. (1987a).   Intergroup behaviour, self-stereotyping and the salience of social categories. *British Journal of Social Psychology*, **26**, 325–40.

Hogg, M. A., & Turner, J. C. (1987b).   Social identity and conformity: A theory of referent informational influence. In W. Doise & S. Moscovici (Eds), *Current Issues in European Social Psychology* (Vol. 2, pp. 139–82). Cambridge: Cambridge University Press.

Hyakawa, S.I. (1950).   Recognizing stereotypes as substitutes for thought. *A Review of General Semantics*, **7**, 208–210.

Judd, C. M., & Park, B. (1988).   Out-group homogeneity: Judgments of variability at the individual and group levels. *Journal of Personality and Social Psychology*, **54**, 778–88.

Judd, C. M., & Park, B. (1993).   Definition and assessment of accuracy in social stereotypes. *Psychological Review*, **100**, 109–28.

Karlins, M., Coffman, T. L., & Walters, G. (1969). On the fading of social stereotypes: Studies in three generations of college students. *Journal of Personality and Social Psychology*, **13**, 1–16.

Katz, D., & Braly, K. (1933). Racial stereotypes of one hundred college students. *Journal of Abnormal and Social Psychology*, **28**, 280–90.

Keil, F. C. (1987). Concepts, Kinds and Cognitive Development. Cambridge, MA: MIT Press.

Kelly, C. (1989). Political identity and perceived intragroup homogeneity. *British Journal of Social Psychology*, **28**, 239–50.

Klineberg, O. (1951). The scientific study of national stereotypes. *International Social Science Bulletin*, **3**, 505–15.

Laviolette, F., & Silvert, K. H. (1951). A theory of stereotypes. *Social Forces*, **29**, 257–62.

Leyens, J-P., Yzerbyt, V., & Schadron, G. (1994). *Stereotypes and Social Cognition*. London: Sage.

Linville, P. W., Salovey, P., & Fischer, G. W. (1986). Stereotyping and perceived distributions of social characteristics: An application to ingroup-outgroup perception. In J. F. Dovidio & S. L. Gaertner (Eds), *Prejudice, Discrimination and Racism*. New York and Orlando, FL: Academic Press.

Lippmann, W. (1922). *Public Opinion*. New York: Harcourt Brace.

Mackie, D. M., Worth, L. T., & Ascuncion, A. G. (1990). Processing of persuasive ingroup messages. *Journal of Personality and Social Psychology*, **58**, 812–22.

McCauley, C., & Stitt, C. L. (1978). An individual and quantitative measure of stereotypes. *Journal of Personality and Social Psychology*, **36**, 929–40.

McCauley, C., Stitt, C. L., & Segal, M. (1980). Stereotyping: From prejudice to prediction. *Psychological Bulletin*, **87**, 195–208.

McGarty, C., & Grace, D. (1996). Categorization, explanation and group norms: Evidence for the social mediation of a cognitive process. Unpublished manuscript, The Australian National University.

McGarty, C., Haslam, S. A., Hutchinson, K. J., & Turner, J. C. (1994). The effects of salient group memberships on persuasion. *Small Group Research*, **25**, 267–93.

McGarty, C., Turner, J. C., Oakes, P. J., & Haslam, S. A. (1993). The creation of uncertainty in the influence process: The role of stimulus information and disagreement with similar others. *European Journal of Social Psychology*, **23**, 17–38.

McIntyre, D. R. (1995). Understanding the shared nature of object categories: The role of theories and social identification in categorization. Unpublished thesis: The Australian National University.

Medin, D. L., Wattenmaker, W. D., & Hampson, S. E. (1987). Family resemblance, conceptual cohesiveness, and category construction. *Cognitive Psychology*, **19**, 242–71.

Meenes, M. (1943). A comparison of racial stereotypes of 1935 and 1942. *Journal of Social Psychology*, **17**, 327–36.

Moscovici, S., & Zavalloni, M. (1969). The group as a polarizer of attitudes. *Journal of Personality and Social Psychology*, **12**, 125–35.

Moscovici, S. (1984). The phenomenon of social representations. In R. M. Farr & S. Moscovici (Eds), *Social Representations*. Cambridge: Cambridge University Press.

Oakes, P. J. (1987). The salience of social categories. In J. C. Turner, M. A. Hogg, P. J. Oakes, S. D. Reicher & M. S. Wetherell (Eds), *Rediscovering the Social Group*. Oxford: Blackwell.

Oakes, P. J. (1996). The categorization process. Cognition and the group in the social psychology of stereotyping. In W. P. Robinson (Ed.), *Social Groups and Identity: Developing the Legacy of Henri Tajfel*. Oxford: Butterworth-Heinemann.

Oakes, P. J., Haslam, S. A., Morrison, B., & Grace, D. (1995). Becoming an ingroup: Re-examining the impact of familiarity on perceptions of group homogeneity. *Social Psychology Quarterly, 58*, 52–61.

Oakes, P. J., Haslam, S. A., & Turner, J. C. (1994). *Stereotyping and Social Reality*. Oxford: Blackwell.

Oakes, P. J., Haslam, S. A., & Turner, J. C. (in press). A consideration of prototypicality from the perspective of self-categorization theory. In J-C. Deschamps, J. F. Morales, D. Paez & H. Paicheler (Eds), *Current Perspectives on Social Identity and Social Categorization*. Barcelona: Anthropos.

Oakes, P. J., & Reynolds, K. J. (1997). Asking the accuracy question: Is measurement the answer? In R. Spears, P. J. Oakes, N. Ellemers & S. A. Haslam (Eds), *The Social Psychology of Stereotyping and Group Life*. Oxford: Blackwell.

Oakes, P. J., & Turner, J. C. (1990). Is limited information processing the cause of social stereotyping? In W. Stroebe & M. Hewstone (Eds), *European Review of Social Psychology* (Vol. 1, pp. 111–35). Chichester: Wiley.

Park, B., Ryan, C. S., & Judd, C. M. (1992). Role of meaningful subgroups in explaining differences in perceived variability for ingroups and outgroups. *Journal of Personality and Social Psychology, 63*, 553–67.

Park, B., & Judd, C. M. (1990). Measures and models of perceived group variability. *Journal of Personality and Social Psychology, 59*, 173–91.

Reicher, S. D. (1996). Social Identity and social change: Rethinking the context of social psychology. *Social Groups and Identity: Developing the Legacy of Henri Tajfel*. Oxford: Butterworth-Heinemann.

Reicher, S. D., Hopkins, N., & Condor, S. (1997a). Stereotype construction as a strategy of influence. In R. Spears, P. J. Oakes, N. Ellemers & S. A. Haslam (Eds), *The Social Psychology of Stereotyping and Group Life*. Oxford: Blackwell.

Reicher, S. D., Hopkins, N., & Condor, S. (1997b). The lost nation of psychology. In C. Barfoot (Ed.), *National Stereotypes and Racial Purity*. DQR Studies in Literature. Amsterdam: Rodopi.

Rojahn, K., & Pettigrew, T. F. (1992). Memory for schema-relevant information: A meta-analytic resolution. *British Journal of Social Psychology, 31*, 81–109.

Rosch, E. (1978). Principles of categorization. In E. Rosch & B. B. Lloyd (Eds), *Cognition and Categorization*. Hillsdale, NJ: Erlbaum.

Ruscher, J. B., Hammer, E. Y., & Hammer, E. D. (1996). Forming shared impressions through conversation: An adaptation of the continuum model. *Personality and Social Psychology Bulletin, 22*, 705–20.

Schneider, D. (1996). Stereotype research: Unfinished business. In C. N. Macrae, C. Stangor & M. Hewstone (Eds), *Stereotypes and Stereotyping*. New York: Guilford.

Schoenfeld, N. (1942). An experimental study of some problems relating to stereotypes. *Archives of Psychology, 270.*

Schuman, H. (1966). Social change and the validity of regional stereotypes in East Pakistan. *Sociometry, 29*, 428–40.

Sherif, M. (1936). *The Psychology of Social Norms*. New York: Harper.

Sherif, M. (1967). *Group Conflict and Co-operation: Their Social Psychology*. London: Routledge and Kegan Paul.

Sherif, M., & Cantril, H. (1947). *The Social Psychology of Ego-involvements, Social Attitudes and Identifications*. New York: Wiley.

Sherif, M., Harvey, O. J., White, B. J., Hood, W. R., & Sherif, C. W. (1961). Intergroup Conflict and Cooperation: The Robbers Cave Experiment. Norman, OK: University of Oklahoma.

Sigall, H., & Page, R. (1971). Current stereotypes: A little fading, a little faking. *Journal of Personality and Social Psychology, 18*, 247–55.

Simon, B. (1992). The perception of ingroup and outgroup homogeneity: Reintroducing the social context. In W. Stroebe & M. Hewstone (Eds), *European Review of Social Psychology* (Vol. 3). Chichester: Wiley.

Simon, B. (1995). Majority–minority status and perceived ingroup variability revisited: A reply to Bartsch and Judd. *European Journal of Social Psychology, 25*, 463–8.

Simon, B., & Brown, R. J. (1987). Perceived intragroup homogeneity in minority–majority contexts. *Journal of Personality and Social Psychology, 53*, 703–11.

Simon, B., & Hamilton, D. L. (1994). Self-stereotyping and social context: The effects of relative in-group size and in-group status. *Journal of Personality and Social Psychology, 66*, 699–711.

Simon, B., Pantaleo, G., & Mummendey, A. (1995). Unique individual or interchangeable group member? The accentuation of intragroup differences versus similarities as an indicator of the individual self versus the collective self. *Journal of Personality and Social Psychology, 69*, 106–19.

Smith, J. D. (1993) (Ed.). *Anti-Black thought* (Vol. 1, pp. 1863–1925). New York: Garland.

Spears, R, & Haslam, S. A. (1997). Stereotyping and the burden of cognitive load. In R. Spears, P. J. Oakes, N. Ellemers & S. A. Haslam (Eds), *The Social Psychology of Stereotyping and Group Life*. Oxford: Blackwell.

Stangor, C., & Lange, J. (1994). Mental representations of social groups: Advances in understanding stereotypes and stereotyping. In M. P. Zanna (Ed.), *Advances in Experimental Social Psychology* (Vol. 26, pp. 357–416). New York: Academic Press.

Stangor, C., & McMillan, D. (1992). Memory for expectancy-congruent and expectancy-incongruent information: A review of the social and social developmental literatures. *Psychological Bulletin, 111*, 42–61.

Stangor, C., & Schaller, M. (1996). Stereotypes as individual and collective representations. In N. Macrae, C. Stangor & M. Hewstone (Eds), *Foundations of Stereotypes and Stereotyping*. New York: Guilford.

Taft, R. (1959). Ethnic stereotypes, attitudes, and familiarity: Australia. *Journal of Social Psychology, 49*, 177–86.

Tajfel, H. (1969). Cognitive aspects of prejudice. *Journal of Social Issues, 25*, 79–97.

Tajfel, H. (1978). Interindividual behaviour and intergroup behaviour. In H. Tajfel (Ed.), *Differentiation Between Social Groups*. London: Academic Press.

Tajfel, H. (1981). Social stereotypes and social groups. In J. C. Turner & H. Giles (Eds), *Intergroup Behaviour*. Oxford: Blackwell.

Tajfel, H., Flament, C., Billig, M. G., & Bundy, R. F. (1971). Social categorization and intergroup behaviour. *European Journal of Social Psychology, 1*, 149–77.

Thorndike, R. L. (1977). Content and evaluation in ethnic stereotypes. *Journal of Psychology, 96*, 131–40.

Turner, J. C., & Giles, H. (1981). Introduction: The social psychology of intergroup behaviour. In J. C. Turner & H. Giles (Eds), *Intergroup Behaviour*. Oxford: Blackwell; Chicago: University of Chicago Press.

Turner, J. C., & Oakes, P. J. (1989). Self-categorization theory and social influence. In P. B. Paulus (Ed.), *The Psychology of Group Influence*. Hillsdale, NJ: Erlbaum.

Turner, J. C. (1982).   Towards a cognitive redefinition of the social group. In H. Tajfel (Ed.), *Social Identity and Intergroup Relations*. Cambridge: Cambridge University Press.

Turner, J. C. (1985).   Social categorization and the self-concept: A social cognitive theory of group behaviour. In E. J. Lawler (Ed.), *Advances in Group Processes* (Vol. 2). Greenwich, CT: JAI Press.

Turner, J. C. (1987).   The analysis of social influence. In J. C. Turner, M. A. Hogg, P. J. Oakes, S. D. Reicher & M. S. Wetherell (Eds), *Rediscovering the Social Group: A Self-categorization Theory*. Oxford: Blackwell.

Turner, J. C. (1991).   *Social Influence*. Buckingham: Open University Press.

Turner, J. C., Hogg, M. A., Oakes, P. J., Reicher, S. D., & Wetherell, M. S. (1987).   *Rediscovering the social group: A self-categorization theory*. Oxford: Blackwell.

Turner, J. C., Oakes, P. J., Haslam, S. A., & McGarty, C. A. (1994).   Self and collective: Cognition and social context. *Personality and Socal Psychology Bulletin,* **20**, 454–63.

Vinacke, W. E. (1956).   Explorations in the dynamic process of stereotyping. *Journal of Social Psychology,* **43**, 105–32.

Wetherell, M. S. (1987).   Social identity and group polarization. In J. C. Turner, M. A. Hogg, P. J. Oakes, S. D. Reicher & M. S. Wetherell (Eds), *Rediscovering the Social Group: A Self-categorization Theory*. Oxford: Blackwell.

Wetherell, M. S., & Potter, J. (1992).   *Mapping the Language of Racism: Discourse and the Legitimation of Exploitation*. Hemel Hempstead: Harvester Wheatsheaf.

Wilder, D. A., & Thompson, J. E. (1988).   Assimilation and contrast effects in the judgements of groups. *Journal of Personality and Social Psychology,* **54**, 62–73.

Wisniewski, E., & Medin, D.L. (1994).   On the integration of theory and data in concept learning. *Cognitive Science,* **18**, 221–82.

Yzerbyt, V. (1997).   Steoreotypes as explanations. In R. Spears, P. J. Oakes, N. Ellemers & S. A. Haslam (Eds), *The Social Psychology of Stereotyping and Group Life*. Oxford: Blackwell.

Chapter 8

Outgroup Prejudice in Western Europe

Thomas F. Pettigrew
University of California, Santa Cruz
James S. Jackson
University of Michigan
Jeanne Ben Brika and Gerard Lemaine
l'École des Hautes Études en Sciences Sociales
Roel W. Meertens
University of Amsterdam
Ulrich Wagner
Philipps-Universität, Marburg
Andreas Zick
Bergische Universität, Wuppertal

ABSTRACT

Outgroup prejudice has been a major area for social psychological applications. Yet European social psychology has not widely studied prejudice against the continent's new minorities. These groups provide a useful comparison with which to test generalizations concerning prejudice derived largely on African-Americans. This chapter advances two interrelated hypotheses: (1) The *universality hypothesis* predicts that social psychological factors operate in similar ways across nations and target groups though the macro-contexts vary widely; (2) the *mediation hypothesis* predicts that key social psychological predictors of prejudice serve as critical mediators of the effects on prejudice of social factors. We test these hypotheses and more specific phenomena with analyses of the rich data of the 1988 Euro-Barometer 30 survey. We find considerable support for both hypotheses. There are remarkable consistencies, with some distinctive features, in prejudice

European Review of Social Psychology, Volume 8. Edited by Wolfgang Stroebe and Miles Hewstone.
© 1998 John Wiley & Sons Ltd.

phenomena that operate across nations and outgroups. The chapter highlights
the comparable operation of psychological processes acting as proximal causes
of prejudice and mediators for social factors operating as distal causes.

Historically, social psychology has utilized intergroup relations as a primary
area for applications. Yet most of these applications have focused on Black–
White conflict in the USA. This situation is atypical of intergroup relations
around the world on many dimensions. African–Americans endured two cen-
turies of slavery and another century of legal segregation. To this day, they
endure intense racial boundaries. They remain the most residentially segregated and have the lowest intermarriage rates with Whites of any American
minority (Pettigrew, 1988).

Paradoxically, Black Americans nonetheless "belong" in the USA (Landes,
1955). Not even the most racist of White Americans suggest their removal.
Moreover, African-Americans share a language, religion and a broad national
culture with other Americans. Indeed, they have disproportionately contributed to those elements of American culture that are most distinctive in the
Western world. The dynamics involving the millions of new Latino- and
Asian-Americans more closely resemble many minorities elsewhere; but they
have received scant attention from American social psychology.

In short, no other minority group shares such a position with African-
Americans. Yet this is the intergroup situation upon which much of social
psychology's study of prejudice rests. This circumstance raises questions concerning the generalization of social psychology's findings on outgroup prejudice to other intergroup situations around the globe. Thus, our principal focus
is on the generalization of psychological principles of prejudice across societies and target groups.

OVERVIEW OF OUTGROUP PREJUDICE IN WESTERN EUROPE

Western Europe has many native minorities—such as the Scots and Welsh of
the UK, the Bretons and Corsicans of France, and the Frisians of The Netherlands and Germany (Foster, 1980). This chapter, however, focuses on attitudes toward the new minorities who arrived during the past four decades.
Western European states have a long history of immigration, stretching back
to their colonial expansion into the Third World. Yet this recent immigration
involves larger numbers than before. Adding to the new immigration is a
sharp increase in those who flee to Western Europe to escape wars, political
persecution and economic disasters. And for some countries, especially Germany, there has also been a large increase in refugees from eastern Europe.

By the 1980s, the size and permanence of "guest-worker" communities
made the term a misnomer. Augmented by rising numbers of refugees, the

new minorities elicited an increasingly hostile reaction from threatened sectors of the native populations. Extreme right-wing political groups seized on the threat as their central issue. Franz Schoenhuber and his Republikaners in Germany, Jean-Marie Le Pen and his National Front in France and successors to Enoch Powell in the UK all became more strident in their opposition to the new minorities. Even in The Netherlands, a misnamed Centrum Party formed in 1980 to exploit the new threat.

While these far-right efforts have gained only minimal power directly, they have succeeded in shifting the entire political spectrum to the right on the issue. Left-wing parties have equivocated. Conservative parties, fearing the loss of supporters to the far right, have made repeated concessions to anti-minority sentiments (Thraenhardt, 1995). Prime Ministers Margaret Thatcher and John Major in the UK, Chancellor Helmut Kohl in Germany, and now President Jacques Chirac in France have all espoused restrictions on citizenship and the new minorities that partly meet the far right's demands. These events recall 1968 in the USA, when an avowed racist, Alabama Governor George Wallace, created a climate that moved President Richard Nixon to the far right on civil rights. The Republican Party has openly played "the race card" in American politics ever since, and converted the White South into a major source of support (Carmines & Stimpson, 1989).

Not surprisingly, this political shift witnessed a rise in anti-minority violence. Attacks on the new immigrants and refugees have rapidly risen in recent years throughout Western Europe. The most publicized have occurred in Germany. In September 1991, a mob attacked and besieged for days a residence of asylum seekers in Hoyerswerda. Many of the city's middle-class residents applauded the action. Soon imitative acts of brutality erupted, the worst being the riots and murders in Rostock, Molln, Solingen and Magdeburg. Initially, this wave of violence primarily targeted Asian and African refugees. Later, Turks, the dominant ethnic minority, also became victims (Wagner & Zick, 1997).

Shrill political debates on the constitutional rights of asylum seekers and refugees preceded these attacks (Gerhard, 1992; Zick & Wagner, 1993). Yet the official political reaction to the initial attacks was to deny the problem. Germany, officials repeatedly declared, was a nation with sympathy for foreigners. One can speculate about the effects of such positions by European governments. Solid empirical evidence, however, establishes the existence of widespread prejudice and discrimination in Western Europe (Hill, 1993; Wiegand, 1992). This chapter's analyses of 1988 survey data provide further evidence. Thus, 37% of our European respondents agreed there were too many people of other races in their countries. On a measure of blatant prejudice, West German interviewees voiced the strongest outgroup rejection—3 years before the mob violence at Hoyerswerda.

Research also uncovers widespread discrimination (Luck, 1975; Sissons, 1981). Klink and Wagner (1998) recently conducted 14 field experiments in various parts of Germany in which either a German or a foreign confederate asked for help (e.g., for directions, applying for a rental of a flat). The study also used Milgram's (Milgram, Sabini, & Silver, 1992) "lost letter" technique with either a German or foreign sender or receiver. In nine of the 14 tests, the foreigner received worse treatment than the German. A meta-analysis of the experiments shows that discrimination was stronger when there was greater social distance between the subjects and the confederates. Such tests in other European nations yield similar results (Den Uyl, Choenni, & Bovenkerk, 1986). Their results closely resemble those of studies of subtle discrimination in the USA (Crosby, Bromley, & Saxe, 1980).

European social psychologists have conducted considerable research using the social identity approach (Abrams & Hogg, 1990; Wagner, 1994a)—a body of theories highly relevant for intergroup relations. Yet only a small proportion of these social identity studies have directly examined minority relations in Europe (for notable exceptions, see Sanchez-Mazas, Roux, & Mugny, 1994; Masson & Verkuyten, 1993). Excluding our own analyses of Euro-Barometer data, we reviewed all publications during the past 10 years in the 12 leading English-language journals in social psychology. We found only 18 papers that examined prejudice and discrimination against Europe's new minorities. Of these scant 18, 10 used Dutch samples. Three papers involved German subjects, two British subjects, and one each Belgian, French or Swiss subjects. No thematic priority emerges; studies addressed a variety of topics. Neither do the papers refer to each other, save for the Dutch publications.

Although there may be additional publications in non-English-language journals, social psychology is clearly missing an opportunity to provide a distinctively European perspective on racism, prejudice and discrimination. It is a distinctive perspective needed by the discipline to correct for the research literature's reliance on the highly atypical African-American situation. Furthermore, the prolific publications on the subject from other social sciences in Europe (e.g., Heitmeyer, 1987; Miles, 1989; van Dijk, 1991; Wieviorka, 1991) show that social psychology in particular suffers from this deficit. So we hope this chapter's analyses will arouse further research interest in this area.

THEORETICAL OVERVIEW

Our theoretical framework centers on two interrelated questions:

1. Do the psychological principles of outgroup prejudice generalize across societies and target groups?

2. If so, how does this psychological universalism exist in the context of societal differences in prejudice and discrimination?

We take a multi-level, normative approach to these questions (Pettigrew, 1991b, 1996a). At the macro-institutional level of analysis, broad historical, demographic, economic and political factors shape intergroup norms and situations. These norms and situations vary across societies and outgroups, leading to different degrees of prejudice. The meso-situational and micro-individual levels of analysis—the basic levels of social psychology—are important as mediators of the macro-level causes. We hold these mediating processes to be similar across societies and outgroups. To be sure, direct, unmediated causal paths from macro-variables may remain. But this framework holds that such direct effects represent processes whose meso- and micro-mediation is simply not yet understood by social psychology. In short, broad social forces at the macro-level are *distal causes* of prejudice, while meso- and micro-level phenomena serve as *proximal causes*. Hence, complete models of prejudice, in this framework, would consist of the specification of distal social causes and their mediation via situational and individual causes.

We can test two major and interrelated implications of this framework in the present study. We shall call them the *universality hypothesis* and the *mediation hypothesis*.

1. The *universality hypothesis* predicts that social psychological factors operate in similar ways across nations and target groups although the macro-contexts vary widely. For this purpose, we will compare findings across seven samples, four Western European nations and six different target groups. For a few items, we also can compare these European data with American data on attitudes toward African-Americans.
2. The *mediation hypothesis* predicts that key social psychological predictors of prejudice serve as critical mediators of the effects on prejudice of distal social factors. So we shall check for such mediation throughout much of our analyses. For example, for two social location variables, education and social class, we shall test four suggested mediating processes.

The Euro-Barometer 30 survey offers unique tests of this framework. Since it focuses on the new minorities of Western Europe, its target groups present a sharp contrast with much-studied African-Americans. These new groups are relatively recent arrivals, and they were never slaves or legally segregated. Yet they often do not fully share religious and other cultural elements with their host populations, and many question their "belongingness". Moreover, the six European target groups covered in our data set vary widely among themselves—from Asians and Turks to North Africans and Caribbeans.

OUTLINE OF THE STUDY

In the fall of 1988, the Commission of the European Community conducted an extensive Euro-Barometer survey of intergroup attitudes in its 12 member nations. In four of these nations—France, UK, West Germany, and The Netherlands—we added a module of additional items. A subset of our module replicated items from the 1986 National Election Study in the USA. Collected across the four European countries and the USA, these data form a unique data resource on the prejudice of dominant groups toward subordinate groups. Rarely have social psychologists had the opportunity to study these phenomena in such a comparative, cross-national, and multiple outgroup context.

Reif and Melich (1991) provide complete details of the survey, and the data are available from the University of Michigan's Inter-university Consortium for Political and Social Research. The Paris Gallup affiliate, *Faits et Opinions*, constructed the questionnaires and coordinated the fieldwork. We checked the translations of our questions in the four languages for accuracy. Gallup affiliates in each nation conducted the actual sampling and field work. They drew representative samples of the adult populations 15 years of age and older within each country. The sampling designs were a mixture of multi-stage national probability and national stratified quota procedures. Appropriate weights for the samples in each country and for the entire study were developed. The full sample sizes before removal of minority respondents were: France ($n = 1001$), UK (1017), The Netherlands (1006), and West Germany (1051). The part of the 1986 American National Election Study that we used for comparative purposes numbered 964 respondents (Kinder, 1986).

We selected two outgroups within each country, except in West Germany, using a split-ballot technique: Southeast Asians and North Africans in France, Asians and West Indians in the UK, Surinamers and Turks in The Netherlands, but only Turks in Germany. This procedure provides two randomly-drawn samples within each nation that reacted to one of two groups. This allowed us to examine relationships, not only across countries, but also within countries for different groups.

These rich data yield interesting results on a wide variety of intergroup topics. To date, we have investigated most thoroughly the distinction between blatant and subtle forms of outgroup prejudice, the predictors of prejudice, the effects of intergroup friendship and social class on prejudice, comparisons between European and American data, and the role of phenotype in outgroup prejudice. Focusing on the issue of generalization, this chapter provides an overview of our findings in each of these realms.

TWO FORMS OF PREJUDICE—BLATANT AND SUBTLE

Considerable work in the USA has centered on conceptualizing and studying more elusive, indirect forms of outgroup prejudice (Pettigrew, 1989). Two traditions have developed. *Symbolic* or *modern racism* research has typically used surveys, and *aversive racism* research laboratory experiments. Symbolic racism, inspired by work on symbolic politics, emphasizes that racist symbolism, rooted in childhood socialization, is more important than individual self-interest (McConahay, 1983; Sears, 1988). It is triggered by "moral feelings that Blacks violate . . . traditional American values . . ." (Kinder & Sears, 1981, p. 416). It rejects gross stereotypes and blatant discrimination; but it rationalizes opposition to racial change with ostensibly non-racial beliefs. For example, most White Americans today favor inter-racial schools. Yet many oppose the "bussing" of students necessary to achieve such schools, on the unfounded belief that such bussing is highly dangerous.

The second tradition has psychoanalytic roots. Kovel (1970, p. 54) defined aversive racism as "an intrapsychic battle" between White superiority beliefs and "a conscience which seeks to repudiate them . . ." Given this internal struggle, aversive racists avoid the issue by avoiding Black people. When they cannot avoid interracial contact, their behavior is polite and removed. Deeper and more subtle than the symbolic form, aversive racism is most likely to emerge in situations without clear norms. This formulation has inspired the most persuasive laboratory support for the phenomenon by Dovidio, Gaertner and others (Dovidio & Gaertner, 1986; Dovidio, Mann, & Gaertner, 1989). Closely related, too, is the experimentation on ambivalence and amplification of Katz and his colleagues (Katz, Wackenhut, & Glass, 1986).

Following this work, we began our analysis by distinguishing between blatant and subtle forms of prejudice—a blend of the two American traditions. Blatant prejudice is the traditional, often studied form; it is hot, close and direct. Subtle prejudice is the modern form; it is cool, distant and indirect. As various European writers had proposed (Barker, 1984; Bergmann & Erb, 1986; Essed, 1984), the distinction proves as useful in our analysis of European data as in North American data.

Prejudice Measures

Two ten-item scales measure BLATANT and SUBTLE prejudice (Pettigrew & Meertens, 1995). Table 8.1 shows the scales in English. (Dutch, French and German versions are available.) We used standard Likert-scale scoring, with item responses scored 0, 1 (no 2), 3 and 4 on a strongly disagree, somewhat disagree, somewhat agree and strongly agree dimension. Higher scores indicate greater prejudice. Five items are reversals in which we scored disagreement in the prejudiced direction (items 2, 3 and 4 of the ANTI-INTIMACY subscale and the two items of the AFFECTIVE subscale).

From more than 50 items, we chose 10 to measure each type of prejudice based on our conceptualization of the two forms and factor analyses. Using principle components analyses, exploratory factor analyses yield similar

Table 8.1 The BLATANT and SUBTLE prejudice scales and their five subscales

Threat and rejection factor items: the BLATANT scale
1. West Indians have jobs that the British should have (strongly agree to strongly disagree)
2. Most West Indians living here who receive support from welfare could get along without it if they tried (strongly agree to strongly disagree)
3. British people and West Indians can never be really comfortable with each other, even if they are close friends (strongly agree to strongly disagree)
4. Most politicians in Britain care too much about West Indians and not enough about the average British person (strongly agree to strongly disagree)
5. West Indians come from less able races and this explains why they are not as well off as most British people (strongly agree to strongly disagree)
6. How different or similar do you think West Indians living here are to other British people like yourself—in how honest they are (very different, somewhat different, somewhat similar, or very similar)?

Intimacy factor items: The BLATANT scale
1. Suppose that a child of yours had children with a person of very different color and physical characteristics than your own. Do you think you would be very bothered, bothered, bothered a little, or not bothered at all, if your grandchildren did not physically resemble the people on your side of the family?
2. I would be willing to have sexual relationships with a West Indian (strongly agree to strongly disagree) (reversed scoring)
3. I would not mind if a suitably qualified West Indian person was appointed as my boss (strongly agree to strongly disagree) (reversed scoring)
4. I would not mind if a West Indian person who had a similar economic background as mine joined my close family by marriage (strongly agree to strongly disagree) (reversed scoring)

Traditional values factor items: SUBTLE scale
1. West Indians living here should not push themselves where they are not wanted (strongly agree to strongly disagree)
2. Many other groups have come to Britain and overcome prejudice and worked their way up. West Indians should do the same without special favor (strongly agree to strongly disagree)
3. It is just a matter of some people not trying hard enough. If West Indians would only try harder they could be as well off as British people (strongly agree to strongly disagree)
4. West Indians living here teach their children values and skills different from those required to be successful in Britain (strongly agree to strongly disagree)

Cultural differences factor items: SUBTLE scale
How different or similar do you think West Indians living here are to other British people like yourself (very different, somewhat different, somewhat similar, or very similar):
1. In the values that they teach their children?
2. In their religious beliefs and practices?
3. In their sexual values or sexual practices?
4. In the language that they speak?

Affective prejudice items: SUBTLE scale
Have you ever felt the following ways about West Indians and their families living here (very often, fairly often, not too often, or never):
1. How often have you felt sympathy for West Indians living here? (reversed scoring)?
2. How often have you felt admiration for West Indians living here (reversed scoring)?

results across samples. For the BLATANT scale, two orthogonal factors emerge after varimax rotation in each sample (eigenvalues > 0.98): four INTIMACY and six THREAT AND REJECTION items. For the SUBTLE scale, three orthogonal factors emerge after varimax rotation in each sample (eigenvalues > 1): four TRADITIONAL VALUES, four CULTURAL DIFFERENCES, and two AFFECTIVE PREJUDICE items. Such structural stability across samples lends initial support for our universality hypothesis.

Sears' (1988) survey work on symbolic racism inspired the first of these SUBTLE subscales, TRADITIONAL VALUES. The second, CULTURAL DIFFERENCES, builds on the laboratory work of Rokeach (1960) on belief dissimilarity. We based the third subscale, AFFECTIVE PREJUDICE, on the laboratory findings of Dovidio, Mann and Gaertner (1989). Consistent with their American findings, the two positive emotions (sympathy and admiration) scaled, but two negative emotions (irritation and fear) did not.

The median alphas for these scales and subscales across the samples reach adequate or marginal levels: BLATANT (median alpha = 0.90), SUBTLE (0.77), REJECTION (0.77), ANTI-INTIMACY (0.81), TRADITIONAL VALUES (0.63), CULTURAL DIFFERENCES (0.66), and AFFECTIVE PREJUDICE (0.67). Pettigrew and Meertens (1995) provide further details.

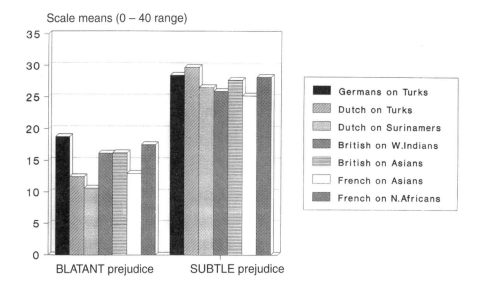

Figure 8.1 BLATANT and SUBTLE prejudice across seven samples

Aggregate Results

Figure 8.1 shows the BLATANT and SUBTLE scale means for the seven samples. Three trends emerge: (a) target differences within two nations— significantly greater French prejudice against North Africans than South-East Asians, and significantly greater Dutch prejudice against Turks than Surinamers; (b) a distinctive Dutch pattern of lower BLATANT but higher SUBTLE means; and (c) much higher SUBTLE than BLATANT scale means. We will discuss the first trend later.

The Dutch data are distinctive. The Dutch are significantly lower on BLATANT prejudice, but not on SUBTLE prejudice. The contrast is striking when we compare similar target groups. The Dutch BLATANT mean for Turks is significantly lower than that of the Germans for Turks. And the Dutch BLATANT mean for Surinamers is significantly lower than that of the British for West Indians—both Caribbeans largely of African ancestry. Yet the Dutch SUBTLE means are higher than these comparisons. In normative terms, this distinctive pattern outlines the famed "tolerance" of The Netherlands. We posit a stern Dutch norm against BLATANT prejudice. But SUBTLE prejudice slips in under the norm, unrecognized as prejudice (Pettigrew & Meertens, 1996).

SUBTLE scale means are consistently higher than those of the BLATANT scale, because the items are more socially acceptable (Pettigrew & Meertens, 1996). This allows an analysis of three types of prejudice (Figure 8.2). We divided high from low prejudice in Figure 8.2 at the central point of the scales (20), not the empirical means. So one quadrant drops out (type 0), with less than 2% of the respondents scoring high on BLATANT and low on SUBTLE. Types 1 (low on both scales) and 3 (high on both) are the familiar *Equalitarians* and *Bigots* long studied in social psychology. Of special interest is Type 2—the *Subtles*, who score high on the SUBTLE but low on the BLATANT measures. They reject crude expressions of prejudice. Still, they view the new minorities as "a people apart" who violate traditional values and for whom they feel little sympathy or admiration.

Attitudes toward Immigration Policy

As a test of our universality hypothesis, we find that differences between the types in attitudes toward immigration policy are consistent across all samples (Pettigrew & Meertens, 1995). Thus, *Bigots* are disproportionately among those who wish to restrict immigrants' rights further. *Equalitarians* disproportionately favor extending the rights of immigrants. By contrast, the *Subtles* assume a middle, ostensibly non-prejudicial position; they simply wish to leave the issue as it is.

Our supplement to the Euro-Barometer 30 schedule also included a six-item Guttman scale of immigration positions that allowed multiple responses:

BLATANT prejudice

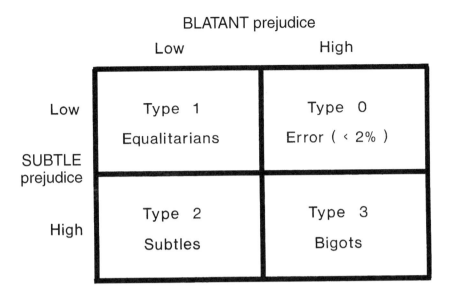

	Low	High
Low	Type 1 Equalitarians	Type 0 Error (< 2%)
High	Type 2 Subtles	Type 3 Bigots

SUBTLE prejudice

Figure 8.2   Typology of prejudice

There are a number of policy options concerning the presence of (outgroup) immigrants living here. In your opinion, which is the one policy that the government should adopt in the long run? The government should: (1) send all (outgroup), even those born in (the country), back to their own country; (2) send only those (outgroup) who were not born in (the country) back to their own country; (3) send only those (outgroup) back who are not contributing to the economic livelihood of (the country); (4) send only those (outgroup) who have committed severe criminal offenses back to their own country; (5) send only those (outgroup) who have no immigration documents back to their own country; (6) the government should not send back to their own country any of the (outgroup) now living in (the country).

Differences between the types also appear on this measure. *Bigots* typically favour sending all immigrants home; *Equalitarians* often favor not sending back any of the immigrants. *Subtles*, however, typically favor sending immigrants home only when there is a seemingly non-prejudicial reason for doing so—if they have committed crimes or do not have their documents. Again, in support of the universality hypothesis, these differences among the three types are statistically significant in all seven samples.

This immigration policy index provided an informative measure for testing the effects of our prejudice scales. In contrast with most of the prejudice data, this policy question elicited sharp and significant differences among the samples. German respondents most often and the Dutch least often adopted punitive immigration policies. Yet only small numbers in any nation endorsed the most generous policy alternative—refusing to send back any immigrants (ranging from 9% in Germany to 17% in the UK). Major differences also emerged between responses to outgroups within the same nation. Again, the Dutch were more harsh toward Turks than Surinamers, the French more harsh toward North Africans than Asians. Hence, 27% of the French favoured sending back all North Africans not born in France, as opposed to only 11% favouring such a policy for Asians.

For additional tests, we ran a series of regression analyses (Jackson *et al.*, 1995). A consistent pattern emerges for the predictors of the immigration policy positions. Various combinations of the prejudice indicators and outgroup unfavorability ratings from a 0–100 thermometer measure, plus GROUP RELATIVE DEPRIVATION, account for much of the variance in views about immigration policy. The consistency of these findings across countries and outgroups is exceptional. The standardized coefficients within each sample reveal that the rankings of the most important factors are similar across all countries and outgroups. This consistency provides further support for our universality hypothesis. While prejudice levels and immigration policies differ widely, our various prejudice measures still relate at comparable levels to immigration attitudes.

Sociodemographic factors and left/right political orientation exert few *direct* effects on opinions about government policy. Hierarchial regressions reveal that these factors influence policy attitudes largely through their *indirect* effects on our prejudice measures and (especially for the Dutch) GROUP RELATIVE DEPRIVATION. Hence, prejudice and economic threat serve as critical mediators of the effects on policy attitudes of such distal variables as EDUCATION and AGE. Consistent with our mediation hypothesis, then, the psychological variables serve as the proximal predictors, mediating the effects of broader social variables.

THE CORRELATES OF PREJUDICE

We found further constancy across samples in the correlates of the two prejudice scales. Eight variables emerged as unfailing predictors of prejudice. These relationships are consistent with both our universality hypothesis and the research literature on prejudice, most of it using African-Americans as the target.

Figure 8.3 provides the mean effect sizes from eight-variable regressions that predict both BLATANT and SUBTLE prejudice. We use Cohen's *d* as our effect size measure. This metric represents the difference between the means of the groups being compared given in standard score units (or, in correlational terms, $d = 2r/\sqrt{(1 - r^2)}$) (Rosenthal, 1991, pp. 16–20). By averaging the samples' effect sizes, we see the relative strength of each predictor holding

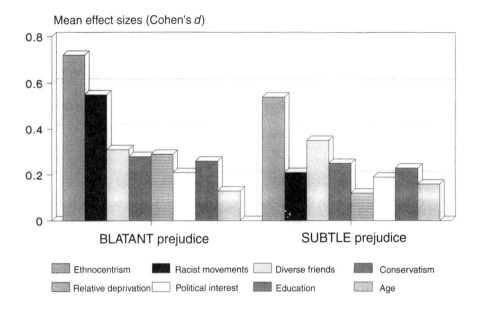

Figure 8.3   Prejudice predictors. Data from Pettigrew & Meertens, 1995

constant the other predictors. Six of these 16 mean effects are heterogeneous, that is, only six have significantly different effect sizes across the seven independent samples. All 16 mean effects are highly significant ($p < 0.0001$).

Ethnocentrism

For both scales and all samples, a measure of ETHNOCENTRISM proved the strongest correlate. This measure derives from a feeling thermometer used for a variety of groups in the Euro-Barometer 30 survey. ETHNOCENTRISM is an index of unfavorability ratings of three highly diverse groups not covered by other measures—southern Europeans, Black Africans and Jews. It served as our measure of generalized prejudice. Its robust positive effects recalls the authoritarian personality findings on the high correlations between prejudices against Jews, Blacks and Mexican-Americans (Adorno *et al.*, 1950).

Political Conservatism

Based on a 10-point self-rating, political CONSERVATISM related positively with both types of prejudice. These results allow us to test contentions in a current debate about subtle prejudice. Sniderman and Tetlock (1986a, 1986b; Sniderman *et al.*, 1991; Tetlock, 1994) question whether subtle prejudice is

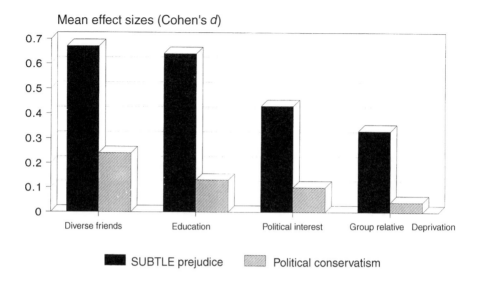

Figure 8.4 Predictors of subtle prejudice and conservatism. Data from Meertens & Pettigrew, 1997

distinct from traditional forms, or even if it is prejudice at all. They focus on Sears' (1988) symbolic racism. Central to their position is their concern that analysts have confounded symbolic racism with political conservatism and unfairly indicted conservatives as racists.

These European data refute these claims (Meertens & Pettigrew, 1997). Contrary to Sniderman and Tetlock's expectations, correlations between the BLATANT and SUBTLE scales with CONSERVATISM partialed out still range between +0.46 and +0.67. True, both prejudice scales relate positively to CONSERVATISM. Yet, again contrary to Sniderman and Tetlock's concerns, CONSERVATISM is significantly *more* related to BLATANT than SUBTLE prejudice ($t = 2.24$; $p < 0.03$). Moreover, Figure 8.4 shows that SUBTLE prejudice and CONSERVATISM differ sharply in their relationships with other variables (unlike Figure 8.3, these are zero-order correlations). When compared with CONSERVATISM, SUBTLE prejudice is significantly more closely associated with less EDUCATION, less POLITICAL INTEREST, not having DIVERSE FRIENDS, and feeling more GROUP RELATIVE DEPRIVATION.

Diverse Friends

This index of close contact refers to the respondents' reports of having friends from a religion, culture, nation, race or social class different from their own. It relates negatively with both BLATANT and SUBTLE prejudice (Figure 8.3). This variable allows a test of Allport's (1954) intergroup contact hypothesis (Pettigrew, 1997) (for another such test using these data but different analytic techniques, see Hamberger & Hewstone, 1997). Figure 8.5 shows that this measure relates strongly and negatively with all five prejudice subscales with or without seven co-varying controls (EDUCATION, AGE, CONSERVA-TISM, national PRIDE, POLITICAL INTEREST, community size, and GROUP RELATIVE DEPRIVATION). Note that DIVERSE FRIENDS relates most strongly with the two affect-laden subscales—ANTI-INTIMACY and AFFECTIVE PREJUDICE.

More surprising is the generalization of this effect to policy preferences and other groups *not directly involved in the initial contact*. With the same seven controls, DIVERSE FRIENDS consistently relates with more favorable im-migration attitudes—immigration is a good thing, all immigrants should be allowed to stay, immigration rights should be extended and citizenship should be made easier. These attitudes apply to immigrants of all groups—not just those represented among the respondents' friends.

Figure 8.6 reveals that mean DIVERSE FRIENDS effects extend to a variety of groups. Like the ETHNOCENTRISM measure, these data come from the feeling thermometer that asked for ratings, 0–100, of favorability toward an array of outgroups. Inspection of the effect sizes for individual samples further supports the conclusion that these data reflect wide

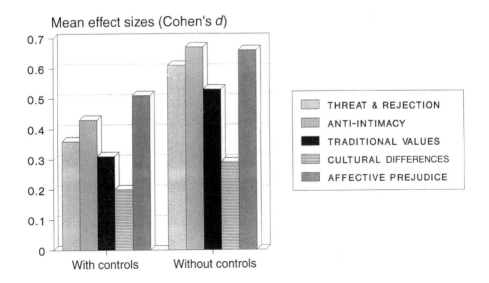

Figure 8.5 Intergroup friendship and prejudice. Controls: education, age, city size, conservatism, national pride, political interest, group relative deprivation

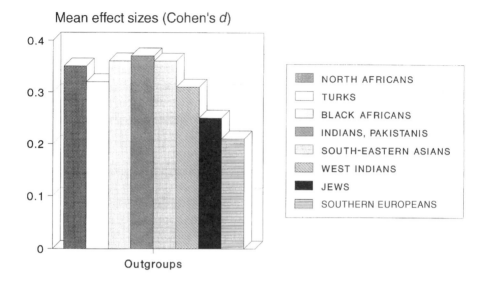

Figure 8.6 Intergroup friendship and outgroup ratings. Controls: education, age, city size, conservatism, national pride, political interest, group relative deprivation

generalization of reduced prejudice. Thus, Turks are a major minority in both Germany and The Netherlands, but not in France and the UK. In the latter two countries, then, it is highly unlikely that respondents would have Turkish friends. Yet the mean effect of DIVERSE FRIENDS for the French and British samples on ratings of Turks is identical to that of the German and Dutch samples. North Africans are not as large a group in Germany and the UK as they are in France and The Netherlands; but the mean effects of these two sets of samples are also the same. Similarly, Black Africans are far less common in Germany and The Netherlands than in the UK and France; yet the mean effects of these two sets are also the same.

These results raise the causal sequence problem that plagues cross-sectional studies. Does intergroup friendship reduce prejudice? Or do the prejudiced simply avoid intergroup friends? Figure 8.7 provides the best estimates possible with cross-sectional data (Pettigrew, 1997a, 1997b). It depicts a non-recursive model, using standardized path coefficients for the total sample of 3806 (Bentler, 1989; Bollen, 1989; Heise, 1975, pp. 160–68).

The rectangles at the bottom of the diagram represent the 10 measured variables with their estimated error terms that comprise the analyzed matrix. Variables 1, 2 and 3 tap reports of having neighbors of different cultures, races or religions. Variables 4–8 are the reports of having friends of a different culture, race, religion, nationality or social class. Variables 9 and 10 are the two affective prejudice items of Table 8.1. These variables estimate three

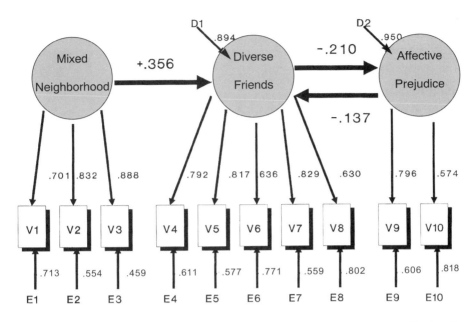

Figure 8.7   Diverse friends and prejudice. Total sample (n = 3806); standardized paths

latent variables (shaded circles): MIXED NEIGHBORHOOD, DIVERSE FRIENDS and AFFECTIVE PREJUDICE. Living in a mixed neighborhood provides the opportunity to have diverse friends, as shown by the +0.356 path. Living in such a neighborhood, however, does not relate to affective prejudice.

The critical results of the model are the two paths between diverse friends and affective prejudice. The model's maximum likelihood estimates reveal that both paths are significant. Prejudiced people do avoid intergroup contact. But this selection bias path (−0.137) is significantly weaker than the friendship-reducing-prejudice path (−0.210). Since having diverse friends meets Allport's (1954) conditions for beneficial intergroup contact, these data support his hypothesis. Moreover, this result suggests that the *potential of an intergroup situation for cross-group friendship* is a critical condition for reducing prejudice.

Figure 8.7 illustrates a central result of our analysis in testing our mediation hypothesis. Mixed neighborhoods serve as a distal social factor influencing AFFECTIVE PREJUDICE. Although it has no direct effects on prejudice, it makes having DIVERSE FRIENDS significantly more likely. In turn, having such friends from other groups acts as a proximal factor and is directly related to AFFECTIVE PREJUDICE. Such macro-variables at the institutional level of analysis as mixed neighborhoods vary greatly across the four nations. Yet their effects on prejudice are mediated in similar fashion through such situational and individual variables as DIVERSE FRIENDS—a finding that supports both our hypotheses.

Group Relative Deprivation

GROUP RELATIVE DEPRIVATION correlates positively and significantly with prejudice, particularly with the BLATANT scale (Figure 8.3). We used a single item to measure it: "Would you say that over the last 5 years people like yourself in (the UK) have been economically a lot better off, better off, the same, worse off, or a lot worse off than most (Asians) living here?" INDIVIDUAL RELATIVE DEPRIVATION, comparing self with the national ingroup, did not relate significantly with either BLATANT or SUBTLE prejudice.

Additional Correlates

A measure that tapped APPROVAL OF RACIST MOVEMENTS and disapproval of anti-racist movements was a significant and positive correlate of the BLATANT scale (Figure 8.3). POLITICAL INTEREST consisted of two items recording the respondents' interest in politics in general and European Community politics in particular. It was significantly and negatively associated with BLATANT and SUBTLE prejudice. AGE related significantly and positively with both scales. Years of EDUCATION also related significantly and negatively with the two scales—a relationship that we now analyze in depth.

EDUCATION, SOCIAL CLASS AND PREJUDICE: THE POOR-WHITE RACISM EFFECT

One of the most reliable results in prejudice research finds formal education negatively related to the rejection of outgroups (Allport, 1954; Bagley & Verma, 1979; Blank & Schwarzer, 1994; Wagner, 1983). Although less consistently, social class membership correlates negatively with prejudice. This negative correlation of both formal education and social class with outgroup prejudice comprises the *poor-White racism effect.*

Our data offer an excellent test of both our mediating and universality hypotheses as they pertain to education (Wagner & Zick, 1995). Using their reported years of schooling, we classified respondents into low or high education categories. According to their self-categorization, they were also classified as members of the working or middle class. We then used these dichotomous variables of formal education and subjective social class membership as independent variables in 2×2 ANOVAs with three dependent variables: the BLATANT and SUBTLE prejudice scales and the rating of the sample's target outgroup on the feeling thermometer. As in Figures 8.3 and 8.4, the results for EDUCATION are clear. In all 21 analyses (three in each of the seven samples), EDUCATION relates to prejudice significantly and negatively.

The results for subjective social class are more complex. In six samples, class differences in prejudice were in the predicted direction. The exception was antipathy against West Indians in the UK. Yet this difference reached significance only in the large German sample with BLATANT prejudice as the dependent variable. In only one analysis (Dutch BLATANT responses to Surinamers) did a significant interaction of EDUCATION and class emerge. This lone interaction, however, had no influence on the data pattern of the main effects (Wagner & Zick, 1995).

We clarify this mixed picture for subjective social class effects when we calculate objective social class from the respondents' occupations (Zick, 1996). With all samples and the three dependent variables, blue-collar workers revealed, as predicted, greater prejudice than white-collar workers. Only in the German sample were these differences not statistically significant. However, self-employed and freelance workers in four samples from The Netherlands, France and the UK are nearly as prejudiced as blue-collar workers. Thus, these data clearly replicate the poor-White racism effect with EDUCATION. By contrast, the relation of both subjective and objective social class to attitudes toward outgroups is less reliable. When it does emerge, it is often non-linear in some samples and with particular target groups.

Cognitive and Motivational Explanations

There are several explanations for how the poor-White racism effect is mediated. Peter Schoenbach and his co-workers, as well as others (Sidanius & Lau, 1989; Sniderman, Brody, & Tetlock, 1991) propose that we can explain at least the educational effect by different cognitive capacities. They offer data to support the hypothesis that the effects of education on prejudice are mediated by the better educated having greater associative flexibility (Schoenbach, 1970; Schoenbach et al., 1980) and cognitive complexity (Wagner, 1983; Wagner & Schoenbach, 1984). A higher cognitive complexity may facilitate access to liberal and egalitarian values and norms (Ehrlich, 1973; Lipset, 1983).

Wagner (1983; 1994b) offers a motivational explanation for class differences in prejudice. Adopting Tajfel and Turner's (1979) social identity theory, he assumes the working-class are more likely to develop a negative social identity than those of higher class standing (see also Deschamps, 1982). Thus, working-class people compare themselves with lower-status immigrants and refugees, and use the devaluation of these groups to re-establish their threatened social identity. Experimental studies by Schiffmann and Wagner (1985) and Spears and Manstead (1989) support this assumption.

Our 1988 survey data allow us to explore further these mediating explanations. Several correlates of prejudice are of special relevance to these educational and social class effects. These include CONSERVATISM, INDIVIDUAL and GROUP RELATIVE DEPRIVATION, disturbance elicited by the presence of outgroups, outgroup contact, and national PRIDE. These variables significantly correlate with prejudice in all samples. In decreasing strength, the more disturbed by outgroups, the more CONSERVATIVE, the stronger sense of GROUP RELATIVE DEPRIVATION, the less contact, and the more national PRIDE, the higher their scores on all three prejudice indicators. In addition, less educated respondents were more disturbed by outgroups, more politically CONSERVATIVE, more often reported both GROUP and INDIVIDUAL RELATIVE DEPRIVATION, less often reported outgroup contact, and more often felt national PRIDE. Accordingly, path analyses show that we can explain an important part of the variance between EDUCATION and the three prejudice indicators in all samples with these psychological variables—further support for both our hypotheses.

On average, the differences between blue- and white-collar respondents parallelled those of the two education groups. The white-collar workers, compared with blue-collar workers, were less disturbed by outgroups, less group-deprived, reported more contact (except in Germany) and were less nationally proud and individually deprived. Only in France and the UK were they slightly more CONSERVATIVE on average than their blue-collar comparison group. As with EDUCATION, differences in these psychological variables mediate much of the disparity in prejudice between blue- and white-collar respondents.

The means of the self-employed and freelancers in disturbance, contact, individual deprivation and national PRIDE fall in between those of blue- and white-collar workers. However, in the Dutch and French samples, the self-employed and freelancers revealed extremely high CONSERVATISM means. Moreover, CONSERVATISM in these samples is one of the strongest predictors of prejudice. Thus, we can partly explain the strong rejection of Surinamers in The Netherlands and of Asians and North Africans in France by the self-employed and freelancers by their high CONSERVATISM. The comparably strong rejection of Asians by the self-employed and freelancers in the UK, however, did not relate to CONSERVATISM. British respondents rated themselves on average more conservative than other European samples. And the British self-employed and freelancers did not exceed the general CONSERVATISM of the country significantly. In addition, British CONSERVATISM is not a strong predictor of prejudice. Instead, a feeling of severe GROUP RELATIVE DEPRIVATION may at least partially cause the self-employed and freelancers' high outgroup rejection in the UK. Thus, the explanation of the sample- and target-specific co-variation of occupation and prejudice requires that we consider specific circumstances—a limitation of the consistency across samples predicted by the universality hypothesis.

Summarizing from this and other studies, psychological variables importantly mediate poor-White racism. Yet no one study has yet incorporated all the relevant cognitive and motivational variables. While the co-variation of education and prejudice and its mediating variables are reliable in Western countries, subjective and objective class effects on prejudice vary somewhat across different populations and target groups.

An Impression Management Explanation

Another explanation for poor-White racism consists of an impression management hypothesis. Thus, the educational and class differences in prejudice may simply reflect a greater sensitivity and need for socially appropriate responses among upper-status people. We conducted two tests of this possibility, using both survey and experimental data.

First, we compared the prejudice scores on the BLATANT and SUBTLE prejudice scales. If the SUBTLE scale uncovers more hidden prejudice with its more socially acceptable items, the impression-management hypothesis predicts that educational differences in SUBTLE prejudice should be markedly less than with BLATANT prejudice. A repeated measures ANOVA with the two prejudice scales as dependent variables does in fact reveal a significant interaction between the scales and EDUCATION. The differences between the educational groups were significantly larger for the BLATANT than the SUBTLE scale scores. However, there remains a substantial educational effect even for the SUBTLE scale scores, so the self-presentation phenomenon can alone account for only part of the poor-White racism effect (Wagner & Zick, 1995).

A second test of the impression management explanation involved a bogus-pipeline experiment (Wagner & Zick, 1995). This technique convinces subjects that an impressive computer procedure can detect their true attitudes (Jones & Sigal, 1971). Indeed, this procedure shifts subjects' self-reports toward veracity (Roese & Jamieson, 1993). Accordingly, we found our better educated subjects did reveal more negative attitudes toward minorities. But less educated subjects changed even more in the bogus pipeline compared to the paper-and-pencil condition. Again, the results do not support the impression management argument that the poor-White racism effect is merely an artifact.

An Abstract vs. Concrete Explanation

Finally, we tested Jackman's (1978) related argument that the better educated give more support for abstract democratic principles, but do not differ from others in their support for specific policies. The immigration policy index described previously allows a test of this explanation. Even with these items, educational differences emerged. Again, the better educated were more liberal and more often refused to send back minority residents than the less educated. The same educational difference emerged in a separate study of 794 German students. Half of the pupils attended the Hauptschule, Germany's lower educational level, and half-attended the more advanced Gymnasium. When asked for their behavioral intentions to act aggressively against immigrants, the Hauptschule students revealed greater aggression (Schneider, 1994; Wagner & Zick, 1997; Zick, 1996). These data, then, fail to support Jackman's hypothesis. Yet we lack research on differential educational and social class responses to immigrants under conditions of threat. For example, would there still be educational differences if they had to approve a home for refugees in their immediate neighborhood?

Such critics as Jackman (1978), who reject empirical demonstrations of the poor-White racism effect, stress the influence of the political elite on prejudice and discrimination. Yet there is no necessary contradiction between these positions. Often, as in recent European immigration debates, the process by which outgroups become a popular topic is top-down (Pettigrew, 1991a, 1996a). It is the elite who sets the immigration theme, makes minorities salient and a target of prejudice, and even employs negative outgroup stereotypes. Then the poor-White racism phenomenon can emerge if those with less education and social status prove more susceptible to such political messages.

COMPARISONS BETWEEN EUROPE AND THE UNITED STATES

American surveys have not used most of our BLATANT and SUBTLE prejudice items. We did select, however, a few items from the 1986 American National Election Study. This overlap allows a comparison of our European data with a broad American sample. Figures 8.8 and 8.9 illustrate mean differences across the eight samples for selected variables.

Ratings

As assessed by reversing the 0–100 feeling thermometer data, Blacks in the USA and Surinamers in The Netherlands receive significantly the *least* unfavorable ratings. And, as with the BLATANT and SUBTLE scales, significant differences emerge in Figure 8.8 within France between North Africans and Asians and within The Netherlands between Turks and Surinamers. Also, as in Figure 8.1's BLATANT prejudice results, French feelings toward North Africans and German feelings toward Turks are especially and significantly negative.

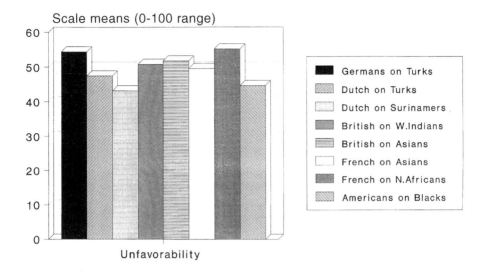

Figure 8.8 Unfavorability ratings across eight samples. From Euro-Barometer 30 survey (1988); American National Election Study (1986)

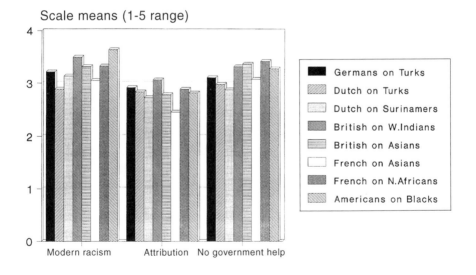

Figure 8.9 European and American comparisons on key variables. From Euro-Barometer 30 survey (1988); American National Election Study (1986)

Modern Racism

We constructed a modern racism index of two items asked in all eight samples. They concerned "welfare" (Table 8.1's item 2 of the Threat and Rejection subscale) and "work their way up" (item 2 of the Traditional Values subscale). Figure 8.9 provides the results. Here a different pattern emerges. Now two Black minorities—African-Americans and West Indians—receive significantly the *most* negative responses.

Group Attribution

Some theorists hold attributions to be a core component of prejudice (Apostle *et al.*, 1983). So we constructed a three-item measure that taps the respondents' tendency to blame a minority's problems on the outgroup itself. These items are the "should try harder" and "wrong values and skills" questions (items 3 and 4 of the Traditional Values subscale), and the "less able race" question (item 5 of the Threat and Rejection subscale). Figure 8.9 shows that such negative attributions are significantly stronger for British beliefs about West Indians, while French views of Asians are significantly the most charitable.

Government Help for Outgroups

One item in all samples posed the proposition: The government should make every effort to improve the social and economic position of (the outgroup) living in (this country). As Figure 8.9 shows, the Dutch are significantly the most willing to have the government aid their minorities, while the British are significantly the least willing to help their minorities. The French are far more inclined to help Asians than North Africans. American resistance to government efforts is comparable to the more resistant European samples.

Summary of Comparisons

White American attitudes toward African-Americans are not distinctively different from European attitudes toward the new minorities on these indicators. While scoring highest on the index of modern racism, the American sample was more favorable in its ratings on the feeling thermometer.

PHENOTYPE, SOCIAL DISTANCE AND ATTRIBUTIONS

Our analyses to this point have dealt only with aggregated data, using scales and entire samples of respondents. Yet the rich data of the Euro-Barometer

30 survey invite finer-grain tests of detailed phenomena. The effects of physical appearance on prejudice offers an example. Following up earlier work (Lemaine & Ben Brika, 1988, 1989, 1994), we explored the role of the target population's physical appearance and concerns over the phenotype of intergroup offspring (Lemaine & Ben Brika, 1996). This is an old issue in the intergroup relations literature. Consider Park's (1928) concept of "visibility", Hoetink's (1967) notion of "somatic norm image", and Dignan's (1981) and Memmi's (1982) emphasis on color, physical diversity and phenotype as major obstacles to assimilation. Drake and Cayton (1945), Fredrickson (1972) and Jordan (1968) noted its special significance for US race relations, and Mc-Crone (1937) for South African race relations. The point, repeatedly made in many contexts, is that group identity is grounded in part on physical appearance and the homogeneity of lineage. Yet social psychologists have virtually ignored the subject.

At first glance, the aggregated results of our 1988 data appear to support the critical importance of culture rather than physical appearance. As noted throughout, the French consistently favor Asians to North Africans and the Dutch favor Surinamers to Turks. Figure 8.10 shows this trend in more detail. Here we compare the two French samples with the German sample on five relevant items. At the left of the figure, we see the results on the key

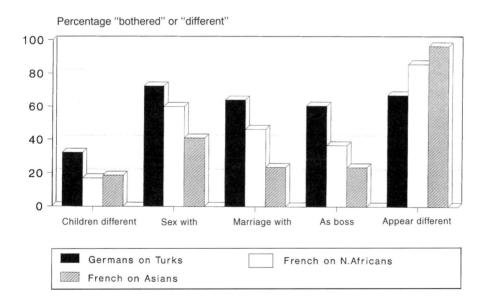

Figure 8.10 Intimate social distance and phenotype in France and Germany. From Euro-Barometer 30 survey (1988)

phenotype item: Suppose that you have children with a person of very different color and physical characteristics than your own. Do you think that you would be very bothered, bothered, bothered a little, or not bothered at all if the children do not typically resemble the people on your side of the family? The next three items in Figure 8.10 measure intimate social distance (Table 8.1's Intimacy Subscale items 2, 3, and 4). These items concern having a target group member as a sexual partner, a family member through marriage or a boss at work. With one minor exception, the three samples form the same rank order. Intimate contact bothers Germans significantly the most, and the French more with North Africans than Asians.

Yet the reverse rank order emerges in response to the question: How different or similar do you think (outgroup) living here are to other French people like yourself—in their physical features like their skin colors, nose, eyes, hair, and lips? Very different, somewhat different, somewhat similar, or very similar? Although Germans view Turks as more similar in appearance to Europeans, Turks remain the least accepted for intimate contact. Likewise, the French regard Asians as appearing the most different yet the most accepted.

A detailed analysis of the most extreme French respondents reveals that both cultural and physical characteristics play vital, inter-related roles in outgroup prejudice. We developed two sub-groups of French respondents with a two-stage procedure. Using Benzecri's (1992) factorial analysis of correspondence, we first selected 21 outgroup items for their strong loadings on both the direction and intensity of their anti-outgroup attitudes. Then, using Rouanet and Le Roux's (1993) analysis of structured data, we isolated French sub-samples of extreme *racists* (n = 104; 81 toward North Africans, 23 toward Asians) and *non-racists* (n = 72; 30 toward North Africans and 42 toward Asians). For larger samples, we combined the two French samples for these analyses.

As expected, the two sub-sets differ in their sensitivity to the physical appearance of outgroups. While only one non-racist reported being "bothered" if his mixed-race children did not resemble his family, over half of the racists would be "bothered". All respondents saw Asians as having a different appearance from them. Yet for North Africans, 91% of the racists, compared with 63% of the non-racists, reported them as different in appearance.

The two groups also differed markedly in their outgroup attributions. We used two questions to tap this dimension. Respondents agreed or disagreed with two statements that directly pose racial and cultural inferiority attributions: (a) (Outgroup) living here may not do as well as French people in France because (outgroup) comes from less able races . . . (item 5 of the THREAT AND REJECTION subscale); (b) because the cultures of the home countries of (outgroup) are less developed than that of France (not in scale).

In Figure 8.11, racists often agreed with both items or with just the cultural item. Non-racists emphatically disagreed with both items. Only one respondent agreed with the racial but disagreed with the cultural attribution. Note

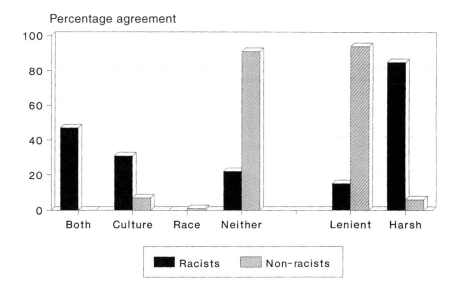

Figure 8.11 Attributions and immigration attitudes of extreme French respondent. From Euro-Barometer 30 survey (1988)

how sharply the two sub-groups differed on immigration policy. To dichoto-mize our immigration index, we defined "lenient" views as agreement to let all immigrants stay or send back only those who lack papers or who have committed crimes. "Harsh" immigration attitudes include wanting to send all immigrants back or those who were not born in France or are economically unproductive. With this split, the racists overwhelmingly adopted harsh immi-gration attitudes, the non-racists more lenient views.

CONCLUSIONS

We have reviewed the contours of prejudice—its social patterning across predictors, outgroup targets and nations. With several exceptions and qualifications, these survey data provide initial support for both of our broad hypotheses.

The Universalistic Hypothesis

Constructs and measures largely developed in the USA in the context of Black–White relationships have remarkable currency in Western Europe. In particu-lar, the distinction between BLATANT and SUBTLE prejudice proves useful on both sides of the Atlantic (Table 8.1). And these types of prejudice are clearly distinguishable from political CONSERVATISM (Figure 8.4). Moreover, European and American data on the same survey items are comparable (Figures 8.8 and 8.9).

Similarly, the findings reveal marked consistencies across the seven European samples and six contrasting outgroups. The two key scales for BLATANT and SUBTLE prejudice rendered essentially the same factor structure in the seven European samples. The same social and psychological variables predict the prejudice measures at roughly comparable levels across the samples (Figure 8.3). When we looked more closely at several of these predictors—CONSERVATISM, DIVERSE FRIENDS, EDUCATION, subjective social class, occupational status and the outgroup's physical appearance—we again found close parallels across the samples (Figures 8.4, 8.5, 8.6 and 8.10). In addition, while prejudice levels and views on immigration policies differ across outgroups and nations, our various prejudice measures still relate in the same direction and at comparable levels to attitudes toward immigration.

Nonetheless, there are qualifications we must place on the universalistic hypothesis. The most obvious limitation is that our data cover only Western, industrialized countries. Comparable work in non-industrialized nations is badly needed. In addition, each nation and outgroup target features distinctive phenomena that deserve attention. The mean levels of our indicators often varied widely across the samples, even while their predictive values remained relatively constant. Thus, the self-employed and freelancers were especially prejudiced in four samples, but not in three others. The British samples proved more politically conservative, and the German sample more resistant to intimate contact with the outgroup (Figure 8.10). The French revealed considerably less prejudice toward Asians than North Africans, the Dutch less towards Surinamers than Turks (Figures 8.1 and 8.10). Finally, the Dutch samples' extremely low means on the BLATANT prejudice scale together with high SUBTLE prejudice means proved to be the most striking national profile.

The Mediating Hypothesis

Throughout our results, psychological variables typically act as proximal causes of outgroup prejudice. They generally serve as mediators for the effects of social variables acting as distal causes. For example, in explaining poor-White racism, we saw how education's effects on prejudice were mediated in all seven European samples by such variables as political CONSERVATISM, GROUP RELATIVE DEPRIVATION, intergroup contact and national PRIDE. Similarly, Figure 8.7's structural model showed for the total sample how mixed neighborhoods increased the probability of having intergroup friends that in turn reduced AFFECTIVE PREJUDICE. On a broader scale, we also noted how prejudice and GROUP RELATIVE DEPRIVATION mediated the effects of AGE and EDUCATION on attitudes toward immigration in all samples.

These results recall a similar conclusion reached by Alex Inkeles (1969; 1978; Inkeles & Smith, 1974) in his research on modernity in six developing countries. He found sharp differences among the nations in industrialization and in the degree of modernity attained. Yet the relationship between industrialization and the psychological processes leading to modernity were strikingly similar. Inkeles concluded that industrialization leads to similar forms of social organization across societies. These modern organizations in turn shape face-to-face situations that produce similar patterns of modern beliefs and values. Likewise, we posit that similar social processes pattern majority–minority relations in industrial countries. In turn, these processes shape similar intergroup situations, behavior and attitudes. Mean levels of such political variables as attitudes toward immigration can vary sharply, yet their relationships with prejudice remain relatively stable.

ACKNOWLEDGEMENTS

We wish to thank Dr Anna Melich for her valuable help with the survey; the University of Michigan's Center for Group Dynamics and the Friedrich-Ebert Stiftung for their financial support; and the Rockefeller Foundation for its fellowship to the Bellagio Study Center for the first author.

REFERENCES

Abrams, D., & Hogg, M. A. (1990). *Social Identity Theory*. London: Harvester Wheatsheaf.

Adorno, T. W., Frankel-Brunswik, E., Levinson, D. J., & Sanford, R. N. (1950). *The Authoritarian Personality*. New York: Harper & Row.

Allport, G. W. (1954). *The Nature of Prejudice*. Reading, MA: Addison-Wesley.

Apostle, R. A., Glock, C. Y., Piazza, T., & Suelzle, M. (1983). *The Anatomy of Racial Attitudes*. Berkeley, CA: University of California Press.

Bagley, C., & Verma, G. K. (1979). *Racial Prejudice, the Individual and Society*. Westmead: Saxon House.

Barker, M. (1984). *The New Racism: Conservatives and the Ideology of the Tribe*. Frederick, MD: Aletheia Books.

Bentler, P. M. (1989). *EQS: Structural Equations Program Manual*. Los Angeles, CA: BMDP Statistical Software.

Benzecri, J.-P. (1992). *Correspondence Analysis Handbook*. New York: Marcel Dekker.

Bergmann, W., & Erb, R. (1986). Kommunikationslatenz, moral und offentliche Meinuing. *Kolner Zeitschrift fur Soziologie und Sozialpsychologie*, **38**, 223–46.

Blank, T., & Schwarzer, S. (1994). Ist die Gastarbeiterskala noch zeitgemass? Die Reformulierung einer ALLBUS-Skala. *ZUMA-Nachrichten*, **34**, 97–115.

Bollen, K. A. (1989). *Structural Equations with Latent Variables*. New York: Wiley.

Carmines, E. G., & Stimpson, J. (1989). *Issue Evolution: Race and the Transformation of American Politics*. Princeton, NJ: Princeton University Press.

Crosby, F., Bromley, S., & Saxe, L. (1980). Recent unobtrusive studies of black and white discrimination and prejudice: A literature review. *Psychological Bulletin*, **87**, 546–63.

Den Uyl, R., Choenni, C. E. S., & Bovenkerk, F. (1986). *Mag het ook an buitenlander wezen?: Discriminatie bij uitzendburo's*. Utrecht: National Bureau Against Racism.

Deschamps, J. C. (1982). Social identity and relations of power between groups. In H. Tajfel (Ed.), *Social Identity and Intergroup Relations* (pp. 85–98). Cambridge, MA: Cambridge University Press; Paris: Editions de la Maison des Science de l'Homme.

Dignan, D. (1981). Europe's melting pot: A century of large scale immigration into France. *Ethnic Racial Studies*, **4**, 137–52.

Dovidio, J. F., & Gaertner, S. L. (Eds) (1986). *Prejudice, Discrimination and Racism*. New York: Academic Press.

Dovidio, J. F., Mann, J., & Gaertner, S. L. (1989). Resistance to affirmative action: The implications of aversive racism. In F. Blanchard & F. Crosby (Eds), *Affirmative Action in Perspective*. New York: Springer-Verlag.

Drake, St. C., & Cayton, H. (1945). *Black Metropolis*. New York: Harcourt, Brace.

Ehrlich, H. J. (1973). *The Social Psychology of Prejudice*. New York: Wiley.

Essed, P. (1984). *Alledaags racisme*. Amsterdam: Sara.

Foster, C. R. (Ed.) (1980). *Nations within a State: Ethnic Minorities in Western Europe*. New York: Praeger.

Frederickson, G. M. (1972). *The Black Image in the White Mind: The Debate on Afro-American Character and Destiny*, 1817–1914. New York: Harper Torch Books.

Gerhard, U. (1992). Wenn Fluchtlinge und Einwanderer zu 'Asylantenfluten' werden—zum Anteil des Mediendiskurses an rassistischen Pogromen. *Osnabrucker Beitrage zur Sprachtheorie*, **46**, 163–78.

Hamberger, J., & Hewstone, M. (1997). Inter-ethnic contact as a predictor of prejudice: Tests of a model in four West European nations. *British Journal of Psychology* **36**, 173–90.

Heise, D. R. (1975). *Causal Analysis*. New York: Wiley.

Heitmeyer, W. (1987). *Rechtsextremistische Orientierungen bei Jugendlichen Empirische Ergebnisse und Erklarungsmuster einer Untersuchung zur politischen Sozialisation*. Weinheim: Juventa.

Hill, P. B. (1993). Die Entwicklung der Einstellungen zu unterschiedlichen Auslandergruppen zwischen 1980 und 1992. In H. Willems (Ed.), *Fremdenfeindliche Gewalt. Einstellungen, Tater, Konflikteskalation* (pp. 25–67). Obladen: Leske & Budrich.

Hoetink, H. (1967). *Caribbean Race Relations*. London: Oxford University Press.

Inkeles, A. (1969). Making men modern: On the causes and consequences of individual change in six developing countries. *American Journal of Sociology*, **75**, 208–25.

Inkeles, A. (1978). National differences in individual modernity. *Comparative Studies in Sociology*, **1**, 47–72.

Inkeles, A., & Smith, D. (1974). *Becoming Modern: Individual Change in Six Developing Countries*. Cambridge, MA: Harvard University Press.

Jackman, M. R. (1978). General and applied tolerance: Does education increase commitment to racial integration? *American Journal of Political Science, 25*, 302–24.

Jackson, J. C., Lemaine, G., Ben Brika, J., & Kirby, D. (1995). Individual outgroup rejection: Western European and United States comparisons. Unpublished manuscript, Institute for Social Research, University of Michigan.

Jones, E. E., & Sigal, H. (1971). The bogus pipeline: A new paradigm measuring affect and attitude. *Psychological Bulletin, 76*, 349–64.

Jordan, W. D. (1968). *White over Black: American Attitudes toward the Negro, 1550–1812*. New York: Norton.

Katz, I., Wackenhut, J., & Glass, D. C. (1986). An ambivalence-amplification theory of behavior toward the stigmatized. In S. A. Worchel & W. Austin (Eds), *The Social Psychology of Intergroup Relations* (2nd Edn, pp. 103–17). Chicago: Nelson-Hall.

Kinder, D. R. (1986). The continuing American dilemma: White resistance to racial change forty years after Myrdal. *Journal of Social Issues, 42*, 151–72.

Kinder, D. R., & Sears, D. O. (1981). Symbolic racism versus racial threats to the good life. *Journal of Personality and Social Psychology, 40*, 414–31.

Klink, A., & Wagner, U. (1998). Discrimination against ethnic minorities in Germany: Going back to the field. *Journal of Applied Social Psychology* (in press).

Kovel, J. (1970). *White Racism: A Psychohistory*. New York: Pantheon.

Landes, R. (1955). Biracialism in American society: A comparative view. *American Anthropologist, 57*, 1253–63.

Lemaine, G., & Ben Brika, J. (1988). Racisme et descendance. *Information sur les Sciences Sociales, 27*, 237–64.

Lemaine, G., & Ben Brika, J. (1989). Identity and physical appearance: Stability and desirability. *Revue Internationale de Psychologie Sociale, 2*, 325–38.

Lemaine, G., & Ben Brika, J. (1994). Le rejet de l'autre: Purete, descendance, valeurs. In M. Fourier & G. Vermes (Eds), *Ethnicisation des Rapports Sociaux: Racismes, Nationalismes Ethnicismes et Culturalismes* (pp. 196–235). Paris: Editions L'Harmattan.

Lemaine, G., & Ben Brika, J. (1996). Distance sociale et phenotype: Des attitudes aux intentions d'exclusion. Unpublished manuscript, Écoles des Hautes Études en Sciences Sociales, Groupe d'Études et de Recherches sur la Science, Paris.

Lipset, S. M. (1983). *Political Man*. London: Heinemann.

Luck, H. E. (1975). *Prosoziales Verhalten*. Cologne: Kiepenheuer & Witsch.

Masson, C. N., & Verkuyten, M. (1993). Preudice, ethnic identity, contact and ethnic group preferences among Dutch young adolescents. *Journal of Applied Social Psychology, 23*, 156–68.

McConahay, J. B. (1983). Modern racism and modern discrimination: The effects of race, racial attitudes, and context on simulated hiring decisions. *Personality and Social Psychology Bulletin, 9*, 551–8.

McCrone, I. D. (1937). *Race Attitudes in South Africa: Historical, Experimental and Psychological Studies*. London: Oxford University Press.

Meertens, R. W., & Pettigrew, T. F. (1997). Is subtle prejudice really prejudice? *Public Opinion Quarterly, 61*, 54–71.

Memmi, A. (1982). *Le Racisme*, Paris: Gallimard.

Miles, R. (1989). *Racism*. London: Routledge.

Milgram, S., Sabini, J., & Silver, M. (Eds) (1992). *The Individual in a Social World: Essays and Experiments* (2nd edn). New York: McGraw-Hill.

Park, R. E. (1928; 1950). The bases of race prejudice. In R. E. Park (Ed.), *Race and Culture* (pp. 230–43). Glencoe, IL: Free Press.

Pettigrew, T. F. (1988). Integration and pluralism. In P. A. Katz & D. Taylor (Eds), *Eliminating Racism: Profiles in Controversy* (pp. 19–30). New York: Plenum.

Pettigrew, T. F. (1989).   The nature of modern racism in the United States. *Revue Internationale de Psychologie Sociale*, **2**, 291–303.

Pettigrew, T. F. (1991a).   Advancing racial justice: Past lessons for future use. In H. J. Knopke, R. J. Nowell & R. W. Rodgers (Eds), *Opening Doors. Perspectives on Race Relations in Contemporary America* (pp. 165–78). Tuscaloosa, AL: The University of Alabama Press.

Pettigrew, T. F. (1991b).   Normative theory in intergroup relations: Explaining both harmony and conflict. *Psychology and Developing Societies*, **3**, 3–16.

Pettigrew, T. F. (1996).   *How to Think like a Social Scientist.* New York: Harper Collins.

Pettigrew, T. F. (1997a).   The affective component of prejudice: Empirical support for the new view. In S. A. Tuch & J. K. Martin (Eds), *Racial Attitudes in the 1990s: Continuity and Change* (pp. 76–90). Westport, CT: Praeger.

Pettigrew, T. F. (1997b).   Generalized intergroup contact effects on prejudice. *Personality and Social Psychology Bulletin*, **23**, 173–85.

Pettigrew, T. F., & Meertens, R. W. (1995).   Subtle and blatant prejudice in western Europe. *European Journal of Social Psychology*, **25**, 57–75.

Pettigrew, T. F., & Meertens, R. W. (1996).   The *verzuiling* puzzle: Understanding Dutch intergroup relations. *Current Psychology*, **15**, 3–13.

Reif, K., & Melich, A. (1991).   *Euro-barometer 30: Immigrants and Out-groups in Western Europe*, October–November 1988 (ICPSR 9321). Ann Arbor, MI: Inter-University Consortium for Political and Social Research.

Roese, N. J., & Jamieson, D. W. (1993).   Twenty years of bogus pipeline research: A critical review and meta-analysis. *Psychological Bulletin*, **114**, 363–75.

Rokeach, M. (Ed.) (1960).   *The Open and Closed Mind.* New York: Basic Books.

Rosenthal, R. (1991).   *Meta-analytic Procedures for Social Research* (Rev. Edn). Newbury Park, CA: Sage.

Rouanet, H., & Le Roux, B. (1993).   *Analyse des Donnees Multidimensionnelles: Statistique en Sciences Humaines.* Paris: Dunod.

Sanchez-Mazas, M., Roux, P., & Mugny, G. (1994).   When the outgroup becomes ingroup and when the ingroup becomes outgroup: Xenophobia and social categorization in a resource allocation test. *European Journal of Social Psychology*, **24**, 417–23.

Schiffmann, R., & Wagner, U. (1985).   Wie gehen benachteiligte Gruppen miteinander um? *Grupperdynamik*, **16**, 43–52.

Schneider, S. (1994).   Vorurteile Gegenüber ethnischen Minderheiten in Ost- und West-Deutschland. Unpublished diploma thesis, Ruhr-Universität, Bochum.

Schoenbach, P. (1970).   *Spräche und Attituden.* Bern: Huber.

Schoenbach, P., Gollwitzer, P., Stiepel, G., & Wagner, U. (1980).   *Education and Intergroup Attitudes.* London: Academic Press.

Sears, D. (1988).   Symbolic racism. In P. A. Katz & D. A. Taylor (Eds), *Eliminating Racism: Profiles in Controversy* (pp. 53–84). New York: Plenum.

Sidanius, J., & Lau, R. R. (1989).   Political sophistication and political deviance: A matter of context. *Political Psychology*, **10**, 85–109.

Sissons, M. (1981).   Race, sex and helping behavior. *British Journal of Social Psychology*, **20**, 285–92.

Sniderman, P. M., Brody, R. A., & Tetlock, P. E. (Eds) (1991).   *Reasoning and Choice: Explorations in Political Psychology.* New York: Cambridge University Press.

Sniderman, P. M., Piazza, T., Tetlock, P. E., & Kendrick, A. (1991).   The new racism. *American Journal of Political Science*, **35**, 423–47.

Sniderman, P. M., & Tetlock, P. E. (1986a). Symbolic racism: Problems of motive attribution in political debate. *Journal of Social Issues,* **42**, 129–50.

Sniderman, P. M., & Tetlock, P. E. (1986b). Reflections on American racism. *Journal of Social Issues,* **42**, 173–87.

Spears, R., & Manstead, A. R. S. (1989). The social context of stereotyping and differentiation. *European Journal of Social Psychology,* **19**, 101–21.

Tajfel, H., & Turner, J. C. (1979). An integrative theory of intergroup conflict. In W. G. Austin & S. Worchel (Eds), *The Social Psychology of Intergroup Relations* (pp. 33–47). Monterey, CA: Brooks/Cole.

Tetlock, P. E. (1994). Political psychology or politicized Psychology: Is the road to hell paved with good moral intentions? *Political Psychology,* **15**, 509–30.

Thraenhardt, D. (1995). The political uses of xenophobia in England, France and Germany, *Party Politics,* **1**, 321–43.

Van Dijk, T. A. (1991). *Racism and the Press.* London: Routledge.

Wagner, U. (1983). *Soziale Schichtzugehorigkeit, formales Bildungsniveau und ethnische Vorurteile.* Berlin: Express.

Wagner, U. (Ed.) (1994a). *International Review of Social Psychology,* **7**(1) (special issue on the social identity approach).

Wagner, U. (1994b). *Eine sozialpsychologische Analyse von Intergruppenbeziehungen.* Gottingen: Hogrefe.

Wagner, U., & Schoenbach, P. (1984). Links between educational status and prejudice: Ethnic attitudes in West Germany. In N. Miller & M. B. Brewer (Eds), *Groups in Contact* (pp. 29–52). Orlando, FL: Academic Press.

Wagner, U., & Zick, A. (1995). The relation of formal education to ethnic prejudice: Its reliability, validity and explanation. *European Journal of Social Psychology,* **25**, 41–56.

Wagner, U., & Zick, A. (1997). Ausländerfeindlichkeit, Vorurteile und diskriminierendes Verhalten. In H. W. Bierhoff & U. Wagner (Eds), *Aggression und Gewalt.* Stuttgart: Kohlhammer.

Wiegand, E. (1992). Zunahme der Auslanderfeindlichkeit? Einstellungen zu Fremden in Deutschland und Europa. *ZUMA-Nachrichten,* **31**, 7–28.

Wieviorka, M. (1991). *L'Espace du Racism.* Paris: Editions du Seuil.

Zick, A., & Wagner, U. (1993). Den Turken geht es besser als uns. Wie Fremde zu Feinden werden. *Psychologie Heute,* **20**, 48–53.

Zick, A. (1996). *Vorurteile und Rassismus: Eine sozialpsychologische Perspektive.* Münster: Waxman.

Author Index

Abate, M., 215
Abelson, R.P., 35, 38, 191
Abrams, D., 87, 97, 178, 216, 244
Adorno, T.W., 138, 208, 253
Aebischer, V., 184
Ajzen, I., 35, 38, 39, 44, 45, 57
Alba, J.W., 113, 120
Allport, G.W., 176, 209, 255, 257, 258
Altarriba, J., 94
Alvaro, E.M., 176, 177, 179, 184, 187,
    188, 189, 192, 194
Amir, Y., 207
Anderson, N.H., 82, 96
Anderson, J.R., 191
Arcuri, L., 156
Arkes, H.R., 108, 113
Arnold, M.B., 67
Aronson, E., 1, 2, 3, 15, 18
Asch, S.E., 142, 189, 210, 216
Ashmore, R.D., 204
Asuncion, A.G., 179, 216
Attig, M.S., 113, 120

Baddeley, A.D., 78
Baeyens, F., 68, 82
Bagley, C., 258
Bak, P., 73
Baker, S.M., 181
Bales, R.F., 155
Ballachey, E.L., 69
Banaji, M.R., 69, 74, 78, 80, 94
Bar-Hillel, M., 47
Bar Tal, T., 211

Bargh, J.A., 34, 70, 76, 77, 77, 78, 82, 83,
    84, 93, 94, 95, 96
Barker, M., 247
Baron, J., 43, 49
Baron, R.M.., 151
Barsalou, L.W., 231
Bartsch, R.A., 213
Bassok, M., 142
Batson, C.D., 148
Baumeister, R.F., 2
Bazerman, M.H., 43
Beattie, J., 47
Beauvois, J.L., 2, 5, 6, 8, 9, 10, 11, 12, 14,
    15, 18, 19, 20, 21, 22, 24, 25, 26, 28,
    29
Bekerian, D.A., 107
Bell, D.E., 43, 45, 46, 48, 59
Bellezza, F.S., 78, 94
Belli, R.F., 109
Bem, D.J., 3, 7
Ben Brika, J., 265
Bentler, P.M., 256
Benzecri, J.-P., 266
Bergmann, W., 247
Berrien, F.K., 215
Besner, D., 76
Beyth, R., 106, 119
Birnbaum, M.H., 58
Blank, T., 258
Bless, H., 36
Bogardus, E.S., 207
Bohm, G., 39
Boles, T.L., 47

Bollen, K.A., 256
Boudreau, L.A., 151
Bovenkerk, F., 244
Bower, G.H., 70, 82, 82
Braly, K., 204, 205, 206, 207, 209, 218, 223, 230
Branscombe, N.B., 48
Breckler, S.J., 35, 36, 37, 39
Brehm, J.W., 2, 3, 5, 7, 10, 15, 23, 26
Brewer, M.B., 176, 179
Briand, K., 84
Brigham, J.C., 204, 205, 208, 209
Brilmayar, A.G., 185, 186, 187
Brody, R.A., 259
Bromley, S., 244
Brown, R.J., 212
Brunetti, F., 5, 10, 11, 12
Buchner, A., 115, 125
Buck, R., 58
Bungert, M., 18, 21, 22

Cacioppo, J.T., 36, 136, 139, 177, 179, 187, 192, 193
Campbell, D.T., 176
Campbell, J.D., 108, 113
Cantril, H., 211
Carlsmith, J.M., 5, 16, 17, 26, 27
Carlston, D.E., 72
Carmines, E.G., 243
Carr, Th.H., 77
Casaer, S., 94
Cayton, H., 265
Chaiken, S., 60, 76, 136, 137, 176, 186
Chan, D.K.-S., 38
Chandler, J.A., 178
Choenni, C.E.S., 244
Christensen-Szalanski, J.J.J., 106, 108
Cialdini, R.B., 3
Clark, H., 78, 95
Clark, R.D. III, 178, 193
Clore, G.L., 59
Coffman, T.L., 205, 207, 218
Cohen, A.R., 2, 5, 7, 15, 23
Cohen, J.D., 89, 155
Cohen, L.J., 45
Condor, S.G., 205, 209, 215, 218, 219, 220, 227, 228, 232
Cook, T.D., 187
Cooper, J., 2, 3, 4, 15, 17, 27
Costa, P.T.Jr., 138

Crano, W.D., 176, 177, 178, 179, 181, 182, 184, 187, 188, 189, 192, 194
Cratylus, 145, 163
Crites, S.L. Jr., 37, 38, 57
Crosby, F., 244
Crown, S., 209
Crutchfield,R.S., 69
Czapinski, J., 72

D'Andrade, R., 191
Dagenbach, D., 77
Dannenbring, G., 84
David, B., 216, 225, 232
Davies, M.F., 113
Davis, M.H., 147
de Dreu, C.K.W., 181, 184, 186, 187
De Grada, E., 155, 167, 168
de Groot, A.M.B., 84, 87
de Houwer, J., 68, 77, 78, 83, 94, 95
de Vries, N.K., 40, 41, 42, 43, 49, 50, 51, 52, 53, 54, 55, 57, 59, 60, 181, 184, 186, 187
Dehn, D., 115
Del Boca, F.K., 204
den Heyer, K., 84
Den Uyl, R., 244
Deschamps, J.P., 213, 225, 259
Devine, P.G., 10, 98, 204, 209, 218
Diab, L.N., 207, 210
Dignan, D., 265
Dijksterhuis, A.P., 145
Doise, W., 213, 225, 226
Doms, M., 185
Doosje, W., 213, 217
Dovidio, J.F., 70, 74, 95, 247, 249
Draine, S.C., 78, 87, 90, 92, 93, 97
Drake, St.C., 265
Drever, J., 166
Driscoll, D.M., 204, 209
Driver, B.E., 57
Dunbar, K., 89

Eagly, A.H., 37, 39, 41, 136, 137, 176, 186
Eckert, H., 120, 121
Edwards, K., 34, 36, 38, 39
Edwards, W., 44
Eelen, P., 68, 77, 82, 83, 94, 95
Ehrlich, H.J., 259
Eisentadt, D., 2
Ellemers, N., 213, 217
Ellen, P.S., 38

Eller, F., 118, 119, 125
Elliot, A.J., 10, 204, 209, 218
Ellis, A.L., 178, 178
Erb, R., 247
Erber, R., 149
Erdfelder, E., 115, 125
Eriksen, B.A., 88
Eriksen, C.W., 88
Essed, P., 247
Evans, N., 70, 74, 95
Eysenck, H.J., 138, 209

Fabrigar, L.R., 37, 38, 57
Fazio, R.H., 2, 3, 4, 15, 17, 27, 49, 70, 71, 72, 73, 74, 75, 76, 77, 80, 82, 83, 93, 96
Feldman, S., 7
Fernandez, J.K., 59
Festinger, L., 1, 3, 4, 5, 7, 16, 26, 27, 46, 153, 176, 185, 187, 189
Fiedler, K., 151, 152
Findley, C., 148, 163
Fink, E.L., 191
Finlay, J.C., 205
Fischer, G.W., 212, 214, 229
Fischhoff, B., 106, 107, 109, 111, 113, 119, 126, 127
Fishbein, M., 38, 39, 44, 45
Fisher, W.A., 35
Fishman, J.A., 209
Fiske, S.T., 149, 209
Fointiat, V., 10
Ford, T.E., 146, 154, 162
Forgas, J.P., 70
Foster, C.R., 242
Franklin, P.E., 76
Fredrickson, G.M., 265
Frenkel-Brunswik, E., 138
Freud, S., 137
Freund, T., 136, 139, 142, 143, 145, 158, 164, 166
Freyd, J.F., 231
Frijda, N.H., 43

Gaertner, S.L., 247, 249
Gallois, C., 39
Gardner, R.C., 205, 205, 218, 232
Gawlik, B., 128
Gerard, H.B., 193
Gerhard, U., 243
Ghiglione, R., 5, 6, 28

Gilbert, G.M., 205, 207, 218
Gilbert, D.T., 143, 144, 194
Giles, H., 211
Gilovich, T., 48
Girandola, F., 16, 17
Glass, D.C., 247
Gleicher, F., 48
Goldstone, R., 232
Gorenflo, D.W., 178
Gorkin, L., 10
Gotz, J., 10
Gotz-Marchand, B., 10
Grace, D., 216
Greenberg, J., 10
Greenwald, A.G., 2, 69, 73, 74, 78, 79, 80, 87, 90, 91, 92, 93, 94, 97, 110
Gruder, C.L., 180

Haberkorn, G., 178, 193
Hager, W., 78
Hamberger, J., 255
Hamilton, D.L., 127, 204, 209, 212, 232
Hammer, E.D., 206
Hammer, E.Y., 206
Hammersley, R.H., 107
Hampshire, S., 46
Hampson, S.E., 231
Hannula-Bral, K.A., 176, 178, 182
Hansen, C.F., 72
Hansen, R.D., 72
Hardin, C., 216
Harless, D.W., 46
Harmon-Jones, E., 18
Harris, M.J., 143, 187
Hasher, L., 113, 120
Haslam, S.A., 206, 207, 208, 209, 210, 211, 213, 214, 215, 216, 217, 219, 220, 221, 222, 224, 225, 227, 231, 232
Hasselhorn, M., 78
Hastie, R., 106, 114, 120, 127, 129
Hawkins, S.A., 106, 119, 129
Heaton, A., 142, 162
Hedderly, D., 38
Heider, F., 69
Heise, D.R., 256
Heitmeyer, W., 244
Hell, W., 107, 113
Henderson, M., 184
Hermans, D., 68, 77, 78, 79, 80, 82, 83, 90, 91, 94, 95
Herr, P.M., 49

Hewstone, M., 184, 255
Higgins, E.T., 146, 148, 216
Hill, A.B., 93
Hill, P.B., 243
Hoch, S.J., 113, 118
Hodges, S.D., 53
Hoetink, H., 265
Hoffman, M.L., 29, 107, 109, 112
Hofstede, G., 137
Hogg, M.A., 178, 212, 215, 216, 244
Homer, P.M., 180
Hopkins, N., 215, 218, 220, 227, 228, 232
Hovland, C.I., 35, 179
Hyakawa, 207

Inkeles, A., 269
Irle, M., 10
Irvin, J., 148, 163
Isenberg, D.J., 168

Jackman, M.R., 261, 262
Jackson, J.C., 252
Jamieson, D.W., 145, 158, 162, 261
Janis, I.L., 46, 50, 52, 179
John, O.P., 72, 73
Johnson, M.K., 73
Jones, E.E., 7, 143, 146, 178, 261
Jordon, W.D., 265
Joseph, J.G., 60
Josephs, R.A., 47
Joule, R.V., 2, 5, 6, 8, 9, 10, 11, 12, 13, 14,
    15, 16, 17, 18, 24, 25, 26, 28, 29
Judd, C.M., 191, 204, 209, 212, 213, 214,
    215, 228
Judice, T.N., 165, 166

Kabili, D., 151
Kagan, J., 138
Kahle, L.R., 180
Kahneman, D., 45, 47, 48, 59, 69, 120,
    121, 143
Kanki, B., 193
Kaplan, M.F., 178
Kaplowitz, S.A., 191
Karlins, M., 205, 207, 218
Katz, D., 127, 204, 205, 206, 207, 209,
    218, 223, 230, 247
Keefe, D.E., 84, 87
Keil, F,C., 231
Kelley, H.H., 178, 179
Kelly, C., 212

Kelly, J., 168
Kelsey, D., 48, 59
Kemp-Wheeler, S.M., 93
Kenny, D.A., 151
Kenrick, D.T., 178, 191
Kiesler, C.A., 2, 15, 23
Kinder, D.R., 246, 247
King, G., 185
Kirby, D.M., 205
Klauer, K.C., 69, 74, 78, 79, 80, 82, 84, 87,
    88, 91, 92, 95
Klem, A., 141, 152, 156, 160, 162, 163,
    164, 165, 168
Klineberg, O., 207
Klinger, M.R., 78, 79, 80, 91, 92, 97
Klink, A., 243
Köhnken, G., 109
Kort, J., 69
Kovel, J., 247
Krech, D., 69
Krosnick, J.A., 68, 68, 176, 191
Kruglanski, A.W., 133, 134, 136, 138, 139,
    140, 141, 142, 143, 144, 145, 146, 149,
    152, 153, 154, 155, 156, 157, 158, 159,
    160, 162, 163, 164, 165, 166, 168, 176
Krull, D.S., 143, 144
Kuipers, P., 43
Kunda, Z., 134
Kwan, J., 177, 186

Lage, E., 176, 193
Landes, R., 242
Landman, J., 46, 48
Lange, J., 205, 206, 209, 217, 227
Larrick, R.P., 47
Lau, R.R., 259
Laughlin, P.R., 178
Laviolette, F., 209
Lazarus, R.S., 36, 58, 67, 68
Le Roux, B., 266
Legrenzi, P., 177
Leippe, M.R., 2
Leirer, V.O., 127
Lemaine, G., 265
Lempert, R.O., 114
Leo, G., 185
Lepper, M.R., 69
Lévèque, L., 5
Levey, A.B., 67, 68, 69
Levine, J.M., 176
Leyens, J.-P., 178, 205

Liberman, A., 60, 136, 137
Linville, P.W., 212, 214, 229
Lippmann, W., 209, 217
Lipset, S.M., 259
Liu, Th.J., 78, 79, 91, 92
Loewenstein, G., 43, 53, 113, 118
Loftus, G.R., 108
Loftus, E.F., 107, 108, 109, 112
Logan, G.D., 73, 89
Loomes, G., 43, 45, 46, 59
Lord, C.G., 69
Luck, H.E., 243

Maass, A., 156, 176, 178, 178, 191, 193
McCamish, M., 39
McCaul, K.D., 38
McCauley, C., 208, 209
McClelland, J.L., 89
McCloskey, M., 108, 109, 110
McConahay, J.B., 247
McCrae, R.R., 138
McCrone, I.D., 265
McFarland, C., 49
McGarty, C., 216, 216, 223, 229
McGrath, J.E., 168
McGuire, C.V., 177
McGuire, W.J., 177
McIntyre, D.R., 231
Mackie, D.M., 176, 179, 181, 216
McKoon, G., 74, 87
MacLeod, C.M., 72, 89, 90, 98
McMillan, D., 205
McNamara, T.P., 94
Madden, T.J., 38
Malone, P.S., 194
Mandler, G., 80
Mann, J., 247, 249
Mann, L., 46, 50, 52
Manstead, A.S., 39, 52, 57, 260
Mariette, P., 18, 21, 22
Mark, M.M., 108
Marques, J.M., 178
Martin, L., 67, 69, 94
Martin, R., 177
Masson, C.N., 244
Mayseless, O.,140, 141, 142, 149, 162
Mazursky, D., 113, 118
Medin, D.L., 231
Medvec, V., 48
Meenes, M., 210
Meertens, R.W., 247, 249, 250, 253, 254

Melich, A., 246
Mellor, S., 108
Memmi, A., 265
Merikle, P.M., 92
Meyer, G., 213, 225
Middlestadt, S.E., 38
Mikulincer, M., 151
Miles, R., 244
Milgram, S., 244
Millar, M.G., 2, 36
Millar, K.U., 36
Miller, D.T., 48
Minsk, E., 49
Mladinic, A., 37, 39, 41
Monahan, J.L., 68, 95
Morton, J., 107
Moscovici, S., 176, 180, 181, 185, 186,
    193, 216, 227
Moscowitz, G.B., 166
Mucchi-Faina, A., 176
Mugny, G., 176, 179, 180, 184, 185, 186,
    187, 188, 192, 193, 244
Mummendey, A., 212
Murphy, S.T., 34, 68, 69, 82, 95, 98
Musch, J., 78, 79, 80, 82, 84, 87
Myoshi, H., 76

N'gbala, A., 48
Naccarratto, M.E., 166
Naffrechoux, M., 176, 193
Neely, J.H., 70, 74, 75, 81, 82, 83, 84, 87,
    94
Nemeth, C.J., 177, 185, 186, 187, 193
Neter, E., 47
Neuberg, S.L., 165, 166, 167
Newsom, J.T., 165, 166, 167
Niedenthal, P.M., 68, 95
Nisbett, R.E., 69

Oakes, P.J., 206, 208, 209, 210, 211, 213,
    215, 217, 220, 223, 225, 227, 232
Ofir, C., 113, 118
Oliver, P.V., 151
Olson, J.M., 178
Ortony, A., 43, 59, 68
Osgood, C.E., 67, 69, 191
Otto, S., 37, 39, 41
Oulette, J.A., 59

Page, R., 208
Pantaleo, G., 212

Papastamou, S., 179, 192, 193
Park, B., 127, 204, 209, 212, 213, 214, 215, 228
Park, R.E., 265
Parker, D., 38, 39, 52, 57
Parker, K.H., 166
Pattison, D.A., 157, 158, 163, 165
Peeters, G., 72
Pelham, B.W., 143, 144
Perdue, C.W., 70, 74, 95
Pérez, J.A., 176, 179, 180, 184, 185, 186, 187, 188
Peri, N., 160, 162
Personnaz, B., 185
Personnaz, M., 185
Pettigrew, T.F., 182, 205, 242, 245, 246, 247, 249, 250, 253, 254, 255, 256, 262
Petty, R.E., 36, 37, 38, 56, 58, 136, 139, 176, 177, 179, 181, 187, 187, 191, 192, 193
Pfister, H., 39
Pierro, A., 155, 163, 167
Pieters, R.G.M., 108, 113, 118
Pohl, R.F., 108, 115, 128
Polley, R.B., 155
Posner, M.I., 74, 82, 83, 90
Potter, J., 219
Pratkanis, A.R., 180
Pratto, F., 70, 72, 73, 77, 78, 96

Quattrone, G.A., 143, 178

Rabbie, J.M., 5
Rainis, N., 5, 8
Rajecki, D.J., 25
Rasinski, K.A., 191
Rasinsky, K., 35
Ratcliff, R., 74, 87
Reicher, S.D., 211, 215, 218, 219, 220, 227, 228, 232
Reif, K., 246
Reingold, E.M., 92
Rempel, J.K., 35, 39
Reynolds, K.J., 208, 215, 220
Rholes, W.S., 146
Rice, G.E., 166, 167
Richard, R., 40, 41, 42, 43, 49, 50, 51, 52, 53, 54, 55, 57, 59, 60
Richter, L., 139, 142, 162, 164
Ritov, I., 46, 49
Robalo, E.M., 178

Rocha, S.A., 178
Roelofsma, P.H.M.P., 53
Roese, N.J., 261
Rojahn, K., 205
Rokeach, M., 138, 191, 249
Ronis, D.L., 2, 58
Rosch, E., 210
Roseman, I.J., 43
Rosenberg, M.J., 35, 73, 191
Rosenthal, R., 187, 252
Roskos-Ewoldsen, D.R., 71, 72, 73
Ross, M., 49, 69, 84
Roßnagel, C., 78, 79, 80, 82, 84, 87
Rothermund, K., 73
Rothman, G., 191
Rouanet, H, 266
Roux, P., 244
Rubini, M., 151, 152, 155, 159, 163
Rugs, D., 178
Ruscher, J.B., 206
Russo, E.M., 176
Ryan, C.S., 228

Sabini, J., 244
Sage, A.P., 48
Salovey, P., 212, 214, 229
Sanchez-Mazas, M., 244
Sanford, R.N., 138
Saxe, L., 244
Schadron, G., 205
Schaller, M., 166, 167, 206
Schepanski, A., 48, 59
Scherer, K.R., 68
Schiffmann, R., 260
Schifter, D.B., 38
Schneider, D., 206
Schneider, S., 262
Schoenbach, P., 259
Schoenfeld, N., 207, 218
Schooler, J.W., 109
Schpitzajzen, A., 142, 162
Schuh, E., 78, 79, 80, 92, 97
Schumann, H., 215
Schwarzer, S., 258
Sears, D., 247, 254
Segal, M., 208, 209
Seligman, C., 35
Semin, G.R., 151, 152
Shelton, J.R., 94
Shepherd, R., 38
Sheppard, J.A., 59

Sherif, M., 176, 179, 182, 209, 211, 216, 231
Sherman, S.J., 10, 49
Short, J.C., 138
Shupe, E.I, 178
Sidanius, J., 259
Sigall, H., 208, 261
Silver, M., 244
Silvert, K.H., 209
Simon, B., 212, 213
Simon, L., 10
Simonson, I., 46, 56, 60
Sinclair, A., 226
Sissons, M., 243
Skowronski, J.J., 72
Slovic, P., 107, 113
Smith, J.D., 203, 269
Smith, M.C., 76
Snell, J., 45, 47
Sniderman, P.M., 253, 254, 259
Snyder, C., 74, 82, 83, 90
Sorrentino, R.M., 137, 138, 185
Sparks, P., 38
Spears, R., 208, 260
Spranca, M., 49
Staats, A.W., 68
Staats, C.K., 68
Stahlberg, D., 108, 114, 115, 116, 117, 118, 119, 119, 120, 121, 122, 124, 125, 128, 156
Stangor, C., 205, 206, 209, 217, 227
Starmer, C., 46
Steele, C.M., 2
Steiner, I.D., 22, 123
Stern, E., 87, 88, 91, 95
Stimpson, J., 243
Stitt, C.L., 208, 209
Stolz, J.H., 84
Stradling, S.G., 52
Stroessner, S.J., 204, 209
Suci, G.J., 67, 69
Sugden, R., 43, 45, 46
Swartz, T.S., 43
Swedlund, M.,193

Tafarodi, R.W., 194
Taft, R., 205, 207
Tajfel, H., 182, 206, 209, 216, 217, 220, 226, 227, 231, 259
Tammeo, B., 115
Tannenbaum, P.H., 69, 191

Taylor, S.E., 209
Tedeschi, J.T., 2
ter Schure, E., 43
Terry, D.J., 39
Tesser, A., 108, 113
Tetlock, P.E., 144, 253, 254, 259
Theodor, L., 76
Thompson, M.M., 43, 146, 154, 162, 166, 167, 213
Thorndike, R.L., 205
Thraenhardt, D., 243
Timko, C., 35
Tourangeau, R., 191, 195
Treisman, A., 69
Triplett, N., 175
Trolier, T.K., 232
Trope, Y., 142
Trost, M.R., 178, 191
Tuchin, M., 109
Tucker, D.M., 58
Turner, J., 43, 59, 68, 177, 178, 181, 206, 208, 209, 210, 211, 212, 213, 214, 215, 216, 217, 219, 220, 223, 225, 229, 232, 259
Tversky, A., 45, 48, 59, 120, 121, 143
Tversky, B., 109
Tyler, T.R., 35
Tyler, R.B., 70, 74, 95

van Avermaet, E., 185
van der Pligt, J., 40, 41, 42, 43, 49, 50, 51, 52, 53, 54, 55, 57, 59, 60
van Dijk, T.A., 244
van Knippenberg, A., 213
Verkuyten, M., 244
Verma, G.K., 258
Verplanken, B., 108, 113, 118
Vinacke, W.E., 207, 209, 210, 229

Wackenhutt, J., 247
Wagenaar, W.A., 109
Wagner, U., 243, 244, 258, 259, 260, 261, 262, 262
Walster, E., 46
Walters, G., 205, 207, 218
Wassermann, D., 114
Wattenmaker, W.D., 231
Webster, D.M., 138, 139, 141, 142, 144, 146, 148, 152, 153, 154, 156, 157, 158, 160, 162, 163, 164, 165, 166, 168
Weiner, B., 49

Weisz, C., 73
Wendt, D., 113, 118
Wentura, D., 73, 77, 88, 90, 93, 98
West, S., 165, 166
Wetherell, M.S., 219, 227
Wetzel, C.G., 69
White, F.B., 48
Wicklund, R.A., 2, 3, 15, 26
Wiegand, E., 243
Wiest, C., 43
Wieviorka, M., 244
Wiggins, E.C., 35, 36, 37, 39
Wilder, D.A., 213
Wilhelmsen, A., 77
Willham, C., 106, 108
Williamson, J., 73
Wilson, T.D., 53, 69
Wisniewski, 231
Wood, G., 106

Wood, W., 178, 180, 184, 185, 193, 195
Worth, L.T., 179, 216
Wyer, R.S., 95

Yinon, A., 151
Yzerbyt, V., 178, 205, 220

Zajonc, R.K., 7, 25
Zajonc, R.B., 34, 35, 44, 56, 58, 68, 69, 70, 82, 84, 95, 98
Zakai, D., 160, 162
Zanna, M., 35, 39, 145, 158, 162, 178
Zaragoza, M.S., 108, 109, 110
Zavalloni, M., 227
Zbrodoff, N.J., 73, 89
Zeelenberg, M., 43, 46, 47, 49
Zick, A., 243, 258, 259, 261, 262
Zillig, M., 69

Subject Index

abstract questions, closure and, 151
abstract/concrete explanation, prejudice
    and, 261–2
accessibility effects, 146
act rationalization, dissonance theory,
    10–15
action, closure and, 135
activation, spreading, 94
active coordination, stereotypes, 215
active reconstruction, 126
   pervasiveness of, 124–9
actor effect, 48
actualization hypothesis, destructive, 107
affect, 33–60
   attention and, 71–3
   attitude-behaviour models, 38–44
   decision-making, 44–9
   definitions of, 56
affect/attention summary, 73
affect-cognition distinction, 57
affect-cognition interface, 34
affect/evaluation
   definitions of, 39
   as synonyms, 38
   time perspective, 40
affect-evoking objects, attention and,
   71–2
affective/cognitive information
   processing, 34
affective connotation, Stroop paradigm,
   89
affective/emotional information, 35
affective priming, 67–97

basic findings, 73–81
consistency proportion errors, 86(fig.)
explanations of, 81–91
masked stimuli and, 91–3
in response latencies, 85(fig.)
affective reactions, anticipated
   postbehavioural, 40
agreement, posterior probability of,
   223
almanac paradigm, 126
ambiguity
   closure and, 138
   trait meaning, 228
analytic cognition, affect and, 58
anchoring effects, 143
   automatic, 120–2
anthropomorphism, commitment
   cognitions, 28
anticipated affect, 41, 42(fig.)
anticipated postbehavioural affective
   reactions, 40
   increased salience of, 53–6
anticipated regret, 45
   as determinant, 51(fig.), 52(fig.)
   planned behaviour and, 49–53
argumentation, attitude change and, 5–7
assimilation hypothesis, immediate, 107
association strength, attitude
   accessibility, 71
attention, affect and, 73
attention attraction
   affect-evoking objects and, 71–2
   negative information and, 72–3

attitude accessibility
  association strength and, 71
  role of, 76–7
attitude-assessment phase, affective
  priming, 75
attitude-attribution task, closure, 144
attitude-behaviour models, 57
  affect and, 38–44
attitude change
  argumentation, 5–7
  counter-attitudinal advocacy and,
    6(table)
  indirect, *see* indirect attitude change
  multidimensional scaling analysis and,
    189
  negative feedback and, 7–10
  post-test, 190(fig.)
attitude-congruent information, affective
  priming, 70
attitudes
  compliance commitment and,
    21(table)
  conditioning, 68
  non/chosen issues and, 19(table)
  research, 69
  structure, context/comparison model,
    191
  tedious tasks, 17(table)
attractiveness conditions, closure, 144
authoritarian personality, 208
automatic anchoring effects, 120–2
automatic evaluation effect, affect and,
  35
automatic spreading activation, 82
aversive consequences, 27
  dissonance theory and, 17

balance theorists, dissonance theory, 25
basic emotions, 43
behaviour
  anticipated regret, 49–53
  discomforting, 12(table)
  fear-arousing messages, 37n
  perception and, 206
  subjective expected utility, 39–40
  trivialization, 10
  valence, linguistic abstraction,
    157(table), 158(table)
behaviour-attitude models, 57
behaviour/internal-state correspondence
  principle, 7

behavioural alternatives, utilitarian
  beliefs and, 57
behavioural change, 56
  risky behaviour, 60
behavioural expectations, anticipated
  post-behavioural affective
  reactions, 41
behavioural style, context/comparison
  model, 193
beliefs
  consensually held, 204
  crystallization, closure and, 158–61
  uniformity of, 205
between-attitude consistency, context/
  comparison model, 191
biased-recognition model, hindsight bias
  and, 111(fig.)
biased reconstruction, 108–13
  memory impairment and, 112–13,
    114–15, 129
  response bias and, 113
bigots, 250–1
blatant prejudice, 246–52
  scales, 248(table), 249(fig.)

capacity-restriction concept, closure, 164
categories, social action and, 214–16
caught-in-the-gears procedure,
  dissonance theory, 11
causality hypothesis, closure, 164
central attitudes, 179–81
certainty-orientated individuals, closure,
  137
change strategy, closure, 153
choice
  dissonance theory and, 21
  regret-minimizing, 47
classical conditioning, 68
closed-mindedness, 137–8
closure, cognitive, 133–68
  consequences of, 159(table)
  continuum, need for, 135
  need for, combination of sources, 168
  need to avoid, 141
  and simple structure, 165–7
closure-motivation
  antecedents of, 135–9
  interpersonal consequences of, 146–53
cognition
  emotions and, 59
  generating, 26

most-change-resistant, 26
cognition/affect
    distinction, 57
    interface, 34
cognition-based attitudes, changes in, 36
cognitive/affective information
        processing, 34
cognitive appraisal models, of emotion,
        68
cognitive capacity
    causality hypothesis and, 164
    motivation comparison and, 163–5
cognitive closure, *see* closure, cognitive
cognitive-defense theory, dissonance
        theory as, 2, 15
cognitive dissonance, *see* dissonance,
        cognitive
cognitive explanations, prejudice and,
        259–61
cognitive information, affect and, 35
cognitive miser metatheory, 209
cognitive processes, in context/
        comparison model, 186
cognitive responses, multidimensional
        scaling analysis and, 189
cognitive/structural adjustments, 195
colour-naming latencies, 72–3
commitment
    cognitions, 25, 27–9
    compliance, 18–22
    external, 2
    factors, 23
commitment-to-compliance/non-chosen
        issue situation, 20
common informational input model, 217
common sense, dissonance theory and, 3
comparative basis, of stereotyping
        consensus, 218–25
comparative context, stereotypes and,
        214(table), 221(table)
compliance
    commitment and, 18–22, 21(table)
    double, 26
    forced contract, 18
compliance/conversion, 181
concrete/abstract explanation, prejudice
        and, 261–2
concurrent load, effects of, 77–8
confidence interval, hindsight bias and,
        111
confidence level, closure and, 162(table)

consensually held beliefs, 204
consensus co-efficient, 223
consensus issue, 206–8, 216–30
conservatism
    predictors of, 254(fig.)
    prejudice and, 253–4
consistency
    closure and, 156
    dissonance theory and, 5–15
consistency proportion, 84, 91
    affective priming, 85(fig.), 97
    errors, 86(fig.)
    evaluative inconsistency, 88
consonant cognitions, dissonance theory
        and, 21
constraint, free choice and, 22
construct accessibility effects, closure,
        146
constructs, closure and, 138–9
context/comparison model, of social
        influence, 175–96
contract hypothesis, stereotyping and,
        207
convergent processing, 186
    positive to negative arguments and,
        187
conversion, 178
    majority and, 181
cooperation, task-orientation and, 154–5
correspondence bias, closure, 143–5
counter-argument, attitude change, 180
counter-attitudinal advocacy, 16, 26
    attitude and, 6(table)
    essay writing, 19
    non/chosen issues and, 19(table)
counter-motivational behaviour,
        acceptance of, 14
counterfactual thinking, regret and, 48
cross-group friendships, prejudice and,
        257
cue utilization, 142–5
cultural stereotypes, 204
current attitude accessibility, 77

decision-making
    affect and, 44–9
    regret and, 45–7
decision utility, 45
default assumption, 118
depersonalization, self-categorization
        and, 212

destructive actualization hypothesis, 107
direct change, indirect influence and,
    194–6
disappointment, predictive power of,
    59
discrimination, 243
discussion, closure and, 160(table)
dissonance, cognitive, 1–29, 46
    calculation of, 23, 26
    increase, truth telling and, 16–18
    ratio, calculation, 25–7
    reduction, 10, 13, 14, 25
    theory, 1–29, 46
        consistency and, 5–15
        morals and, 15–22
        reformulations, 3–22
distal causes, outgroup prejudice and,
    245
divergent thinking, 186
diverse friends, 254–8, 257(fig.)
double compliance, 26
double minorities, 193
dual memory traces model, 107

education, prejudice and, 258–62
elaboration likelihood
    affect, 36
    closure, 136
emergent stereotype consensus, 203–32
emotions
    basic, 43
    evaluation and, 68
    as needing cognitions, 59
empathy
    mean perspective, 150(table)
    mental fatigue, 149(table)
    perspective taking, 147–51
empirical relations, closure and, 138–9
equalitarians, prejudice, 250–1
ethnocentrism, 253
Euro-Barometer 30 survey, 241, 245, 250
Europe/United States comparison,
    prejudice, 262–4
evaluation/affect, as synonyms, 38
evaluations
    anticipated affect, 41
    definition of, 36
    norms, primes selected on basis of,
        78–9
evaluative attitude, affective priming
    and, 70

evaluative decision task, Stroop
    paradigm, 90
evaluative inconsistency
    consistency proportion, 88
    Stroop paradigm, 90
evaluative processes, as automatic,
    75
evaluative-response mechanisms
    affective priming, 68, 81
    consistency proportion, 84
    postlexical mechanisms, 87
evaluatively polarized stimuli, affective
    priming, 96
expectancy
    affective priming, 83
    list-context effects, 83–7
expectancy-based mechanisms, 91
    affective priming, 97
    consistency proportion, 84
expectancy-value models
    affect and, 56
    regret and, 58
experience, socially mediated, 232
experienced utility, 45
extended-range conditions, 220
external commitment, definition of, 2

fatigue, mental, 148, 149(table)
    closure and, 140
favourableness, feedback and, 224(table)
Fazio studies
    affective priming, 74–6
    extensions of, 76–81
fear-arousing messages, behaviour and,
    37n
feasibility, context/comparison model,
    193
feedback
    current recall and, 125
    favourableness and, 224(table)
    hit rates, 114–15, 115(table),
        119(table), 125
    initial estimates, 116, 117
    negative, see negative feedback
    pre-post differences, 121(table)
    regret and, 48
    stereotype-consistency of, 222(table)
    stereotypic differentiation and,
        224(table)
    on tedious tasks, 9(table)
forced compliance contract, 18

formation effects, knowledge and, 139–42
free choice, 23
    constraint and, 22
    dissonance theory, 21
    manipulation of, 18
'freezing'
    closure and, 158–61
    consequences of, 147(table)
friends, diverse, 254–8

government help, for outgroups, 264
group(s)
    attribution, prejudice and, 264
    consensualization, 232
    emergent stereotype consensus, 203–32
    interaction, closure and, 153–5
    judgments, and individual judgement comparison, 122–4
    origins, stereotypes and, 209
    prejudice, 252
    relative deprivation, 258
group-based dynamics, stereotype-consensualization, 225–30

hindsight bias, 105–29
    biased recognition, 111(fig.)
    distortions, outcome knowledge and, 125
    misleading information, 109(fig.)
hit rates, 117(table), 123
    feedback and, 114–15, 115(table), 119(table), 125
    memory impairment and, 112
    pre-post differences, 121(table)
homogeneity, social identity salience and, 216
hypothesis generation, closure, 141
hypothetical design, 106

ideals
    dissonance theory, 4
    individual, see individual ideals
immediate assimilation hypothesis, 107
immigration policy, 250–2
impression formation
    instruction, 128
    memory comparison, 129(table)
    primacy effects, 142
impression-management theory, 2

prejudice and, 261
inconsistency
    behavioural mode of dissonance, 14
    dissonance as, 25
indirect attitude change, 175–96
    context/comparison model, 192–4
indirect influence, 184–7
    direct change and, 194–6
    study of, 187–90
individual ideals
    differences, closure and, 137
    dissonance theory, 4
    group judgment comparison, 122–4
    stereotypes, 204, 209
individual/group judgments, 124(table)
information
    attention and, 72–3
    misleading, hindsight-bias design, 109(fig.)
    original estimates, 110
    past behaviour, affect and, 35
    processing
        affective priming, 70
        closure, 135, 135
        extent of, 139–40
        types, closure and, 141–2
        valence, closure and, 134
informational base, closure and, 160(table)
ingroup minority, 177, 193
ingroup–outgroup categories, 210, 214
initial estimate, outcome feedback and, 116, 117
interaction process analysis, closure, 155
intergroup effects, closure, 155–8
intergroup friendship
    outgroup ratings and, 256(fig.)
    prejudice and, 254(fig.)
internal-state/behaviour correspondence principle, 7
internalization, rationalization in, 29
interpersonal communication, closure and, 151–2
intimate social distance, prejudice and, 265(fig.)
intolerance, closure and, 138
intragroup–intergroup distinction, 228
involvement, closure and, 136–7

judgment(s)
    attitude research, 69

judgment(s) (*cont.*)
  biases, affective priming, 93
  individual/group, 122–4, 124(table)
  meta-cognition and, 120
  stereotypes and, 145

Katz–Braly checklist, 218, 220, 221, 226
  self-categorization and, 213
'knew-it-all-along' effect, *see* hindsight
    bias
knowledge formation effects, 139–42
  closure, 145–6

'language-as-fixed-effect' fallacy, 78, 95
latent-manifest distinction, indirect
    influence, 185
leniency contract, 179–80
lexical decision task, 88
  affective priming, 93–4
linguistic abstraction
  behaviour valence, 157(table),
      158(table)
  closure, 152
linguistic intergroup bias, closure, 155–8
list-context effects
  expectancy and, 83–7
  Stroop paradigm, 89
low-ball/accomplished-act procedure, 13

majority effects
  central attitudes, 180–1
  norm formation, 178–9, 184
majority-inspired concerns, 176
masked primes, affective priming, 91–3,
    97
mean judgments, response trials and,
    183(fig.)
mean perspective taking, empathy and,
    149(table), 150(table)
mediation hypothesis, 241, 268–9
  outgroup prejudice and, 245
memory
  dual traces model, 107
  impairment, 107–8, 117
    active reconstruction, 126
    biased reconstruction, 112–13,
        114–15, 129
    indications of, 128
    impression formation comparison,
        129(table)
    improvement, 122

stereotypes and, 145
mental fatigue, closure and, 140, 148
message elaboration, 194
  attitude change and, 189
  context/comparison model and, 181
meta-cognition, 118–20
  biased reconstruction, 112, 125
  response bias, 114
meta-contrast, self-categorization and,
    211
minorities, 176
  double, 193
  central attitudes and, 179–80
  delayed, 195
  indirect measures, 184
  and norm formations, 177–8
misleading information, hindsight-bias
    design, 109(fig.), 110
modern racism, 247, 264
mood, affect and, 36
morally void situations, dissonance
    theory, 22
morals, dissonance theory and, 4, 15–22
motivation, cognitive capacity
    comparison, 163–5
motivational biases, closure and, 134
motivational consequences, causality
    hypothesis and, 164
motivational explanation, 108
  prejudice and, 259–61
motivational tension, dissonance theory
    and, 10
multidimensional scaling analysis, 188–9
mutual influence, stereotypes and, 215

negative feedback
  attitude change and, 7–10
  on tedious tasks, 9(table)
negative information, attention and, 72–3
negative/positive affects, dichotomy in,
    57
negative postbehavioural affective
    consequences, awareness of, 56
network models, context/comparison
    model, 191
non-directional motivational biases,
    cognitive closure and, 134
norm formation, 177–9, 182–4
normative basis, of stereotyping
    consensus, 218–25
novel response norm, 182, 184

openness factor, closure and, 138
opinion deviates, rejection of, 153–4
original estimates, biased reconstruction, 110
outcome feedback, *see* feedback
outgroups, 179
   consensus effect, 228
   government help for, 264
   prejudice
      overview of, 242–4
      in Western Europe, 241–69
   ratings, intergroup friendship and, 256(fig.)

paradigmatic situation, multi-processes, 23
perceived responsibility, regret and, 48
perceiver readiness, self-categorization, 211, 212(fig.)
perception, coordination with behaviour, 206
permanence strivings, closure and, 139, 152, 156, 167
Personal Need for Structure scale, 165–6
personal reality testing, 215
personal worth, dissonance theory, 3
perspective taking, empathy and, 147–51
persuadability, closure and, 152–3
persuasive messages, context/comparison model, 192
phonological loop, 78
planned behaviour
anticipated regret and, 49–53
   theory of, 38, 39
political conservatism, 253–4
poor-white racism effect, 258–62
positive to negative arguments, 43, 57
   convergent processing and, 187
post-decisional regret, 46
post-test attitude change, standardized pretest to, 190(fig.)
postbehavioural affective reactions
anticipated, 40
   increased salience of, 53–6
posterior probability of agreement, 223
postlexical mechanisms, 87–8
power relations, rationalization in, 29
predictive power
   of disappointment, 59
   hit rates and, 119(table)
   of regret, 58

of rejoicing, 59
preferences, affect and, 34
prejudice, 247–9
   blatant, *see* blatant prejudice
   correlates of, 252–8
   diverse friends, 257(fig.)
   intergroup friendship, 254(fig.), 256(fig.)
   outgroup, 241–69
   overview of, 242–4
   predictors, 253(fig.)
   stereotyping, 207
   typology of, 251(fig.)
primacy effects, in impression formation, 142
prime-target pairs, 74
primes, evaluation norms and, 78–9
priming effects, 77
   affective priming and, 75, 96
   experiments, 74
   stimulus onset asychrony and, 79(fig.)
problem-solving groups, closure and, 154–5
processing
   speed, Stroop paradigm, 90
   unconscious, 92
pronunciation task, affective priming and, 94–5, 97
psychologization, context/comparison model, 192

questions, closure and, 151

racism, 247
   modern, 247, 264
   poor-white effect, 258–62
radical views, dissonance theory and, 22–9
rapport, closure and, 151–2
reality
   social categories and, 208–14
   testing, 215
reasoned action, theory of, 38
recall
   advantage, groups, 123
   outcome knowledge and, 125
reconstruction
   active, 124–9
   biased, 108–13
regression analysis
   affective priming, 92, 97

regression analysis (*cont.*)
    prejudice, 252
regret
    antecedents of, 47–9
    anticipated, *see* anticipated regret
    decision-making and, 45–7
    expectancy-value models, 58
    planned behaviour and, 49–53
    predictive power of, 58
    research on, 46–7
regret-minimizing choices, 47
rejoicing, predictive power of, 59
response
    alternatives, 116(fig.)
    bias hypothesis, 108, 113
    latencies, affective priming and,
        85(fig.)
    norm, novel, 182
    trials, mean judgments and, 183(fig.)
responsibility, regret and, 48
restricted-range conditions, 220
reverse sleeper effect, 195
risky behaviour, behavioural change and,
    60

salience, social identity and, 225, 226, 229
'seizing'
    closure and, 158–61
    consequences of, 147(table)
selective retrieval hypothesis, 107–8
selective-attention studies, affective
    priming and, 96
self-affirmation, 2
self-categorization theory, 2, 7, 208–16
    critique of, 219
self-stereotyping, 206, 229
    self-categorization and, 212
    uniformity of, 207
semantic priming, 70, 74
    affective priming and, 81–8, 97
    postlexical mechanisms, 87
sensitivity hypothesis, closure and, 168
simple structure, closure and, 165–7
situational determinants, closure and,
    135–7
smoking, abstinence, 11(table), 13,
    14(table)
social categories, 214–16
    self-categorization and, 210–11, 219
    as variable representations of reality,
        208–14

social distance, 264–9
social identity
    conflict, 223
    consensus and, 232
    judgements, 69
    prejudice and, 244, 258–62
    pressure to comply, 180, 181
    salience, 216, 225, 226, 229
    tradition, 219
social influence, 208–16
    context/comparison model, 175–96
social realities, 207, 214
    testing, 215
socially mediated experience, 232
source derogation, attitude change,
    180
source evaluation, multidimensional
    scaling (MDS) analysis and, 189
spreading activation, 91
    affective priming and, 82–3, 94
status quo, majority-inspired concerns
    and, 176
stereotype-consensualization, group-
    based dynamics of, 225–30
stereotyping, 208–16
    affective priming and, 93
    consensus
        analysis of, 216–17
        basis of, 218–25
        group and, 203–32
    consistency, feedback and, 222(table)
    differentiation, feedback and,
        224(table)
    judgments, closure and, 145
stimulus onset asynchrony, 74–5
    priming effects as function of, 79(fig.)
    role of, 79–80
stimulus-level
    affective priming, 81
    expectancy mechanisms, 83
    spreading activation, 82
Stroop paradigm, 72, 88–90
structural/cognitive adjustments, 195
structure
    closure and, 165–7
    context/comparison model and, 191–6
subject-experimenter rapport, 29
subjective confidence, closure and, 141
subjective evaluative response, 68
subjective expected utility, 44–5
    behaviour and, 39–40

subjective–objective task manipulation,
183
subliminal presentation, of affective
primes, 34
subtle prejudice, 246–52
predictors of, 254(fig.)
scales, 248(table), 249(fig.)
symbolic racism, 247
syncretic cognition, affect and, 58
Systematic Multiple Level Observation
of Groups (SYMLOG), 155

task condition, closure, 144
task-orientation, cooperation and, 154–5
tedious-task paradigm, 8
attitudes towards, 17(table)
feedback on, 9(table)
threshold hypothesis, closure and, 168
time
perspective, affect/evaluation
distinction and, 40
stereotypes and, 221(table)
time-pressure, closure and, 145
total dissonance, calculation of, 23
trait meaning, ambiguity and, 228

trans-situational consistency, closure, 156
truth telling, dissonance theory, 16–18

unconscious processing, affective
priming, 92
unfavourability ratings, prejudice and,
263(fig.)
uniformity of belief, stereotypes, 205
United States/Europe comparison,
prejudice, 262–4
universality hypothesis, 241, 267–8
outgroup prejudice and, 245
unvested attitudes, 177
urgency tendencies, closure, 139
utilitarian beliefs, behavioural
alternatives, 57
utility, 45, 46

valence of information, closure, 134
value-expectancy models, 58
variable representations of reality, social
categories and, 208–14
vested attitudes, 179–81

weak attitudes, 177

Indexes compiled by A. C. Purton

European Review of Social Psychology

Contents of Previous Volumes

VOLUME 1 — 1990

Chapter 1   Mood-dependent Selectivity in Social Cognition
Klaus Fiedler

Chapter 2   Positive–negative Asymmetry in Evaluations: The Distinction Between Affective and Informational Negativity Effects
Guido Peeters and Janusz Czapinski

Chapter 3   Frames of Reference, Judgment and Preference
Joop van der Pligt and Els C. M. van Schie

Chapter 4   Consensus Estimation in Social Context
Russell Spears and Antony S. R. Manstead

Chapter 5   Is Limited Information Processing Capacity the Cause of Social Stereotyping?
Penelope J. Oakes and John C. Turner

Chapter 6   Social Identity and Intergroup Differentiation Processes
Ad van Knippenberg and Naomi Ellemers

Chapter 7   A Social Psychology of Reputation
Nicholas Emler

Chapter 8   Social Identification, Self-Categorization and Social Influence
Dominic Abrams and Michael A. Hogg

Chapter 9   Majority and Minority Influence: A Judgmental Process Analysis
Arie W. Kruglanski and Diane M. Mackie

Chaper 10   The Minimal Group Paradigm: Theoretical Explanations and
Empirical Findings
Michael Diehl

Chapter 11 Affiliation and Helping Interactions within Organizations: A
Critical Analysis of the Role of Social Support with Regard to
Occupational Stress
Bram P. Buunk

Chapter 12 Meeting the Handicapped: A Case of Affective-cognitive
Inconsistency
Wolfgang Heinemann

VOLUME 2 — 1991

Chapter 1   The Linguistic Category Model, Its Bases, Applications and
Range
Gün R. Semin and Klaus Fiedler

Chapter 2   Context Effects in Attitude Surveys: Applying Cognitive Theory
to Social Research
Norbert Schwarz and Fritz Strack

Chapter 3   A Conversational Model of Causal Explanation
Denis J. Hilton

Chapter 4   How to Make Cognitive Illusions Disappear: Beyond "Heuristics and Biases"
Gerd Gigerenzer

Chapter 5   Logical, Statistical, and Causal Reasoning: Compartmentalized
or Generic Processes?
Yechiel Klar

Chapter 6   Greed, Efficiency and Fairness in Resource Management
Situations
Henk A. M. Wilke

Chapter 7   Intergroup Biases and the Cognitive Dynamics of Stereotype
Formation
Anne Maass and Mark Schaller

Chapter 8   Social Categorization and the Representation of Variability
Information
Bernadette Park, Charles M. Judd and Carey S. Ryan

Chapter 9   The Different Effects of Simple and Crossed Categorizations: A Result of the Category Differentiation Process or of Differential Category Salience?
Norbert Vanbeselaere

Chapter 10 Social Psychological Issues in the Study of Rape
Barbara Krahé

VOLUME 3 — 1992

Chapter 1   The Perception of Ingroup and Outgroup Homogeneity: Reintroducing the Social Context
Bernd Simon

Chapter 2   On the Overestimation of Between-group Differences
Joachim Krueger

Chapter 3   Accuracy and Expectancy-confirming Processing Orientations and the Development of Stereotypes and Prejudice
Charles Stangor and Thomas E. Ford

Chapter 4   The Social Judgeability Approach to Stereotypes
Jacques-Philippe Leyens, Vincent Y. Yzerbyt and Georges Schadron

Chapter 5   The Discontinuity Effect in Interpersonal and Intergroup Relations: Generality and Mediation
John Schopler and A. Insko

Chapter 6   The Role of Event Prototypes in Categorization and Explanation
Mansur Lalljee, Roger Lamb and Robert P. Abelson

Chapter 7   Affect and Social Perception: Research Evidence and an Integrative Theory
Joseph P. Forgas

Chapter 8   Long-lasting Cognitive and Social Consequences of Emotion: Social Sharing and Rumination
Bernard Rimé, Pierre Philippot, Stefano Boca and Batja Mesquita

Chapter 9   Paradoxical Effects of Praise and Criticism on Perceived Ability
Wulf-Uwe Meyer

Chapter 10   Evolution of the Self Concept in Adolescence and Social Categorization Processes
Augusto Palmonari, Maria Luisa Pombeni and Erich Kirchler

VOLUME 4 — 1994

Chapter 1   The Common Ingroup Identity Model: Recategorization
and the Reduction of Intergroup Bias
*Samuel L. Gaertner, John F. Dovidio, Phyllis A. Anastasio,
Betty A. Bachman and Mary C. Rust*

Chapter 2   The Influence of Socio-structural Variables on Identity Management Strategies
Naomi Ellemers

Chapter 3   Group Identification, Intergroup Perceptions and Collective
Action
Caroline Kelly

Chapter 4   Group Cohesiveness: A Critical Review and Some New
Directions
Michael A. Hogg

Chapter 5   Self-enhancement and Superiority Biases in Social Comparison
Vera Hoorens

Chapter 6   Goal Achievement: The Role of Intentions
Peter M. Gollwitzer

Chapter 7   Deviance in Primary Groups: The Social Negotiation of Personal Change
Arie Nadler

Chapter 8   On the Experience of Injustice
Gerold Mikula

VOLUME 5 — 1995

Chapter 1   Are People Prejudiced against Women? Some Answers from
Research on Attitudes, Gender Stereotypes, and Judgements of
Competence
Alice H. Eagly and Antonio Mladinic

Chapter 2   The 'Black Sheep Effect': Social Categorization, Rejection of Ingroup Deviates, and Perception of Group Variability
José M. Marques and Dario Paez

Chapter 3   Revision and Change of Stereotypic Beliefs: In Search of the Elusive Subtyping Model
Miles Hewstone

Chapter 4   Trait Inferences, Impression Formation, and Person Memory: Strategies in Processing Inconsistent Information about Persons
Roos Vonk

Chapter 5   The Functional Value of Realistic Attributions
Friedrich Försterling

Chapter 6   Subjective Assessments and Evaluations of Change: Some Lessons from Social Cognition Research
Norbert Schwarz, Michaela Wänke and Herbert Bless

Chapter 7   Social Comparison Processes under Stress: Towards an Integration of Classic and Recent Perspectives
Bram P. Buunk

Chapter 8   Expectation States Theory and the Motivational Determinants of Social Influence
Dick de Gilder and Henk A. M. Wilke

Chapter 9   Why Groups are Less Effective than their Members: On Productivity Loss in Idea-generating Groups
Wolfgang Stroebe and Michael Diehl

Chapter 10   Group Socialization: Theory and Research
John M. Levine and Richard Moreland

VOLUME 6 — 1995

Chapter 1   It's About Time: Optimistic Predictions in Work and Love
Roger Buehler, Dale Griffin and Michael Ross

Chapter 2   The Interplay of Heuristic and Systematic Processing of Social Information
Gerd Bohner, Gordon B. Moskowitz and Shelly Chaiken

Chapter 3   Evaluating and Extending the Theory of Planned Behaviour
Anthony S. R. Manstead and Dianne Parker

Chapter 4   Outcome Frames in Bilateral Negotiation: Resistance to Concession Making and Frame Adoption
Carsten K. W. De Dreu, Peter J. D. Carnevale,
Ben J. M. Emans and Evert van de Vliert

Chapter 5   Social Remembering: Individual and Collaborative Memory for Social Information
N. K. Clark and G. M. Stephenson

Chapter 6   A Social Identity Model of Deindividuation Phenomena
S. D. Reicher, R. Spiers and T. Postmes

Chapter 7   Intergroup Biases in Multiple Group Systems: The Perception of Ethnic Hierarchies
Louk Hagendoorn

VOLUME 7 — 1996

Chapter 1   Shared Reality in the Self-system: The Social Nature of Self-regulation
E. Tory Higgins

Chapter 2   Control, Interdependence and Power: Understanding Social Cognition in Its Social Context
Susan T. Fiske and Eric Dépret

Chapter 3   Mood and Stereotyping: Affective States and the Use of General Knowledge Structures
Herbert Bless, Norbert Schwarz and Markus Kemmelmeier

Chapter 4   Asymmetries in Judgements of Ingroup and Outgroup Variability
Thierry Devos, Loraine Comby and Jean-Claude Deschamps

Chapter 5   Majority and Minority Influence: A Dual Role Interpretation
Nanne K. De Vries, Carsten K.W. De Dreu, Ernestine Gordijn, and Mieke Schuurman

Chapter 6   Group Polarization and Repeated Attitude Expressions: A New Take on an Old Topic
Markus Brauer and Charles M. Judd

Chapter 7   "Does My Contribution Really Matter?": Efficacy in Social Dilemmas
Norbert L. Kerr

Chapter 8   Social Psychology and Health Education
Gerjo Kok, Herman Schaalma, Hein de Vries, Guy Parcel and Theo Paulussen

Essential reading for social psychologists...

European Journal of
Social Psychology

CHIEF EDITOR:
PROFESSOR FRITZ STRACK

The **European Journal of Social Psychology** is an international forum for theoretical and empirical research. It was founded and is sponsored by the European Association of Experimental Social Psychology, and is therefore dedicated to fostering communication among social psychologists in Europe and to providing a bridge between European and other research traditions. The Editors invite researchers from all over the world to contribute to the Journal.

The Journal has become the natural home for work on intergroup relations, social identity and influence processes. However the editors welcome innovative, well-designed research in all areas of social psychology.

Articles published in the Journal, whether empirical or theoretical, address fundamental issues in social psychology. The Journal seeks to promote a better understanding of social psychological phenomena through a variety of approaches. Published papers include:

- Social Categorization as a Function of Priming - *M. van Twuyver and A. van Knippenberg*
- Racial Categorization and Preference Among Older Children in the Netherlands - *M. Verkuyten, K. Masson and H. Elffers*
- Feelings of Injustice After Violation of Succession Rules in Simulated Organizations - *J. Bruins and H. Wilkie*

Contact Wiley for current subscription details or to place your order...

☎ **Phone**: UK/Europe: +44 (0) 1243 843282 or USA: + 1 212 850 6645

🖹 **Fax**: UK/Europe: +44 (0) 1243 843232 or USA: +1 212 850 6021

✉ **Write** to: Journals Administration/EJSP, John Wiley & Sons Ltd, 1 Oldlands Way, Bognor Regis, West Sussex, PO22 9SA, UK or Subscription Dept 'C', John Wiley & Sons Inc., 605 Third Avenue, New York, NY 10158-0012, USA

🖥 **e-mail**: cs-journals@wiley.co.uk